Edexcel Level 3 Diploma

Children's Learning and Development
Early Years Educator

Brenda Baker

Kate Beith

Louise Burnham

Elisabeth Byers

Alan Dunkley

Sue Griffin

Wendy Lidgate

Hayley Marshall

PEAR

Published by Pearson Education Limited, Edinburgh Gate, Harlow, Essex, CM20 2JE.
www.pearsonschoolsandfecolleges.co.uk

Text © Pearson Education Limited 2014
Typeset by Tek-Art, West Sussex
Original illustrations © Pearson Education Limited
Cover design by Pearson Education Limited
Picture research by Caitlin Swain
Indexing by Wendy Simpson

The rights of Brenda Baker, Kate Beith, Louise Burnham, Elisabeth Byers, Alan Dunkley, Sue Griffin, Wendy Lidgate and Hayley Marshall to be identified as authors of this work have been asserted by them in accordance with the Copyright, Designs and Patents Act 1988.

First published 2014
18 17 16 15 14
10 9 8 7 6 5 4 3 2 1
British Library Cataloguing in Publication Data
A catalogue record for this book is available from the British Library
ISBN 978 1 447972 44 0

Printed in Italy by Lego S.p.A.

Copies of official specifications for all Edexcel qualifications may be found on the Edexcel website: www.edexcel.com

A note from the publisher

In order to ensure that this resource offers high-quality support for the associated Edexcel qualification, it has been through a review process by the awarding organisation to confirm that it fully covers the teaching and learning content of the specification or part of a specification at which it is aimed, and demonstrates an appropriate balance between the development of subject skills, knowledge and understanding, in addition to preparation for assessment. While the publishers have made every attempt to ensure that advice on the qualification and its assessment is accurate, the official specification and associated assessment guidance materials are the only authoritative source of information and should always be referred to for definitive guidance.

Edexcel examiners have not contributed to any sections in this resource relevant to examination papers for which they have responsibility. No material from an endorsed book will be used verbatim in any assessment set by Edexcel.

Endorsement of a book does not mean that the book is required to achieve this Edexcel qualification, nor does it mean that it is the only suitable material available to support the qualification, and any resource lists produced by the awarding organisation shall include this and other appropriate resources.

Picture Credits

The publisher would like to thank the following for their kind permission to reproduce their photographs:

(Key: b-bottom; c-centre; l-left; r-right; t-top)

Alamy Images: Golden Pixels LLC 72, Mark Richardson 159, PhotoAlto 216, Picture Partners 138, 283; **Corbis:** Mika 191; **DK Images:** Ruth Jenkinson 257; **Getty Images:** Ariel Skelley / Stone 61, Blend Images 31, Chris Schmidt 207, Christopher Futcher 8, 83, David Tipling 235, Don Smetzer 79, jo unruh 92, 107, Jupiterimages 267, Luka 309, marcduf 35, Oleksiy Maksymenko 293, Riser 96, Vetta 126; **Imagestate Media:** BananaStock 164, 220, 299, 301; **Pearson Education Ltd:** Studio 8 13, 21, 46, 65, 121, 129, 157, 170, 214, 222, 260, Lord and Leverett 6, 24, MindStudio 201, Roddy Paine 247, Tudor Photography 62, Jules Selmes 10, 26, 104, 155, 167, 189, 193, 198, 228, 233, 239, 244, 286, 291, 298, Ian Wedgewood 88, Susie Williams 113; **Shutterstock.com:** Emese. 236, Kzenon 74, Monkey Business Images 135, Rob Marmion 197, Serhiy Kobyakov 1, Tomasz Markowski 75; **SuperStock:** Phanie / Phanie 43; **Veer / Corbis:** flashon 38, Kzenon 5, Leda 115, michaeljung 185, naumoid 258, nruboc 180, TatyanaGl 225, Yliv 172

All other images © Pearson Education

The publisher would also like to thank Maddie James for her kind permission to use her illustration on the cover of this book.

This book contains public sector information licensed under the Open Government Licence v1.0.

Every effort has been made to trace the copyright holders and we apologise in advance for any unintentional omissions. We would be pleased to insert the appropriate acknowledgement in any subsequent edition of this publication.

Contents

About the authors

Brenda Baker has worked in early years settings and as a primary teacher. She taught childcare and education and, for a number of years, managed the Health and Social Care Department in an FE college. In recent years she has contributed to textbooks and support materials for learners and teachers of early years and teaching assistant qualifications.

Kate Beith has a wide experience in early years: as a teacher, head teacher, trainer, adviser, author and assistant director of schools for an international organisation following the EYFS framework and National Curriculum. In her current role, Kate is responsible for quality assurance in early years, professional development and training.

Louise Burnham currently works as an early years and primary teacher. She also led teaching assistant training and worked on childcare and teaching courses at a London FE college for a number of years as a tutor and assessor. Louise has written many books for early years and teaching assistant qualifications, and continues to work with early years and teaching assistant students.

Elisabeth Byers worked as an early years educator before becoming a lecturer in early years. She has taught on a range of early years programmes from entry level to Level 5. In recent years she has contributed to textbooks and written teaching and learning resources. She is currently teaching higher education students and is programme director for the Foundation Degree in Early Years. She is also completing a Doctorate in Education.

Alan Dunkley has an academic background in psychology and sociology and currently works as the Learning Manager for early years at Banbury and Bicester College. He has worked with children of different ages in different settings, including primary schools. He spent 10 years at the Department of Pedagogy at Warsaw University, Poland, where he taught trainee primary school teachers specialising in English Language. Alan has written learner and teacher support materials for early years courses and has also supported the development of a Foundation Degree in Early Years.

Sue Griffin has worked in a variety of roles in the field of early years training for over 30 years, mostly with playgroups and childminders. When she was at NCMA (now PACEY), she developed qualifications for childminders. Sue has written a range of distance learning materials for the National Extension College and is now a freelance writer and author.

Wendy Lidgate worked as a health visitor before teaching childcare and health and social care students in an FE college. She has extensive experience in developing qualifications and assessments for awarding organisations, including those for Level 2 and Level 3 childcare and education. Wendy has also written resources and training materials to support teachers delivering childcare and education programmes. She currently has a senior role in external assessment of childcare programmes.

Hayley Marshall worked in early years settings for many years before becoming a lecturer in early years and childcare. She has taught a wide range of early years courses from entry level to Foundation Degree in FE colleges. She was head of the childcare department at a secondary school and has previously written books and teaching and learning resources for early years qualifications. Currently, she is an early years inspector.

Introduction

It is an exciting time to be training for work in the early years sector. Recent changes to practitioner qualifications as well as to the Early Years Foundation Stage framework have put early years and childcare high on the political agenda; and, as part of this important workforce, you will play a key role in supporting the needs of children and their families.

Studying the Level 3 Diploma will help you to develop the high level of professionalism that you will need to work with children and families. Although the work is responsible and demanding, it is extremely rewarding and our children deserve a well-trained workforce that is able to work consistently to high standards. During your study you will gain new skills and knowledge that will help you in your everyday life, as well as in your professional work with children and families.

The Level 3 Diploma overview

The Pearson Edexcel Level 3 Diploma in Children's Learning and Development is supported by The National College for Teaching & Leadership (NCTL) and meets the NCTL Early Years Educator (Level 3) Qualifications Criteria. It is made up of units of assessment. You need to achieve a minimum of 64 credits to gain your qualification; 46 credits must be achieved from mandatory units (Units 1 to 9) and the remaining 18 credits from optional units (there are 14 different optional units to choose from).

Optional units cover many specialist areas, such as disability or working with babies. What is available to you will depend on your interest and what is being offered by your centre or training provider.

How to use this book

This book contains all nine mandatory units and four of the optional units. All the chapters are matched to the specifications of each unit in the qualification and follow the unit learning outcomes and assessment criteria closely, making it easy for you to work through the criteria and be sure you are covering everything you need to know.

Key features of the book

- Jargon buster – clear, easy-to-understand definitions of key terminology used.
- Reflect – opportunities for you to reflect on your own skills and performance and to consider different ways of doing things.
- Theory in action – activities and suggestions for linking theories and key principles to your everyday practice.
- Case study – real-life scenarios exploring key issues to broaden your understanding of key topics.
- Find the balance – suggestions/tips to help you achieve that all-important work–life–study balance.

Understand children's early years education and development

As you work with young children and get to know them, you will notice that all children develop in different ways and at different rates. It is important that you have a good knowledge and understanding of different aspects of children's development from birth up to the age of 8 years so that you can meet their individual needs. In this way, you can move quickly to support them if there are any concerns.

Before you start

Think about the abilities of different children with whom you work. What do you notice about the development of the children in your care?

Learning outcomes

By the end of this unit you will:

1. understand patterns of children's development from birth up to 8 years
2. understand evidence-based approaches to child development
3. understand the significance of attachment to children's development
4. understand how to support children's speech, language and communication
5. understand how transitions and significant events affect children's lives.

1 Understand patterns of children's development from birth up to 8 years

All children develop differently, but the stages they pass through are broadly the same. If you work with children of the same age, you will start to recognise similarities in their levels of development. This will help you to identify those children who are working at a significantly higher or lower level than others in the group. The pattern of children's development falls into different areas, although many of these are interlinked.

From birth to 5 years
Cognitive, neurological and brain development

Cognitive development refers to the development of the mind and intellect, whilst neurological development refers to the development of the brain. Neurological development includes the growth and reinforcement of neural pathways. Between birth and the age of 5 years, babies' and children's brains will undergo the most rapid changes.

Neural pathways carry electrochemical messages between different regions of the brain. They act in different ways. The first of these is to carry instructions from the nervous system to the brain. An example of this might be a signal from the brain telling an individual to move part of the body, such as an arm, or the control of sensation from the body to the brain, for example when feeling pain or temperature. Another is to make connections between different areas of the brain, through neurons.

In the very earliest stages of life, these pathways between neurons need to be constantly developed and reinforced. Experiences that children have in the earliest years assist with regular forming and reforming of these connections between neurons, so that the pathways can be developed.

It is essential that these pathways are reinforced regularly in the child's early years to enable them to retain informaton later on. Every interaction which a baby or young child has with an adult will form connections. The pathways that are regularly used are those which are retained and developed, so those who have limited early experiences will be at a disadvantage. A baby's brain has significantly more neurons than an adult brain, as those that are not used will not survive. Recent research has shown that 90 per cent of brain development occurs in the first 3–5 years of life, so this is a crucial time for the development of neurons in the brain and for our cognitive development.

Jargon buster

Cognitive – to do with acquiring knowledge.

Neurological – to do with nerves and the nervous system.

Birth to 6 months
Babies will develop rapidly as they use their senses and start to become aware of what is happening around them. They will be aware of physical sensations such as hunger and will start to recognise their carers, responding to physical stimuli such as smiles. From an early stage, babies will start to make simple associations, for example starting to recognise the soothing voice of a parent or the routines when feeding and sleeping.

6 to 12 months
Babies will be starting to understand tone of voice and some key words such as 'mama' or 'dada'. They will also be able to recognise some objects, such as a favourite toy, and know to search for it when it is hidden.

1 to 2 years
Children will continue to explore different objects to find out what they do. They will start to use objects appropriately: for example, trying to use a hairbrush or cup. Their language will be developing rapidly and they will be able to use around 40 words, as well as understanding more than this.

2 to 3 years
Children's vocabulary will be expanding rapidly and they will start to understand more abstract thoughts. They will have more awareness of others and will be able to understand the consequences of their own actions. They will also be starting to learn nursery rhymes and familiar songs.

3 to 4 years
Children's understanding of the abstract will continue to develop. They will continue their fascination with why things happen. They will be starting to understand the passing of time – what has happened in the past or will happen in the future.

4 to 5 years
Children will be able to give reasons for their actions and solve problems. Their memory skills will be increasing. They will be able to remember events such as Christmas or what happened in the summer break. Children will be able to sort and categorise objects by criteria, such as colour and size. They may also be able to state their name and address.

Speech, language and communication development

This refers to the way in which children start to understand and process language so that they can communicate with others. The first five years of life are crucial as children start to make sense of the world and their place in it.

Birth to 6 months
Babies will start to interact with adults by looking and listening, and by starting to vocalise through gurgling or cooing at people they recognise. Young babies may respond to their name when they are as young as a few weeks old, but this is more likely to be because they recognise the voice of their parent or carer. They may respond to speech by smiling, or cry when they have a need.

6 to 12 months
Babies will be starting to recognise key voices, understand simple language and recognise their own

name. They will be starting to experiment with speech by making sounds, babbling or talking to themselves.

1 to 2 years

Babies will be starting to understand simple instructions ('have a drink') when accompanied by gestures (being given a cup). They will be able to identify a few objects and will start to increase their spoken vocabulary. They may also be echoing what others say to them, known as echolalia.

2 to 3 years

Children will know and speak over 200 words and will begin to put them together. They will often talk to themselves as they do things, and will name different objects when they recognise them.

3 to 4 years

Children will become more aware of their own thoughts. They will start to be able to count by rote, recognise and say nursery rhymes, and have basic conversations.

Jargon buster

By rote – by memorising and repeating, often without really understanding.

Echolalia – echoing what others say over and over.

Fine motor skills – skills that involve small muscle movements, such as using a pencil.

Gross motor skills – skills that involve large movements of the arms, legs, feet or entire body, such as running.

Sensory development – growth of awareness through the senses (sight and sound, touch and texture, smell and taste, and also body position sense).

---

4 to 5 years

Children will be able to reason about different things, solve problems and talk with fluency. They will now have a large vocabulary and be able to use tenses, although they may sometimes be unaware of more irregular ways of speaking.

Literacy and numeracy development

As soon as young children learn to speak and understand language, they are starting to develop their literacy and numeracy skills. This area of development is closely linked to both speech and language development.

Speech and language are linked to numeracy because so many of children's earliest numerical experiences will depend on their ability to use language and be able to put their experiences into words. For example, if children do not recognise and understand the words 'more' and 'less', they will find it difficult to recognise and understand the concept.

Similarly, the development of language is closely related to the development of literacy skills.

At the age of 2 years, children will be starting to understand and use language themselves.

2 to 3 years

It is important for young children to put words together and start using sentences. They will understand the significance of different objects, and so be able to recognise similarities and categorise items later when working on mathematical activities.

3 to 4 years

As children start to remember and repeat songs and rhymes, they will be exploring patterns in language and will enjoy hearing similar sounding and nonsense words.

4 to 5 years

Children of this age will have an increasing enjoyment of books and sharing them with adults. They will be starting to learn their sounds and recognise some simple words.

Physical development

Physical development covers sensory as well as fine and gross motor skills. Children will develop at their own rate so many of these key points, such as learning to crawl and walk, and in particular potty or toilet training, will depend on the child's readiness.

Birth to 6 months
A newborn baby's physical development will progress quickly. From basic reflexes, they will soon be able to make jerky movements with their arms and legs, keep their head up and move it deliberately to look around them.

6 to 12 months
Babies will be able to push themselves up if lying on their front, using their arms. They will also be able to roll over and kick their legs. They will continue to develop their strength, and may be able to bear much of their weight when supported and sit unsupported for brief periods. They may be starting to find ways of moving. They will also be able to pick things up.

1 to 2 years
Babies will be able to bring themselves to a sitting position. From pulling themselves up using furniture, they will gradually learn to walk steadily as their balance develops. Their coordination will be developing and they will be able to pick up small objects, turn the pages of a book, and begin to feed themselves using a spoon. They may be starting to use a potty.

2 to 3 years
At 2 years, children will be able to run, climb and throw a ball. They may be using a tricycle; by 3 years they will also be able to use pedals. They will be able to drink from a cup and use a spoon more confidently, and may have a preferred hand for feeding and drawing.

3 to 4 years
Children will have a greater spatial awareness and ability to move around objects. They will be able to use stairs, jump off a low step and kick a ball. They will be developing their ability to use a pencil and draw simple representations of people.

4 to 5 years
Children's physical skills will be well developed. They will be starting to use a knife and fork, thread beads and hold a pen or pencil correctly. They will have a good sense of balance and be confident when walking and running.

Figure 1.1: What activities will help children to develop their strength and coordination?

Theory in action

Consider why early years practitioners need to take the developmental needs of children into account when planning the learning environment. How is the environment relevant to different areas of children's development?

Emotional and social development

Birth to 12 months
It is important to ensure that babies receive positive emotional experiences in their first year. This is because they are starting to learn about relationships with others. Babies are likely to be easily distressed if their primary carer leaves and to be wary of unfamiliar people. Babies of this age will enjoy cuddles and attention.

1 to 2 years
Babies will still be shy with unfamiliar adults but will be starting to develop their independence. They will become frustrated if they cannot express themselves. Babies will enjoy socialising and playing alongside others.

2 to 3 years

Children will be learning to say how they are feeling, although at times they will find it difficult to control their feelings and may have tantrums. They will still depend on adults emotionally. They may start to share with other children, while still enjoying solitary play.

3 to 4 years

Children will be starting to express likes and dislikes. They will be developing their own personal identity and starting to perceive that their own perspectives may differ from those of others. They will be developing in confidence and independence. They will be starting to make friends and enjoy playing with others.

Figure 1.2: At what age do children begin to enjoy playing together?

4 to 5 years

Children's confidence will continue to increase and they will enjoy the company of other children. They will enjoy their independence and will enjoy helping adults. They will be more likely to share with others and take turns, although they may still exert their own wishes and desires.

From 5 to 8 years

Development between these ages will be less rapid, but children will still be developing in different areas and will need support from adults. This age group covers the period up to the child's eighth birthday.

Cognitive, neurological and brain development

At this stage, children will be starting to think in a more abstract way due to the development of their language skills. Consequently they will be able to understand topics such as rules and to discuss points of view. They will be able to concentrate for increasing periods and be starting to categorise and sort objects according to multiple features. For example, children may sort a pile of toy animals by colour, type of animal, how they move or other features.

Speech, language and communication development

Children of this age are likely to be fluent speakers who are easily understood and can follow instructions. Their language will be grammatically correct and they will have a good grasp of tenses, being able to use language in different ways. They will be starting to talk about abstract words and will enjoy listening to stories, often acting them out later and being able to distinguish between fantasy and reality. Their thinking skills will be developing as they are more able to organise their language, and they will understand time concepts such as 'tomorrow' and 'yesterday'. They will be starting to read, recognise and write their own name, and know their left and right.

Literacy and numeracy development

Children will be developing their literacy and numeracy skills rapidly during this period. They will be able to read and write on their own and structure well formed sentences. Their counting skills will be developed and they will be able to count money and tell the time.

Physical development

Between the ages of 5 and 8 years, children will grow rapidly and have increasing agility and muscle coordination (for example, starting to ride a bicycle). They will also develop their fine motor skills, being able to use a knife and fork, have good control over pens and pencils, and copy complex shapes and pictures.

Milk teeth will start to fall out and permanent teeth will appear.

Emotional and social development

Children of this age will be developing in confidence and independence, and have a greater perception of their own individual, unique identity and self-concept. They will have more understanding of the thoughts and feelings of others, showing greater sympathy and concern for others who are hurt or upset. They will be able to play cooperatively with each other and form loose friendships, as well as demonstrating a competitive spirit. Their attention span will continue to grow and they will be forming a sense of humour.

Jargon buster

Holistic development – all areas of development, including moral, cultural and wellbeing.

Peer – someone who is equal in terms of age, status or ability to another specified person.

Self-concept – the way in which you see and think about yourself.

The importance of different aspects of development

The different aspects of children's development are interlinked and co-dependent, so they will each be important to the child's holistic development. Children's overall development and educational needs will be affected by the way in which they develop in key areas. As children grow and pass different milestones or key points, they will gradually become more independent and less reliant on those around them in preparation for the future.

The three key areas of children's development are personal, social and emotional, physical, and speech and language development – the Early Years Foundation Stage (EYFS) framework refers to them as the three prime areas, ('speech and language' is 'communication and language' in the EYFS framework document). If children are slower to develop in these areas, further development in other areas such as literacy and numeracy will take longer to achieve.

Speech, language and communication

This aspect of development is important for children's holistic development. Through the development of speech and language, children will learn to socialise and express their preferences and their needs, and be able to make sense of the world. In turn, the ability to communicate will support the development of their confidence and self-esteem. It is important that young children have as much opportunity as possible not only to listen to others but also to put their own language skills to use. Adults should make sure that young children are given praise when they achieve, as well as frequent feedback.

Children who have limited speech and language skills will have corresponding difficulties in expressing themselves, which in turn may lead to frustration, poor understanding, inability to express themselves and limited social skills.

Personal, social and emotional development

This aspect of children's development is related to their confidence and self-esteem. Babies and children need to have positive interactions and form firm attachments from the earliest stages, and feel reassured emotionally by the adults around them. Children who are given praise, encouragement and guidance as they grow will develop a greater sense of self-worth. Children will in turn be able to form positive relationships and friendships with their peers through their interactions. (For more information about attachments and attachment theories, see learning outcome 3 in this unit.)

Physical development

As well as physical growth, this aspect involves children's health, physical strength, mobility and sensory abilities. They will need to have opportunities to exercise and develop both fine and gross motor skills so that they can gain full control over their muscles. The more opportunities children have to develop muscular strength and physical skills, the greater their stamina. Some children may be limited by a physical condition or disability, or have a sensory impairment which hinders their progress. (For information on the effects of atypical development, see later on in this learning outcome under 'The impact of atypical development'.)

Jargon buster

Atypical – not typical; unusual; not following the expected pattern.

How different factors can affect children's learning and development

Children's learning and development may be affected by a wide range of factors. Their background, their health and the environment in which they are growing up will all have an impact, as each will affect all areas of development. You should know how children may be affected so that you can encourage them to develop and reach their potential.

Personal factors

The personal factors that affect children's learning and development are based around their environment and their relationships with primary carers. Some of the causes and effects are outlined below.

Encouragement

Children need to be encouraged and given positive praise by primary carers as they learn and develop in different areas, to build confidence and self-esteem.

Figure 1.3: What opportunities can you give children to develop their muscle coordination?

This is true of all areas of development. If they form poor attachments with little encouragement from adults, it is likely that they will develop anxieties and insecurities about their own abilities and have a need for reassurance. They may lack motivation or adopt attention-seeking behaviour. They may also suffer from separation anxiety – a fear of being apart from their primary carer – due to their own poor self-confidence and self-concept.

Limited resources

Children who are from backgrounds where there are limited resources may have less time with their primary carers, or have limited life experiences. This may be as simple as having trips to different areas to broaden their knowledge, or having access to different experiences.

Role models

Children may have ineffective role models in different areas of their development. Those who look to adults with poor social and communication skills may have difficulty in developing their own, as the adults do not form positive relationships with others. Children who have limited opportunities to develop their own communication skills may also demonstrate poor behaviour or a poor attention span if they become frustrated due to an inability to communicate.

Expectations

Expectations of children can vary depending on the past experiences of adults in their family. Some children may have parents or carers who have had poor experiences in the education system and in turn may have low expectations for their own children.

External factors

External factors affecting children's learning and development are likely to be concerned with more limited access to services and support where it is needed. Parents or carers may not be aware of the different services available or may not be able to find out about them.

Access to resources and services

Some children may have reduced access to healthcare or social services, and so have less support if they have a slower rate of development.

Ill health

Children who suffer from ill health on a regular basis may develop more slowly. On its own, or alongside other factors such as limited support, this may cause longer-term issues such as failure to grow or thrive.

Case study 1.1

Minal is in your school's nursery and has a large extended family. She seems very busy and regularly attends different clubs and activities after school with her brothers and sisters. She is usually collected by her mother or her aunt, who both support the school PTA. She is very confident and talkative.

Michael is from a small family and has to travel some distance to the nursery. You do not know much about his home circumstances except that his mother is bedridden and he is cared for by his father. He is regularly late and his father seems very shy and not keen to communicate.

1. How might the learning and development of these two children be affected by some of the factors above?
2. What could the nursery staff do to support Michael's father?

Opportunities and choice

Children who are from more disadvantaged backgrounds and who have limited support may be offered fewer external opportunities from others, or have fewer support systems in place.

Influence of others

The smaller the social circle and the fewer opportunities to develop social skills, the more likely children are to be dependent on parents and carers. This may also lead to poor communication skills and low self-image or lack of confidence.

Consistency in education

Children who move around to different schools and areas, for example foster children, children in traveller families, children whose parents are in the military, immigrant children or children whose family routine is otherwise disrupted, may find their development is adversely affected. The impact may not only be on their educational outcomes but also their social and language development. They may have more difficulty forming and maintaining friendships or fitting in with different cultures and social groups. These developmental issues may be harder to identify or may not be acted upon because of changes of address and high mobility.

Monitoring of development

Where children's development is not monitored effectively, any failure to grow, thrive or develop will not be picked up, so the intervention available will be limited.

The impact of atypical development

If young children are developing differently from their peers in one or more areas, this is likely to have an impact on other aspects of their progress. Two key areas where this may happen are physical and communication development, although it may also impact on their social and emotional development.

Physical development

Atypical physical development may mean that a child has a slower or faster rate of development than other children, or has a physical impairment.

However, if a child is growing at a much faster or slower rate than their peers, they may feel different to other children, which may affect their social and emotional development. Adults will need to ensure that this kind of issue is discussed with parents so that the child's health status can be checked and services accessed.

Children who have a physical impairment may be affected in different ways. Physical impairments are usually related to mobility or coordination, but may also be sensory – related to vision or hearing.

Problems with, for example, mobility may also have an impact on a child's social and emotional development as they develop feelings about themselves and other people. The effects may be negative if the child starts to have low self-esteem or confidence, and adults will need to provide positive support.

Figure 1.4: How can you ensure that children with physical disabilities feel included?

Case study 1.2

Amara has a condition that means she is much taller than all the other children in her year. She does not seem to be unduly concerned, but as her childminder, you have heard other children in the school passing comments on her size as you leave the playground.

1. Should you do anything in this situation if Amara is not concerned?

2. What might be the effects of Amara's condition as she goes through the school?

Communication development

Children whose communication development is atypical may have a variety of needs. Communication development may be affected by a sensory impairment such as poor vision or hearing, but can also be due to speech and language issues such as a language disorder, or a cleft palate – or simply a slower rate of development. Communication and language are vital aspects of children's learning, so it is important that a slower rate of communication development is addressed as soon as possible.

In the early stages of communication development other aspects may be unaffected, but as children grow older their rate of communication development may lead to delayed cognitive development, anxiety, poor behaviour and possible social exclusion by their peers.

In all of these cases, you should discuss any effects of atypical development with parents so that they can get the support they need, in order to benefit the child.

Reflect

Consider the needs of children with whom you have worked in your setting. How has their development been affected by different factors?

The effect of stage of development

Children's learning and development will be affected by the stage of development they have reached. They will need to pass the milestones in sequence, although not necessarily at exactly the same age. For example, learning to walk may occur at around the age of 1 year, but some children walk at 10 months, and others not until 16 months.

If a child completes a stage in one area sooner than their peers, they are likely to continue to progress more quickly and this may impact on other areas of development. For example, a child of 18 months who has spent time in the company of adults or older children may have learned some action songs and nursery rhymes. These will promote their communication and conversation skills, and so their confidence and self-concept is likely to be greater.

A child who has not formed an attachment or bonded with a primary carer, or whose attachment has been disrupted, may also be affected, as their feeling of personal identity and security will not be so developed. (For more information on attachment, see learning outcome 3 in this unit.)

How interventions can promote positive development

As children grow and develop, they will undergo checks at different times. For example, the progress check at age 2, which takes place between the ages of 24 and 36 months, gives a breakdown of children's development in the three prime areas – personal, social and emotional, physical, and communication and language. These checks are designed to give parents and healthcare professionals a clear picture of the child's development so that they can identify any areas in which children are developing slower or faster than is expected.

Following observations and assessment judgements, a child may be referred to a specialist to assess and support their further development. The specialist will then advise teaching and support staff. Parents will be told about the kind of service provision and opportunities available to support their child. In this way, targeted intervention can promote positive development, and appropriate support can be put in place. If children are not making expected progress or achieving milestones, intervention should happen as early as possible.

With the right intervention, children are likely to be more motivated and have a greater self-concept, which will enhance their overall development. Their progress will then continue to be monitored by setting and reviewing targets on a regular basis.

Case study 1.3

Following her progress check at age 2, Ramola has been referred to a speech and language therapist as her communication skills are very poor. Her mother is not keen to take her because she does not want her to be 'labelled' and has spoken to you about it.

1. What would you say to Ramola's mother?

2. Why is it important that Ramola attends the appointment?

2 Understand evidence-based approaches to child development

How babies and children learn and develop

The way in which babies and young children learn and develop is a continuous process involving a number of factors, many of which are linked and incorporate different aspects of development. The pattern of development starts with more simple actions and goes on to more complex ones as the child grows up.

Use of senses and exploration

As soon as they are born, babies begin to use their senses to explore their new world. They will be taking in a huge amount of information and are alert, looking and listening when they are awake. As they grow and develop, the use of their senses will continue to be an important aspect of their development.

Continuous interaction and communication

The communication development of babies and young children will need to be stimulated by continuous interaction and communication with others. In this way they will learn the norms of interaction: for example, taking turns to speak, making eye contact and using facial expressions.

Resources

Access to resources will support children's development as they explore and begin to talk about different materials and their properties. They will need to have access to sensory materials such as sand, water and dough, items that support their physical development such as tricycles, balls and pencils, and items they can explore and play with as they become more independent. This will also support their communication and language development as they talk to others about what they are finding out.

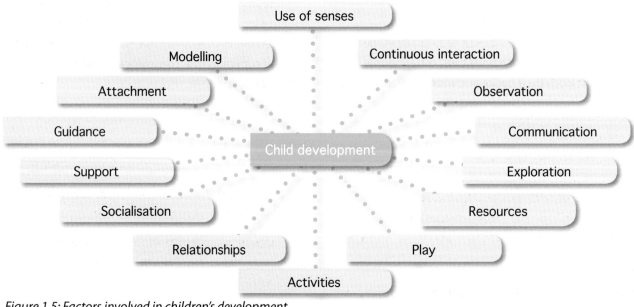

Figure 1.5: Factors involved in children's development.

Figure 1.6: What resources can you use to stimulate children's development?

Play and activities

Play and different activities will support all areas of development. Young children will need to socialise with others and explore their environment through play and a variety of different activities.

Relationships and socialisation

As children grow and develop, they will form relationships with others, socialising with adults and their peers. They will learn about their place in the world and the way in which we treat other people. This will support both their social and moral development.

Guidance and support

Babies and young children will need guidance and support from adults as they grow and develop. This may take different forms, such as praise and encouragement or through demonstration, such as showing them how to catch a ball. Young children will continuously ask questions as they start to find out about the world.

Attachment

Babies and young children will need to have a positive attachment to a parent or primary carer to support their social and emotional development. This is because they will need to feel secure and protected as they begin to explore their world, as they will always have a reassuring presence to return to. (For more information on attachment theory, see learning outcome 3 in this unit.)

Modelling and observation

Babies and young children will learn by observing adults and others modelling different aspects of behaviour. For example, they will pick up language by listening to others and copying the way in which they speak, or recognise the correct way to behave by observing adults.

Theories and models of child development

Various theories of development will influence the way we approach our work with children. Psychologists have different ideas about how children learn and develop. Some feel that a child's ability is innate, while others think it depends on the opportunities that they are given. This is often called the 'nature versus nurture' debate.

Sigmund Freud

Freud stated that our personalities are made up of three parts – the id, the ego and the superego. Each of these will develop with the child and will be subconsciously driven by childhood events and experiences. Freud focused on the relationship between the id (the instinctive part of our personality) and the superego (the conscience), which develops later in childhood.

Jargon buster

Innate – inborn, natural; an innate ability is something you are born able to do.

Modelling – a technique by which adults show children what is expected by doing it themselves.

Erik Erikson

Erikson was greatly influenced by Freud. He stated that we pass through eight psychosocial stages throughout our entire lives. At each stage, our psychological needs will conflict with those of society.

John Bowlby

Bowlby stated that early attachments are crucial to a child's healthy mental development and are a key part of the way in which we build relationships later. (For more information on attachment theory, see learning outcome 3 in this unit.)

Jean Piaget

Piaget thought that children think differently to adults. He believed that the way children think and learn is governed by their age and stage of cognitive development, because learning is based on experiences they build on as they become older. As children's experiences change, they adapt their beliefs. For example, a child who only ever sees green apples will believe that all apples are green. Children need to extend their experiences in order to extend their learning. They will eventually take ownership of this themselves so that they can think about experiences that they have not yet developed.

Albert Bandura

Bandura's 'social learning' or 'modelling' theory stated that learning takes place through observing others rather than being taught. Children will often simply copy adults and their peers without being told to do so, meaning that their learning is spontaneous.

Lev Vygotsky

Vygotsky believed that culture and social factors both play a crucial role in a child's development, and that cognitive functions will be affected by the beliefs and values of the society in which children grow up. He also believed that children learn actively, from hands-on experience through interaction with another more competent peer or adult. Vygotsky believed that children's learning of language was heavily reliant on the amount of time spent communicating with others and the interplay of the growth between thought and language.

B. F. Skinner

Skinner believed that children learn through experience or conditioning. He promoted the theory that our learning is based on a consequence following a particular behaviour. We will repeat experiences that are enjoyable and avoid those that are not. This applies to learning too. For example, a child who is praised for working well at a particular task will want to work at the task again. Skinner called this positive reinforcement. Skinner also produced one of the earliest explanations of language development in the 1950s, called 'language acquisition theory'. In it he stated that children's language acquisition is heavily influenced by their environment and by others around them positively reinforcing their correct use of language. For example, a child's mother smiling and bringing a drink when they ask for one is a rewarding outcome and will make them want to speak more.

Noam Chomsky

Chomsky heavily criticised the work of Skinner and stated that relying on language input from others would not be sufficient for children to learn language. He outlined his own theory for the acquisition of language, based on grammar, and stated that we are born with an innate system which he called a 'Language Acquisition Device'. This enables us to break down nouns, objects and verbs into phrases; we are so tuned in to these features of language that we are able to predict how they will be used.

Jerome Bruner

Bruner rejected Chomsky's view and supported that of Vygotsky. That is, he believed that children learn language through social interaction and at the same time will learn the rules of grammar. The role of others is to 'scaffold' children's language so that they are supported as they start to communicate with others.

Ivan Pavlov

Pavlov put forward the idea of classical conditioning, which he discovered by accident when carrying out research using dogs. The dogs would salivate when one of Pavlov's assistants entered the room, even if they did not feed them, as the dogs expected it to happen. He then started to ring a bell whenever the dogs were fed; eventually ringing a bell produced the same response. Because this response was learned, it was called a conditioned response. Classical conditioning is often used today to treat phobias and anxiety problems, by helping people form new associations. In the same way, children can be taught to associate positive experiences with learned behaviour.

Urie Bronfenbrenner

Bronfenbrenner developed a theory known as ecological systems theory. This emphasises the importance of different environmental factors on a child's development, from people in the child's immediate environment to the influence of national forces such as cultural change.

Howard Gardner

Gardner introduced the theory that all individuals learn in different ways based on their own aptitudes, and not by a single general ability of intelligence. He stated that different 'intelligences' do not all progress at the same time, so children may be at a different stage in their understanding of number compared to their ability with language, for example. Gardner originally outlined eight intelligences, although he subsequently added two more.

Information-processing theory

Information-processing theory was developed during the 1950s and 1960s, influenced by the concept of the computer. It states that individuals process information in much the same way as a computer does, by coding, storing and using information. This is a model used by cognitive psychologists.

Reggio Emilia

This approach, developed in the 1940s, is based around the child being the initiator in their own early learning. When it was first introduced, it was a progressive model of early years care as it had never been done before. Children will follow their own interests, which will be fostered and developed with support from parents, teachers and the wider community. It speaks of 'the hundred languages of children' – children explore their world and express their thoughts in many different ways, all of which should be nurtured.

Jargon buster

Classical – in this context, to do with an unlearned reflex such as salivating.

Progressive – in this context, a reform or change in the way in which education is delivered.

Psychosocial – to do with how social factors and individual behaviour interact.

How to apply theories and models to support children's development

You will need to be able to consider how different theories support the development of young children. In your workplace it is likely that you will be able to see evidence of different ways in which they influence your practice.

Table 1.1: Links between childcare practice and theories of child development.

Aspect of practice	Links to	How it is applied
Observation and assessment	All	All theories of child development are based on observation and the way in which children react in different situations. You will need to observe children so that you can assess their progress and plan for their future needs.
Planning and evaluation	Piaget	Piaget emphasised the importance of extending children's experiences, so that they are able to see things in different ways and challenge their ideas. This theory may influence the way in which you plan and evaluate work with children.
Effective communication	Bowlby Skinner	Bowlby's attachment theory affects the way in which our confidence develops and we are able to relate to others. This may be seen in the way in which young children can develop relationships and communicate with others. Skinner's language acquisition theory emphasises the importance of positive communication in order to develop children's confidence and use of language. This may be seen in the inclusion of communication and language as a prime area and subsequently in the importance of spoken language in the literacy aspect of the national curriculum.
Behaviour analysis	Skinner Pavlov	Behaviour analysis is based on the way in which the child's behaviour is affected by the environment and how we respond to their behaviour. Both Skinner and Pavlov's theories show that we can influence behaviour in different ways.
Planning or structure of educational programme	Gardner Bronfenbrenner	Both Gardner's and Bronfenbrenner's influence affects the way in which we present activities to children and shows the importance of doing this in different ways to appeal to different learning styles and environmental stimuli.
Consultation and intervention	Pavlov	Pavlov's influence can be seen in the use of intervention as it shows that some aspects of behaviour and development can be taught or modified.
Environment and resources	Reggio Emilia Bronfenbrenner	Reggio Emilia's influence can be seen particularly in the EYFS framework, which emphasises the importance of children's own interests being followed. Bronfenbrenner's influence can be seen in the development of the learning environment, particularly the outside classroom.
Partnership working and referral	All	Where children are a cause for concern and all agencies work together to support them, there is potential for all theories to influence practice, depending on the needs of the child.

Theory in action

Look at each of the aspects in Table 1.1 and think about how they affect your own practice. Can you think of any other ways in which the theories of development relate to the aspects of practice on the left?

How evidence-based approaches can inform your practice

It is important that you keep up to date with current research and practice so that you are aware of any new findings around children's development. You should read around the subject and regularly attend courses so that you can review any areas you need to update. Within your setting or network you should have opportunities to discuss and review your practice, to ensure consistency and effectiveness in different areas.

Planning, the curriculum and evaluation of practice

Evidence-based approaches and research findings will affect your day-to-day practice through changes to the curriculum or framework you follow in your setting. You will need to be aware of any changes well in advance so that you can anticipate how this will affect your planning. Regularly review and evaluate your practice to ensure that it is up to date.

Use and effectiveness of interventions and strategies

Research findings may affect the way in which you target interventions in your setting. There may be new research into how children respond to interventions, or more support may be available.

Safety of practice and risk assessment

Issues around safety – safeguarding and child protection as well as general health and safety – are key in informing your practice. Make sure you have procedures in place so that you can keep up to date with regular training.

Reflect

1. How do you ensure that you stay up to date with current practice?
2. What is available to you within your setting and the wider area? How do you find out about it?

3 Understand the significance of attachment to children's development

Theories of attachment

There are a number of different theories of attachment that you should be aware of when considering children's overall development. Attachment is important as it affects a child's long-term social and emotional development.

John Bowlby's theory of attachment

John Bowlby was a psychoanalyst like Freud. He recognised and devised one of the most important theories, which is that of attachment. He stated that a child is influenced the most by their relationship with their primary carer (in most cases, their mother). Here are the main aspects of his theory.

- Babies have an innate need to attach to one main person. This is called a monotropic attachment, and will need to be established during the first 6 months of life.

- Bowlby originally stated that a child will need to have continual care from this person for around the first two years of life; this is a critical period. Any kind of disruption during this period will have long-lasting effects on the child's overall development, such as depression, increased aggression or affectionless psychopathy (showing no guilt for antisocial behaviour).

- He later revised his ideas to state that children were capable of forming multiple attachments and that it was important for them to have attachments with at least one caregiver in their early years.

Mary Ainsworth's studies of attachment behaviour

Following John Bowlby, other theories have emerged around attachment. Mary Ainsworth, a student of Bowlby, was a psychologist who devised an experiment that focused on the different forms of attachment shown between mothers and infants. In this experiment, called 'The Strange Situation', the behaviour of a child aged 12–18 months was observed in a series of seven different situations.

1. Parent and infant alone.
2. Stranger joins parent and infant.
3. Parent leaves infant and stranger alone.
4. Parent returns and stranger leaves.
5. Parent leaves; infant left completely alone.
6. Stranger returns.
7. Parent returns and stranger leaves.

Ainsworth wrote about three main attachment styles.

- **Anxious-avoidant** – The baby largely ignores the parent, and continues to play when the parent leaves, showing little distress. The baby ignores or avoids the parent when they return. The baby doesn't like being alone but can be comforted by a stranger.

- **Securely attached** – The baby plays while the parent is present, but plays less when the parent leaves, showing some distress. When the parent returns, the baby is comforted easily and carries on playing. The baby cries when alone but can be comforted to some extent by a stranger. The baby's reactions towards parents and strangers are noticeably different.

- **Anxious-resistant** – The baby is wary and explores less than other types. The baby is very distressed when the parent leaves and actively resists the stranger's attempts to comfort. When the parent returns, the baby wants immediate contact but is ambivalent, showing frustration and anger alongside clinginess; for example, wanting to be held but then immediately struggling to get down.

Ainsworth thought that the child's behaviour was determined by their early attachment to their mother. For example, where parents could predict their baby's needs and frustrations, the baby showed securely attached behaviour, happy to explore a strange environment, knowing that their parent was a safe 'base' for them to return to. Ainsworth found that a high percentage of children (70 per cent) formed a secure attachment like this. However, when upset by the departure of their parent, they will only be comforted by the parent's return.

Hazan and Shaver: the applicability of attachment theory to adult relationships

Hazan and Shaver (1987) investigated the influence that attachment has on adult relationships. They put forward the idea that there are the same kinds of interaction between adult romantic partners as there are between primary carers and infants. Their research with different couples looked at the way they responded to one another and in particular to different situations. They drew the conclusion that romantic relationships and infant-carer relationships are based on the same system, although in adult partnerships the attachment and caregiving roles are often exchanged.

Main and Solomon's attachment style

Main and Solomon (1986) wrote about the characteristics of disorganised-insecure attachment. They describe this as children's behaviour that is mixed in response to caregivers. This is caused by inconsistent behaviour by parents: for example, carers who both frighten and comfort the child. Subsequent research has stated that this may occur in situations of abuse or neglect.

Theory in action

Deliver a training session to other staff in your setting explaining different theories of attachment. Make sure that you cover strategies for promoting positive attachments and why a positive attachment is so important for children.

Include handouts analysing the impact on children of not forming positive attachments.

Why positive attachment is important

Forming a positive attachment is important for children for a number of reasons. It supports children's development as it is through a secure attachment that children gain a feeling of security and have a reassuring base from which to explore the world. This will gradually enable them to develop the confidence to start exploring things for themselves and gain their own sense of competence. When children have the security and stability of a secure attachment, they will be more able to develop a positive and non-threatening view of the world. This will in turn lead to the development of an individual who is more likely to have good self-esteem and self-concept, as well as the ability to self-regulate (self-control). An inability to form effective attachments can lead to an inability to form meaningful relationships with others and there is evidence to suggest that this also affects their ability to establish friendships in later life.

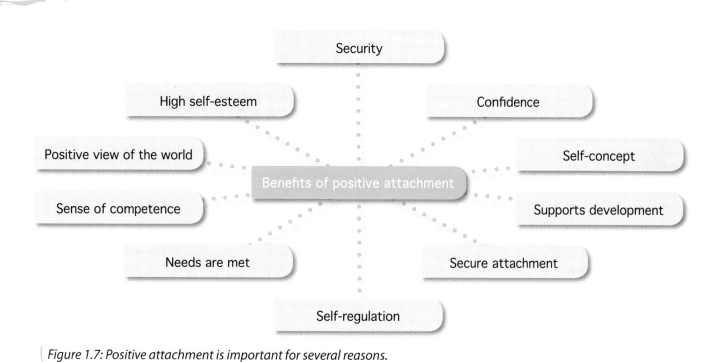

Figure 1.7: Positive attachment is important for several reasons.

If we look at Maslow's hierarchy of needs in Figure 1.8, we will see that our basic human needs are those of shelter, safety, belonging and esteem from ourselves and others. Children in particular will be unable to reach their potential without these needs being met.

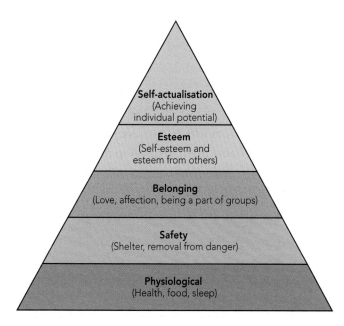

Figure 1.8: Maslow's hierarchy of needs.

The impact on children of not forming positive attachments

Not forming positive attachments with adults can be very damaging for children and their social and emotional development. If their primary carer has not been a reliable attachment who reassures and gives them a sense of security, they may well develop negative traits. These are likely to include:

- lack of trust and wariness of strangers
- low self-esteem and lack of self-affirmation
- anxiety
- developmental delay
- a negative view of the world.

These kinds of issues will impact on their future development and the opportunities available to them, as children need to have a secure base from which to develop relationships and grow feelings of trust.

Theory in action

Johnnie is 3 years old and has been in care for most of his life. He has recently started at your nursery and is collected by different adults at different times. You can see that Johnnie lacks confidence and is usually quite 'clingy', particularly when he first comes into the nursery.

1. How could you support Johnnie's social and emotional development as his key person?

2. Why is it important that you make this a priority?

Strategies for promoting positive attachments

Children's social and emotional development depends on positive attachments being formed in the early years. However, even without this they will benefit from the nurturing and consistency available to them through your setting. One of the benefits of the key person system is that children have reliable contact with an adult who will get to know them and develop a relationship with them and their families. A key person will be able to provide continuity and reliability for the child; in turn they will learn to build trust with others.

Here are some key ways in which positive attachments can be built.

- **Effective communication and openness** – Adults should ensure that they communicate with all children on a regular basis, but in particular with those who have limited experience of positive attachments. This will support the child in building regular socialisation and developing relationships with others.

- **Observing and being responsive to children's needs** – All adults should as far as possible be responsive to the needs of children through observing and getting to know them so that they develop confidence in seeking help or approval.

- **Understanding individuality** – As adults get to know children, they will start to recognise their own individual preferences and traits. This will help children to develop positive attachments and relationships with the adults who care for them.

- **Being consistent** – Children respond to routines and consistency as they benefit from knowing what will happen next. They need to have clear expectations from adults. This also leads to a sense of security.

4 Understand how to support children's speech, language and communication

The communication development needs of children

In order to develop their speech, language and communication skills effectively, babies and young children will need to have supportive carers around them who interact with them and each other and encourage them to do the same through speaking and responding.

Birth to 2 years

From the earliest stages, adults should try to communicate with babies even though they are not yet able to understand what is said to them. This is because babies need to be stimulated and have an interest shown so that they will learn to interact with others. They should have opportunities to listen and respond to normal language as well as different forms of communication such as soothing voices, songs and rhymes, hand gestures and simple board and cloth books. If babies are neglected and do not spend time interacting with adults at this time, they will find it difficult to learn the skills of effective communication later.

2 to 5 years

Children of this age should continue to have many opportunities to communicate and interact in different ways, through a variety of experiences as their circle widens. As they grow and develop they will ask many questions as they seek to find out about their world, and adults will need to support them by answering and showing an interest. As well as opportunities to speak and listen to others and develop their social skills, children should continue to look at books with adults and be starting to learn to read and write. Adults should encourage them in all areas and give them positive praise and feedback as they name different objects and start to use a pencil to draw and write.

5 to 8 years

Children of this age will continue to look to adults to model correct use of language and give them feedback as they become more mature and develop their skills in socialisation. They will continue to enjoy sharing books and reading as well as playing games, which will also develop their ability to take turns and wait for one another, as in conversation. Adults will need to actively listen, give guidance, respond and question children sensitively so that they continue to develop their communication skills.

Figure 1.9: How can you interact with a baby who is not able to talk?

Early intervention criteria

Early intervention will be based on the criteria shown in Figure 1.10.

How the child is passing through the different stages of language development

Observations of the child both in the setting and at home

Assessment of the child's level of language development

Diagnosis and reference-based analysis of any speech and language or communication needs

Standards to support the development of early communication skills

Guidance, collaboration and specialist intervention

Figure 1.10: There are various criteria that may highlight a need for early intervention.

As children develop through different stages, it may become apparent through observation and interaction with them that they need specialist intervention. Specialists will then assess their communication skills so that they can give a diagnosis and a basis for intervention.

The earlier the diagnosis of speech and language or communication needs, the easier it will be for professionals and others to target the child's language so that they can give support – and the more beneficial for the child, as the early years are a time of rapid learning and development. Specialists will be able to work with early years teams and collaborate to support the child. You will then need to ensure that you have opportunities to meet with them regularly in order to discuss the child's progress.

It is important to act quickly to support children who have speech and language or communication needs, as language is crucial to learning and enables us to store our thoughts in an organised way. Children with language delay may also find it harder to form relationships with others; as a result they may become frustrated, leading to possible behaviour problems. Very young children in particular will not have the experience to recognise the reason for their feelings. If you are working with a child who has a diagnosis of communication delay or disorder, you should be sent on specific training or be given guidance so that you have support strategies to help you in your work with them.

Case study 1.4

Mike is working in a reception class and often works with a group of children who need to develop their confidence in speaking and listening. Sasha is working well in this group and seems to have a good level of understanding, but she seems to find it difficult to express her ideas, even in a small group. Mike has noticed that Sasha is increasingly reluctant to speak to others.

1. What should Mike do?

2. Can you think of any other ways in which Mike can support Sasha?

How multi-agency teams work together

If you are working with a child who has speech, language and communication needs, you may come into contact with a number of other professionals. This is called a multi-agency team. They may come together as a team to discuss and share expertise and resourcing, to see how the child's needs can best be met and to monitor their progress. In this way, early years practitioners will gain ideas and support to help them assess and plan for children with communication and language needs. Other professionals may also come and observe the child in the setting, feeding back to one another about how the child is managing and looking at the support being given. They will then meet again after a set period to look at outcomes and review the child's progress.

Who is involved will depend on the specific needs of the child, but may include speech and language therapists, educational psychologists, sensory support teachers and local authority representatives. They will always include parents or carers, teachers or key people and support assistants, and children themselves where appropriate. Teams will share information and give advice to education staff and parents about how best to support the child and their needs while encouraging their communication skills. (For more information on partnership working, see Unit 9.)

The systematic synthetic phonics approach to reading

Synthetic phonics is a method of teaching reading that focuses on the link between letters and sounds. This approach is based on breaking down and blending letters so that children learn to link sounds with individual letters and phonemes. The sound system is more complex and inconsistent in English than in other languages. There

Jargon buster

Decipher – decode, work out the meaning of.

Multi-agency – involving different services, agencies and teams of professionals working together.

Phoneme – a distinct unit of sound, such as the 'p' in 'pad'.

are more than 40 different phonemes in spoken English, and there can be a number of different phonemes to represent the same sound (for example, 'f' and 'ph'). Phonics helps us to look at the different letter patterns together, along with their sounds.

Synthetic phonics puts the teaching of letters and sounds into an orderly framework. It requires the reader to learn simpler individual sounds first, then start to put them together to form words, and finally progress to the most complex combinations. The sounds are taught in a particular way, not to sound like the letters – for example, the sound for 't' would be taught as this short sound and not as 'tee' or 'tuh'. The simpler and most commonly used sounds will be the first to be taught, as these are also straightforward (s, a, t, l, p and n). These can then be put together to form many simple three-letter words, which can be sounded out by children from a relatively early stage (for example, 'p-i-n' or 'c-u-p'). Children's confidence usually develops quickly and they can sound out different words quite easily as they start to blend combinations of sounds together – an important stage of this process. As children become more skilled at blending, they will also start to develop word recognition skills until they gradually become more fluent readers.

Strategies for developing early literacy and mathematics

Learning to read and write is a complex process, incorporating speaking and listening to others, phonemic awareness and deciphering text. Mathematics is also a broad subject area covering many aspects of learning, including measuring, using money and telling the time. You will need to think about different areas in order to develop early literacy and mathematics skills.

Planning and preparation

Thorough planning and preparation is important when considering how you will carry out literacy and mathematics activities with children. You will need to develop long-term plans to ensure coverage over a period, and think about how you can link different areas of learning together. For example, if your topic is based around stories you will be able to incorporate all other areas of learning, including mathematics.

Theory in action

Write a report for parents about the way in which your setting teaches phonics to children. Does it follow a specific scheme?

	Shared reading text	Communication and language/ literacy activities	Communication and language/literacy goals	Numeracy activities	Numeracy goals
Week 2: Health workers (doctors/nurses/ dentists/opticians)	Miss Dose the Doctor's Daughter Going to the Doctors Ness The Nurse Funny Bones **Role-play area:** Doctors' surgery/hospital – writing prescriptions/appointment book/height charts Post office	Phonics Individual and shared reading Weekend News – discussion Handwriting Appointment book/ prescriptions in role-play area Reading optician's board in role play Labelling parts of the body	They listen to stories, accurately anticipating key events and respond to what they hear with relevant comments, questions or actions. They answer 'how' and 'why' questions about their experiences and in response to stories or events. Children express themselves effectively. Children enjoy rhythmic activities. Distinguishes between different marks they make. They use phonic knowledge to decode regular words and read them aloud accurately. Children read and understand simple sentences.	Class height chart – outside Independent: Sorting bandages – long to short Counting activities Sing 'Five little monkeys jumping on the bed...' Continue – Odd and even Numicon	Children count reliably with numbers from one to 20, place in order and say which is more or less. Records, using marks that they can interpret and explain. Orders and sequences familiar events. Measures short spaces of time in simple ways. Begins to use the vocabulary involved in adding and subtracting. Using quantities and objects they add and subtract two single-digit numbers and count on or back to find the answer.

Figure 1.11: What are the benefits of careful planning of literacy and mathematics activities?

Speaking and listening

From Figure 1.11 you will be able to see many different opportunities for speaking and listening. Children should be encouraged to talk about what they have done or are doing with adults, or to report back to their peers afterwards. This reinforces their learning and develops their confidence. Speaking and listening are just as important for developing mathematical skills as children will need to work on and talk about mathematical concepts and develop their vocabulary before going on to more abstract activities.

Reading and writing

It is important to expose young children as much as possible to books and language to encourage their natural curiosity and promote their literacy development. Both fiction and non-fiction books should be available to children, as they should be exposed to as much variety as possible. You will probably have a reading and writing area in your setting, and displays and texts should be at children's level. Word banks and labelling activities are good ways to encourage children to look at print in their environment. It is important that adults point out these kinds of area and use them as much as possible so that children are able to develop their literacy skills.

You should provide children with a range of resources and activities so that they have different opportunities to develop their literacy skills. Although they are often doing this through play, children are very imaginative and will use these skills to develop further. Engaging children's imaginations is an excellent way to encourage them to learn.

Here are some resources and activities you might use.

- **Story sacks** – Children will enjoy using story sacks that contain different elements of a familiar story. For example, a 'Little Red Riding Hood' story sack might include a red cloak, a small stuffed wolf, a basket of fruit, a granny's hat, and so on. Story sacks encourage discussion and develop children's vocabularies as they talk about the text.

Figure 1.12: What games can you use to help children to develop their mathematical skills?

- **Storytelling** – Young children love stories and they should start to be able to retell their favourite stories in their own words. This will help them to sequence their ideas.
- **Role play** – All early years settings should have a role-play area that changes regularly. This will give children opportunities to develop their speaking and listening skills in different contexts, as well as their confidence and imagination.
- **Story and music CDs** – Early years settings usually have a listening corner where children can sit quietly and listen to stories, rhymes and music. They should also regularly sing songs with other children and have opportunities for dance and drama.
- **Small-world play** – When children play with small-world toys, such as building blocks, toy towns and other small figures, they are encouraged to use spoken language and their imagination as they 'act' stories out.

You need to be able to use different strategies and resources in order to develop mathematical skills in young children. You can do this through focused activities as well as using the learning environment to stimulate children's learning.

The kinds of resources you use for developing mathematical skills depend on what is being learned. For example, when working on measuring, weighing or capacity you will need to use specific equipment. When working on numbers and counting, resources can range from playing cards and board games to using counting songs.

Counting

As well as counting with young children as much as possible so they are used to hearing numbers in order, numbers should be displayed indoors and outdoors so that children can see them being used. They should also be part of children's play activities or included in class routines. For example, create a 'car park' in the outside play area with numbered spaces and ask children to park toys or bicycles in the correctly numbered space.

Games

Games are another important part of developing children's mathematical skills as they help them to identify numbers and shapes as well as consolidating their learning. Board games and more physical games such as hopscotch will help them recognise and use their knowledge of number.

Reviewing and evaluating

You should always review plans and activities you have carried out in any area of the educational programme, rather than repeat them in a cycle without considering their effectiveness. This is particularly important with mathematical activities, as children may have found the approach difficult to understand or follow up.

How play and activities support speech, language and communication development

Play experiences can enhance all areas of learning and development. They can be directed specifically to address individual areas such as speaking and listening, or can be used more generally to support all areas as they are interlinked. Play is an ideal way to engage children to communicate with others, as they can interact in a non-pressured environment. You can plan for, monitor and assess different areas of learning using play.

As they grow older, children will still need to be given the chance to enjoy activities and equipment that support their play, creativity and learning across the programme of teaching and learning. It is important that they are given opportunities to use their own initiative, work with others and develop in all areas. These can often be used to best effect when children are introduced to new ideas in practical, imaginative and stimulating ways. Giving children a project or getting them to decide in a group how they are going to solve a problem can be very beneficial. For example, you could ask them to come up with a design for a house for a fictional character that they all know. They would then need to justify what features it might need and why, and present this to a group.

Figure 1.13: How can you use puppets to encourage children's communication development?

Much of our communication with others is expressed non-verbally. It is important for children to be able to recognise and respond to non-verbal signals from others. Children who are autistic, for example, may well have difficulty in recognising and interpreting non-verbal signs. If you are working with a child who has communication and interaction needs, you will probably be using different non-verbal strategies to support them, giving them an additional aid to understanding.

The kinds of strategy you could use include:

- **gestures** – this could be something as simple as a 'thumbs up' or beckoning the child to come over

- **pointing to objects** – you can help children to understand by giving concrete examples of what you are discussing, and encouraging children to point to different objects in a similar way

- **facial expressions** – a smile or nod can show approval, while you can also indicate excitement, disapproval, happiness and other emotions

- **eye contact** – this is essential, as is coming down to a child's level to communicate wth them

- **body language** – you can show that you are giving the child your attention through the way in which you sit or stand.

You may also need to be specific and ask children what particular gestures or signals from others might mean if they are unable to interpret them.

A number of visual and auditory approaches can also be used to enhance communication and will give additional support to young children.

- **Puppets** are always popular with young children. They can be used to model language and will often hold a child's attention. Children may be invited to interact with the puppet and their responses will often be more relaxed than when speaking directly to an adult.

- **Pictures** can be a good starting point for initiating or supplementing conversation. The child can select a picture if they need to communicate something or show adults what they want to say.
- **Games** are often used successfully to initiate children's speech and involve them in social interactions with others.
- **Signs** are used to support children who are unable to communicate verbally. However, other children will also enjoy learning different signs as well as teaching them to one another.
- **Technologies** such as story tapes, CDs, computer programmes and interactive whiteboards are useful ways to stimulate children's communication skills.
- **Modelling language** is important as it gives children the chance to hear the correct use of language.
- **Songs and rhymes** are used in primary classrooms and are another excellent way of reinforcing language.

Case study 1.5

Cassie, who is 4 and a half years old, has been in school for two terms since starting school in September, but does not speak at all to adults. She interacts verbally with her peers, and both you and the class teacher will speak to her as to other children, but her only responses have been to nod or shake her head.

1. What strategies might you use to encourage Cassie to communicate, both verbally and non-verbally?
2. How could you work with others to support Cassie in school?

Communicating with others is an important aspect in the development of confidence and self-esteem. As we

grow up, we interact with others, which reinforces our understanding of who we are and how we fit into our own families and the wider community. As children develop it is important that they have opportunities to socialise and work with others and to feel part of different situations. Children who have communication and interaction needs will need to have support and encouragement and should be included in all activities alongside other children.

5 Understand how transitions and significant events affect children's lives

The potential effect of transitions and significant events

As well as passing through different stages, young children's development may be affected by transitions and significant events. Young children feel more secure and confident when they can predict routines and know about what is going to happen; any unpredicted incident may affect their behaviour, self-esteem and wellbeing. However, there are also some events for which adults can prepare them.

Jargon buster

Significant event – any event that causes disruption to the normal routine or situation.

Transition – a period of change.

Moving to school

For some children, moving to school can cause a level of anxiety that affects their behaviour and how they relate to others. They may become tearful and clingy towards parents and carers, lose their appetite or withdraw. This will mean that the transition becomes more stressful for both children and parents, and can cause upset and lack of concentration at school.

Unit 1

27

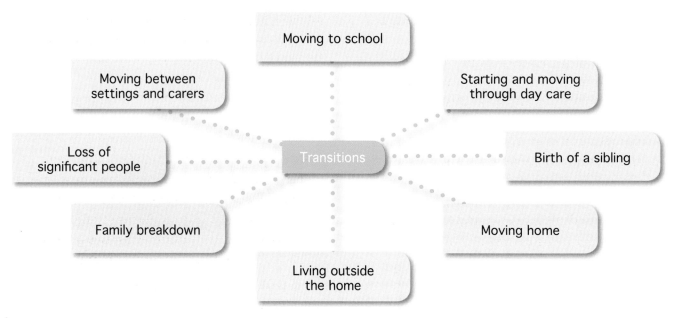

Figure 1.14: How can you help children to cope with the different transitions shown here?

Starting and moving through day care

This can also be traumatic and cause upset for children, depending on their age and how much they are used to being at home with a parent or carer.

Birth of a sibling

In most cases, the birth of a sibling is an exciting event for a young child. However, after the initial excitement has worn off, young children's behaviour may change as they become unsure about their place in the family and seek attention for themselves. They may be angry, have an increased need for affection, regress in behaviour or develop low self-confidence.

Jargon buster

Regress – go backwards.

Moving home

Moving home is likely to unsettle young children as familiar surroundings and routines will be affected.

This may lead to clinginess, confusion and feeling unsettled until they become used to their new home and routines.

Living outside of the home

If young children live outside of the home for any reason, their routines will be disrupted and they will feel unsettled. This may coincide with other incidents – for example, family breakdown or parental illness – which may compound the problem.

Family breakdown

Family breakdown can be traumatic for young children. One parent is likely to move out of the family home and children will be aware of bad feeling between adults. Young children sometimes feel that the breakdown of their parents' relationship is their fault, which can cause further problems in the long term. Family breakdown can also affect children's confidence and self-esteem. This can be exaggerated if one or both parents immediately or soon has a new partner, which will put a strain on existing relationships.

Loss of significant people

We are all deeply affected by the loss of significant people in our lives and young children will be particularly so. They will need support from other close family members and significant adults to help them through this traumatic time. Children who lose significant people may have a number of reactions including lack of sleep or concentration, loss of appetite or motivation, and withdrawal.

Moving between settings and carers

This situation can disrupt routines and make children anxious, as they will be unsure about where they will be. This may cause emotional outbursts or affect their behaviour.

Preparing and supporting children

Where children are experiencing transitions and significant events, adults close to them should anticipate and support them in different ways so that they are reassured as much as possible.

Open communication and discussion

It is vital that children feel able to talk about what will be happening to them and can discuss any anxieties with adults. When children feel unable to voice their feelings, they are likely to be more affected by what is happening.

Routines that reassure

Adults should retain as many routines as possible to reassure children and so that they can feel they have some knowledge of what will happen next.

Familiarisation visits

Where children will be transferring between settings or starting school, they should have the opportunity to visit the new setting beforehand. They will be able to meet other children and the adults, including their key person, and become familiar with the new place that they will be attending.

Encouraging questions

Adults should encourage children to ask as many questions as they need so that they will be able to alleviate anxieties as they arise.

Case study 1.6

Max, aged 4 years, has recently found out that his parents are separating and that his mother has a new partner. Although Max has been told about what is happening and the setting is aware, he has recently started displaying some aggressive behaviour towards other children.

1. What would you do in this situation as Max's key person?

2. How could you support the family in managing Max's behaviour?

The effect of stable relationships

Stable relationships are important to young children as they bring consistency and a feeling of stability and reassurance. If these adults are supportive and communicative, it is likely that children will feel less anxious about what is going to happen during periods of transition. Children are also less likely to feel anxious if they undergo further changes, and will be better able to cope with unexpected events in their lives later on.

Find the balance

Jane Adams, Early Years Leader: 'When I first started my course, I found it difficult to balance work and study, particularly as I have enrolled on a maths course as well. My family has always come first and we have all had to look at different ways in which we can work together. However, studying maths with my 15 year old has been great for both of us, and has helped us to spend more time together.'

Case study 1.7

Selinica, aged 4 years, is from a single-parent family. Her mother does not have other support in the UK as she is from Albania.

Raj aged 5 years, has been at school in reception class since September and lives in a large family.

You have just heard that, in both cases, the children are to move away to a different area, and will be changing schools and moving house. Selinica's mother has said that she is not going to tell her about it until it happens, as she is worried about the effect it will have on her. Raj's parents have come to see you and have talked about the new school and moving house. They will be taking Raj to meet his new teacher and explore the new area.

1. What might you say to each family?

2. How could you support them in each case so that the children have minimal disruption during their transition?

Further reading and resources

Publications

- Athey, C. (2007) *Extending Thought in Young Children: A Parent–Teacher Partnership* (2nd ed.), London: Sage Publications

- Donaldson, M. (1986) *Children's Minds,* London: HarperCollins

- Fraley, R. C. (2010) *A Brief Overview of Adult Attachment Theory and Research* – good summary of attachment theory, with information on Bowlby, Ainsworth, and Hazan and Shaver – available online at http://internal.psychology.illinois.edu/~rcfraley/attachment.htm

- Gerhardt, S. (2004) *Why Love Matters: How Affection Shapes a Baby's Brain,* Oxford: Routledge

- Lindon, J. (2012) *What Does It Mean To Be Two?* (3rd ed.), London: Practical Pre-School Books

- Lindon, J. (2012) *Understanding Child Development: 0–8 years: Linking Theory and Practice* (3rd ed.), London: Hodder Education

- Thornton, S. (2008) *Understanding Human Development: Biological, Social and Psychological Processes from Conception to Adult Life*, Basingstoke: Palgrave Macmillan

Websites

- Children's Play Information Service: www.ncb.org.uk/cpis – national information service on children's play with reference library and free enquiry service

- Common Threads: www.commonthreads.org.uk – a worldwide community of practitioners, trainers, development and support workers, authors, academics and theorists that promotes playwork theory and practice

- Department of Education: www.gov.uk/childrens-services/early-learning-childcare – committed to providing high-quality early education and support for parents, children and young people

- Early Education: www.early-education.org.uk – believes every child deserves the best possible start in life and support to fulfill their potential

- International Play Association: www.ipaworld.org – forum for exchange and action to promote children's right to play

- KIDS: www.kids.org.uk – provides opportunities and support to children with disabilities, young people and their families

Articles and magazines

- *Early Years Educator* (EYE magazine): www.magonlinelibrary.com/toc/eyed/current – a good source of articles and information

- *Nursery World*: www.nurseryworld.magazine.co.uk – useful articles, information and job advertisements

Implementing the Early Years Foundation Stage

Implementing the Early Years Foundation Stage

This unit introduces you to one of the most important documents you will come across in your work with children. The Early Years Foundation Stage is a framework that all early years practitioners in England have to follow. You will see how this framework ensures that you meet the diverse needs of all the children in your setting, helping each of them to fulfil their potential.

Before you start

Why do you think safeguarding is a major part of the EYFS? What are the major differences between planning for a 2 year old and a 4 year old? How can you support a child's learning during child-initiated play? What will you have to consider when planning an adult-led activity?

Learning outcomes

By the end of this unit you will:

1. **understand the Early Years Foundation Stage (EYFS)**
2. **understand how to apply the safeguarding and welfare requirements within the EYFS**
3. **be able to implement the education programme within the EYFS**
4. **be able to support children's progress towards EYFS outcomes.**

1 Understand the Early Years Foundation Stage (EYFS)

The Early Years Foundation Stage – or EYFS, as you will often hear it called – is the framework that sets standards for learning, development, safeguarding and welfare for children in England from birth to 5 years.

Working in an early years setting, you must have a detailed understanding of its:

- scope and legal status
- overall structure
- principles and themes.

You also need to understand how your setting will be inspected, and how and when children's development is assessed.

The EYFS aims to ensure that those working with children from birth to 5 years provide:

- **quality and consistency** in all early years settings, so that every child makes good progress and no child gets left behind
- **a secure foundation** through learning and development opportunities which are planned around the needs and interests of each individual child and are assessed and reviewed regularly
- **partnership working** between practitioners and with parents and/or carers
- **equality of opportunity** and anti-discriminatory practice, ensuring that every child is included and supported.

(Source: Statutory Framework for the Early Years Foundation Stage, Department for Education, 2014, p.5)

Scope and legal status

The EYFS was initially introduced in 2007 and became statutory in 2008, with the aim of improving outcomes for all children in the early years. It is mandatory – so there are legal requirements on you to make that the standards in the framework are met.

The legal status of the EYFS is based on several different pieces of legislation, which are discussed in more detail later in this book:

- For the Children Act 1989 and 2004 – see Unit 8, learning outcome 1.
- For the Data Protection Act 1998 – see Unit 7, learning outcome 1.
- For the Childcare Act 2006 – see Unit 7, learning outcome 1.
- For the Safeguarding Vulnerable Groups Act 2006 – see Unit 8, learning outcome 1.

Since 2012, it has been a legal requirement for all early years providers in maintained schools and non-maintained schools or independent schools to implement the EYFS, as well as all those on Ofsted's Early Years Register, which includes childminders and other childcare providers.

The settings working within the EYFS framework include:

- children's centres
- daycare nurseries
- maintained nursery schools
- reception classes in schools
- preschool groups
- home-based care.

Some settings providing care for children under 5 years, such as centres offering wrap-around and holiday care, do not need to meet all the learning and development requirements. However, they need to be guided by EYFS standards and encouraged to think about how they can complement the learning children gain where they spend most of their time.

Jargon buster

Legislation – a law or group of laws.

Maintained school – school maintained by a local authority, funded by public money.

Mandatory – required by law; not optional.

Non-maintained or independent school – school that is privately run and privately funded.

Safeguarding – all areas of keeping children safe, including considering the adults who work with them, health and safety, suitable environments, behaviour, outings, medication and child protection.

Statutory – having a legal status.

Overall structure

The overall structure of the EYFS is designed as a framework for practitioners working with children under 5 to follow. Whichever curriculum is used, the setting must meet the standards for children's development, learning and care.

The EYFS is divided into three sections:

- learning and development requirements
- assessment
- safeguarding and welfare requirements.

Learning and development requirements

The EYFS outlines how children will learn and develop skills according to their age – although remember that children develop at different rates, so a child not yet walking at 14 months is not necessarily a concern. The framework covers the education and care of all children in early years provision, including children with special educational needs and disabilities.

Every child is expected to learn skills, acquire new knowledge and show their understanding through seven areas of learning and development.

- **Three prime areas**:
  - » communication and language
  - » physical development
  - » personal, social and emotional development.
- **Four specific areas**:
  - » literacy
  - » mathematics
  - » understanding the world
  - » expressive arts and design.

For more on these areas, see learning outcome 3 in this unit.

At the end of each area of learning there is an early learning goal, which children should meet by the end of their reception year.

You will need to consider how children learn. The characteristics of learning are:

- playing and exploring
- active learning
- creating and thinking critically.

They should be reflected in all areas of your assessment, observation and planning.

Assessment

The EYFS recognises the importance of assessment as part of the planning cycle so that you can meet each child's needs and plan appropriate activities. Formative and summative assessments are made using the early years outcomes as outlined within the prime and specific areas of learning. Children are assessed at two points during the EYFS:

- between 24 and 36 months – called the progress check at age 2
- at the end of the final term of the academic year when the child becomes 5 years old – called the EYFS profile.

Safeguarding and welfare requirements

All early years providers, including childminders, must make sure that children are always healthy, safe and secure. The standards offer clear guidance on how to do this. Some of the key areas are:

- child protection
- suitable people
- staff qualifications, training and support skills
- key person
- staff:child ratios
- health
- suitability and safety of premises.

Principles and themes

The EYFS contains four guiding themes, each of which has a principle behind it. These aim to ensure that every child is looked after in an environment where they feel safe, able to learn and make progress.

The themes and principles give you guidance on how you look after each child in your care and work with parents and colleagues. They also help you to provide a range of activities that will enable each child to reach their potential.

Here are the four EYFS themes and principles.

- **A unique child** – Every child is a unique child, who is constantly learning and can be resilient, capable, confident and self-assured.
- **Positive relationships** – Children learn to be strong and independent through positive relationships.
- **Enabling environments** – Children learn and develop well in enabling environments, in which their experiences respond to their individual needs and there is a strong partnership between practitioners and parents and/or carers.
- **Learning and development** – Children develop and learn in different ways and at different rates. The framework covers the education and care of all children in early years provision, including children with special educational needs and disabilities.

(Source: Statutory Framework for the Early Years Foundation Stage, Department for Education, 2014, p.6)

Here is how these four principles impact on your practice.

Treating each child as unique

Each baby and child will develop in their own way and at their own pace. You need to give each area of their development equal importance, in a way that recognises that particular child. In our diverse culture, you need to value all individuals, families and communities and not discriminate. You also need to recognise that young children are vulnerable and safeguard them, ensuring their wellbeing. A child's health is an important part of their development, so be aware of this in your practice too.

Positive relationships

Your relationship with the children you are caring for should be respectful and show a clear awareness of the feelings of both the child and their family. Parents are the people who usually spend the most time with their child, and you should have a shared approach to their education. In this way you can have a positive impact on children's learning.

As a key person, you have an important role in making a special link between the child's home and your setting. Your actions will help build positive relationships with the parents through a shared knowledge of the child.

Enabling environments

Your learning environment should reflect each child's needs and allow them to make choices. Your routines or schedules should take into account the development levels of the children: for example, making sure that babies can sleep when they need to, rather than at a scheduled time. Create activities that are age-appropriate, but always challenge a child to develop their learning.

Your environment should be rich in resources and accessible to the child – but still a safe place in which they can explore and learn new concepts. Think about the child's wider world – their home, community and culture – when planning and updating the environment in your setting.

Learning and development

You will need to plan for all areas that the EYFS prescribes, while still considering the particular interests and stages of the children in your care. The different areas of their learning and development are interconnected, so they will learn in a **holistic** way – and your planning needs to take this into account. The educational programme at your centre should be play-based and contain a variety of adult-led and child-initiated activities throughout the day. Children's individual needs should be supported in planning and all planning should be based upon the observations made by the practitioners.

Figure 2.1: How do forest schools help children to explore and respond to challenging opportunities?

Jargon buster

Early learning goal – one of 17 EYFS goals covering each of the seven areas of development, giving the level of progress children should be expected to attain by the end of the EYFS.

Formative assessment – part of daily practice that informs how you can meet each child's requirements on an ongoing basis.

Holistic – making links across different areas of learning and development.

Summative assessment – assessment carried out at a specific period, such as the progress check for 2–3 year olds, that informs you of where the child is in their learning development and sums up the evidence gathered throughout the formative assessment process.

It is important to recognise that there are different approaches to young children's learning. Some settings will follow a different approach but still meet the standards of the EYFS framework.

Theory in action

The EYFS is a framework of expected standards that can be met through a variety of approaches to learning. The framework may not be quite what you are used to, but the same standards apply. Montessori, HighScope and Steiner use slightly different approaches but they all follow the standards set out in the EYFS framework. You can find out more on the websites listed at the end of this unit.

Think about the similarities and differences between your setting and one of these three approaches. For example, observing children is at the centre of any Montessori programme of teaching and learning. What else is similar? What is different?

How settings are inspected

All early years settings will be inspected to make sure they continue to meet the requirements of the EYFS, and assessed to see how well they are doing.

The body responsible for these inspections is Ofsted – the Office for Standards in Education, Children's Services and Skills. As well as looking at the overall quality and standard of provision, including teaching and learning, Ofsted will consider three areas:

- how your setting meets the needs of the range of children who attend
- how well the provision contributes to each child's wellbeing
- the quality of the leadership and management in your setting.

Methods

Ofsted inspectors use observations and other evidence to reach their judgement about a setting's provision.

Observations

Inspectors spend time observing a range of different care routines and activities. They may conduct joint observations with managers, and they may use evidence of your own observations.

Other evidence

Inspectors gather evidence to evaluate the progress children are making towards the early years goals. This could include planning and observation notes or progress checks. Inspectors may track the progress of specific children, for example those who need intervention. They may refer to a setting's policies and procedures, and safeguarding and welfare practices, and may talk to the manager, staff and children, and any parents or carers present.

Judgements and grades

Ofsted inspectors have clear criteria against which to make their judgements. They take into account different contexts, such as the age of the children, the amount of time children spend there or the number of children who attend other settings too.

There are four possible grades that your setting could achieve:

- grade 1 (outstanding)
- grade 2 (good)
- grade 3 (requires improvement)
- grade 4 (inadequate).

Results are posted on the Ofsted website so that they are available to anyone, including parents and carers. Settings that do not meet the required standards will be given a timeframe and guidance to improve before a further inspection.

Case study 2.1

Jeralyn had attended a two-day course, learning about how recognising children's schemas is so important for their learning. When the inspector visited, he could see that the children in her 12–24 month unit were well provided for and engaged in learning through schemas. He looked at the children's individual planning sheets, which showed how these schemas influenced the way the setting supported each child. He also looked at some learning journals where schemas were observed and parents had shared their observations at home, and saw video clips of children's schemas, used to help understand children's current learning. Displays showed learning stories of different schemas. When talking to Jeralyn, the inspector found out that she had regular sessions with parents looking at their children's learning and sharing their knowledge. The feedback from the parent surveys was very positive about this area.

1. What do you think the inspector will think about the way Jeralyn is working with parents?

2. How do you think he will comment on the way that the individual children's learning needs are met?

3. How will the inspector evaluate the impact that Jeralyn's professional learning and knowledge about schemas has had on children's learning?

Jargon buster

Schemas – patterns of thoughts or repeated behaviour that can be noticed when observing young children's play. More information on this can be found in Unit 4, learning outcome 4.

Theory in action

To accurately assess and support young children, you need to understand how they develop and how to support them at each stage. *Early Years Outcomes*, from the Department for Education, is a non-statutory guide that will help you to assess whether a child's stage of development is typical for their age. Remember that children progress at different rates.

1. Look at page 11 of *Early Years Outcomes*. How would you assess the physical development of a child aged between 22 and 36 months, to establish their ability to:

   » run safely on the whole foot?

   » squat with steadiness to rest or play with an object on the ground, and rise to their feet without using hands?

   » climb confidently and begin to pull themselves up on nursery play or climbing equipment?

How children's development is assessed

The EYFS requires two main assessments of children's development:

- a progress check at age 2
- an assessment at the end of the EYFS.

Progress check at age 2

This is carried out in the child's setting. It enables practitioners to understand and reflect on where the child is in their development, celebrate success and highlight any areas that might need further discussion or support. It is important that parents are engaged throughout the process, knowing that their child will be supported if they need further help.

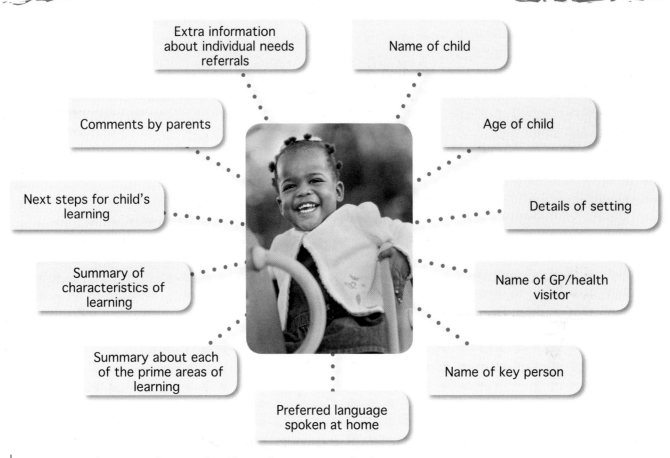

Figure 2.2: Information that you should record in a progress check at age 2.

There is no special method that you have to use when checking children of this age. However, you should only use the prime areas of learning and development for this check.

Figure 2.2 shows what has to be included in this progress check. If you are not involved in these checks yourself, ask your manager if you can see a sample from your setting.

When assessing 2 year olds you will be expected to provide a report of a child's stage of development at a given time around their second birthday. This should include evidence of what they can do or are learning to do in each of the prime areas: for example, sharing a book or putting two words together.

You should also:

- support your assessment through evidence of a child's progress, such as observations, photos or examples of work

- highlight any areas where a child might be developing at a faster or slower pace than expected, such as a child being able to count everyday items accurately

- note a child's schemas – their patterns of play

- share observations with the child's parents, perhaps by discussing video clips or sharing a child's learning journal

- encourage parents to share observations they have made

- consult with other professionals where appropriate.

As a part of the Government's Healthy Child Programme, health visitors will usually carry out a review on a child's health around the age of 2 years. Parents may share the setting's progress check with the health visitor as it might contain useful information: for example, if it identifies concerns that the child does not always seem to hear noise around them.

COMMUNICATION AND LANGUAGE		
Listening and attention	**Understanding**	**Speaking**
Birth–11 months, 8–20 months 16–26 months, 22–36 months 30–50 months, 40–60+ months	Birth–11 months, 8–20 months 16–26 months, 22–36 months 30–50 months, 40–60+ months	Birth–11 months, 8–20 months 16–26 months, 22–36 months 30–50 months, 40–60+ months

Summary of observation

Isla loves to take part in familiar songs and rhymes, and is really enjoying Old MacDonald at the moment. She shows a real interest in animals, often pointing to pictures in books, making animal noises and articulating animal names such as 'dog' and 'cat'.

Isla also enjoys sitting in the cosy area, sharing a book with an adult or looking at a book on her own. Her mother has observed that a favourite activity at home is sharing a book with her father.

Isla copies actions of songs such as 'wind the bobbin' in nursery. Her mum says she is often doing these actions and singing the songs at home.

Isla can engage for some time in activities such as playing with the small world animal farm set, often making noises of the animals as she plays.

She is beginning to play with other children and talks to them when playing. She brought a photo of her granny's dog, Ivy, to nursery and pointed to her collar, saying, 'Ivy likes walks'.

Figure 2.3: What key information can you identify in the following progress check?

Figure 2.3 is an extract from the progress check at age 2 for a girl called Isla, focusing on her communication and language.

The EYFS profile

This should be carried out in the final term of the year in which the child reaches the age of 5 years. It ensures a smoother transition between the foundation stage and school, particularly for children who may have any additional needs.

The EYFS profile is assessed against the 17 early learning goals, which are mapped to the seven areas of learning and development. This profile aims to:

- give practitioners, parents, carers and teachers a holistic picture of the child's development
- assess the child's knowledge, skills and understanding
- indicate if children are meeting the early learning goals
- give teachers in Year 1 of primary school a view of where the child is in their learning.

Three terms are used to summarise the child's level of development:

- **expected** – the child is learning and developing at the right level for his/her age
- **exceeding** – the child is achieving at a higher level than the early learning goal
- **emerging** – the child has not yet reached the expected level.

If you are completing the assessment, you must make sure that it is supported by ongoing observations carried out in your setting, and that it reflects all records the setting holds.

The voice of the child

The EYFS profile also needs to include the voice of the child. You can do this by involving even young children in their assessment, encouraging them to think about their own learning. A young 2 year old could comment on photos of themselves engaged in an activity, gesturing if they do not yet have the language skills to say that they enjoyed it.

Kim was making jiaozi in a cooking pot. He pointed and said, 'Look! It's a dumpling. It's sticky and white. My granny eats this. Smell it!' He offered it to me and I said, 'That smells good, Kim. How are you going to cook it?' He said, 'We'll put it in very hot bubbly water with the wire cage. It will be very hot, so Nolan will help us and we'll watch.'

Greg drew a very detailed picture of a monster and explained all the details to me. He held his finger up and said, 'Ssh. The googly monster is about to have a baby so we have to be quiet when I draw it.' Me: 'Do you have to be quiet around your baby brother, Greg?' Greg: 'Yes, we do quiet things because he cries a lot when he's awake because he's so little. When he's big like me, he won't cry so much.'

James and Daisy were building a railway on the edge of a table.
James: 'This is a railway on a hill. I went on one like this with my Mum and Dad. I could see the snowy mountains and I slept there.'
Daisy: 'My mum goes on a train every day to work but it's flat I think. Tomorrow, she won't go on the train because it's the weekend.'
James: 'Is she scared?'
Daisy: 'No, she reads lots.'

Figure 2.4: What can you observe about the learning that is taking place in these children's play?

Reflect

Consider how the informal notes made by the practitioner in Figure 2.4 could provide evidence that children were meeting the following early learning goal 3: Communication and language – Speaking. *Children express themselves effectively, showing awareness of listeners' needs. They use past, present and future forms accurately when talking about events that have happened or are to happen in the future. They develop their own narratives and explanations by connecting ideas or events.*

(Source: Statutory Framework for the Early Years Foundation Stage, Department for Education, 2014, p.10)

Moderation and data

To ensure consistency, local authorities have a moderation process which registered providers may be required to take part in. Not all settings will be involved, but local authorities may visit up to 25 per cent of settings in their area. If necessary, they can arrange for training in completing the EYFS profile.

The Foundation Years website offers a range of documents that tell you more about the progress check at age 2 and the EYFS Profile, including a 'how to' guide.

2 Understand how to apply the safeguarding and welfare requirements within the EYFS

The EYFS framework stresses the importance of keeping children safe. It gives detailed guidance for providers to ensure that they meet the requirements for the safety and wellbeing of each child, including the following areas:

- child protection
- suitable people
- staff qualifications, training, support and skills
- key person
- staff:child ratios
- health
- managing behaviour
- safety and suitability of premises, environment and equipment
- managing information and records about children.

The key requirements

The third section of the EYFS framework demands a focus on children's safety and wellbeing, to ensure that your setting is a safe place.

There are strong reasons why the safeguarding and welfare requirements in the EYFS are statutory. Children are more likely to do well and to learn in a safe environment, where they are cared for by people who have their best interests at heart. A setting that understands and complies with these requirements will be a safe, secure and healthy place where children feel listened to and respected, and parents and carers are confident that their children are being properly cared for.

These requirements ensure a minimum standard of safety, and address areas that are of particular concern these days. Adults working with children must now be screened more effectively, as must visitors to your setting. Parents in vulnerable situations can also be assured of a better framework of support.

Most importantly, the requirements make sure that the child's voice is respected, and that any child can report concerns about their safety with confidence.

Child protection

Suitable policies must be in place to make sure that children are protected from any form of abuse. These will cover safe recruitment, safe working practices, professional learning, lines of communication and recording procedures.

People, qualifications, training, support and skills

Effective recruiting procedures – including a criminal record, reference and qualification check – must screen out any people who may not be suitable to work with children.

The Government has the authority to stop people from working with children. Providers or practitioners can be barred from working in early years settings, or a manager may be prevented from leading a setting if they do anything that might harm or endanger the safety of a child.

The 2012 report of the Nutbrown review made recommendations to ensure that staff working with children are appropriately qualified and have access to professional learning opportunities. The report includes guidance about supervision requirements and record-keeping skills. At least one person in your setting needs to hold a current paediatric first aid qualification.

Staff:child ratios and a key person for each child

The EYFS states that a key person should be assigned to every child to ensure a smooth transition between home and the setting and to meet their individual needs.

The number of staff on duty in a setting is a legal requirement, and you have to follow the statutory guidance. Having the appropriate number of adults will ensure that children are adequately supervised and that the environment is safe and secure.

Table 2.1 summarises the EYFS guidance on ratios.

Table 2.1: Staff:child ratios required under the EYFS.

Provider	Age of child	Minimum staff:child ratio	Qualifications and experience
Any, excluding childminders	Under 2 years	1:3	• At least one member of staff to have a full and relevant Level 3 qualification • At least half of all other staff to have a full and relevant Level 2 qualification • At least half of all staff must have specified training in the care of babies • Head of under-2s room must have suitable experience of working with under-2
Any, excluding childminders	2 years	1:4	• At least one member of staff to have a full and relevant Level 3 qualification • At least half of all other staff to have a full and relevant Level 2 qualification
Early years setting	3 years +	1:13	Where a person with Qualified Teacher Status, Early Years Professional Status, Early Years Teacher Status or another suitable Level 6 qualification **is** working directly with the children there must be: • at least one other member of staff with a full and relevant Level 3 qualification
Early years setting	3 years +	1:8	Where a person with Qualified Teacher Status, Early Years Professional Status, Early Years Teacher Status or another suitable Level 6 qualification is **not** working directly with the children there must be: • at least one member of staff with a full and relevant Level 3 qualification • at least half of all other staff must hold a full and relevant Level 2 qualification
Independent school	3 years +	1:30 for classes where the majority of children will reach the age of 5 or older within the school year 1:13 for all other classes	Where a person with Qualified Teacher Status, Early Years Professional Status, Early Years Teacher Status or another suitable Level 6 qualification, an instructor, or another suitably qualified overseas trained teacher, **is** working directly with the children there must be: • at least one other member of staff with a full and relevant Level 3 qualification
Independent school	3 years +	1:8	Where there is **no** person with Qualified Teacher Status, Early Years Professional Status, Early Years Teacher Status or another suitable Level 6 qualification, **no** instructor, and **no** suitably qualified overseas trained teacher, working directly with the children: • at least one member of staff must hold a full and relevant Level 3 qualification • at least half of all other staff must have a full and relevant Level 2 qualification
Maintained nursery schools and nursery classes in maintained schools (not reception)	3 years +	1:13	• At least one member of staff must be a school teacher • At least one other member of staff must hold a full and relevant Level 3 qualification

(Source: Statutory Framework for the Early Years Foundation Stage, Department for Education, 2014, pp.22–24)

Health, safety and security of each child

Medicine

There must be a policy and procedure for administering medicines, both those prescribed by a doctor or for everyday medicines such as Calpol. Staff must be trained to administer medication and special equipment such as Epipens® for allergic reactions.

Food and drink

The setting must ensure that all meals and snacks are balanced and nutritious.

Accident or injury

The setting must ensure that first aid boxes are accessible and up to date, that all accidents are recorded and that parents are informed.

Managing behaviour

Your setting's policy on behaviour management should focus on positive behaviour. It is important to note that corporal punishment is an offence. If for some reason you have to use physical intervention, the parents must be informed immediately and the incident must be recorded.

Premises, environment and equipment

Your setting must comply with the following requirements.

- Premises should be fit for purpose and comply with health and safety legislation.
- Evacuation procedures should be clearly communicated and followed.
- Safety equipment should be checked and maintained regularly.
- Smoking should not be allowed.
- Facilities should include suitable indoor and outdoor space, adequate toileting facilities and areas to meet parents.
- Clear and secure procedures for picking up children should be in place.

- Suitable sleeping space should be provided for younger children, with overnight sleeping arrangements as appropriate.
- Public liability insurance should be in place.
- Risk assessments must be carried out.

Figure 2.5: Why is it important to have clear procedures for collecting children from a setting?

Equal opportunities

Your setting must have policies and procedures to promote equal opportunities for the children in its care, including support for children with special educational needs or disabilities. Your policy must cover a wide range of areas, including how the setting will encourage children to value and respect others.

Information and records

Your setting must keep clear and accessible records, and maintain a regular two-way flow of information with parents and carers. While these records must be accessible, they must always be kept secure and you must always respect the setting's rules about confidentiality and privacy. You must give parents and carers access to all records about their child, provided that there are no exemptions under the Data Protection Act.

Case study 2.2

At the Lake Street preschool, Niamh, an art student, was coming to spend a month in the setting. She was a cousin of a mum in the setting, doing a project about collaborative art with young children. It was planned that Niamh would take small groups into the shared space and work with them on large canvases. Everyone else working in the setting had police checks and had some safeguarding training. The manager contacted the Disclosure and Barring Service (DBS) and helped Niamh to complete her check, which she submitted. The manager also gave her some training about safeguarding although they were not due to do any for three months.

1. Why do you think the manager checked Niamh even though she was the cousin of a mum who was known to them?

2. What do you think Niamh should have found out in her training?

3. How do you think the children, staff and parents could be prepared for Niamh's visit?

Meeting the requirements

To ensure that children are safeguarded, there are other specific things your setting must do to meet the requirements of the EYFS.

A safeguarding policy

Your setting must have a safeguarding policy, which is shared and visible to the whole community, and available on its website. The governing body must agree the policy, and nominate a member to have a safeguarding focus. The policy must be reviewed and updated annually and must be made available to any stakeholder on request.

Designated staff member for safeguarding

Your setting must have a designated staff member who is responsible for safeguarding issues. They should be the first line of communication if you have any concerns about a child. They have to have special training so that they can support any expression of concern and identify, understand and know how to respond to any concerns about possible neglect. You should know who the designated staff member is and what you should do if you are concerned about the safety or welfare of a child in your care.

Disclosure

Every adult should know what the procedures are if a child or an adult makes a disclosure. Your setting must be clear as to how it will communicate with an agency such as social services in case of any concerns. A whistle-blowing policy will protect any staff member disclosing information about a colleague, the person experiencing an allegation and, of course, the child concerned.

Good safeguarding practice

Your setting should promote and encourage good safeguarding practice in every area of its work. This should be emphasised through staff meetings, individual meetings and parent meetings.

Staff, parents, volunteers and visitors should be informed that they can raise concerns about poor or unsafe practice with regard to children and young people.

Jargon buster

Disclosure and Barring Service (DBS) – the service that checks an individual's criminal record and issues certificates to adults wanting to work with children and young people.

Whistle blowing – raising concerns about the actions of an individual, group or organisation.

3 Be able to implement the education programme within the EYFS

The EYFS education programme has a number of requirements that you will need to meet. A good understanding of the framework and what it aims to achieve will help you to plan and work effectively.

The scope of the areas of learning

As you saw in learning outcome 1 of this unit, there are seven areas of learning within the EYFS. These cover all different areas of a child's development, and you need to take them into account when you are planning play and activities in your setting.

The areas of learning are clear, but they allow you to consider the individuality of the children you work with, the different environments they learn in, the different relationships they form and the different ways in which they learn. The areas have 'typical behaviours' attached which describe how you might expect a child to react or engage in the areas described, for example:

Communication and Language – Listening and attention

A child of 11 months turns towards a familiar sound then locates a range of sounds with accuracy.

There are three prime areas and four specific areas of learning in the EYFS.

The prime areas

These areas form the foundations for children's future progress, and ensure that they are ready for school.

- **Communication and language development** – involves ensuring that children experience a rich language environment, develop their confidence and skills in expressing themselves, and speak and listen in a range of situations.
- **Physical development** – involves providing opportunities for young children to be active and interact with both peers and adults to develop their

coordination, control and movement. Children must also be helped to understand the importance of physical activity, and to make healthy choices in relation to food.

- **Personal, social and emotional development** – involves helping children to develop a positive sense of themselves and of others. They need to be given opportunities to form positive relationships and develop respect for others, develop social skills and learn how to manage their feelings. You also need to enable them to understand appropriate behaviour in groups and to have confidence in their own abilities.

Reflect

Lara, aged 2 years, has taken some time to settle into her setting. Her key person, Assam, observes Lara using single words as she puts a bag on her arm and says 'work' and happily waves 'bye' to Assam.

1. Why do you think that Lara is doing this?
2. Which of the prime areas does her play cover?
3. How could Assam use this observation to draw Lara's parents' attention to the three prime areas of development?

The specific areas

These areas apply and reinforce the prime areas, and have a closer link with National Curriculum subject areas.

- **Literacy** – Involves encouraging children to link sounds and letters and to begin to read and write. You must give children access to a wide range of reading materials (books, poems and other written materials) to inspire their interest.
- **Mathematics** – Involves providing children with opportunities to develop and improve their skills in counting, understanding and using numbers, to calculate simple addition and subtraction problems, and to describe shapes, spaces and measures.

- **Understanding the world** – Involves guiding children to make sense of their physical world and their community through opportunities to explore, observe and find out about people, places, technology and the environment.

- **Expressive arts and design** – Involves enabling children to explore and play with a wide range of media and materials, as well as providing opportunities and encouragement for sharing their thoughts, ideas and feelings through a variety of activities in art, music, movement, dance, role play, and design and technology.

(Source: text adapted from Statutory Framework for the Early Years Foundation Stage, Department for Education, 2014, p.8)

Figure 2.6: Why is it important to build good relationships with the children in your care?

Case study 2.3

Helen and Louise were planning a texture walk with a group of 4 to 5 year olds in their reception class. The children had been looking at different textures in the environment, such as different ground textures and textures of walls. The five children each had a mini iPad and each took a lot of photos in the playground, the forest area, the learning areas outside the classroom and the front area of the school. When they returned they put the photos onto a slideshow and talked about the photos. Helen put captions on the photos of their comments and they shared the slideshow in circle time at the end of the day, describing the photos and recalling their visit. When planning the activity Helen and Louise referred to communication and language, understanding the world, physical development and expressive arts and design.

1. Which of the 'typical behaviours' of the areas of learning and development considered, as outlined in *Early Years Outcomes*, might have been observed?

2. Are there any other areas of learning and development that you think were covered in this activity?

How the four specific areas relate to the three prime areas

The prime areas act as the foundations for the rest of a child's development and learning. They are fundamental to a child's ability to learn and form relationships, as well as for their general wellbeing – so these will be the areas you focus on when working with the youngest children, up to 3 years of age.

At around the age of 3 years, as children become increasingly competent in the three prime areas, they need to build, develop and broaden their skills. The four specific areas aim to do this through literacy, mathematics, understanding the world and expressive arts and design. Confidence in the prime areas will provide a platform for successful learning in these wider, more specific areas.

By the time children get to the end of the Foundation Stage, they should be spending roughly the same amount of time on each of the seven areas of learning.

In all cases you need to consider the individual child and the fact that each child is unique and progresses at their own pace within expected stages of development.

The three characteristics of effective learning

You will know that children learn in different ways and by doing different things. The EYFS identifies three characteristics of learning:

- playing and exploring
- active learning
- creating and thinking critically.

These characteristics are part of the EYFS profile assessment, so you need to show that you understand them in your work with children.

Play activities to support the prime areas of learning

An important part of our role as adults working with children is to facilitate play activities that provide ample opportunity for them to develop in the prime areas of learning.

0 to 3 years

When considering children under 3 having opportunities for the prime areas of learning it is important to understand how they learn so you can best support them and what they can do.

You can do this by:

- observing the way they learn and planning for each child's individual needs and interests
- building a relationship with their main carers to find out as much as you can about the child and their needs
- supporting each child's individual routines
- providing an environment indoors and outdoors that allows them space and the ability to follow their interests, remembering the importance of the three characteristics of learning
- remembering that children under 3 learn through sensory experiences so a variety of textures are important for them, such as different sorts of fabric, wood, smelly objects, shiny objects, etc.

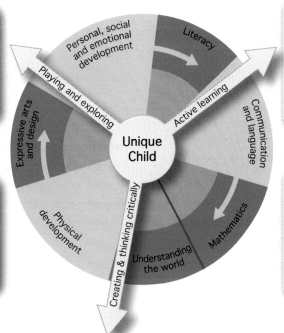

The unique child reaches out to relate to people and things through the characteristics of effective learning, which move through all areas of learning:
- playing and exploring
- active learning
- creating and thinking critically.

Children develop in the context of relationships and the environment around them.

This is unique to each family, and reflects individual communities and cultures.

Prime areas are fundamental, work together, and move through to support development in all other areas.
- Personal, social and emotional development
- Communication and language
- Physical development

Specific areas include essential skills and knowledge for children to participate successfully in society.
- Literacy
- Mathematics
- Understanding the world
- Expressive arts and design

Figure 2.7: The different areas of the EYFS are all interconnected.

- facilitating social interactions so that children can begin to interact with each other, for example by sharing a favourite story with a small group of children or singing a song together.

Children may try the same action on a variety of different objects (think of the child who 'transports' books, bricks and sometimes a doll in a pushchair!). Through their schemas children try to find out how things work and often come up with their own ideas or theories. You will notice that a child usually has more than one schema. Sometimes the schema lasts for a long time and sometimes it is quickly over.

Case study 2.4

Sanita, a trainee in a daycare setting, is planning an activity that ensures that Billy and Evie, both aged 2 years, are encouraged to enjoy and achieve through learning by listening and responding. Sanita has noticed that Billy and Evie love taking items out of the basket and shaking them. She collects a basket of objects that make different sounds for them to play with. Billy laughs when Sanita makes a 'whooshing' sound and joins in. Sanita, Evie and Billy spend a happy ten minutes listening and responding to the sounds of the objects in the basket.

1. How was Sanita providing an enabling environment for Billy and Evie?

2. How were they being encouraged to play and explore?

3. Which prime areas of learning could be observed in this activity?

3 to 5 years

For children aged 3 years or more you should also consider the four specific areas of learning. You should still closely observe the way they learn, facilitate social interactions, build their confidence and build

a relationship with their main carers. You should also ensure that children:

- have opportunities for independent learning and individual choice
- have access to group and individual reading
- can develop gross motor skills in the outdoors through ball play and outdoor challenges
- can develop fine motor skills such as using a pencil, scissors, etc.
- try new things and speaking to peers in activities such as circle time
- develop a phonic awareness
- have opportunities to write, from mark making to recognisable words and sentences
- learn rules and take turns through a variety of games
- learn about their environment
- use IT equipment to enhance their learning
- enjoy singing and rhymes
- use a variety of techniques and skills through creative activity.

Theory in action

Plan a morning in a setting for a 2 year old who shows schemas in transporting and enveloping. Make sure that the morning considers learning opportunities through:

- child-initiated learning
- sensory activities
- appropriate adult-led activities
- routines
- meaningful interactions with adults.

Using observations to plan for progress

To really appreciate how to support the children you work with, you need to have a deep understanding of how they learn. One of the best ways to do this is to carry out observations, which are a type of formative assessment.

An observation does not need to be long. You might make a short observation at the end of a day that makes an important contribution to your planning for that child. Regular observations can help you see how a child is progressing. The more observations you can draw on, the fuller your picture of each child will be – and the better informed your plans will be as you work to meet their needs.

Types of observation

There are different ways to observe children. Which you use will depend on your setting and what is most appropriate for each situation.

- **Free description** – A narrative recording of what you see over a brief period – this can be effective for looking at holistic development.
- **Time sample** – Looking at a child doing an activity over a set period of time or at set intervals – you can use this to see how a child interacts or is involved in the environment.
- **Event sample** – Looking at a particular occurrence or event – this allows you to record the circumstances in which something happens, often relating to behaviour (for example, when a child gets angry about something).
- **Target child** – A series of observations of a particular child, where you can record all the information you need – this can help you to get a picture of a child's holistic development.
- **Parental observations** – Contributions by parents, such as a learning journal – these can be useful evidence about something a child has achieved at home.

Sharing results of observations

It is important that you share and discuss your observations with others, including colleagues, other professionals, parents and carers. They may well have important or interesting information about a child, which will help you build a clearer picture of them – and this will enable you to create, shape and build on activities to meet their needs.

Theory in action

Getting the most from an observation

First make sure that you are aware of the general stage of development the child is at. Have a clear aim for your observation, and decide how you want to record your observations – a pad of sticky notes can be useful, your setting may have a record sheet for you to use, or you may want to devise your own. You may want to observe an activity the child is already familiar with, or you could plan to observe a child while they are learning a new concept. You could use concepts such as:

- putting on shoes/doing up buttons/putting on a coat
- pouring a drink
- mixing some paint
- estimating the weight of objects.

Start by playing or working with the child. Step back and let the child work alone and then intervene, perhaps with some open-ended questioning. An open-ended question encourages a full response rather than a one-word answer; they often begin with 'Why' or 'How'. Continue to support their learning as required, in one session or over a period. Analyse the way that you supported the child and the effect you think this had on their learning.

1. What were they doing?

2. What was the context?

For example, 'Tom was in the sandpit and adding sand to the water to ensure his sand shapes did not fall apart.'

When you are with your colleagues, share your observation. Talk about how you could respond to it. For example, what could you add to the sandpit the next day to extend Tom's interests?

The child's voice in planning

Including a child in planning is probably one of the most beneficial things you can do. By working with a child to find out what they want you can take their learning in some amazing and imaginative directions. For example, you could have a 'sticky note board', and set aside a time for children to stick their ideas on it; you can then consider these ideas in your planning.

Consider the two sticky notes in Figure 2.8 about 3-year-old Gem who is new to the setting and has a circular schema. She is still developing relationships with the other children.

Gem is 3. She was sitting on the floor with her key person, using a large crayon to draw circles on the paper. She looked at her key person and said 'round and round' while she did this.

Gem spent time putting the railway together in a circle. Tom was handing her the trains and people. He had made a circle too.

Figure 2.8: Your observations can be brief – you simply need to record the key points.

Gem appears to have a circular schema, so to plan for her this interest has been added to a planning sheet, shown in Figure 2.9.

Balancing adult-led and child-initiated activities

You will be aware of the need to balance child-initiated activities with adult-led ones. In your setting, you will see a range of activities of both types.

The EYFS talks about the need for play to be a key part of children's learning, saying that adults should encourage them in choosing activities, to help them become more independent. However, the EYFS also expects that, as children grow and develop, the balance will ensure that adult-led activities support a smooth transition into Key Stage One. For example, with the learning of phonics, it is best practice that a child's learning will continue to encourage independent learning, problem-solving and sustained shared thinking.

Jargon buster

Adult-led activity – activity set up and directed by the adult, with a specific learning aim in mind.

Child-initiated activity – activity chosen by the child and led by them.

Sustained shared thinking – when adults and children or groups of children engage in learning together, to talk about or explain their ideas and develop their thinking.

Individual child	Age	Interests/patterns of learning	Next steps
Gem	3 yrs 1 month	Gem is engaged in a circular schema (repeats drawing circular patterns), making circles from the wooden railway and playing with the small world figures and trains.	Give Gem opportunities to develop her schema with painting, the railway, etc. Model language alongside Gem. Encourage Gem to engage Tom in these activities.

Figure 2.9: The observation of Gem's schema is recorded on her individual interest record.

To support child-initiated activities, you will need to provide plenty of resources so that the children can make choices that reflect their interests and the developmental stage they are at. They will be able to choose to learn with other children, developing friendships and enjoying the challenges of working with their peers.

While children should choose the resources they use, it is part of your role to make sure that each child has an equal opportunity to take part and be included in all that your setting has to offer. All of the children should have access to all the resources – and you will have to help this happen.

You will also need to plan adult-led activities to meet the needs of the children for specific groups or for children to choose to come to. These might be connected to a specific interest that the children are following – such as 'pirates' or 'transport' – or they may aim to support the development of skills such as mathematical language – for example, for weighing during a cooking activity.

However this balance is achieved, you should be able to show your contribution to finding the right balance in your plans.

Reflect

Imagine you visit a nursery class of 3- to 4-year-old children attached to a small primary school. The areas of the classroom are clearly accessible. At the moment, areas of the classroom reflect the children's interest in trains, with a ticket office role-play area, paintings of train drivers and conductors on the wall, and learning stories about a recent visit. The children went on a local train and were allowed to look inside the driver's cabin. A range of recycled material is available, with clearly labelled drawers for tape, staplers, string and glue. Two boys are busy making a train. An adult nearby is encouraging them to think deeply about their modelling, showing them photos of their trip and discussing parts of the train they went on. Four children are sharing books in the book corner. Five children are engaged in block play and have gathered some small world people and trains to make a big station. They are trying to work out how to build a bridge. Six other children are in the sand kitchen outside, busy cooking and making food with water and all the equipment. Six other children are cooking train biscuits with one of the adults and are weighing the ingredients out. Three girls are in the creative area painting a large picture with big brushes. An adult nearby asks, 'I wonder why this has turned green?' when a child adds yellow to a large blue circle.

1. Can you identify the child-initiated learning?

2. Why do you think the children were so engaged in their own learning?

3. How do you think the adult may have been encouraging the children to think more deeply about their models?

4. Which areas of learning do you think the adult-led cooking activity could be promoting?

4 Be able to support children's progress towards EYFS outcomes

In the year that children are 5 years old they are expected to reach the early learning outcomes of the EYFS. Not all children will have reached these outcomes by the time they are 5. There are outcomes defined at each stage of development. It is your role to ensure that you are providing developmentally appropriate activities and learning environments to enable children to develop according to the specific outcomes. Remember that each child is unique and children will develop at different rates.

The EYFS outcomes

In 2013 the Department for Education produced a simplified document, *Early Learning Outcomes*, highlighting all the outcomes we want children to achieve before they enter Key Stage One of the National Curriculum. These outcomes are a guide to help practitioners support children's development to reach the early learning goals – a statutory requirement for each child at the end of the school year in which they are 5.

In the document, the early years outcomes are defined by the areas of learning and are listed in specific age bands. You will notice that the age bands overlap: this is because children develop at their own pace and in their own ways. The typical behaviour statements and the order in which the outcomes appear are not necessary steps for individual children, so don't use them as checklists.

Table 2.2 shows the areas of learning and the outcome areas.

Table 2.2: Areas of learning and outcomes.

Area of learning	Outcome areas
Language and communication	• Listening and attention • Understanding • Speaking
Physical development	• Moving and handling • Health and self-care
Personal, social and emotional development	• Self-confidence and self-awareness • Managing feelings and behaviour • Making relationships
Literacy	• Reading • Writing
Mathematics	• Numbers • Shape, space and measures
Understanding the world	• People and communities • The world • Technology
Expressive arts and design	• Exploring and using media and materials • Being imaginative

Evaluating children's progress

In learning outcome 1 of this unit, you read about the EYFS requirements for assessing children's development. To meet these, you need to be involved in a continuing process of evaluating their progress.

You will need to embed the following evaluation cycle in your practice.

1. You observe children's interests, engage parents in observation, make records and add evidence from the child, such as annotated comments, photos or mark making.

2. Together with parents or carers, you identify and record areas to develop in the setting and at home.

3. You plan appropriate activities to meet the child's interests to develop the areas identified.

Figure 2.10: How can you use this cycle to help your evaluations?

As well as the official EYFS progress checks, you can evaluate children's progress in a number of ways.

- **Ongoing assessment on a daily basis** that informs planning of activities or child's individual planning for the next day. For example, 3-year-old Kate may have been fascinated by pouring water into containers in the water tray so it is recommended that an adult asks some questions to extend her thinking when she is next at the water tray, such as, 'I wonder what would happen if you poured water from the big jug into the small cup?'

- **Sharing observations with colleagues** and talking about individual children's progress and how they could be specifically supported in an area of their development. For example, 3-year-old Aziz has been using a palmar (whole-hand) grasp to hold his pencil or crayon. He loves drawing but does not have good control. It was agreed to encourage him to use a tripod (three-finger) grasp to hold his pencils or crayons to give him more effective control.

- **Sharing observations with parents** through talking about children's progress as evident in their learning journal, sharing video clips of similar activities from home and school and asking parents to contribute their own observations.

- **Ensuring that observations are carried out on the environment** to see if it is enabling children's progress in specific areas, such as having access to a range of blocks and small-world play.

- **Regularly reviewing the progress of summative assessment** such as the early learning goals to see if there are areas of a child's development that you may need to focus on. For example, 5-year-old Patrick is soon to leave reception but is reluctant to ask for help if he needs it.

- **Tracking the profile in the final year of the EYFS** while making sure that assessment for children with educational needs or disabilities is adjusted as needed.

- **Taking part in EYFS profile moderation activities** in your setting and local area, to help maintain the quality of your assessment.

You can analyse your plans on a daily or weekly basis to review activities for the next day or the immediate future. You need to be able to adapt at any stage of the process, changing your plan according to your evaluations – don't worry too much about immaculate presentation! It is good practice to write comments on your planning documentation to help you analyse the effectiveness of the plan – this is called annotated planning.

Jargon buster

Annotated planning – planning that has handwritten comments on it to show that it has been adapted daily according to the needs and interests of children observed.

In learning outcome 1 you saw how a child's progress against the early learning goals is described according to three attainment levels: expected, exceeding or emerging.

You will need to develop a deep understanding of their progress against all the expected outcomes. By evaluating children's learning and development in this way, you will be able to provide appropriate activities that will improve a child's learning considerably.

Planning an adult-led activity

When implementing an activity you will need to consider a variety of issues to ensure that it works. Remember that children and young people have different ways of processing information – and planning must take these into account. A mixture of learning styles might be displayed, or children might move from one style to another. We all use a range of learning styles and might have a preference for one, but it can depend on the context. It is important for you to be aware of children's learning styles when planning activities for them.

A **visual learner** will:

- watch people speak as well as listen to them
- look for shape and form in words and numbers
- enjoy pictures in books
- enjoy visual descriptions.

An **auditory learner** will:

- retain and recall spoken words
- enjoy the spoken word
- enjoy different voices
- enjoy an involved explanation
- enjoy communicating with others
- speak aloud when reading.

A **kinaesthetic** leaner will:

- sense relative position and movement
- examine touch and feel in order to learn.

A **sequential learner** will:

- learn and remember things in order
- often be organised in their learning.

A **holistic learner** will:

- have a combination of all styles.

The implementation of any plan for children will involve:

- preparation and setting up of environment/activities
- supporting and facilitating (experiment/problem-solve/challenge)
- positive intervention
- modelling

- engaging and interacting
- sustaining shared thinking
- extending children's learning through open questions
- planning with children
- allowing time for children to learn and develop relationships
- encouraging friendships and quality interactions.

Planning the environment

As you have seen, observations involving children or young people can support the planning of the environment or activities. The environment must also be safe and healthy for children's learning to take place.

Make sure that your planning reflects independence by encouraging things such as:

- self-registration (when children arrive in the morning and perhaps find a photo of themselves and place it on a wall or make a mark against a photo)
- appropriately labelled resources
- accessible resources for the children to choose from
- a range of resources for the children to enjoy free choice in their play
- areas in which to socialise and make friends, such as snack areas or quiet areas in the garden.

Theory in action

Choose one of the following scenarios:

- a 2 year old who has just started nursery
- a 4 year old who loves playing in the construction area
- a boy of 5 years who is not interested in books but loves to play outdoors.

Plan an activity for your chosen scenario. Consider how you would use the environment and meet the needs of the individual child. How will you evaluate the activity?

Identifying children's needs and interests

To plan and provide effectively for the next steps in a child's learning you need to bring together:

- knowledge about individual children
- knowledge about what they can learn.

Knowledge about individual children

Children develop their own thinking and encounter new ideas through play in which they take the lead and make choices. They strive to make sense of how things work in their world and are keen to manage it for themselves.

Watch what children play with and the way they play. By allowing time for children to learn and develop their interests you can encourage them to complete activities at their own pace and revisit their learning or continue an activity at another time. This will encourage a deeper level of learning and thinking.

During the day you may take the opportunity to make brief notes that contribute to your planning for the next day, or you might plan an observation as part of the assessment of individual children. This will ensure that you meet the needs of each child and that they experience a balance of meaningful adult-led and child-initiated activities.

Knowledge about what children can learn

Documents such as *Early Years Outcomes* or *Development Matters* will ensure that you understand the importance of valuing and extending children's spontaneous play, respecting that babies and young children are strong, able and independent characters in their learning.

Planning effectively

A plan is only effective if it reflects and supports each child's learning needs. When differentiating for children in your care you should consider:

- their learning and health needs
- their individual learning plans

- the needs of children whose home language is not English
- children who may be advanced in aspects of their learning
- the actual stage of development of each child
- transient (temporary) needs such as a child whose parents have separated.

Jargon buster

Individual learning plan – a plan to support the specific learning needs of a child, developed by practitioners, parents and any relevant professionals who may support the child.

Making links to the areas of learning

All areas of learning can be linked. For example, a 3 year old may be sharing an animal story and helping to turn the pages. This creates a link between communication and language and physical development (moving and handling: *turns pages in a book*). During the story he points to four cows and says, '1 cow, 2 cows, 3 cows, 4 cows.' This links to mathematics (number: *recites some number names in sequence*).

Remember that the prime and specific areas of learning are underpinned by the four EYFS principles and the three characteristics of effective learning. You should highlight the principles and characteristics in your planning and observations, and show how you can make links to all the areas of learning.

Table 2.3 shows how areas of learning can be linked to each other. This is a progressive chart, starting with the EYFS principles, which are the basis of everything, and ending with an appropriate activity.

Table 2.3: Areas of learning can be linked through various activities.

EYFS principle	Characteristic of effective learning	Prime area of learning	Activity
Every child is a **unique child**, who is constantly learning and can be resilient, capable, confident and self-assured	**Playing and exploring** Children experience and investigate things, and 'have a go'	**Communication and language** • Listening and attention • Understanding • Speaking	• Greeting and exchanging information with parent or carer in the morning • Block play • Home corner • Sparkly play dough • Collaborative painting on large paper • Key family snack time • Washing hands • Transporting items in a trolley around the nursery such as cars, bricks or teddies • Sharing a book • Singing a nursery rhyme in a small group and following actions • Playing with shells and pebbles in the water tray • Using hats, bags and scarves • Looking at their reflections in a large mirror • Pouring water to drink • Climbing onto the slide • Crawling though a tunnel • Making circular movements with a large brush using water poured onto a patio • Making jelly • Playing with small-world figures and adding them to sand play
Children learn to be strong and independent through **positive relationships**	**Active learning** Children concentrate and keep on trying if they encounter difficulties, and enjoy achievements	**Physical development** • Moving and handling • Health and self-care	
Children learn and develop well in **enabling environments**, in which their experiences respond to their individual needs and there is a strong partnership between practitioners and parents and/or carers	**Creating and thinking critically** Children have and develop their own ideas, make links between ideas, and develop ideas for doing things	**Personal, social and emotional development** • Self-confidence and self-awareness • Managing feelings and behaviour • Making relationships	
Children develop and learn in different ways and at different rates. The framework covers the education and care of all children in early years provision, including children with special educational needs and disabilities			

Making sure activities are playful

Playful learning is made up of both child-initiated play and adult-led play, ensuring that children can reach deep levels of thinking in a well-balanced play-based programme of teaching and learning. Children need to engage in free play to develop their language and social skills, but adults can also support children in reaching specific outcomes through guided play.

It is your role to ensure that children can engage in a range of meaningful play, whatever their age. Sometimes this is through adults' guidance and sometimes through providing an enabling environment where children can access quality resources independently both indoors and outdoors. For very young children your support is essential: for example, using gestures, sounds, movement or objects such as puppets to support and develop their play.

For older children it is your role to respond to their needs and scaffold their learning at a point where you can extend their thinking, judging when to join in and teach them something new.

Theory in action

Plan a maths activity relating to shape for a group of 4 year olds. Consider the following ideas:

- Which areas of development and learning in mathematics will you consider?
- How will you plan for the needs of each child?
- Which behaviours will you use as a guide?
- How will you encourage children to make links in their learning?
- Where will you set the activity up?
- What are the resources that you will need?
- How will you ensure that the children can learn independently during this activity?
- How will you encourage sustained shared thinking?
- How will you ensure that the activity is playful?
- How will you evaluate the activity and assess the children's learning?

Jargon buster

Scaffolding – a process by which an adult or a more competent child builds on a child's existing knowledge and skills.

Find the balance

Junita had just completed her qualification and started to work with a group of 2 year olds in Planwell children's centre. She was made a key person for a group of children. She knew from her recent training that it is important to observe children as much as possible to ensure that she can provide a range of opportunities for them. Junita likes her work to be well presented so spends a great deal of time typing up her daily observations on the computer and placing them in each child's learning journey, a portfolio that shows their progress in the prime areas of development. Junita works long hours and found that she was spending a lot of time doing this. Her manager suggested that Junita carried a pad of sticky notes with her and wrote her observations onto these, then placed them in the learning journal, also adding a piece of work as alternative evidence or photos with brief captions underneath. The work setting had some stickies with the areas of learning pre-printed on them so that Junita could highlight the areas observed. She placed these on the wall next to the child's name and used her non-contact time each week to update the journals. Junita was relieved to change the way she was doing things. She was less tired and anxious, and she had positive comments from the parents about the learning journeys.

Further reading and resources

Publications

- Birth to Three Matters (2012) – a framework to support practitioners working with this age group – available for download from www.foundationyears.org.uk/files/2012/04/Birth-to-Three-Matters-Booklet.pdf

- Department for Education publications: www.education.gov.uk –

  - *Working Together to Safeguard Children* (2013)

  - *Keeping Children Safe in Education* (2014)

  - *Setting the Standards for Learning, Development and Care for Children from Birth to Five* (2014)

  - *Statutory Framework for the Early Years Foundation Stage* (2014)

  - *Early Years Outcomes* (2013) – non-statutory guide for practitioners and inspectors, to help inform understanding of child development through the early years – available online at www.gov.uk/government/publications/early-years-outcomes

- Early Education (2012) *Development Matters in the Early Years Foundation Stage (EYFS)* – non-statutory guidance material for practitioners implementing the statutory requirements of the EYFS – available online at www.foundationyears.org.uk/files/2012/03/Development-Matters-FINAL-PRINT-AMENDED.pdf

- Lindon, J. (2013) *The Key Person Approach: Positive Relationships in the Early Years* (2nd ed.), London: Practical Pre-School Books – a practical guide, written by a child psychologist, on how to both work in and lead a key person system in the early years setting

Websites

- Foundation Years: www.foundationyears.org.uk – for a broad range of information and resources developed by government, professionals and the voluntary and community sector, plus the latest news

- Early Education: www.early-education.org.uk – believes every child deserves the best possible start in life and support to fulfil their potential

- HighScope: www.highscope.org – a quality approach to early childhood care and education shaped and developed by research and practice

- Montessori: www.montessori.org.uk – information about Montessori, teacher training, jobs, schools, quality standards and more

- Steiner Waldorf Schools Fellowship: www.steinerwaldorf.org – UK website for schools following the Steiner ethos

Diversity, equality and inclusion in early years settings

Unit 3

Diversity, equality and inclusion in early years settings

Any form of work with people must be underpinned by values that are clearly understood and shared by all practitioners. Promoting diversity, equality of opportunity and inclusion upholds the rights of children to fair chances in life and helps them to make progress in all areas of development, in an emotionally secure and supportive environment. These principles are at the heart of work with children and families.

Before you start

If the young children and their families who come to your early years setting do not feel welcome and included, what impact could this have on the children's development and achievements? How can you open up opportunities for the future of all the children in your care? How can you protect them from the effects of prejudice and discrimination?

Learning outcomes

By the end of this unit you will:

1. understand the importance of promoting diversity, equality and inclusion
2. be able to use practice that reflects cultural differences and family circumstances
3. be able to promote equality of opportunity and anti-discriminatory practice
4. be able to support children with additional needs in early years practice.

1 Understand the importance of promoting diversity, equality and inclusion

When children spend time in settings that promote diversity, equality of opportunity and inclusion, they can make progress in all areas of development, in an emotionally secure and supportive environment.

Diversity, equality and inclusion

Diversity

Our society is made up of people with a wide range of characteristics and backgrounds. There are differences between individuals and groups that come from gender, ethnic origin, culture, social or religious background, family structure, disability, sexuality, age and appearance.

This is what we call diversity. Sadly, diversity is often seen as a problem, even though it gives a community strength.

The children you work with throughout your career will come from a variety of ethnic, social and cultural backgrounds and will live in families with a wide range of lifestyles. Exploring the diversity in our society enables you to understand and value the individuality of each unique child, and so help them progress along the pathway of development and learning.

Equality of opportunity

Each child should have access to equality of opportunity. Equality of opportunity means each individual in society having opportunities to achieve and flourish that are as good as the opportunities other people experience.

Every child has a right to have opportunities to develop and learn, while their physical and emotional safety and wellbeing are protected – and this access must be offered equally to all children.

Inclusion

To promote the positive aspects of diversity and to offer children equal chances in life, all settings for children should work towards inclusion. Inclusion means actively trying to meet the needs of different individuals and creating an environment where everyone can take part and feel respected. For children, this means giving them access to appropriate provision and experiences that support their wellbeing, development and learning.

Laws and codes of practice

The way we interact with one another in society is regulated by laws. These laws establish a framework for what is considered to be appropriate or inappropriate behaviour. The UK also signs up to international conventions that set out principles and rights.

The Equality Act 2010 brought together all previous anti-discrimination legislation and built on it. The act requires providers of services to promote equality of opportunity, and to protect people with 'protected characteristics' from discrimination and harassment. 'Protected characteristics' include:

- race (ethnicity)
- religion or belief
- gender
- disability
- sexual orientation.

The Children and Families Act 2014 updated local authorities' responsibilities for children with special educational needs. The UN Convention on the Rights of the Child, which the UK signed up to in 1991, declares that all children have a right to be protected from abuse and discrimination.

Laws and codes alone cannot influence the way people think or change prejudiced attitudes, but they tend to reduce practical aspects of discrimination. Good inclusive practice goes beyond what the law demands.

Your setting must comply with laws and codes. To be able to play your part in this, you need to:

- understand how and why discrimination has such negative effects on children's lives
- be committed to developing your professional practice so you protect children from the effects of discrimination, and positively promote equality of opportunity.

The effects of prejudice and discrimination

The rights of children can be adversely affected by prejudice and discrimination, which are significant barriers to inclusion. Differences between people in our diverse society can become a source of suspicion, may lead to divisions and conflict, and may create prejudice. Prejudice may lead to the view that some people are inferior to others, and of less worth and significance.

Jargon buster

Culture – the attitudes and values behind the traditions and customs that determine everyday aspects of life.

Disability – the long-term and substantial adverse effect of an impairment on a person's ability to carry out normal day-to-day activities.

Discrimination – treating someone less or more favourably because they or their family are seen as belonging to a particular group in society.

Impairment – a condition caused by an injury or illness, or present from birth, which might lead to disability.

Prejudice – a judgement or opinion, often negative, of a person or group, made without careful consideration of accurate, relevant information.

Prejudice can lead to assumptions such as:

- some people (defined by their skin colour, gender, impairment, sexuality or appearance) are of less value, are inferior to or are less capable than others

- one culture or religion or social group is superior to another, representing the 'right' way to live

- if a family is not a two-parent family, with parents of different genders and the same ethnicity, it is not 'normal'.

Prejudice has harmful effects. When children experience prejudiced attitudes, there is a danger that their emotional wellbeing will be damaged. Prejudice can also lead to discrimination.

Even very young children can experience discrimination as the result of:

- the colour of their skin and other aspects of their ethnicity

- the traditions and way of life of their family, arising from culture and religion

- their disability

- their gender

- their social background – the class or socio-economic group of their family

- the structure or composition of their family.

Jargon buster

Self-esteem – valuing ourselves, and seeing ourselves as being of value in other people's eyes.

Socio-economic – relating to a mix of social and economic factors.

Stereotypes – generalisations about a person; assumptions (usually inaccurate) about an individual because they are part of a particular group.

When children are discriminated against, they are harmed because:

- they are denied the advantages others have, so they do not have the chance to fulfil their potential

- they do not progress and experience success in their lives, and the negative effect this has on their self-esteem may make them less motivated to learn

- they are excluded from certain roles.

All of this means that their potential is lost to society.

Figure 3.1: How can prejudice damage children's self-esteem?

Many people have to endure prejudice, discrimination and lack of respect as a daily part of life, expressed in many ways, such as:

- racism in all its forms, ranging from petty insults to violence

- dismissal of the significance of 'female' roles and qualities, and the undervaluing of the contribution made to society by women (this can lead to unfair differences in pay and fewer opportunities for women to reach the top in the world of work)

- buildings and public transport that people with disabilities find difficult to get into or to move around in
- homophobic bullying or abuse.

Discrimination and prejudice interfere with:

- children's rights to have access to equality of opportunity
- children's wellbeing and learning opportunities
- promoting positive aspects of diversity.

Prejudice and discrimination have no place in settings for children.

Barriers to equality

Potential barriers to implementing equality of opportunity in early years settings arise when children are not seen as individuals. Each of us has a set of physical and psychological characteristics that makes us a person, different from all other people. Some of those characteristics may be similar to other people's, but our own collection of characteristics is different to anyone else's. Each of us also has our own mix of ethnicity, cultural and social background, gender, age, sexuality and perhaps impairment or disability. This is what gives us our unique identity.

Equal but different

It is vital that you acknowledge children's diversity and see each child as a unique individual, different from all other children. To treat children equally, you will need to organise provision for their daily care and learning in ways that take account of the differences between them – whether these differences come from gender, ethnicity, disability or cultural and social background. If you treat children 'all the same', you will not offer each child opportunities to achieve and flourish that are as good as the opportunities other children have.

For example, there seem to be some differences in the way many boys develop from the ways in which many girls develop. Young boys (under the age of

seven) may have their learning opportunities limited if they have to spend too much of their day indoors, doing activities that adults initiate where their physical activity is restricted. When an activity requires them to sit for long periods under the direction of an adult, they may just switch off and not participate. Boys' play and learning styles are often seen as noisy, disruptive and generally undesirable. Instead, we can acknowledge the value of their games as ways to help them explore their ideas and understanding.

Theory in action

Think about what we now understand about the natural learning styles of many boys – exploratory, physical, involving movement. Consider the widespread attitude that learning is only really happening when children are sitting quietly.

1. Is boys' boisterous play valued? Are there attempts to control and suppress some of it?

2. What is your own attitude to boys' fantasy games involving superheroes? Do you see it as mostly about fighting and exerting power over others? Do your observations reveal a lot of imagination and creativity in this sort of play?

Stereotypes

Of course, not all boys are more physically active, noisy and boisterous than girls, and it is important to guard against thinking in that way. A major barrier to promoting equality of opportunity is to fall into the trap of stereotypes, which tend to prevent us from seeing each child as an individual. Stereotypes can make you assume that, because a child is part of a particular group, they will have certain characteristics, have the same needs as all other members of that group or behave in a particular way.

Stereotyping can lead us, without our realising it, into making assumptions about what an individual child can achieve, based on one aspect of who they are. That stops us nurturing the all-round development of the child. If we think about children in stereotyped ways instead of seeing them as unique individuals, we may be limiting the expectations and aspirations we – and they – have for:

- their abilities
- how they should behave
- their future achievements.

These limited expectations are likely to stop us promoting equality of opportunity because we may fail to:

- offer challenging and stretching opportunities for learning suited to the individual child
- encourage children to have ambitious aims for their future.

It is important to develop your awareness of stereotyped thinking. Think about stereotypical expectations you have observed other people making about a child or family (or you have found yourself making). These might include:

- what girls and boys can do or ought to do
- characteristics of children of various ethnic origins or cultural groups
- what disabled children are capable of
- the roles people can play in adult life if they are male or female, white or black, disabled or non-disabled
- the behaviour that might be expected of children from particular social groups or specific areas, or who speak with a particular accent.

Language

One potential barrier to promoting equality is not taking sufficient care about the language we use. Some people will dismiss attempts to use words in a careful way as 'just being PC (politically correct)', but do not let this distract you from being thoughtful about what you say and how you say it.

Language reflects and also influences how we think about ourselves and others. The words we use to express ourselves affect our ability to think clearly and fairly, and can affect the concepts, values and attitudes we develop; they mould the way we think and may lead us to distorted or limited opinions. Language can have a negative effect, leading us to develop prejudiced and stereotyped ideas – or it can have a positive effect, helping us to think more constructively and to treat others respectfully, without discrimination.

For example, using a term like 'the disabled' lumps all people with impairments together and suggests that they will all have identical needs and requirements. Obviously this is not so: meeting the needs of a wheelchair user requires different resources and strategies from meeting those of someone with sensory impairment or learning difficulties.

Supporting others

You can and should support the other adults in your setting – parents and colleagues – to understand and promote diversity, equality and inclusion.

Parents

Children's future development might be restricted because they have not had an equal opportunity to try a wide range of activities and experiences – but their parents' up-bringing and expectations may mean that they have not thought about this. You can help the parents broaden their way of thinking.

Colleagues

You may come across other practitioners who have limited understanding of the significance of inclusion and equality, and who may not yet appreciate the need to implement their setting's policies consistently. In some settings, team meetings are used to highlight ways of implementing policies that give all children equal chances in life. Confronting and accusing people is likely to make things worse. However, by expressing your view in a calm, professional and constructive way, you can help colleagues develop their understanding and change their practice.

Case study 3.1

When welcoming new parents, Maz spent a little time with a small group, outlining the inclusion and equality policy of the preschool. This included explaining that she wanted to give girls and boys equal opportunities to participate in the full range of activities. She explained that girls were encouraged in physical play, construction and using technology, and boys were encouraged in creative and imaginative activities and to try out domestic roles in home play.

One father said, 'I don't want my son to play with dolls or play at cooking and ironing. That's women's work. He should be in with the cars, like a proper boy.' A mother said, 'But we want our daughter to grow up in the culture of our religion to become a mother and homemaker like me, not to get ideas of a career.'

Maz talked to the father about taking a wider view of gender roles in society today and how they may change even further by the time the child had grown up. She wanted to respect other people's religions but she was concerned about limiting children's opportunities – especially for girls. She explained the setting's position about giving children choices in life, but she chose her words very carefully and tried to show respect for the family's traditional views.

1. In what other ways might parents' wishes be different from a setting's policy about offering children opportunities for learning?

2. How would you try to explain to parents the importance of offering children such opportunities, while respecting families' cultural and religious views?

Figure 3.2: How can you overcome stereotypes through play?

Reflect

1. Imagine that a colleague is assuming that the two boys of a black family who are about to join your setting will be a lot of trouble and disruptive. She thinks that all African-Caribbean parents are harsh disciplinarians, and that practitioners will have to 'keep on top of them, like they're used to at home'. How would you go about convincing her that she shouldn't judge a family or make such assumptions about children before she's even met them?

2. Imagine you have a child with learning difficulties in your setting. You hear a parent of another child telling one of your colleagues that they do not want their child to play with 'backward children'. The staff member says, 'OK, I understand'. What would you say to your colleague?

2 Be able to use practice that reflects cultural differences and family circumstances

Showing respect

A key element in promoting positive outcomes for children's wellbeing and their ability to learn and achieve is to nurture their self-esteem and self-confidence. Children with high self-esteem are confident enough to tackle the new activities and experiences that will help them develop and learn.

> **Jargon buster**
>
> **Self-confidence** – feeling able to do things and capable of achieving.

To help children feel good about themselves, it is necessary to show that you value each child as an individual, and also respect their family.

Respecting and valuing families

Families come in many forms, such as:

- 'reconstituted' families containing step-parents and half-siblings or step-siblings
- same-sex parents
- extended families which include grandparents, aunts, uncles and cousins as part of regular daily life
- parents of mixed ethnicity
- teenage parents.

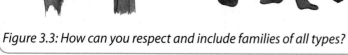

Figure 3.3: How can you respect and include families of all types?

Some of the families that you encounter in your work will have beliefs, cultures, values and preferences about how they run their lives that are very different from your own. It is essential that you communicate with them and speak about them in ways that make them feel you value them and their way of life, and that you do not discriminate against particular families.

By welcoming and valuing all families equally in your setting, you show each child that you don't have negative opinions or feelings about how their family functions. Children need to feel that their parents and the family unit they live in are respected and valued by the other people who are significant in their lives, especially their key person in their early years setting. When your manner towards parents and the way you refer to them in front of their children shows that you respect parents' ways of life, you enhance children's self-esteem. Any indication that you don't quite approve of their parents, or regard their family as odd or 'not normal', would be discriminatory and would undermine children's emotional wellbeing.

You should make it clear that you respect the way all families live and should not imply that one sort of family is superior to others. For example, this can mean taking particular care about preparations for Mothers' Day and Fathers' Day. Don't assume that every child has one mother and one father – be sensitive to single-parent families, step-families and same-sex parent families.

Unit 3

Case study 3.2

Vicky and her colleagues in the children's centre took a critical look at their practice and identified ways to improve how they showed respect for families' beliefs, culture, values and preferences.

- They recognised the significance of the fact that none of the staff could speak any of the languages spoken in the local community.

- They identified how important it was to ensure they addressed people correctly – that they get names right, because names are an important part of our identity and individuality. They improved their efforts to check how to pronounce and spell names they weren't familiar with, especially those from languages other than their own. They stopped using English versions of names from other languages, realising that it shows a lack of respect to use another name just because it seems easier to pronounce.

- They also acknowledged that they needed to find out more about the systems used for names and titles in various ethnic and social groups, so they could address family members in ways seen as courteous in their own culture.

One change they could make quickly was to their admission forms, which asked for a child's 'Christian name'. They changed it to 'First name' so families from other religions or none did not feel that they were unwelcome in the setting.

1. If your first language was Polish, how would you feel if your child's key person greeted you by saying 'dzien dobry'?

2. Imagine you are the parent of a girl called Yetunde, named after your grandmother who died just before Yetunde was born. How would you feel if a practitioner said: 'I just call her Jenny – I can't get my tongue round that foreign name'?

3. How would you respond to a parent who explained that she was concerned about her little girl taking part in vigorous physical play because she wanted her to maintain her modest clothing at all times?

Another aspect of this is to show respect for families' culture. Our culture is reflected in aspects of our life, such as:

- how we see the role of men and women in society, and the way we bring up our children
- the language we speak
- what, when and how we eat, how we dress and how we wash and care for ourselves
- the way we decorate and furnish our homes
- the religious practices we pursue regularly
- how we celebrate special occasions such as weddings and festivals
- our attitudes to death and dying.

Culture is often expressed in drama, music, dance, literature and art.

Language

If we don't pay attention to the way our language may offend people, we show that we don't value or respect them. As citizens living together in society, we should respect one another and avoid giving offence to others. Racism, sexism and other offensive behaviour has no place in a setting where young children are learning to be interested in and appreciate the diversity of their fellow human beings.

Terms like 'the N word', 'Paki' (applied to all people of colour) or 'pikey' (for travellers or gypsies) are used with racist intent, deliberately to offend. But you may also hear white British people referring to people whose skin is not white as 'coloured', which most black British people now find offensive, mainly because of associations with apartheid in South Africa. This is rarely intended to offend: the users of this word may have been brought up to think that this was a polite way of speaking. However, we all need to consider the sensitivity of the people we apply words to. We now talk about people whose parents are of different ethnic backgrounds as being of 'mixed race' or preferably 'mixed heritage'; terms that are more respectful than the old usage of 'half-caste'.

Inclusive practice

An essential aspect of inclusion is that children and families should feel that they are welcome in your setting – that it is expected that they will join in and be readily accepted. Children should feel secure there, able to see and play with things that are familiar and that make them feel linked to their homes. They should be able to play with materials they recognise from their own lives, so they can engage in imaginative play about themselves, their families and their communities with real meaning for them.

Ethnicity and culture

If the puzzles, books and pictures or posters on the walls in your setting show people from the ethnic and cultural backgrounds of the children and families who come to your setting, they will see visual representations of themselves and feel that they 'belong'.

Disability

When disabled children have access to resources including, for example, characters in books or play figures using wheelchairs or with hearing aids, they can see themselves as part of society, accepted and reflected in your setting.

Family groupings

Children with single or same-sex parents or from large extended families also need to see their lives reflected visually in your setting. If they are not, what message is the setting giving them and their families about what is 'normal' and welcomed?

Another approach to inclusion is to extend children's knowledge and understanding of people like themselves and of people different from themselves. You can do this by giving them opportunities to talk about the way they are similar to and different from other people. Presenting differences in a positive way – as interesting and enriching to all our lives – helps children enjoy the diversity of our society and feel included in it.

Case study 3.3

Karen and her colleagues carried out an audit of the resources in the nursery and made plans to ensure that they included:

- dolls, puppets and small-world figures with skin and hair tones and facial features similar to those of the children using the centre

- paint and crayons in a range of skin tones, so that children could make pictures that really looked like themselves and their families

- books and posters in relevant home languages and scripts

- 'pretend play' resources that reflected what was used and worn in the children's families such as:

  » dressing-up clothes including saris and shalwar kameez (the traditional dress of South and Central Asia), skull caps, headscarves and turbans, wrappa (long robes worn by Muslim women in Africa) and dashiki (colourful shirts widely worn by men in West Africa)

» a wok as well as a saucepan

» play food that includes plantains and okra

» food packaging in a range of home languages

» mats and cushions as well as chairs to sit on.

They also resolved to tackle the fact that, although several languages were spoken in the local community, the only language to be seen in the setting was English.

1. How far do the resources in your setting offer a visual welcome?

2. How could you improve this?

3. If you were a parent who read no English, how do you think you would feel about taking your children to the children's centre where the only word over the door was 'Welcome'?

Figure 3.4: How can you provide a welcome to everyone?

Theory in action

Talk with a group of children about the ways they are different from one another and the characteristics they share. Who is tall, who has freckles, who has the darkest hair or the brownest skin? What colour eyes does everyone have? How does their hair grow? What sort of clothes do we and our families wear? What language(s) can each of us speak? Do we say words the same way, or do some of us have different accents? What are we each good at? Guide the conversation so the differences are brought out as interesting and enjoyable, not something to laugh at or be wary of.

3 Be able to promote equality of opportunity and anti-discriminatory practice

Challenging discrimination

You have seen that discrimination and prejudice go against the aims of supporting the development and progress of children, and that early years practitioners have a duty to protect children from discrimination. This means that you must challenge any children or adults who express prejudice or behave in discriminatory ways. You need strategies to challenge what is said or done.

It is necessary to support anyone who is the object of discrimination, but it is also important to try to help the person who is speaking or behaving in a discriminatory way, so that they can change their behaviour for the future. This can be a demanding aspect of practice, and needs careful thought.

Children

Children are influenced by the adult world around them – at home, in their local community and in the media – and can acquire stereotyped and prejudiced views at a surprisingly young age. It would be comforting to think that young children cannot be prejudiced, but the harsh reality is that they absorb attitudes from others, and this affects their behaviour. Even children under 5 sometimes behave in discriminatory ways, making hurtful remarks or excluding others from play because of some aspect of their individuality – gender, ethnicity, family background, disability or appearance.

When you encounter discrimination:

- never ignore or excuse one child's bullying or discriminatory behaviour towards another child, any more than you would ignore or excuse them if they inflicted physical pain on that child

- don't feel that you will make things worse by drawing attention to what has been said and done – if you do not respond, you give the impression that you condone the behaviour

- intervene immediately, pointing out to the child who has behaved in a bullying or discriminatory way that what was said or done is hurtful and that the behaviour cannot be accepted (using words like 'unfair' or 'cruel') – but don't suggest that they will be punished

- if necessary, point out anything that is untrue and give correct information and new vocabulary

- help the child to learn from the situation, to see the consequences of their actions and to understand why their behaviour is regarded as inappropriate (ask 'How would *you* feel?')

- don't leave the child with the feeling that you dislike them personally for what they have said or done – make it clear that what you won't tolerate is what they have said or how they have behaved

- support the child who is the object of the discrimination, reassuring them and helping to maintain their self-esteem.

Reflect

Think about how you would respond in situations like these.

1. A 3-year-old white girl says she won't hold hands with an African-Caribbean boy. She says his hands are dirty and he should wash them properly.

2. A 4-year-old girl is playing with the dolls, cuddling them and putting them to bed. But she won't let the boys anywhere near 'because boys don't play with dolls'.

3. Some children seize the patka of a Sikh boy and throw it around the room, chanting 'J wears a hankie on his head'.

Don't think of name-calling such as 'fatty' or 'four eyes' as a minor or unimportant matter, or dismiss it as merely teasing. When it is repeated and done with intent to hurt, it becomes bullying or harassment. Some adults play down what they see as 'toughening children up for the real world' and don't intervene. But why should a child be expected to endure comments that undermine their self-image and self-esteem? You should be ready to support them in facing torment like this.

Adults

Responding to children's expressions of prejudice or discriminatory behaviour takes patience and a consistent approach. However, responding to the comments and behaviour of adults can be very daunting, requiring strength and, at times, even courage.

If it becomes necessary to challenge adults – whether parents or colleagues – use a similar approach as with children.

- Challenge the remark, politely but firmly.
- Choose your time and place – you may not want to speak strongly in front of children, but you should act as soon as you can.
- Remain as calm as you can but make it clear that you find the remark or behaviour offensive or inappropriate.
- Remember that, if you let the incident pass, you are contributing to the person feeling that it is acceptable to speak or behave in that way.
- Offer support to the person who has been the object of the remark or excluding behaviour.
- Offer accurate information if the person's comments or actions seem to arise from being unaware of the implications of what they are saying or doing.

Figure 3.5: How can you challenge the prejudices of adults?

Applying anti-discriminatory practice

To comply with laws and codes of practice to promote diversity, equality and inclusion you need to adopt anti-discriminatory practice. Anti-discriminatory practice means actively promoting equality of opportunity by being positive about differences and similarities between people, and by identifying and challenging prejudice.

You have already looked at how you might challenge prejudice and discrimination, so here we focus on presenting differences in a positive light.

Being positive about differences

Young children are very observant and notice differences between people from a surprisingly young age. If you help children to have positive attitudes towards those differences, it will be less likely that they will develop prejudiced views.

If you respond readily to children's questions and comments about differences in gender, ethnicity, culture, family and physical appearance, you can help

them grow up with positive and respectful attitudes towards:

- people from ethnic, cultural and social groups different from their own
- people who live in families different from their own
- people with disabilities
- people who look or sound different from themselves.

Don't feel uncomfortable dealing with children's natural curiosity about people who are different from themselves and talking about variations in skin tone, hair texture, shape of features, physical abilities and impairments. Some practitioners find it helpful to use dolls (especially Persona dolls) or puppets to help these discussions.

Figure 3.6: How can puppets be used to help discussion of differences between people?

Celebrating diversity

Taking this positive observation of differences a step further, anti-discriminatory practice involves encouraging children to have positive attitudes towards the wide range of ethnic, cultural and religious groups that make up British society. It is enjoyable to help them begin to learn about cultures other than

Theory in action

Here are some things to consider when you talk about differences with children and respond to their questions or comments.

- Don't ignore a child's question or comment, and don't change the subject. Talk to children openly and honestly. (If a child says, 'That man is riding in a buggy like a baby', explain that maybe he finds it difficult to walk and the wheelchair helps him to get around.)

- Respond in a direct way, tailored to the child's stage of development; keep it simple. (If you're asked, 'Why are Jamila's arms browner than Molly's?' it's better to say something like, 'Because Jamila's mum and dad have darker skin than Molly's parents', than trying to go into a long explanation about skin pigment and sun levels in tropical countries.)

- Give some factually accurate information and introduce appropriate new vocabulary. (Respond to 'Parvati's mummy wears a funny long dress' by explaining that it's called a sari.)

- Offer reassurance if you think the child is anxious or concerned in some way. (If a child says, 'I don't like that thing on Leo's leg', explain that it's called a calliper and is very helpful to Leo by making his leg stronger.)

1. Why do some people find it difficult to talk with children about differences?

2. What differences are there among the children in your setting that you could use as a basis for discussion in a positive way?

their own and to show respect for the way other people lead their daily lives. With younger children, your focus is likely to be on aspects of culture such as food, dress, stories and music.

Learning about various cultures can widen children's horizons, making them aware of the range of ways

people approach the events of everyday life – but there are potential pitfalls. Here are some things you need to take care to avoid.

- References to 'funny' food or 'strange' music, or the suggestion that, for example, it is not very clean to eat with one's fingers. To help children grow up without developing prejudice, show them that you respect all cultures, not valuing one as better than or superior to another.

- Images and information about various cultures presented in an 'exotic' way, or talking about people who live in 'faraway lands' and presenting them as very different from people who live in the UK, with peculiar ways of living their lives.

- The 'tourist curriculum' – giving children information only about the festivals of various cultures, or the sort of 'souvenir' aspects of life that get presented to tourists. Culture is not just about festivals and dress for special occasions; it is primarily about everyday aspects of life.

Reflecting on promoting equality of opportunity

Laws and codes require your setting to promote equality. In learning outcome 1 of this unit, you saw that stereotypes and use of language are two barriers to the promotion of equality of opportunity.

Overcoming stereotypes

You can help to overcome stereotypical expectations about children's potential and possible future roles by providing positive images among the resources in your setting.

Jargon buster

Anti-discriminatory practice – actively promoting equality of opportunity.

Positive images – visual and other representations showing people who are sometimes marginalised or discriminated against in roles and activities that go against stereotypes.

Use positive images of a diverse range of people to show that, for example, black people, women and people with disabilities can take on responsible, active and prominent roles in society, and male people can take on creative, caring and domestic roles. This helps children to develop strong expectations about their own future and what they will be able to achieve in life and the positions of influence and responsibility in society they will be able to take, whatever their ethnicity, gender, cultural or social background or disability.

Case study 3.4

Elena and her colleagues decided to improve their practice in providing positive images. They started by carrying out a thorough review of the resources and activities provided for children in the nursery, looking at:

- pictures, posters and photographs
- books
- puzzles
- DVDs, video tapes and computer games
- board games.

1. Check these resources in your setting. Do they include positive images, showing:
   - girls and women as strong and independent?
   - boys and men as emotional, creative and caring?
   - children and adults with disabilities playing active roles, for example as the 'hero' of a story?
   - black people, women and people with disabilities taking responsible, challenging and influential roles?

2. What would you like to add to extend the range of positive images in your setting?

To make sure that all children have equal opportunities to participate in particular activities, you may have to give some children positive encouragement, making it clear that it is entirely proper and acceptable for them to engage in certain activities, against stereotype.

Reflect

Monitor your own practice over a period of a few weeks. Note occasions when you give positive encouragement, such as giving 'permission' or reassurance that it is perfectly OK for:

- a child with a disability to climb
- a girl to play with technological gadgets
- a boy to wash up.

Perhaps the most powerful positive image is a real-life adult offering children a version of the world that challenges gender stereotypes, such as:

- a male practitioner cooking, reading a book or mending dressing-up clothes
- a female practitioner playing football or mending a broken chair.

Figure 3.7: How can role models help to challenge stereotypes?

Stereotypes about children's behaviour are just as common as expectations about what sort of activities and learning they will want to engage in and succeed at. Not all boys are aggressive, but society does seem to expect males to be more aggressive than females. To some extent, society tolerates more aggression from boys and men than from girls and women. Stereotypes about what behaviour is appropriate or relevant for a child may have a limiting effect on their social and emotional development. Practitioners should never accept that boys will be aggressive and girls won't. You have a role to play in helping children to find non-aggressive ways of settling disputes and dealing with strong feelings.

Reflect

Think about how gender stereotypes about children's behaviour might be influencing your own practice and leading you to have different expectations about the behaviour of boys and girls (be honest!).

1. Do you accept more aggression and noisiness in boys' behaviour than in girls'? Do you emphasise controlled and quiet behaviour more to girls than to boys? Do you expect girls to be able to sustain quiet concentration more effectively than boys? Do you let things go further with boys before you intervene in a dispute than you do if it's girls who are falling out? Do you think that boys won't talk with you about their feelings?

2. Have you observed such varying expectations based on gender in other practitioners?

3. What do you think might be the outcome of different expectations such as these about behaviour on gender lines? Will this influence you to change your practice?

Careful use of language

As you have seen, it is important to pay attention to the way you speak. Try to avoid the many negative uses of the word black, meaning bad, dirty, ugly or evil. For a child who knows they and their family are 'black' and constantly hears the word 'black' used in these negative ways, the cumulative effect can be harmful to their self-esteem. They may learn to think of themselves as undesirable in some way, and become ashamed of their skin colour, wishing that they could be white instead.

Labelling people with disabilities by using terms like 'a Down's child' or 'a diabetic' can limit your thinking about the person so that you focus only on their impairment, rather than acknowledging the needs and requirements of the whole person, including their gender, ethnicity and culture, and social background. Talking about 'a child with Down's syndrome' or 'a person with diabetes' helps you put the person first in your thinking, not their impairment. This way of talking about people with disabilities is more respectful to the individual, seeing their impairment as just one part of them as a person, not the whole of who and what they are.

Figure 3.8: Why is it important to avoid labels when talking about people with disabilities or impairments?

4 Be able to support children with additional needs in early years practice

A child may have an impairment that gives rise to disability and stops them developing their potential and becoming independent. If a child is disabled by their impairment, you may need to meet their needs in different ways from those you usually employ with non-disabled children, recognising that they have specific or additional requirements.

Children with disabilities may have a wide range of impairments or conditions including 'hidden' ones.

- Sensory impairment may consist of hearing loss (deafness) or restricted vision (blindness).

- A physical impairment or learning difficulties may be the result of a genetic inheritance, events before or during birth, an accident or a disease.

- Some children's disabilities relate to learning difficulties that may or may not have a specific title, such as Down's syndrome.

- For others, their difficulties are with emotional or social development, communication and interaction, and behaviour, including conditions such as autism.

- Each child is affected differently by their impairment or condition.

Applying additional needs laws and codes to your own practice

In learning outcome 1 of this unit you read about the Equality Act 2010. Disability is one of the 'protected characteristics' included in this act, so early years settings have a duty to protect children with disabilities from discrimination and harassment. The act also requires settings to make 'reasonable adjustments' to the provision of services to make sure that children with disabilities can be included and participate. The duty to make reasonable adjustments is 'anticipatory'; a setting must not wait until they are asked to offer a place to a child with disabilities, but think ahead about the sort of changes they could make so they would be ready to provide a service for a particular child.

The UN Convention on the Rights of Persons with Disabilities is well worth studying. It requires nations to combat stereotypes and prejudice, and promote awareness of the capabilities of people with disabilities who must be enabled to be independent. It asserts that people with disabilities, particularly children, must have rights equal to those of other people. Children must have equal access to education.

Settings in England are required to comply with the Special Educational Needs and Disability (SEND) Code of Practice issued by the Department for Education. This Code provides practical advice on how to carry out the duties the law requires of settings to identify, assess and make provision for children with special educational needs.

These laws and codes underpin the policies and procedures in your setting. Your practice must be in accordance with them, promoting equality and inclusion and protecting children from discrimination and prejudice.

Models of disability

The medical model of disability and the social model of disability help us to understand the effect of disability on individuals.

Jargon buster

Medical model of disability – a traditional view of disability that treats the person as a sick patient and tends to focus on how to make the person more 'normal'.

Social model of disability – a more modern view of disability which recognises that discrimination against people with disabilities is created by society, not by these people's impairments.

The medical model is a traditional view of disability, that treats the person as a sick patient and their disability as something to be 'cured', even though many conditions have no cure. In this model, the disabled person and their impairment are seen as the problem, while the solution is seen as adapting the disabled person to fit the non-disabled world. The focus is on 'How can we make this person more normal?'

When medical labels are placed on the disabled person (for example, referring to someone with epilepsy as 'an epileptic'), the individual is seen merely in terms of their impairment, not as a whole person.

The social model of disability is a more modern, constructive approach to disability. This model puts the emphasis on the way in which society needs to change (in contrast to the medical model which expects people with disabilities to change to fit into society). It recognises that discrimination against people with disabilities is created by society, not by these people's impairments. The focus is on 'What do we need to do to enable this person to achieve their potential and have a fulfilling life?' The strength of the social model is that it identifies problems that can be resolved if the environment is adapted and the right resources are made available. The medical model dwells on problems that often can't be solved.

The social model asserts the rights of people with disabilities; it involves listening to individuals with disabilities to see what they want and, when there are barriers to their requirements, looking at ways of removing those barriers. The social model has been constructed and promoted by people with disabilities themselves, so it should be respected.

Your work should be guided by the social model, and you should look at how to adapt your setting and practice to the needs of individual children. Avoid the medical model approach of focusing on the child's impairment and seeing the problem as getting them to fit into the environment and routine of your setting – or being marginalised when that proves impossible. Instead, think in terms of how you can adjust the environment, what resources you can use and how you can adapt routines and your practice to offer children with disabilities equality of opportunity.

Planning to meet individual needs

In planning to meet the individual needs of children with disabilities, you should think about:

- how the environment where they spend their time can be adjusted to meet their requirements
- how to make appropriate resources and facilities available to them

Case study 3.5

Bushra attended a training day about inclusion of children with disabilities. During one session, participants shared examples of how they had made changes in their settings to enable children with disabilities to join in activities and benefit from the full range of experiences offered to support their development and learning. She heard about settings that:

- used variations in textures on floor coverings and panels on walls, rough or smooth stones and bricks outdoors, and white strips along the edge of steps to help children with sight impairments find their way around
- used carpets and soft furnishings to avoid hard surfaces and reduce the background noise picked up by the hearing aids of hearing-impaired children, helping them to focus on voices
- paid attention to keeping thoroughfares clear of objects which might get in the way of wheelchair users.

1. Look around your setting and identify any ways it could be adapted to meet the needs of a sight-impaired child, a hearing-impaired child or a wheelchair user.

2. What might be the barriers to make such adaptations (for example, financial, other people's attitudes)?

- how you can help to ensure that the attitudes of the people they meet are positive, and not based on limited assumptions about what they can and cannot do.

Environment

It is not possible to plan an environment to suit the needs of every disabled child. The requirements of a child with visual impairment are different from those of a child who uses a bulky walking frame, and the requirements of two children with the 'same' impairment is unlikely to be identical as their impairment may affect them in different ways or to a different extent. What matters is that the layout of your setting's environment can be flexible and adaptable – and, perhaps even more important, that you are willing and ready to make changes to that layout so you can remove any barriers to the inclusion of children with disabilities.

Resources

Many sophisticated resources are on the market that are liberating for some children with disabilities, such as hand-propelled trikes, but you should also think about how you can use your usual resources with children with disabilities. You may find that, with some imagination and some basic materials, you can adapt some resources, or improvise with what you already have so that you can use them with children with various impairments.

Attitudes

Media stories about people with disabilities often present them as 'tragic' victims to be pitied, and it is often assumed that they will be helpless and dependent. Seeing people with disabilities in this way undermines the view of these people as individuals who deserve respect for what they are capable of achieving. If you have low expectations about the potential of a child with disabilities, or are overprotective of them, you might limit what they achieve. You should always keep a balance between being realistic about the limitations a child's impairments may cause, and having high expectations for their progress and achievements.

Case study 3.6

Nick and Fran looked for simple ways to help some of the children participate in more of the nursery's activities.

- Nick read about using Velcro and rubber suction mats to keep toys and dishes fixed and steady. He got some for the nursery and it transformed the way Chloe, who had cerebral palsy, was able to use puzzles for the first time and even begin to feed herself. He stitched bells onto some gloves so Chloe could join in music-making sessions. He found some foam shapes in the local market, which gave Chloe support so she could reach play equipment.

- Fran made a shape and texture lotto game that Helen, who had visual impairments, could enjoy with other children. She made pieces of various shapes (circles, squares, triangles) with different textured surfaces, using bubble wrap, fur, foil and sandpaper.

- Hasan used a wheelchair and was finding it difficult to join in with painting because he couldn't reach. Fran brought in some long-handled rollers (used for painting behind radiators) to overcome this barrier to him taking part.

1. What equipment do you have in your setting that might be used to help children like Chloe, Helen and Hasan participate in activities?

2. How could you make or adapt other resources to support children with other forms of impairment?

Figure 3.9: Why is it important not to underestimate what children with disabilities are capable of?

Case study 3.7

Sonali works with Brandon, who is 6 years old. She says, 'I try to persuade colleagues not to say things like "developmentally he's like a 3 year old". It's true that his **cognitive** development is at a stage we usually see in younger children, but his chronological age *is* 6, and in other aspects of development, he is like other 6 year olds. His interests are like those of other children of his own age, so it is important not to treat him as though he is only 3. If we talk to him in a babyish way or keep him only in the company of younger children, his self-esteem will be damaged and his development will be held back.'

1. Can you identify your own negative attitudes towards the disability of children you work with?

2. And your positive attitudes?

Probably the main stereotype about adults and children with disabilities views them as helpless and dependent. In the past, some settings have been reluctant to accept children with disabilities because they mistakenly thought they would create extra work and would always need more adult attention. See past these stereotypes and prejudices, and don't be afraid to let children with disabilities 'have a go' for themselves. Allow and encourage them to try to do things that contribute to their own wellbeing, such as looking after their own aids, like spectacles or a walking frame. This helps them to become more self-reliant. If this doesn't happen, the development of children with disabilities may be limited.

Leading activities that meet individual children's needs

Although you may have to adapt your practice to suit the needs of children with disabilities, that doesn't mean working in an entirely different way. Your work with children with disabilities should be based on your usual good practice with all children. Hold on to the same basic principles and expectations and use the strategies you would usually employ with any child, disabled or not. The key is to observe the child and assess their stage of development, just as you would with any other child, so you can plan how to support their development and learning.

With a bit of thought and imagination, many of the usual activities in your setting can be adapted to offer all children opportunities to take part in them.

Jargon buster

Cognitive – to do with acquiring knowledge.

Case study 3.8

Leila described to her colleagues in the pre-school some of the ways that a dance class she belonged to included children with disabilities. She thought these could also be used in their setting.

'We play parachute games with all the children sitting on chairs rather than standing, so Kwasi, who uses a wheelchair, can take part. He joins in the dancing by wheeling his chair around or using streamers of ribbon to dance with his arms and hands. Aidan, who has a hearing impairment, dances in bare feet and picks up the rhythms and pulsations of the music through the vibrations of the floor.'

1. What adaptations like this can you think of to help children with disabilities join in activities in your setting?

2. How will children with disabilities benefit from being able to participate alongside other children?

What matters most is to have positive attitudes about your capacity to provide for disabled children's requirements, and be ready to learn new skills, such as sign language or using the Makaton system.

Some children can only participate fully in the activities in a setting if they make use of specialist aids or equipment. These might include:

- spectacles or a reading light
- a hearing aid or hearing loop

Jargon buster

Makaton – a language programme that uses signs and symbols alongside spoken language.

- a Makaton board or electronic communication aid, perhaps with a head stick or mouth stick, or a voice-activated computer
- a wheelchair, crutches or a walking frame or roller
- a prosthetic limb or a calliper
- a feeding tube or a catheter.

If you need to learn how to use such aids when working with a particular child, listen to advice from the child's parents and other professionals, such as occupational therapists.

If a child in your setting is identified as having special educational needs, specific activities may be planned for them, to help them develop and progress. The Special Educational Needs Coordinator (SENCO) in your setting will take the lead in developing these plans, and you may be involved in implementing the plans, with their support and guidance.

Always see a child with disabilities as a child first and foremost. You may be tempted not to be 'too hard' on children with disabilities, but this is misguided. You will not be doing the child any favours if you let them behave in unwanted ways when they have the capacity to learn positive patterns of behaviour.

Seeking specialist expertise

There will be times in your work with children with disabilities when you need to call on the expertise of specialist professionals outside your setting. You need to be aware of the aspects of support they may be able to offer the child, their family and you and your colleagues in your setting.

Here are some of the specialist professionals you may need support from.

- **Educational psychologists** – assess children's development and learning to identify learning difficulties and special educational needs. They may give guidance on how to support a particular child's developmental progress.
- **Speech and language therapists** – identify the causes of speech and language difficulties. They may devise programmes of activities to improve

Case study 3.9

Rhiannon, who is 4 years old, attended the nursery school where Leanne worked. Since her diabetes was diagnosed, her family had become very protective of her and often let poor behaviour pass unchallenged. Rhiannon and Huw were having a fierce argument in the playground – Rhiannon grabbed Huw, hit him and kicked him.

Leanne intervened immediately to stop the assault and reminded Rhiannon that that sort of behaviour was not accepted in the school. She gave her time to cool down in 'time out' while she made sure that Huw was all right. Later she talked to Rhiannon about not hurting other people and discussed calm ways of sorting out differences and conflicts. She used exactly the same approach to the situation as she usually used with children of Rhiannon's age, making no concessions because of her diabetes.

1. How would you respond to a child with cerebral palsy who used racist language?

---

communication skills for children with a wide range of impairments, including cleft palate and autism.

- **Physiotherapists** – identify physical problems caused by impairment, ill health or injury. They may devise a programme of exercise or treatment to help a child become more mobile.
- **Occupational therapists** – advise on the use of specialist aids or equipment.
- **Portage workers** – devise step-by-step programmes for a child's family to use to help the child develop particular skills in an area of learning.
- **Child psychologists** – identify the underlying causes of disturbed behaviour. They may advise on the use of play therapy.

It can be very demanding for parents to engage with a range of professionals. Perhaps the most positive development in England in recent years for young children with disabilities and their families has been the Early Support Programme. This aims at early identification of children's impairments and better coordinated, 'family focused' services. The programme provides parents with information about living with a child who has a disability and 'the system' – the many agencies they have dealings with relating to health, education, social care, benefits and housing. It explains which professionals they may meet and how such agencies can provide support, as well as giving information about sources of financial support and childcare.

Case study 3.10

Shania's parents find that the Early Support 'family file' is a real help. They hold the file in which they and the professionals involved with Shania record important information. This means that the professionals are aware of the advice and support being provided elsewhere, and can identify priorities for their contribution as part of a whole strategy for Shania, planned jointly with her family.

1. Parents of children with disabilities encounter many different professionals and services. How do you think parents might feel about having to 'tell their story' from the beginning every time they meet a different one?

2. How does the family file help them?

Further reading and resources

Publications

- Gibson, N. (2011) *Guide to the Equality Act and Good Practice*, UK: Pre-school Learning Alliance – guide covering the basic principles, with questions and answers, case studies and ideas to make sure your practice is inclusive and lawful

- Griffin, S. (2008) *Inclusion, Equality and Diversity in Working with Children:* Harlow: Heinemann – easy-to-follow guide to taking an integrated approach to inclusion, equality and diversity in today's childcare settings

- Lindon, J. (2012) *Equality and Inclusion in Early Childhood: Linking Theory and Practice* (2nd ed.), London, Hodder Education – looks at key principles and best practice across the areas of social inclusion: gender, ethnic group and cultural background or faith, disability and health

Websites

- Department for Education: www.gov.uk/dfe – with information on the SEND Code of Practice 2014 (look under schools and colleges, then SEND code of practice: 0 to 25)

- Equality and Human Rights Commission: www.equalityhumanrights.com – for information on the Equality Act 2010

- UNICEF: www.unicef.org – for information on the UN Convention on the Rights of the Child (look under: Our mission – Children's rights)

- United Nations Enable: www.un.org/disabilities – for information on the UN Convention on the Rights of Persons with Disabilities (look under: Disabilities – Convention)

- Persona Dolls: www.persona-doll-training.org – for information on using Persona Dolls in teaching

Plan and provide effective teaching and learning in early years settings

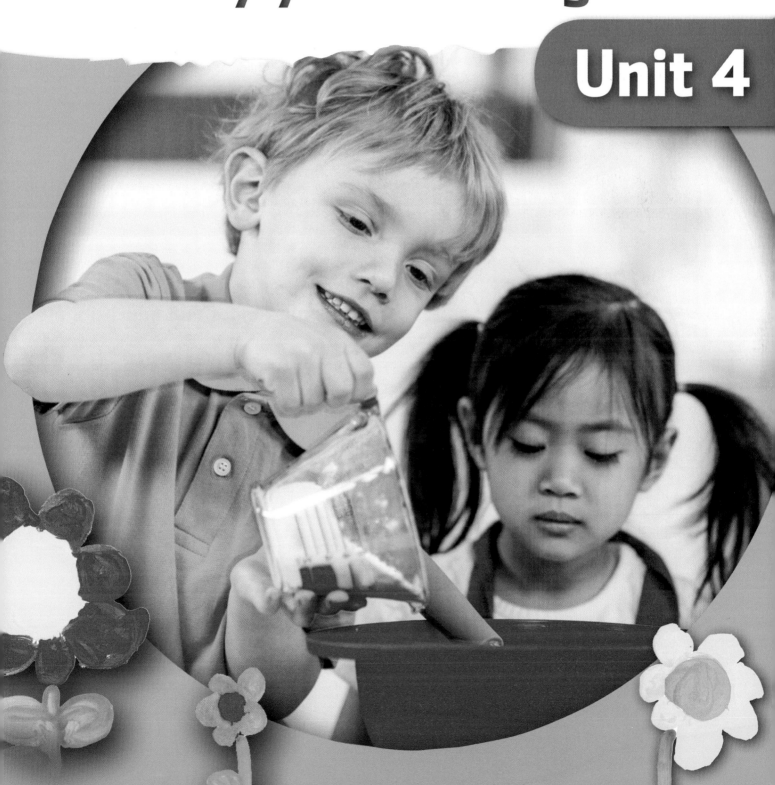

Children learn best in an environment that is stimulating, interesting and reflects their needs and interests. You need to make sure that you offer children a good balance of child-centred activities, led by adults, as well as opportunities to initiate their own learning. You will need a deep understanding of the importance of how children learn individually and in groups, and how you can best support each child to achieve the learning outcomes in each area of development.

Before you start

Imagine a group of 4 year olds from an inner city nursery, engaged in a cooking activity. One of the strong current interests of the children is gardening and they are making cress sandwiches, using cress they have grown. Each child has picked their own cress from the garden and has a knife, butter and bread to use. What do you think they can learn from this activity? How do you think you could help them to do this?

Learning outcomes

By the end of this unit you will:

1. be able to implement purposeful play opportunities, experiences and educational programmes
2. be able to provide environments that support children's learning
3. be able to support children's group learning and socialisation
4. be able to support children's individual learning and development
5. be able to promote positive behaviours expected of children
6. be able to support children to manage their own behaviour
7. understand when a child is in need of additional support.

1 Be able to implement purposeful play opportunities, experiences and educational programmes

Purposeful play refers to play that has meaning and enables children to make sense of their world. When children engage in this sort of play, they can progress in all areas of their development. You will observe that young children who have the opportunity to play in a safe but challenging environment will gain the confidence to try new experiences.

Jargon buster

Purposeful play – play that has meaning and enables children to make sense of the world.

Applying the EYFS principles and themes

In learning outcome 1 of Unit 2, you read that the EYFS contains four guiding themes, each of which has a principle behind it.

- **A unique child** – Every child is a unique child, who is constantly learning and can be resilient, capable, confident and self-assured.

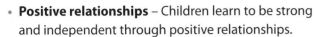

- **Positive relationships** – Children learn to be strong and independent through positive relationships.

- **Enabling environments** – Children learn and develop well in enabling environments, in which their experiences respond to their individual needs and there is a strong partnership between practitioners and parents and/or carers.

- **Learning and development** – Children develop and learn in different ways and at different rates.

Note that this covers all children in early years provision, including those with special educational needs and disabilities.

(Source: Statutory Framework for the Early Years Foundation Stage, Department for Education, 2014, p.6)

Table 4.1 gives examples of how you can embed each principle in your practice.

Table 4.1: How can you embed the four EYFS principles in your practice?

Unique child	• Find out all you can about a child's culture, language, developmental needs and interests before they start in your setting. • Create an individual learning plan for each child. • Make, share and use observations of how each child learns to plan for what that child will learn next. • Follow children's individual interests, such as spiders or pirates. • Make sure children have a range of activities and resources to choose from, to reflect their different interests. • Make sure that all children can be included. • Provide a range of resources such as role-play resources that celebrate diversity.
Positive relationships	• Make sure that everyone in your setting is valued, for example, by displaying photos of children's families, greeting children in their own language and encouraging parents to lead activities about their culture. • Use the key person system to give parents and children a voice and help them share important information. • Show parents that they are respected for their knowledge about their children, for example by sharing video clips of children at home. • Encourage children to manage their feelings by expressing themselves and using stories, songs or items such as Persona dolls. • Find out what children are really interested in and plan activities or provide resources to deepen these interests.
Enabling environments	• Plan activities or extend resources to support your assessments of children, for example add a water wheel to the water tray to extend a child's thinking about how water makes things move. • Encourage children to take part by constantly adapting the environment to suit their changing needs. • Make sure resources are open-ended and rich, both inside and outside. • Ensure children are encouraged to care for their environment by putting things away in clearly labelled areas. • Where possible enable children to flow indoors and out in all weathers. • Provide quiet and reflective spaces for children to use, as well as spaces to socialise and collaborate.
Children develop and learn in different ways	• Get to know documents such as *Development Matters* or *Early Learning Outcomes* to find out more about the stages of child development. • Make sure you think of the EYFS characteristics of effective learning and know how children learn through: 　» playing and exploring 　» active learning 　» creating and thinking critically. • Plan for the prime areas for younger children and build on the specific areas as they get older. • Ensure that activities are varied and support the stages of learning children are at. • Remember that children can learn actively individually, in small and in large groups. • Develop planning that reflects each child and is constantly being adapted based on your observations and assessment. • Make sure that all children can access a range of resources independently. • Make sure that children are assessed with a progress check at age 2 and the EYFS profile at the end of the foundation stage.

Reflect

Professor Ferre Laevers, Director of the Centre for Experiential Education at The University of Leuven, Belgium, has created scales that practitioners can use called the Scales of Involvement and Wellbeing to assess a child's emotional health. The principle is if that a child's wellbeing is low, their level of engagement in learning will be too. You can use these to find out why a child's wellbeing is low and support this. The reasons could be complex – or as simple as the fact that they have not had a good night's sleep. To find out more about the Laevers' scales, ask around local settings or go online.

Developing and extending children's learning and thinking

Engaging with children and enabling them to extend their learning is an important part of your role.

Remember that children learn at their highest level when their play interests and absorbs them.

Take a look at Case study 4.1, in which 3-year-old Sam is engaged for over 20 minutes in creating and playing with a train track. He has just returned from a holiday with his grandparents in New Zealand where they went on a long train journey.

Extending children's learning and thinking often means following the child, rather than leading the activity. Observe what the child is playing with and their train of thought through their actions. Consider placing resources by them to encourage them to extend their thinking further. For example, if they are drawing a pirate ship and chatting about going on a treasure hunt, you could place a container with play money on the table. Think about how you can show a genuine interest in a child's play and intervene sensitively. Use appropriate body language to show you are listening, such as a nod or smile. Always play alongside children if needed, such as drinking a cup of tea a toddler may make you. Remember to use language appropriate to their age and stage of development, always using words in context.

Case study 4.1

Sam is busy getting the pieces of wooden train track out of the box and making a track. He spends time carefully connecting the pieces. Another child sits by him and starts to connect another track. Sam starts to try to make a bridge but is having difficulty. The other child sits by him and they try to fit the piece. Eventually they manage. They carry on. Sam uses up all his pieces and reaches the wall. 'I want my track to go on,' he says. The adult nearby comes and sits near Sam and the other boy joins them. 'I wonder what would happen if you joined your tracks together?' Sam moves his track and says, 'Now we can have a long train ride.' He and the boy then spend time joining the track up, talking about it 'bending' and being a 'circle'. The other boy goes away and Sam gathers small-world figures and trees from another area and lines them up saying, 'Bye bye, Granny and Grandad!' He plays for another ten minutes.

1. How is Sam able to become more deeply involved in his play?

2. How was Sam encouraged to be independent?

3. Which areas of development did Sam display?

4. How did the two children benefit from collaborating?

5. How did the adult support Sam in extending his learning and thinking?

6. How was Sam using his play to explore his own world?

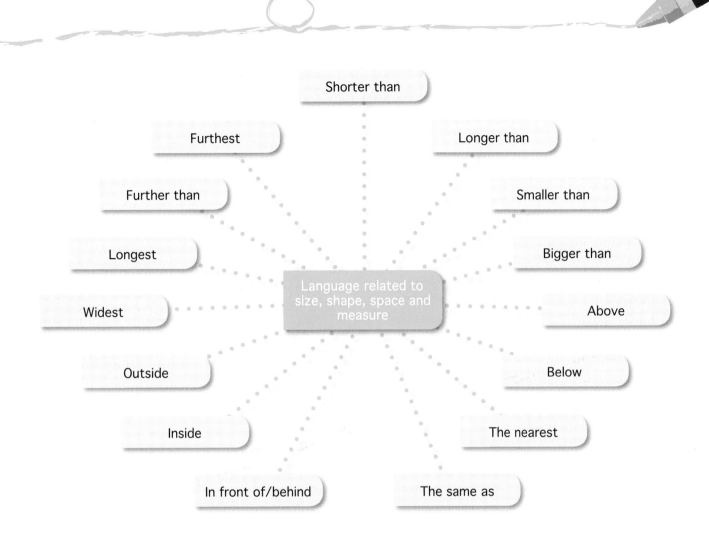

Figure 4.1: What language would you use to draw children's attention to size, shape, space and measure?

Questioning also plays an important part in extending children's thinking. The way you ask a question can encourage them to find their own answers, solving their own problems. One of the most effective ways is to engage children in conversation and use open questions to encourage children to think and find their own answers.

It is sometimes difficult to use questioning effectively, as Table 4.2 shows.

You may need to sit with a child, gain their trust and engage in questioning at the right time – something you will have to practice. Ask a colleague to observe you and give constructive feedback to help you develop the skills of recognising when there is

potential for you to encourage deeper learning. You could also watch more experienced colleagues modelling the type of questioning that extends children's learning and thinking.

Jargon buster

Open questions – encourage children to think deeply and to give their opinions or express their feelings. By using words such as 'how', 'why' or 'I wonder' at the beginning of a question, you will give the child the opportunity to lead the conversation.

Table 4.2: Examples of ineffective and effective questioning and their effect on children's learning.

Ineffective questioning	Example	Negative effect on the child's learning	Effective questioning	Positive effect on the child's learning
Asking too many questions at once	How could you make this tower taller? Which bricks will you use?	Not giving the child enough time to really consider the first concept of how to make the tower taller	How could you make this tower taller?	Gives the child the concept that the tower could be made taller but enables the child to think how it could be done
Asking a question and answering it yourself	I wonder how many pigs are there? Oh look, there are three!	The child may not be inclined to engage in conversation or develop their thinking if you are giving the answer	I wonder how many pigs there are on this page?	Gives the child time to think and find out for themselves and give an answer, therefore engaging in dialogue
Asking irrelevant questions	I can see you are looking at the ladybird on the leaf. Do you like it?	The child may be absorbed in really investigating the ladybird and its habitat and may be distracted by such a limited question	That looks interesting. Can you tell me what you can see?	Acknowledges that it is interesting to the child and asks to share some of their observations
Always asking the same type of question	Are you enjoying the apple?	Could result in limited conversation such as 'Yes I am'	What does the apple taste like?	Enables the child to give a fuller description of the apple such as 'It is juicy' or 'It is very sweet and crunchy'
Ask questions in an intimidating way	Why have you just used red in your picture?	The child may think you are being critical and communication may be limited	The way that you have used a lot of red in your picture is interesting. Can you tell me a little about it?	Shows the child you are interested and encourages them to share their thinking with you

Figure 4.2: Why is it important to take time to engage a child in conversation?

Sustained shared thinking

Your daily conversations with children help build relationships and find out about their interests. However, deeper levels of conversation will help children to learn at a higher level. You may plan activities to develop sustained shared thinking, such as an investigation into what happens when ice melts. Try to follow a child spontaneously and use the opportunity to engage in a deep dialogue. For example, a group of children could be digging a large hole to find Australia that could result in the idea of what they might really find by continuing to dig. Whatever the context, children will need to be absorbed and interested in what they are doing.

There are many benefits for children of using language to further explore their interests or a concept. For instance, this will help them to:

- develop their problem-solving, interpersonal and social skills
- improve their reasoning
- explore concepts at a deeper level
- reach their own conclusions
- process information
- make connections in learning
- join up their ideas.

In Unit 2 you were introduced to the importance of scaffolding children's learning. This important part of your role is a process by which you or a more competent child builds on a child's existing knowledge and skills.

When developing their learning children sometimes need to hear you use language and phrases before they can use them. This modelling will help them extend their learning vocabulary. Recognise what a child says and repeat it, perhaps using the correct grammar or words or expanding a sentence. The following conversation illustrates effective scaffolding.

Child: Look! (Points to a shape in the sand kitchen made using a cake tin)

Adult: You have made a great cake. Who is that for?

Child: Mummy. Mummy like yummy cake. (Pretends to eat and rubs tummy)

Adult: So your Mummy likes yummy cake? I like yummy cake too, with icing on top.

Child: I like yummy icing and 'phew, phew' (doing a blowing action)' on my birthday cake.

Adult: You had a cake with candles for your birthday? How many candles did you have to blow out?

Child: I had (counts fingers) 1, 2, 3 and 4. I had 4 candles.

Planning activities

As you read in Unit 2, observation and assessment are key to how you work out and plan for the next steps in children's learning.

Planning formats will be specific to your setting, but should involve input from your colleagues. They should be flexible and simple enough for any team member to follow. Your plans should be based on observations and reflect each child's needs and interests – but they should always consider the EYFS areas of learning and development, showing progress towards the early learning goals. Make sure you consider the indoor and outdoor environment and the importance of learning through routines.

There are different types of plan that you may use.

Long-term plans

Long-term plans are more relevant in a group environment and tend to offer an overview of the year. They give you the chance to consider static festivals, celebrations or activities that you may want to acknowledge, such as Chinese New Year, Christmas, Divali or the Nursery Fun Day.

Planning for children's needs and interests can make long-term planning a challenge, but the longer perspective can be useful. You should be aware that long-term plans are not effective for children under 3 as they are developing at such a fast pace.

Medium-term plans

Medium-term plans reflect individual children's needs, interests and groups and are often interlinked. For example, an interest in superhero play could be reflected in the medium-term plan through adult-led activities such as making superhero books in the mark-making area or ensuring there are superhero cloaks in the role-play area.

Jargon buster

Scaffolding – a process by which an adult or a more competent child builds on a child's existing knowledge and skills.

Sustained shared thinking – when adults and children or groups of children engage in learning together, to talk about or explain their ideas and develop their thinking.

A medium-term plan should cover a month or half a term, depending on whether your setting is termly or all year round.

Individual plans

Individual plans are a way of gathering information about each child so you know what to provide for them and what their next steps in learning will be. Individual plans should:

- be simple and easy to follow
- reflect observations and the voice of parents or carers
- involve the child in developing the plan
- show what may be the next steps for the coming weeks
- link to patterns of learning, such as schemas.

A PLOD is a possible line of development, which helps you plan where an individual child goes next in their learning. For an example, see learning outcome 4 in this unit.

Short-term plans

Short-term plans are the ones your setting will focus on. These include:

- weekly plans – an overview of adult-led and child-initiated activities and routines for the coming week

> ### Jargon buster
>
> **Continuous provision planner** – planner that reflects how the environment is planned for resources, children's interests and learning, both indoors and outdoors.
>
> **Holistic** – making links across different areas of learning and development.
>
> **PLOD** – possible line of development, used in developing a child's individual plan.

- daily plans – showing adult-focused activities, often used in association with a continuous provision planner.

Table 4.3 looks at how you might plan activities after observing a child's needs.

There is a place for adult-led activities to introduce new knowledge or ideas or to practice skills, offering new stimulus for children to take into their own learning. An activity might be prompted by an interest, or could be an area of learning such as phonics. You can take a lead and introduce new

Table 4.3: Planning activities in response to observations of children's needs.

Observation	Early learning outcome	Activity
A 4 year old is writing his name and phonetically-spelled words in the mark-making area	**Literacy** 40 to 60 months Writes his own name and other things such as labels and captions	A mark-making activity in the shop role-play area where the child has to make shopping lists and label items in the shop with sticky notes
A 30 month old is beginning to play with a ball	**Physical development** Moving and handling 30 to 50 months Can catch a large ball	A small throwing and catching activity in a circle
Some 4 and 5 year olds are beginning to use the names of 2D shapes	**Mathematics** Shape, space and measure 40 to 60+ months Beginning to use mathematical names for solid 3D shapes and flat 2D shapes and using mathematical terms to describe shapes	• Making Christmas decorations using circles, rectangles and squares • Looking at some Christmas gift boxes that are 'cubes'

concepts, with clearly specified learning opportunities matched to children's current learning needs, to consolidate what they know and do.

Activities will often support more than one area of development at once. This is called holistic learning as you saw in Unit 2.

Each area of learning and development of the EYFS is broad. *Development Matters* shows the different ways you can provide appropriate activities and resources for children of each age. Remember that the EYFS framework is centred on the needs of each individual child, enabling children to progress through the prime and specific areas of learning and development. The developmental stages outlined in *Early Years Outcomes* are a guide to help you understand the children you are working with and provide age-appropriate activities.

Take a look at the activity plans in Figures 4.3, 4.4 and 4.5, each of which considers a different area of the EYFS.

Activity for a small group of 5 year olds
Volcanoes and dinosaurs
Aim To respond to children's interest after a trip to the dinosaur museum
Characteristics of learning EAD – Creates simple representations of people, events and objects Other areas of development: KU, CLL
Activity Place bark, pebbles, builder's sand and gravel in a tough spot on the floor. Place a basket of dinosaurs nearby. Help the children to make a dinosaur museum and take photos of their creation. Use key words to describe the dinosaurs' habitat.

Figure 4.4: A sample activity plan for a group of 5 year olds.

Activity for a group of 4 to 5 year olds
Taller and shorter
Aim To develop mathematical language – tall, short, shorter, taller
Characteristics of learning MD – Uses language such as 'greater', 'smaller', 'heavier' or 'lighter' to compare quantities Other areas of development: CLL, PD, KU
Activity Place a variety of construction blocks in the construction area outside. Encourage children to build the highest towers they can. Is the building tall or short? Is it taller than anything else in the room, or is it shorter? Use a camera or iPad and go for a 'tall' walk, taking photos of things that the children think are tall. Back in the classroom show the children a slideshow comparing the photographs taken.

Figure 4.3: A sample activity plan for a group of 4 to 5 year olds.

Activity for a 10 month old
A treasure basket
Aim To encourage hand–eye coordination, exploration, concentration and independence through sensory play
Characteristics of learning PD – Reaches out for, touches and begins to hold objects Other areas of development: PSE
Activity Place a range of natural and household objects in a low basket. These could include: • spoons of different sizes and materials, such as wood, metal and plastic • cardboard kitchen roll tubes • nailbrush, wooden mop • scarves or pieces of textured fabric • metal chain • natural sponge • hand whisk or lemon squeezer • shells and pebbles. Encourage the baby to explore the objects independently. Sit nearby to offer help if necessary but allow the baby to explore without interference.

Figure 4.5: A sample activity plan for a 10 month old.

Leading activities

Adult-led activities should be playful and open-ended, with elements of imagination and active exploration that will increase children's interests and motivation. Adult-led activities can include greeting times, story times, songs and even tidying up.

When leading learning activities, you will need to develop appropriate strategies to make sure that children receive the best learning experience. You will have several roles.

- **Supporter** – You help children learn to make the right choices and then lead their own activities. You can help them develop ways to express their own ideas and collaborate with their peers.

- **Instructor** – When you can see that leading an activity is more appropriate (such as at the woodwork bench), you model a skill, give information, encourage children to think deeply and enable rich opportunities for learning.

- **Guide** – You use pedagogical strategies, knowing which skills to develop and build on.

- **Participator** – You join in with children's play and are led by them, to help you understand the purposes of their play, creating an opportunity to extend children's learning. Children can learn from you if you know how to play with them.

Figure 4.6: How can adult-led activities increase children's interest and motivation?

Spontaneous adult-led activities involve responding to children's learning or encouraging children to participate. Sometimes you may sensitively involve yourself in an activity to take the lead, but you need to ask yourself the following questions.

- Will my involvement change the focus of the play?
- Are the children responding positively to my involvement?
- How is my involvement enhancing the play opportunity?
- Do I know when the children do not need me to be involved?

You may need to model the activity (for example, playing a matching game or rolling glittery play dough). You will also need to:

- show a genuine interest in what children are doing
- praise and acknowledge the achievement of each child
- make sure they have the resources they need.

When planning an activity, consider the following questions.

- Is the activity based on the children's interests or observations by you or other adults?
- How will you ensure that the activity engages the child?
- Do you have enough resources to carry out the activity?
- Is the activity appropriate for the age and stage of development of the children, as outlined in *Early Years Outcomes*?
- Do you know enough about the children who will be involved?
- What skills and knowledge do you want the children to gain?
- How many children do you want to be involved at any one time?
- Is there enough space to carry out the activity?
- How will you make your observations?
- How will you use language to extend children's thinking?

Reflect

Mark is leading a planned cooking activity in a reception class for ten children. Consider the following points.

- Mark was making bread that he had not made before.
- Mark had the recipe but did not have time to create a written plan.
- He had only one bowl, so he did most of the preparation himself.
- The table on which the activity was taking place was against a wall.

- The children did not wash their hands before starting.
- He found it difficult to control the children's behaviour.
- Some of the children were disinterested and walked away.

1. What do you think the children gained from the activity?

2. What advice would you give to help Mark reflect and learn from this experience before planning another activity?

Case study 4.2

In Scarlet Road Nursery Wei Ling had planned an activity about how static electricity can be created and what can happen when it has been. Wei Ling had noticed a few days before that a small group of boys had been rubbing balloons on their jumpers and repeated the activity again and again.

Wei Ling set out a range of different fabrics on a table that the children could easily access. She added a mirror, some aluminium cans and balloons tied on to the table leg with string.

Wei Ling started by showing the children how to create static electricity with the balloons, starting sentences with phrases such as, 'Have you noticed?' and, 'What do you think?' She encouraged the children to try different fabrics and even try their hair. David laughed when he looked in the mirror and saw his hair going

in the air towards the balloon. The other children noticed and copied him. Wei Ling also rolled a can on its side on a table after rubbing a balloon against her jumper and showed the children how the can moved towards the balloon as she pulled it away by the string.

The children had time to play with the materials independently and got very involved.

1. How else could the children present their discovery about static electricity?

2. How could this become an opportunity for a child-initiated activity?

3. What areas of learning and development might the children demonstrate through this activity?

4. How do you think that the children benefited from David's discovery?

5. How else could Wei Ling have extended the children's thinking during this activity?

2 Be able to provide environments that support children's learning

An effective learning environment – the physical environment, the resources and all the people involved – is important to ensure that each child achieves the best possible learning outcomes. This principle in the EYFS refers to an enabling environment.

Preparing the environment

Think carefully about the needs of each child's stage of development as outlined in the EYFS through the prime and specific areas of learning and development. The experiences and opportunities you offer should be appropriate, but the environment should also reflect the context of your setting: for example, woodland surrounding a setting will influence the outdoor learning environment. Children need space to play and

a way of taking ownership of the environment from a very young age.

The following sections describe the key points you should consider when preparing the learning environment for children of different ages.

0 to 1 years

Babies need to feel secure, as this is usually their first experience outside of the home. Your environment needs to adapt to their rapid physical development, from turning over to taking their first steps. It should also consider the three prime areas of learning and development. In addition, you must avoid over-stimulating children, as this can lead to distress. The learning environment should include:

- changes in environment so children have different places to visit

- indoor and outdoor experiences

- a variety of textures, smells, sounds and things to touch
- periods of quiet and areas where children can have one-to-one interactions with an adult
- space to sit, crawl, pull themselves up, stand and explore
- objects they can reach, such as books
- objects such as push-along trolleys to enable mobility
- large resources indoors and outdoors to encourage children to investigate at different heights
- mirrors so children can explore their own reflections
- sensory resources such as treasure baskets
- accessible items that are familiar from home, such as comforters or teddies
- resources to enable schematic learning – the children's patterns of learning that are very evident at this age
- opportunities for personalised and sensitive care routines, such as appropriate nappy changing areas and feeding areas
- photographs in the environment of their families and themselves.

1 to 3 years

Children of this age are increasing their physical coordination, developing relationships with adults and other children, and developing their language. Your environment needs to consider the importance of the three prime areas of learning and development, while also taking the children's interests into account. When preparing the learning environment, you should consider children's patterns of learning and schemas and include:

- outdoor areas rich with opportunities to explore
- quality sensory experiences that encourage sight, smell, sound and touch
- water, sand and other materials and textures which children can explore
- books, puppets and other resources (such as mark-making materials) to support children's literacy skills

- resources that reflect children's home environments and encourage imaginative play
- links to current learning, with learning statements and visual reminders
- children's own work (annotated as needed), reflecting their learning
- photographic evidence of children's engagement in learning.

3 to 5 years

At this stage, it is important to organise the environment in relation to the different needs of children's play and development, adding the four specific areas of learning and development to the three prime areas. You should include:

- different areas of provision that enable high-quality child-initiated play, adult-led activities, and high levels of thinking and problem solving
- resources that children can access independently
- sufficient resources to support each area of learning and development
- resources that provide real value
- resources that develop literacy and numeracy skills
- places for interactions with adults, in small and large groups
- safe places for privacy
- links to current learning, with learning statements and visual reminders
- children's own work (annotated as needed), reflecting their learning
- photographic evidence of children's engagement in learning.

Jargon buster

Schematic learning – the use of previously learned experiences to understand or simply new experiences.

Indoors and outdoors

The indoor and outdoor environments are important for all ages. The lists below will help you to plan for both areas for children from 3 to 5 years. Outdoor learning has long been important in early years but has received a higher profile recently thanks to an increase in quality outdoor learning organisations and professional learning opportunities.

Indoor environments

You can vary indoor environments greatly, using a wide range of resources, such as:

- role-play areas, such as shops or a post office
- a home corner, with real-life props such as hats, bags or real vegetables
- small-world play, such as figures or dinosaurs
- mark-making and writing areas, with a variety of writing materials, sticky notes, staplers, tape and scissors
- a creative area, with paints, collage materials, manipulative materials, woodwork bench and tools, fabrics and junk materials
- musical instruments or music to listen to
- a sensory area, with sand, water, dough and a range of clearly labelled resources
- a construction area, with building bricks and a separate block-play area
- jigsaws, puzzles and other board games
- iPads, interactive whiteboards, remote-controlled cars and robots

Figure 4.7: How can a forest school encourage resilience?

- resources to encourage curiosity, such as magnifying glasses, digital microscopes and wormeries
- a book area with a variety of fiction and non-fiction books.

Outdoor environments

These include:

- sensory areas that encourage reflection and small-world play
- wildlife areas, with bird feeders, magnifiers, plants for children to plant and water and watch growing
- areas with wheeled toys such as bikes, carts, scooters and pushchairs
- mark-making areas, with chalkboards, whiteboards and painting walls
- open-ended play areas, with resources such as cardboard boxes and fabric
- investigative areas with drainpipes, water trays at different levels or pulleys
- story areas, where children can read on their own or with adults
- role-play areas, with shops, building sites or garages
- areas in which children can build shelters or dens
- supervised areas in which children can light pit fires, make cocoa, toast marshmallows or whittle wood
- areas with creative opportunities, where children can weave in trees or on weaving wall frames
- areas with equipment that will encourage physical exploration such as climbing, balancing and crawling.

Reflect

Forest schools offer a way of promoting independence and self-esteem in learning through interacting in a natural environment that provides children with the challenges and opportunities to take risks that are so often absent from their lives. Take time to look at the website www.forestschoolsuk.org.uk.

Reggio Emilia preschools

Reggio Emilia is a famous approach developed at an Italian preschool at the end of the Second World War. The approach has inspired many current early years settings. Reggio considers the learning environment to be a third teacher. Reggio-inspired settings organise a learning environment that is rich and stimulating. Uninterrupted play, exploration and interaction encourage children to make links in their learning, make choices and use a wide variety of materials, working alone and with others through sensory experiences.

Reflect

Find out more about the Reggio approach on the official website at www.reggiochildren.it.

You could also research some other popular approaches to preschool learning, such as Montessori or Highscope.

The role of the adult

The following checklist may help you to consider your role in preparing the environment.

Evaluating the environment's effectiveness

You need to continually evaluate the effectiveness of your provision. Here are some questions you might explore.

Are the children extending their learning and development?

- How long are children focused in different activities?
- What is their level of engagement?
- Did the area meet all the children's needs?
- What else could you add to enrich the play opportunities?
- Could the children interact meaningfully with each other and adults?
- Are the children displaying positive behaviour?
- Is the area enabling children to develop the characteristics of effective learning and the areas of learning and development within the EYFS?

Is the environment enabling high expectations in each child's progress and achievement?

- Are the resources challenging enough?
- Is the layout appropriate – for example, having a round table to promote quality interaction?

Have you:

- ☐ divided the space into accessible areas with continuous provision that enables play to flow, indoors and outdoors?
- ☐ made sure there is enough space between activities to enable children and adults to have quality interactions and levels of engagement?
- ☐ made sure activities are carefully placed to promote development, such as a sufficiently large block-play area where children can work together?
- ☐ made sure access is clear?
- ☐ provided plenty of opportunities for children to make choices, think creatively and solve problems?

- ☐ clearly labelled resources, in pictures and writing?
- ☐ made sure surfaces are stable and washable?
- ☐ reflected diversity and cultural awareness?
- ☐ celebrated learning through displaying meaningful learning statements, children's work and photos?
- ☐ made a clear link between home and school, perhaps in the role-play area?
- ☐ made sure there are safe paths and separate areas for bikes, trucks, scooters and large ball games?

- Is there enough adult interaction and scaffolding?
- Are you really meeting individual children's learning needs?

There are a number of ways to evaluate the effectiveness of the environment. Here are some methods you could use, as a basis for discussion with colleagues.

- Observations of individual children
- A group time sample
- Photos and video clips of children using an area
- Recordings of discussions with children about their learning
- Samples of individual children's learning journals to see evidence of progress
- Sharing evaluations with parents and enlisting their views

Meeting individual children's needs

Throughout this unit you have seen the importance of meeting each child's needs and understanding that each child learns individually. This means carrying out observations sensitively on the child concerned to see how the child is engaged in the environment. For each child, you will need to ask:

- how the child is supported by the adult
- how they engage with other children
- whether they can access activities according to their needs
- whether the activities are challenging enough or too challenging
- how the child is benefiting
- which other professionals should support the child
- how to engage parents to find out about what the child is like at home.

Reflect

Take time to observe one child in your setting who you have noticed is not fully engaged in an area of the environment. Make a note of the activities, play opportunities and areas that the child is interested in. Compare the areas that the child engages in with the rest. How would you improve the environment for that child? Are there any changes you would make to benefit other children?

3 Be able to support children's group learning and socialisation

One of the important aspects of working with young children is to encourage their interactions with each other, and foster respectful and meaningful relationships. Here you will find out how you can plan and implement activities to encourage children to socialise according to their needs and stage of development.

Planning activities

Children have the right to experience relationships that are warm and genuine. Any new child entering your setting should be encouraged to form positive friendships with other children. Your role is to enable this by encouraging activities where children can socialise and learn together. Understanding the stages of social interaction that children go through will help you plan these activities effectively.

Table 4.4 shows some activities you could consider according to the needs and stage of development of the children you work with.

Table 4.4: Which of these activities for group learning and socialisation have you used?

Age	Stage of social interaction	Possible planned activities
0 to 1 year	Gradually develops multiple attachments, which are an important part of their socialisation Often enjoys watching older siblings or other children	• Opportunities to watch others • Mother and toddler or music groups – can be with their main carer but alongside others
1 to 2 years	Gradually begins to play alongside other children	• Small group snack where children can sit with each other • Song or story time
2 to 3 years	Starts to take an interest in other children and play with them Begins to share playthings	• Activities to do together, such as role pay, painting, cooking or sharing a story • Activities that encourage sharing, such as snack time
3 to 4 years	Shares playthings and takes turns Plays with other children – mostly pretend play Begins to show concern for others, such as another child crying Can be affectionate towards other children Plays with both genders Choice of activity often more important than who is playing	Activities that encourage children to share and communicate such as: • matching game • role play • ball game • obstacle course • cooking activity • snack time
4 to 5 years	Stable friendships begin to emerge Seeks out company of chosen children Friends begin to be important – may be upset if friend is not there Begins to choose friends of same gender	• Sharing a book • Cooking activity • Block-play activity where children can solve problems • Investigative activity • Role play • Games that may have rules and boundaries, such as ball games

Use Figure 4.8 to help you plan activities to support children's group learning and socialisation.

Figure 4.8: How could you use these recommendations to plan activities for group learning and socialisation?

Case study 4.3

Laurence planned an activity for a group of 4 to 5 year olds. He found a colourful bag and filled it with a range of interesting, sensory objects that could be recognised without being seen. The objects included:

- a wooden spoon
- a small teddy bear
- a woollen glove
- a velvet hat
- a lemon
- a book
- a metal car.

He asked four children to join him. One of them, Harry, had some difficulty sharing with other children. Ellie had not been at the nursery for long and was reluctant to join in with other children. Shadow and Paula were friendly and happy to join in anything.

Laurence asked the children to take turns taking an item out of the bag. They had to be blindfolded and the other children were not able to tell them what the object was. The child had to feel the object and try to guess. Laurence nodded to a child to give a clue if the child with the blindfold could not guess. Ellie was able to guess the teddy and Laurence praised her. The others also showed they were pleased and Ellie was very happy! Harry wanted to have two turns but was encouraged to wait until all the other children had a turn. Laurence praised him for waiting.

1. How do you think Laurence prepared for the activity?

2. Which aspects of socialisation did the activity aim to develop?

3. Why do you think Laurence chose this particular group of children to join in the activity?

4. What further planned activities could Laurence have used to encourage Harry to share and Ellie to play with others?

Implementing activities

When implementing an activity, you will need to make sure that it is age-appropriate and that you plan appropriate resources. Children should have opportunities to take an interest in each other. It is important that you encourage cooperation and that children make eye contact with each other.

4 Be able to support children's individual learning and development

Planning for individual children is an essential part of your work with young children. Children develop at different rates and have very different needs.

Reflect

Before you read on, take time to remind yourself of how children develop at different ages and stages by looking through learning outcome 1 of Unit 1. Revisit *Early Years Outcomes*, which outlines broad expectations of children's development in the prime areas and specific areas of learning.

Planning activities that show differentiation

Showing differentiation means demonstrating how you are going to effectively meet children's individual needs when planning and implementing learning activities.

In order to differentiate in your planning, you need as much information as possible, from a variety of observations and assessments. You will need to observe children, talk to parents, colleagues and other professionals, and find out about different ages and stages of development. You may be involved in making a formal assessment such as the progress check at age 2, reviewing children's developmental records or recent entries in their learning journeys.

Figure 4.9 shows the information you will need.

Jargon buster

Differentiation – recognising the differences in individual children's needs.

Individual learning plans

A child may have an individual learning plan, which will ensure that their specific needs are met. In some settings every child has an individual learning plan; in others it may be for children who have more specific needs. There is no specific format but it should include:

- name and age of child
- name of key person
- observation and notes
- next steps
- suggested activities and experiences
- adult support
- resources
- links with EYFS characteristics of learning and areas of learning and development.

Schemas

Children sometimes display certain schemas in their play. Some children may display one schema for a length of time whereas others may explore a number of schemas. Children's schemas can be short-lived, but they are important to help us understand how each child learns. Look at Table 4.5 to find out about

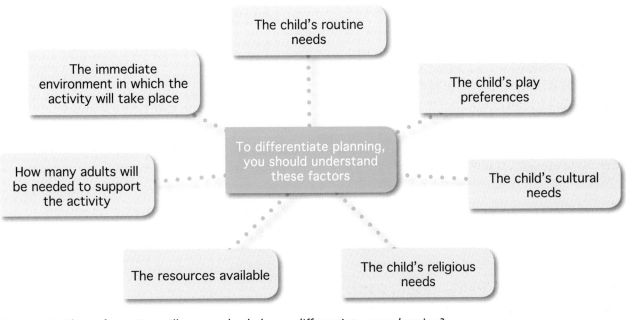

Figure 4.9: What information will you need to help you differentiate your planning?

Table 4.5: Some schemas and examples of how they might be displayed.

Schema	Examples of how they are displayed
Transporting	Carrying cars from one place to another in a pushchair, the bricks from the construction area to the sand pit, or pushing a friend on a bike
Enveloping	A child may wrap objects in blankets and fabric or cover their painting with one colour; they may cover themselves in blankets or scarves
Enclosure/containing	A child could put her thumb in and out of her mouth, fill up and empty containers with water or enjoy being in enclosed spaces such as a play house or den
Trajectory: Diagonal/vertical/horizontal	A baby could continually drop a loved teddy from their cot, a child might make lines with bricks, turn on and play with the water from the taps, line up the cars or trains
Rotation	Play with wheels; a child might love being spun around on a roundabout or enjoy playing circle games
Connection	A child may join train tracks, play with connective toys, use copious masking tape to connect objects such as old shoe boxes
Positioning	Repeat what may seem habits such as always sitting in the same place, not wanting their peas next to their chicken, always putting a bag on their arm when carrying it
Transforming	Adding water to sand or mud, enjoying mixing paint or cooking

some basic schemas and how they can be displayed and supported. Schemas are an important part of creating a child's individual learning plan.

Children whose play is particularly schematic may have particular preferences in your setting for certain activities or resources.

You may have to consult with other professionals if you are planning activities for children with special educational needs and disabilities (SEND). For more information on SEND, see learning outcome 4 in Unit 3 and learning outcome 1 in Unit 9.

Learning styles

Children have different learning styles – they process information in different ways. Although there is debate about learning styles, understanding the different styles will help you to plan appropriately.

Table 4.6 shows different learning styles for older children.

Table 4.6: Which of these learning styles do you recognise?

Visual (seeing)		Auditory (hearing)	
• Watches people and listens to them • Searches for shapes and forms in words and numbers • Benefits from visual descriptions		• Listens and talks • Prefers words • Enjoys listening to a range of voices • Benefits from a detailed verbal explanation • Prefers to communicate verbally with others	
Kinaesthetic (movement)	Sequential (ordering)		Holistic (all round)
• Needs tense relative position and movement • Likes to touch and examine in order to make sense of learning	• Remembers and learns things in order • Organised in learning		• Combination of all styles

Imagine that you have to plan a cooking activity for a group of 5 year olds, taking into account the following:

- one child has a nut allergy
- another child has speech and language delay.

1. How would you make sure that the children's needs are met?
2. Who would you need to consult with before the activity?

Evaluating your plans

Once you have implemented an individual plan for a child it is important to consider how it went and what the next steps are in learning. You will need to provide information as to how the activity has worked as this will most likely inform future planning. You may have a format to do this but the checklist below might also help you evaluate your plan:

- Did the children appear to be engaged and focused for the duration of the activity?
- How much adult support was needed?
- Was this support planned?
- What were the learning outcomes from this activity?
- Was this a planned or an unplanned opportunity?
- What could the next steps of learning be?
- What did individual children gain from the activity?
- How did you help children learn?
- How effective were the resources you used?
- Did you have enough and the right resources?
- Which resources did the children use the most?
- Are there any other resources that could have been used?
- Were there any limitations of this activity?
- What would you change next time?

One way to record each child's learning and next steps is through possible lines of development (PLOD) that build on their interests and needs. PLODs:

- are based around observations or conversations with the child's parents or carers
- inform planning for the environment, activities and experiences
- are the basis for planning adult-led activities
- ensure a child's next steps are identified.

5 Be able to promote positive behaviours expected of children

Promoting positive behaviour is a key part of your role. Like adults, children show how they are feeling through their patterns of behaviour, and you need to help children manage these feelings in a constructive way.

Modelling and promoting positive behaviours

Children learn some of their behaviour from the adults and children they spend time with. The way you model and promote behaviour is an important part of creating a positive environment, where children will develop an understanding of how to behave. You are a role model, and your approach should be consistent. What sort of message are you giving if you are not polite and helpful to your colleagues or disagree in front of children?

Jargon buster

Positive behaviour – the way that children actively show respect and behave well towards themselves, other children and adults.

SEND – Special Educational Needs and Disabilities.

To promote positive behaviour, you need to:

- understand how children develop socially and emotionally
- make managing behaviour part of each child's individual learning plan
- ensure that promoting positive behaviour is an essential part of the educational programme and is celebrated
- create clear and appropriate expectations for how children and adults in the setting treat each other, perhaps by creating your goals together
- make sure that you involve parents in managing children's behaviour through learning journeys, discussions and shared observations.

Your environment plays a part too. Your environment should:

- encourage positive behaviour
- include books and pictures that focus on emotions
- duplicate resources to avoid conflict
- share practice with parents
- provide restful areas for children to have time alone
- use role play to explore feelings
- provide safe places for children to have quiet times.

Figure 4.10: How can you encourage children to work and play positively together?

Applying boundaries and rules

The EYFS sets a goal called 'Managing feelings and behaviour'. To enable children to achieve this goal, you need to follow the policies and procedures within the behaviour framework of your setting.

This framework will guide you on the strategies you can use so that children understand any consequences, and will clarify the importance of including parents and carers and communicating well.

A behaviour policy will make sure that you promote positive behaviour among children, their parents and colleagues. To do this you will model, praise and reward positive behaviour and remind children of what the setting expects of them.

Reflect

It is good practice to regularly review behaviour policies and procedures. Find out how your setting reviews this and how any changes are embedded in practice. How are the policies and procedures monitored?

Tips for applying boundaries and rules

- Be clear if you don't like the behaviour of a child towards you: for example, by saying, 'It makes me feel sad when you push in front of me, Karl.'
- Thank children when they have done something positive: for example, by saying, 'Thank you for pouring the water for Hellen, Parveen.'
- Intervene with a child who has just pushed another: for example, by saying, 'Jo, I know that Bella has the car you like but Bella doesn't want you to push her. That makes Bella feel sad.'

Role modelling behaviour

Children sometimes understand best when an adult shows them how to approach a situation. Here are some examples of how you could model positive behaviour.

- Greet each child in the morning using their name.
- Say 'please' and 'thank you' when children do something helpful.
- Wear an apron during messy play.
- Show how to listen to children when they speak in a small group.
- Tidy up alongside children.
- Sit with children at snack time and take part in the conversation.
- Play a game and take turns.
- Ask a child to share an activity with you.
- Comfort and show concern for a child who is upset.
- Ask a child's permission to show their picture to the class.

Reflect

Think of snack time in your setting. How do you role model how you want the children to behave? Remember meal times are an opportunity to:

- take time to enjoy each other's company
- talk and listen to each other
- develop independence
- develop the skill to choose
- develop social skills such as holding a knife and fork or chopsticks, or eating with your mouth closed
- learn to help others.

1. How well do you think you do this?
2. How could you be a better role model? Think about the developmental stages of the children you are working with.

Your relationship with your colleagues

How you relate to the adults you work with is an important part of modelling positive behaviour to children. You cannot be best friends with everyone you work with, or get on with everybody all of the time – but you should keep any differences out of your setting. Ensure you greet each other, are polite and respectful and always talk calmly. Displaying a good attitude to your work can help to create a positive and respectful environment for the children.

6 Be able to support children to manage their own behaviour

Managing and developing children's behaviour well comes with experience. First you need to have an understanding of each child's development. You can read the stages of social development in learning outcome 1 of Unit 1.

Responding to children's behaviour

Think about these points.

- How often do you smile or acknowledge a child positively?
- How much time do you spend listening to a child?
- What type of activities do you provide to promote positive behaviour?
- Who does the child respond well to?
- How do other adults react to the child?
- In what type of situation is a child likely to display unwanted behaviour?
- How do you encourage children to take responsibility for their own behaviour?
- Are they responding to being bored, frustrated and anxious?
- How do you react to situations of unwanted behaviour?

Skills and techniques for positive behaviour

Different triggers can contribute towards a child's behaviour. Before trying to manage a child's unwanted behaviour, check whether any of these triggers is affecting the situation.

- **Food and water** – Sometimes a lack of food can cause a child to behave in an unusual way – perhaps because they have not had breakfast, need a snack or drink of water or have not had enough lunch.
- **Stimulation** – A child may display negative behaviour, such as distracting other children, if an activity is not interesting them or a story goes on for too long.
- **Friendships** – A child may display unwanted behaviour if another child has rejected them, they are having difficulty making friendships or if a close friend is absent.
- **Sleep** – A child may have recently stopped a daytime sleep, or may not have slept well the night before, so may display unwanted behaviour because they are tired.

Here are some skills and techniques you can use to promote positive behaviour.

- Praise children while they show desired behaviour or afterwards.

- Make sure children understand why they are being rewarded.
- Be frequent with your praise – and be sincere.
- Choose rewards carefully so that a child does not repeat the behaviour just to gain a reward.
- Remind them: 'Do you remember how pleased I was when …'
- Observe that children may enjoy gaining attention from praise.
- Know what a child can achieve for their stage of development.
- Show children what they need to do.
- Give children responsibility to prevent frustration and give confidence.
- Give children a warning and time to change their behaviour.

Children managing their own behaviour

One of the most difficult things that you might have to do is to manage conflict between children. However, situations are usually easily resolved once you have developed the skills and techniques to manage children's behaviour positively.

Remember that using the word 'no' is not usually effective and can form a barrier between you and the child. However, a potentially dangerous situation such as a child hitting another child on the head with a spade may require an adult to say 'no' very quickly – followed with an explanation.

Case study 4.4

Lara was concerned because some children were unkind to George and teasing him for wearing glasses. George was displaying some unwanted behaviour as a result and had been involved in several disagreements.

Lara introduced Liam to the children in a circle time; he is a doll with funky hair and glasses. She whispered to Liam and told the children he had come to play, but it was a bit difficult because he would not wear his glasses, which he needed to see. She asked how they could encourage Liam to wear his glasses. Someone suggested he looked cool. Someone said he should wear them. Lara said he would, but he was afraid children would laugh at him. George sat and listened. Lara produced some glasses for Liam and asked how would they feel if children laughed at them. George joined in with the other children and also asked another child to help him put the glasses on Liam.

1. What do you think Lara hoped to achieve by telling Liam's story?

2. What could the possible effects of the story be on the other children?

You can manage children's behaviour towards each other by following these guidelines.

- Always explain the consequences of their actions: 'That made Billy upset.'
- Use facial expressions, come down to the child's level and make eye contact.

Figure 4.11: How can talking to a child on their level help them to understand?

- Provide a positive environment that encourages sharing, taking turns and listening.
- Use observations to plan how to support a child further.
- Help children to form relationships, showing them how to share and join in.
- If a child does something unacceptable, make sure that the victim is looked after, but make sure the doer realises they are still cared for.
- Help children to negotiate.
- Help children have the vocabulary to express their feelings.
- Develop activities about feelings.
- Consider encouraging a response: 'You hurt Tom but I know you were cross that he took your doll. How can we make you both feel better?'
- Show understanding: 'I know it can be difficult to share your book but …'
- Make sure the child understands you, perhaps by encouraging them to restate what you have said.

Remember that, in order to develop, the brain needs to recall positive experiences of handling situations. Compromise and negotiation can be hard for adults too, so try to help children who need additional support and understand that sometimes you may need support from other professionals.

7 Understand when a child is in need of additional support

Most children will progress well, but some may need extra support, either temporary or ongoing. A child may even enter your setting with recognised needs.

Children may need support at difficult times in their lives, such as after the death of a grandparent or during their parents' divorce. Early intervention and action will give a child the most effective support.

Indicators of a child needing additional support

In *Development Matters* you will notice that the areas of development overlap as follows:

- birth–11 months
- 8–20 months
- 22–36 months
- 30–50 months
- 40–60 months.

The overlap is important as not all children progress at the same rate. You will often see children of the same age achieving at different levels. However, there may be concern if a child:

- continues to develop less than other children in the same age group for a period
- is consistently not achieving some developmental milestones over a period and despite support.

For a child to have an additional assessment you will have to gather evidence to support your concerns, working with parents to do so. However, it is important to first seek the advice of your SENCO or other appropriate person in authority before approaching the parents. This evidence can be gathered using:

- observations and learning journeys
- assessments
- discussions with parents and carers
- records of the child's progress through the early years outcomes
- reviews of any targets in place.

Case study 4.5

Emily is about to start at her local children's centre. She has visual impairment and is partially sighted. Her **portage worker** visits the setting to advise how they could make Emily feel welcome and included. She suggests that they could have a variety of different smells and scents inside and outside to help Emily find her way round. She suggests that a variety of safe textures on floors and outside could help Emily distinguish where she is walking. There are already white strips on all the steps. She also notices that the window blinds are adjustable, which is good as Emily finds it difficult to play in bright light. She suggests some small lamps in the book corner to help Emily enjoy some of the large books and listen to stories.

1. Is there anything else the setting can do to help Emily feel welcome and included?

For most children, concerns can be addressed with appropriate support. However, some concerns can result in further assessment. In this case, the child will receive a diagnosis that will help you support them fully and include them in the setting. This may include help from other professionals.

Jargon buster

Portage worker – someone who helps to develop a programme to support an individual child.

Adapting resources and approaches

While you continue to use the systems of observing, planning and reviewing used for all children, you should record targets on the child's individual learning plan that address the key areas where they need support.

You will need to agree ways to support the child, through experiences and activities that support their learning outcomes. To ensure that these are relevant:

- liaise with any other professionals who are involved with the child
- review the individual learning plan regularly.

Possible additional support and strategies could include:

- small group activities that support the child's learning
- providing appropriate resources, experiences and activities
- adapting some activities so that the child is included and is more likely to progress.

Adult support

You should be aware of the targets and support strategies for the child's learning. An adult can also support a child by:

- being a key person, supporting them and making them feel secure

- planning for the child's learning and recording their progress
- involving the SENCO in planning and reviewing
- including the child in all learning opportunities
- ensuring that learning is flexible
- giving each child time to achieve
- ensuring additional learning opportunities
- providing a variety of developmentally appropriate toys and experiences
- involving the child in any planning and adaptation.

Strategies for working in partnership

It can be difficult for a parent or carer whose child is being assessed for additional needs, so you need to support them sensitively. Work closely with them to share information and create a picture of the child's interests, abilities, needs and successful support strategies. You will need to involve the child and their parents or carers in their individual learning plan.

Figures 4.12, 4.13 and 4.14 relate to the individual learning plan process, which needs to consider the voice of the child, the parents and the professionals and practitioners involved at every stage.

GUIDANCE NOTES FOR WORKING WITH PARENTS	
Setting:	**Name of child:**
	Date of birth:

Strengths and interests

What can the child do now?

Areas for development:

Next steps:

Completed by:	
Signature of parents:	
Date:	

Figure 4.12: Guidance for practitioners.

INDIVIDUAL LEARNING PLAN – EARLY YEARS				
Setting:	Name:	Date of birth:	Early Action	
			Early Action Plus	
		Age:	Plan number	
			Date	
Strengths:		Long term objectives:		
Nature of need:				

Target 1:

Activities / strategies:

Helped by whom:

How often:

Target 2:

Activities / strategies:

Helped by whom:

How often:

Target 3:

Activities / strategies:

Helped by whom:

How often:

Other information:

Other agencies involved:

Parental views and action:

Parental signature:

Completed by:	Review date:

Figure 4.13: An individual learning plan template.

INDIVIDUAL LEARNING PLAN REVIEW – EARLY YEARS				
Name:		**Early Action**	**Plan number**	
		Early Action Plus	**Date**	
Present:				
Targets – fully achieved or working towards?				
1)				
2)				
3)				
Activities / support arrangements				
Additional comments to support review				
Next steps to inform future plans:				
Completed by:			**Parent signature:**	

Figure 4.14: A review plan.

Further reading and resources

Publications

- Athey, C. (2007) *Extending Thought in Young Children: A Parent–Teacher Partnership*, London: Sage Publications – looks at how young children think and explores children's schematic development, to see how educators and parents can best support their learning

- Department for Education (2013) *Early Years Outcomes* – non-statutory guide for practitioners and inspectors, to help inform understanding of child development through the early years – available online at www.gov. uk/government/publications/early-years-outcomes

- Early Education (2012) *Development Matters in the Early Years Foundation Stage (EYFS)* – non-statutory guidance material for practitioners implementing the statutory requirements of the EYFS – available online at www.foundationyears.org.uk/files/2012/03/ Development-Matters-FINAL-PRINT-AMENDED.pdf

- EYFS documentation: www.education.gov.uk/eyfs – information and guidance on using the EYFS

Websites

- Persona Dolls: www. persona-doll-training.org – information about the Persona Doll approach, which encourages children to develop empathy and challenge discrimination and unfairness

- Reggio Emilia: www.reggiochildren.it – information about the Reggio Emilia approach to education from its originators, with information on publications and seminars

Articles and magazines

- Laevers, Dr. F. (2005) *Deep-level-learning and the Experiential Approach in Early Childhood and Primary Education* – available online at http://cego.inform. be/InformCMS/custom/downloads/BO_D&P_Deep-levelLearning.pdf

Make accurate and productive use of assessment in early years settings

Unit 5

Make accurate and productive use of assessment in early years settings

All early years practitioners will have a responsibility to assess the achievement of children in their setting. This unit will help you to be clear on the reasons for assessment and how this supports children's learning and development so that you can do this more effectively. You will also need to be able to work with others in order to monitor and review children's progress.

Before you start

Think about the ways in which you and your colleagues use assessment in your setting. How are assessments recorded? Do all staff have access to them? How do you work with others in assessing children's progress in learning and development? And how do you make sure that the assessments you are involved in are a true representation of each child's progress?

Learning outcomes

By the end of this unit you will:

1. understand how to assess within the early education curriculum framework
2. be able to carry out observational assessment
3. be able to identify the needs, interests and stages of development of individual children
4. be able to use assessment to plan next steps
5. be able to discuss children's progress and plan next stages.

1 Understand how to assess within the early education curriculum framework

One of your main responsibilities as an early years practitioner is to monitor and assess children's learning and development. You need to know how all the children are progressing so that you can plan for the next steps. This knowledge is also important if you are going to be able to report back to parents, other staff and the local authority in a way that is accurate and helpful.

Assessment is an ongoing process – part of your everyday practice rather than a special event. It also has different forms, all of which have particular uses, which you need to understand. For your own professionalism, and for the sake of the children in your care, you will need to be able to use assessment effectively.

The child-centred assessment model

The child-centred model of assessment does something simple but crucial: it puts the child at the centre of your assessments and planning, rather than making them the object of what you are doing. This allows you to understand each child's real needs, actual stage of development and particular interests, so that you can take into account the individuality of each child in your work. Ultimately, this means that you and your setting will be better able to support each child's progress.

This model guides you to encourage children to self-direct – make their own choices and decisions – wherever possible, by providing open-ended tasks that motivate them, stimulate their interest and allow them to learn at their own pace. You can then encourage each child's learning by using effective questioning, and by targeting focused activities towards specific children's needs and interests.

Remember that children pass through different phases depending on their readiness for learning and social and emotional development.

Figure 5.1 illustrates the different factors that contribute to children's learning. Here are some points for you to consider about each of these factors.

- **Motivation** – Children are more likely to be motivated by being offered a range of activities that change regularly and being allowed to explore their environment.
- **Interests** – As you observe a child, you will be able to see the kinds of activities that interest them. For example, some children will regularly go to sensory activities such as dough, messy play or sand, while others may prefer construction, role play or activities in which they use pencils and paper. You may notice that a child has a particular interest in a subject such as football or trains, or needs to have creative activities to stimulate their learning.
- **Stage of development** – A child's stage of development is likely to influence their learning, and this will also have an influence on the activities that you set up for them. You need to see each child's individual stage of development, rather than making any assumptions about them as part of a group.

Figure 5.2: How can children learn through investigative activities?

- **Needs** – All children will have different needs, and it is important for you to recognise those of the children with whom you work. For example, one child may be very happy and settled in your setting, while another may be feeling disrupted by changes to their routine that are impacting on their learning and development. Another child may have developmental needs that mean they need to have tasks and assessment opportunities that take these into account.
- **Opportunities for learning** – You should be able to find many opportunities for learning and assessment when the children are engaged in activities in your setting. For example, if a child is emptying and filling bottles in the water tray, you could question them about what they are doing and encourage their communication and language skills.

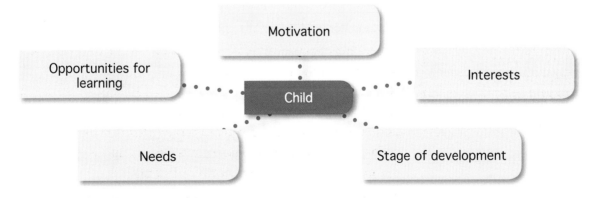

Figure 5.1: Children's learning is affected by several different factors.

Appropriate assessment techniques

Children's learning and development is assessed throughout the Early Years Foundation Stage, and Section 2 of the EYFS statutory framework is dedicated to assessment. It states that: 'Ongoing assessment … is an integral part of the learning and development process' and outlines the ways in which children should be assessed. This should take place through both formative and summative assessment.

- Formative assessment is assessment that is ongoing or continuing, as in daily observations.
- Summative assessment takes place at key points, such as the progress check at age 2.

In your setting, you will need to have an agreed method for ongoing formative assessment on a day-to-day basis through a balance of adult-led and child-initiated activities. (For more information on formative and summative assessment, see learning outcome 4 of this unit.)

Observation and questioning

These are both forms of formative assessment, which means that you will carry them out throughout learning activities. They will be an ongoing part of the teaching and learning process.

Observation

Children are likely to have individual records or folders so that you can note down your observations under:

- the seven areas of learning and development (for more information, see learning outcomes 1 and 3 in Unit 2)
- the three characteristics of effective learning (for more information, see learning outcome 3 in Unit 2).

Your observations may be paper-based, photographed, videoed, or held on computers, but whatever form they take, they should show the way in which children are learning, as well as the progress they are making.

Observations may be short (for example, if a child has made a comment that demonstrates their understanding in a particular area) or longer if you need to describe an activity that a child has

undertaken over time, including photographs of children. The Department for Education has produced some exemplification materials to demonstrate the kinds of observations that you might carry out on children and keep in the children's folders. You can find out more about these materials online at the DfE website (for more information, see the Further reading and resources section at the end of this unit).

Jargon buster

Characteristics of effective learning – the different ways in which children learn: playing and exploring, active learning, and creating and thinking critically.

Questioning

When you are working with children, it is likely that you will carry out assessments through questioning them about what they are doing or what they have found out. You will need to record this as part of the child's learning journal. Questioning helps you build a clearer picture about how children learn, as this sample conversation between an early years practitioner and a child shows:

Elise

'Miss Bennett, this morning the water was frozened, but it's water now.'

'Why did it change?'

'It got hot and melted …it got hot with the sun.'

I asked if the sun had come out, did that mean it was summer?

'No! 'Cos you can't get snow in the summer, and this was snow and iced. Maybe it's a little bit summer but most of it's winter and so it's winter, and that's why.'

Next morning, Elise brought ice into school to show me it was winter.

(Source: EYFS Profile: exemplification materials – Early learning goal 14: the world, Department for Education, 2013, p.15)

Parents should also be encouraged to contribute observations in order to aid practitioners with assessment and to gain a fuller picture of the child over time. (For more information on parental contributions to observations, see learning outcome 3 in Unit 2.)

Summative assessment in the EYFS currently takes place at two points:

- the progress check at age 2
- the EYFS profile – a child's assessment at the end of the EYFS.

These assessments are a review of the child's progress and give a snapshot of the developmental level and needs of the individual child at that time.

Progress check at age 2

This takes the form of a written summary of a child's development in the prime areas of learning (personal, social and emotional development, physical development, and communication and language development). The check should identify any 'emerging significant concerns' so that you and the child's parents or carers can target the child's future learning and development needs. There is no prescribed format for the 2-year check, although some local authorities have produced their own advice and suggested templates. For an example of one of these you can look at Surrey's, which can be found at www.surreycc.gov.uk/eyfs. In addition, a reference to the National Children's Bureau (NCB) guide is given at the end of this unit.

The EYFS profile

This takes place in the final term of the reception year, or the year in which the child turns 5. It gives parents, teachers and early years practitioners 'an overview of the child's knowledge, understanding and abilities', as well as their progress against expected levels, and their readiness for Year 1.

The profile must reflect:

- ongoing observation
- all relevant records held by the setting

- discussions with parents and carers, and any other adults whom the teacher, parent or carer judges can offer a useful contribution.

(Source: Statutory Framework for the Early Years Foundation Stage, Department for Education, 2014, p.14)

At the time of writing, each child's profile should also reflect their abilities and skills in relation to the three characteristics of effective learning, which should be passed on to their Year 1 teacher as well as to their parents or carers. However, this is due to change in 2015 with the introduction of a statutory baseline assessment at the start of the reception year when children enter school. The EYFS profile is likely to become optional.

Using observations and assessments to inform planning

Planning and assessment are part of the teaching and learning cycle. This means that you cannot consider one without the other.

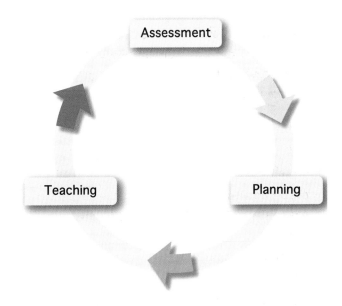

Figure 5.3: The cycle of assessment, planning and teaching.

However your setting carries out its planning, you should be able to work with others to ensure that children's next steps for learning are taken into

Activity and learning objective: To review recognition and ordering of numbers to 20		
Date: 2/5/14		
Adult: JW		
Name	**Management of task**	**Next steps for learning**
Jamal	Able to count out loud to 20 but confuses 6 and 9 / 16 and 19 when placing them in order.	Continue to work on number recognition to 20 through board games, interactive whiteboard sessions, computer, targeted questioning.
Ruthie	Able to count reliably, recognise, order and write numbers to 20 and beyond.	Consolidate counting and recognition and use 100 square to point out patterns and encourage exploration of number.
Emily	Able to count reliably to 12 but then said, 'thirty, forty, fifty, sixty, seventy, eighty' and could not continue.	Continue to count aloud as part of whole class activities and say the words clearly to Emily/ask her to say them alongside an adult or other children.
Ricardo (English as additional language)	Able to count reliably to 20 but cannot place numbers in order or recognise them when shown randomly.	Continue with counting activities alongside an adult as well as targeted intervention to develop number recognition.

Figure 5.4: An example assessment document completed by a practitioner during an adult-led activity.

account. You will need to be able to show how you do this often, through the way in which you assess children as they work and play, and through the records you keep of their next steps for learning.

Where children are carrying out child-led activities, it is more likely that you will record and assess them through observations. When children first come into your setting and before you have got to know them, it is good practice for you to record more observations, so that you can help build up a picture of the child. However, as you get to know the child and their needs better, it may be more manageable for you to record only those situations which are unexpected (ones that you would not have predicted the child would be able to achieve). In this situation, you may be able to write down a child's next steps on observations as well as taught activities.

Case study 5.1

You are working in a reception class with a group of children following a painting activity to make symmetrical butterflies. At the end of the session you have been discussing how you will get some paint back into a bottle, as you don't want to waste any. Melissa, who is of age-related ability, says, 'I know what we can do! I will go and get a funnel and then you can pour the paint back in. Gravity will make it go back in the bottle'.

1. Do you think that this comment is worth noting down?

2. Would you record any next steps if so?

3. How could this inform your team's planning?

Parents' involvement in observation and assessment

Parents have a key role to play in supporting you when making observations and assessments of their children, and you will need to make sure that you take parental contributions and involvement into account. The statutory guidance for the EYFS states that practitioners should 'respond to their own day-to-day observations about children's progress and observations that parents and carers share.' *(Source: Statutory Framework for the Early Years Foundation Stage, Department for Education, 2014, p.13)*

This means that you will need to give parents the opportunity to pass on their own observations about their child's learning and development. They can do this in several ways.

- **Through the key person system** – Getting to know parents and building relationships with them as a key person will put you in a better position to develop an overview of the whole child and their background – and consequently you will understand better how you can support the child's learning and development. You will also be able to note down parental observations about the child following discussions with them.

- **Through welcoming parents into the setting** – Parents should always be welcome to come into your setting – but in addition to the day-to-day routines, there should be specially planned activities and events that enable parents to have contact with both staff and with other parents. These opportunities could be formal or informal. In this way parents will be more likely to develop relationships with you and other adults in your setting, and have the chance to talk to others about their child.

- **Through opportunities to record their observations** – Your setting should make sure that parents are aware of the importance of their input and give them a range of opportunities to make contributions. In the example shown in Figure 5.5,

the setting has distributed 'Wow!' templates to parents and carers, and encouraged them to write on them when their child has done something notable.

Parents should also be aware that they can pass on their observations at any time after something notable has happened, and that they can do so either verbally or in writing.

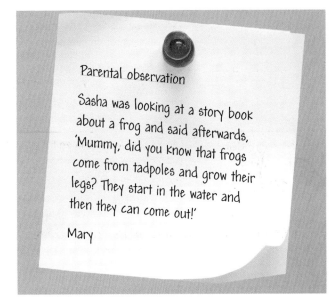

Parental observation

Sasha was looking at a story book about a frog and said afterwards, 'Mummy, did you know that frogs come from tadpoles and grow their legs? They start in the water and then they can come out!'

Mary

Figure 5.5: Why are parental observations important?

How theories of play and development link to assessment

There are a number of different theories of play and development that you will need to be aware of. All theories of development are based on observation and assessment, as they look at the way children react and respond in different situations. However, different theorists focus on different aspects of development, and the views they offer may influence the way in which you consider and carry out your assessments. Table 5.1 outlines some of the key theories of development and how they relate to assessment. (For more information on theories of play and development, see learning outcome 2 in Unit 1).

Table 5.1: How the main theories and approaches to learning and development link to assessment.

Theorist	Theory	How it is related to assessment
Jean Piaget	Cognitive theory	Piaget thought that children's development passes through different stages and that they will not move on to the next until they are ready. This relates to assessment as the stages of children's development are taken into account when planning the educational programme. Children are therefore assessed against what is generally expected for their age group.
Reggio Emilia	Self-guided learning	This approach is based on the child being the initiator in their own learning and following their own interests, which will be fostered and encouraged by adults. In the EYFS, children are encouraged to develop their own interests in this way so that they can learn through play.
John Bowlby	Attachment theory	Bowlby stated that early attachments are crucial to a child's development and will influence the way in which children develop relationships in later life. When carrying out assessments, you will look at the way in which children interact with others in order to assess their social and emotional development.
Albert Bandura	Social learning theory	Bandura's theory states that children will observe the behaviour and learning of others and copy this in their play and behaviour. This is related to assessment as you often see children simply copying what others are doing, and you need to assess what they have initiated themselves.
B. F. Skinner	Behaviour theory Positive reinforcement	Skinner stated that children will respond to positive reinforcement and are heavily influenced by their environment, whether this is for learning and behaviour or for language. He stated that adults can influence the way in which children learn and behave by rewarding more desirable actions. When working on assessment, consider how adults influence children's use of language, behaviour and learning through positive interactions.
Lev Vygotsky Jerome Bruner	Language and communication theory Constructivist learning theory	Vygotsky and Bruner both believed that children's learning and language was developed by scaffolding by adults and social situations. They will learn and communicate with others through being supported and observing how others do things, as well as building on what they know. This relates to assessment as you need to observe whether children are passing through stages in their learning and language development.
Noam Chomsky	Language acquisition device	Chomsky believed that children are born with an innate system which enables them to formulate the rules of grammar. For example, a child who has not learned about irregular verbs might say 'I drinked it' by working out that you add 'ed' to the end of a verb in the past tense. This relates to assessment as you will need to look closely at how children's language is developing and what might influence them.

Theory in action

Sheniz is carrying out an observation on a group of children who are working on a creative activity where they are self-selecting paints. She notices that Anna, who usually enjoys and works well on these kinds of activity, has started to mix two of the colours together on the easel and is talking about it to the others, 'Look! If I mix red and yellow it makes orange!' Marco, on the easel next to her, starts to do the same thing.

1. Should Sheniz note down the responses of both children?

2. What do you notice about this in relation to the theories of learning?

3. Is Anna's response any more valid than Marco's? Give your reasoning.

2 Be able to carry out observational assessment

When you are carrying out observational assessments, you should remember that you are not only observing and recording what is happening: there are a number of other issues that you need to take into consideration. Confidentiality is particularly important, and observations will need to be kept secure within the setting.

Address issues of permission, confidentiality and participant bias when carrying out assessment

You will need to be aware of a range of potentially sensitive issues that are relevant when you are carrying out assessments on young children.

Issues of permission

Your setting may have asked parents and carers to fill in a permission slip when their child first starts there, which enables photographs to be published on the setting's website. You may also keep photographs for observation purposes when you are carrying out assessments. If permission is needed for any other reason, you will need to have regard for this and make sure that you keep any such information on children safe and secure, so that it is not visible to others.

Confidentiality

You need to be aware that any information that you have on children is confidential, and you should not talk about it with others or show it to others outside your setting. You will have to make sure that any paperwork that you keep on individual children remains in the setting or on secure work-based computers. This is because it is important that others do not look at information about children.

Figure 5.6: Why must you obtain parental consent before taking or using any photographs of children in your care?

Participant bias

All staff in your setting should make sure that they are objective when carrying out assessments – including you. This means that you will need to show that you do not record what you think or feel about a child when observing them, but only what you see. This is because your opinions and feelings could distort the observation and make it appear different when read by another person.

Data protection

All records on children will need to be stored and used in a way that complies with the Data Protection Act 1998. Under this act, any organisation that holds information on individuals must be registered with the Information Commissioner. This system is designed to ensure that confidential information cannot be passed on to others without the individual's consent or, in the case of young children, the consent of their parent or carer.

Make accurate and productive use of assessment in early years settings

There are eight principles of practice that govern the storage and use of information. Information must:

- be processed fairly and lawfully
- be used only for the purpose for which it was gathered
- be adequate, relevant and not excessive
- be accurate and kept up to date where necessary
- be kept for no longer than necessary
- be processed in line with the individual's rights
- be kept secure
- not be transferred outside the European Union without adequate protection.

A good rule to remember is that all information is confidential and that you should only discuss information on children with others who need to know.

Carry out observational assessment

In your role, you should be observing children at all times to note how they interact with others, manage their independence and learning, and ensure they are progressing towards the early learning goals. Through observing children informally you will gain information about the kinds of activities that interest them, as well as how they manage the activity and articulate what they are doing. However, you will also need to be able to carry out more formal observational assessments so that you can assess their progress, evaluate their learning and plan the next

steps. You must also make sure that you include and take into consideration observations from parents.

Carrying out observational assessment will be similar in all settings, although the way in which they are recorded and how assessment records are kept is likely to vary slightly from setting to setting. It is important that you understand your own setting's procedures and preferences, and are clear on the format of the observation that you are undertaking. It is also important to be objective in your observations, noting only what you see and hear, not your own thoughts.

Complete assessment records for a given child

Although they may take different formats, all of the different types of record you will be asked to complete will need to show that you are assessing children's progress towards the early learning goals. Here are some of the formats that you may use for assessment records in line with the EYFS.

Checklist

You can use this type of record to check and record whether pupils can carry out a particular activity, quickly and in a straightforward way. They usually require the observer to make a judgement on whether a child is able to achieve a task – for example throwing and catching a ball. Checklists may take different forms and schools can devise their own, depending on what is being observed and whether an adult is supporting them.

PSE/making relationships	Plays alongside others	Plays cooperatively with a familiar adult	Interested in others' play and starting to join in	Seeks out others to share experiences
Ricky	on entry 21/9	with parent 21/9	on entry 21/9	-
Amara	on entry 21/9	with parent 21/9	-	-
Jane	on entry 21/9	with parent 21/9	21/9	21/9
Jamal	-	with parent 21/9	-	-

Figure 5.7: An example of a checklist for personal, social and emotional development (making relationships).

Learning objective check

This may be used when you are leading or guiding a learning activity: for example, if you are looking at whether children are able to count reliably and place numbers to 20 in order. You would ask the children to do the task and then record how they managed the task.

Free description

This enables you to write down everything that happens for the period of the observation – usually between five and ten minutes. Your observation will be completely focused on the child and will need to include what the child says to others, how they express themselves non-verbally and the way in which the activity is carried out. Free descriptions are used when a lot of detail is required, and are usually written in the present tense – *Sarah picks up a ball* rather than *Sarah picked up a ball*.

Stickers or sticky notes

These can be handy when you want to make a quick note when a child has done or said something that is unexpected. You can then stick the sticker or note in the child's assessment folder or learning profile under the area of learning to which it relates. For example, if a child shows understanding of a particular word or idea, you may put this under 'communication and language/ understanding'.

Event samples

These are used to record how often a child displays a particular type of behaviour or activity. If you are carrying out an event sample, you need to make sure that you are not participating in the learning activity in order to remain objective.

Time samples

Time samples occur when the observer has a set amount of time to observe a child and look at how they behave and interact with others during that time. When carrying out time samples, you will need to make sure that you are clear about the exact amount of time needed.

Informal observations

These may come about if you are, for example, asked to 'just keep an eye' on a child, or to watch them at a particular time, and then feed back to other staff. In this case, you can make your own notes – but you should be careful about confidentiality if you are writing things down. Remember not to leave your notebooks lying around, particularly if you have recorded children's names.

The exemplar materials for the EYFS also give good examples of the kinds of observational assessment records you might keep on given children. You can find a link that enables you to access these in the Further reading and resources section at the end of this unit.

Review the effectiveness of plans and planning methods

As you are carrying out assessments, you will need to think about whether your methods support your planning and how they help you to plan children's next steps for learning. In order to do this, your medium-term and daily plans should show learning objectives, so that you keep the children's learning at the forefront of what you are doing as you work with them.

Table 5.2 shows an example of a planning sheet for one week. You will see that it shows learning objectives by subject area. Learning activities are listed in the same order on a previous sheet so that it is clear which objectives relate to which activities. When writing daily plans these are then highlighted so that staff can assess children's learning.

Table 5.2: An example of a planning sheet for one week.

Communication and language / literacy	Numeracy	Expressive arts and crafts	Personal, social and emotional	Understanding the world	Physical development
• Children listen attentively in a range of situations. • They answer 'how' and 'why' questions about their experiences and in response to stories or events. • Children express themselves effectively. • Children enjoy rhythmic activities. • They use phonic knowledge to decode regular words and read them aloud accurately. • Children use their phonic knowledge to write words in ways that match their spoken sounds. • They also write some irregular common words. • Children read and understand simple sentences.	• Children count reliably with numbers from one to 20, place them in order and say which one is more or less. • Using quantities and objects they add and subtract two single-digit numbers and count on or back to find the answer. • Children start to use the vocabulary involved in adding and subtracting. • They use everyday language to talk about size, weight, capacity, position, distance, time and money, and to compare objects and solve problems. • Children order and sequence familiar events.	• They create simple representations of events, people and objects. • Children sing songs, make music and dance, and experiment with ways of changing them. • They construct with a purpose in mind, using a variety of resources. • Children select appropriate resources and adapt work where necessary. • They use what they have learned about media and materials in original ways, thinking about uses and purposes. • Children represent their own ideas, thoughts and feelings through design and technology, art, music, dance, role play and stories.	• They work as part of a group or class, and understand and follow the rules. • Children play cooperatively, taking turns with others. • They take account of others ideas about how to organise their activity. • Children are confident to speak in a familiar group, will talk about their ideas, and will choose the resources they need for their chosen activities. • They adjust their behaviour to different situations. • Children show sensitivity to others' needs and feelings and form positive relationships with adults and other children. • They start to negotiate and solve problems without aggression – for example, when someone has taken their toy.	• They make observations of animals and plants and explain why some things occur, and talk about changes. • Children know about similarities and differences between themselves and others, and among families, communities and traditions. • They know about similarities and differences in relation to places, objects, materials and living things. • Children talk about why things happen and how things work. • They look closely at similarities, differences, patterns and change. • Children complete a simple program on a computer.	• Children experiment with different ways of moving. • They move confidently in a range of ways, safely negotiating space. • Children show increasing control over an object in pushing, patting, throwing, catching or kicking it. • They use simple tools to effect changes to materials. • Children handle equipment and tools effectively, including pencils for writing. • They know the importance for good health of physical exercise and a healthy diet, and talk about ways to keep healthy and safe. • Children can hold a pencil between thumb and two fingers. • They can copy some letters and write some independently.

Reflect

How do you carry out assessments in your setting? What format do they take? How are your plans and planning methods reviewed to take assessment of children's learning into account?

3 Be able to identify the needs, interests and stages of development of individual children

The statutory guidance for the EYFS states: 'Practitioners must consider the individual needs, interests and stage of development of each child in their care, and must use this information to plan a challenging and enjoyable experience for each child in all of the areas of learning and development'. You will be able to use assessment to do this, while also checking any learning and development needs so that you can address them in partnership with parents and carers.

The child's key person will also be well placed to look at their individual needs, interests and stage of development as they will be aware of the background of the child and any issues that are relevant. They will also be able to use formative assessment, which will incorporate all they know about a child, as well as responding to day-to-day situations.

Use assessment to identify the needs of individual children

You will want to use different forms of assessment to identify the needs of individual children. The progress check at age 2 is particularly useful for this. It is designed to look at children's progress against the three prime areas of learning and development, so that parents and carers can be given a short written summary at this stage. This progress check – which takes place at any point between 24 and 36 months – is an opportunity to look at how children are developing as well as to identify any areas in which they may be developing at a faster or slower pace than is expected at their age.

Local authorities publish their own advice and formats for the progress check at age 2. There is no prescribed format, so nurseries and childminders will need to find what works best for them. The Department for Education (DfE) asked the National Children's Bureau (NCB) to support the production of guidance materials for practitioners, to help them complete the assessment. The resulting guide – *A Know How Guide: The EYFS progress check at 2* – is available for you to download at the NCB website.

As children develop and work towards the early learning goals, your formative assessment of them will also be progressing, contributing towards their EYFS profile at the end of the reception year. As each child develops, other learning needs they have may become apparent. It is important that you act on any concerns that you have.

Case study 5.2

You have had some concerns about Charlee's personal, social and emotional development for some time, but have not acted on them. At her progress check at age 2, she is assessed and has come out at 8 to 20 months in all three areas of self-confidence and self-awareness, managing feelings and behaviour, and making relationships.

1. Give two reasons why it is important in this case to act as soon as possible.

2. What might be the consequences of a delay in addressing Charlee's needs?

Figure 5.8: How can you respond to children's needs and interests, to comply with the EYFS?

Use assessment to identify the interests of individual children

While you are carrying out your observations and assessments on children, you will also be able to identify their individual interests. A child's key person will be aware of the kinds of activities that they are likely to choose when they have free choice, as well as those that they are less likely to select.

You can also look through a child's learning journal or folder to note down the kinds of activities that they regularly go to or are stimulated by. Some children's learning journals will have a section in which they write this down separately: for example, under the three characteristics of effective learning.

Identifying individual children's stages of development

The most useful tool for looking at the stages of development is the *Early Years Outcomes* – the document produced by the DfE. This non-statutory guide outlines the different expected outcomes for each age under each 'thread' for each area of learning.

Case study 5.3

Rosie is sitting quietly at the writing table. As her key person, you know that she tends to enjoy solitary play and is not adventurous when self-selecting her activities. She will spend a long time on activities and is persistent, but is often reluctant to come to you when you ask her to join you.

Bella is inquisitive and confident, and will always look all around the room at what is available before fixing on a task. She enjoys looking at different activities and investigates using them, often surprising you with her play.

1. What might you record in each child's learning journal, particularly under the characteristics of effective learning?

2. Should you encourage children to go to tasks that they are less likely to be drawn to?

Communication and language

Table 5.3 sets out what you should be observing a child doing at each stage, if they are developing typically for their age.

Early Years Outcomes is a useful document to help you identify expected behaviour for different stages, as you will be able to see whether or not children are developing at age-related levels. You can also keep relevant extracts from the document in the child's learning journal, to help you measure their progress towards the early learning goals. Some settings will do this by regularly highlighting the relevant information in different colours, by date.

Table 5.3: Typical listening and attention behaviour at different ages. (Source: Early Years Outcomes, Department for Education, 2013, p.4)

Age	Typical behaviour
Birth to 11 months	• Turns towards a familiar sound then locates range of sounds with accuracy • Listens to, distinguishes and responds to intonations and sounds of voices • Reacts in interaction with others by smiling, looking and moving • Quietens or alerts to the sound of speech • Looks intently at a person talking, but stops responding if speaker turns away • Listens to familiar sounds, words or finger plays • Fleeting attention – not under child's control, new stimuli takes whole attention
8 to 20 months	• Moves whole body to sounds they enjoy, such as music or a regular beat • Has a strong exploratory impulse • Concentrates intently on an object or activity of own choosing for short periods • Pays attention to dominant stimulus – easily distracted by noises or other people talking
16 to 26 months	• Listens to and enjoys rhythmic patterns in rhymes and stories • Enjoys rhymes and demonstrates listening by trying to join in with actions or vocalisations • Rigid attention – may appear not to hear
22 to 36 months	• Listens with interest to the noises adults make when they read stories

4 Be able to use assessment to plan next steps

You will need to show how you use assessment to plan the next steps for learning for the children in your care. This may be easier in some cases than in others. For example, you may find it easier to assess a child who is good at expressing their likes and dislikes than to assess a child who is more shy and reluctant to come forward. You will have the support of other professionals as well as parents and carers, and, along with the child, they should be able to demonstrate the next steps that should be taken following assessments in order to support future outcomes.

Collaborating in expressing children's needs

You will need to be able to collaborate with others when planning the next steps for a child's learning, as well as supporting the child in expressing their own needs and aspirations. In addition, the child's key person should be available to discuss their needs and make sure that learning and care is targeted to support them. Other professionals may also visit your setting in order to assess children, or they may come specifically to meet with you and the child's parents or carers, to discuss their needs and the next steps that should be taken to support the child's learning and development. If these other professionals are not available to attend meetings with you they may be asked to submit written reports, outlining the child's progress and their recommendations. It may also be appropriate for the child to be present if they are able to take part in some or all of the discussion, or to have a separate discussion with their key person, which is then fed back during the meeting.

Case study 5.4

A transition meeting is being held at Rehan's new school before he starts in September. Rehan has global learning delay and will be attending a mainstream school. A number of other professionals are invited to the meeting alongside the headteacher – Rehan's new class teacher, his key person from nursery, his physiotherapist and speech and language therapist, and his parents. The physiotherapist is unable to attend the meeting but has submitted a report with details of his most recent assessment and recommendations for physio in school.

1. How will this meeting support Rehan's transition to school?

2. Should Rehan be invited to attend in this case?

The term 'others' in this unit refers to and may include various people, as outlined in Table 5.4.

Table 5.4: People who may be involved in planning children's learning.

Carers and foster carers	Parents and carers or foster carers will be present at meetings as they are likely to have the most knowledge and understanding of the child, and will be able to give background information
Residential and support workers	Residential and support workers will be present if the child is living in residential care, as they will be the child's main carers
Social workers	Social workers may need to be present as they give support and advice to families and will have information on background issues
Psychologists	Psychologists may assess children and possibly their parents if there are issues at home
Doctors	Doctors may be included or be asked to submit reports on children and sometimes on their parents or carers
Police and youth justice	Police and the youth justice team may need to come into your setting if the child or their parents have been in a vulnerable situation
Speech and language therapists	Speech and language therapists may attend meetings about a child in your care to go through work that they have done with them, so that all those working with the child are able to work to the same targets

Using formative assessment to shape learning opportunities

Before you start the next two sections, look back at learning outcome 1 in this unit, and reread the section about formative and summative assessment.

As formative assessment is ongoing, you will need to find a way of using it to enable you to shape learning opportunities within your setting. You may have to act quickly in order to maintain a child's interest in a subject on which they are working. You must always consider the different ways in which children learn so that you can present them with a range of activities. You may look on a daily basis at the ways in which children have responded to different tasks and note down next steps, or wait until you evaluate the week with your colleagues, so that you can think about how you can incorporate your findings into the next week's planning.

However you use formative assessment, it is important that you consider the children's needs as it may be more appropriate and meaningful for them if you act straight away, rather than waiting.

Case study 5.5

Kacper has been very interested in your 'transport' topic and has been bringing in some vehicles from home to show the other children in your setting. He is particularly interested in buses as his dad is a bus driver. You have been given some large old boxes and he has said that he would like to make a bus out of them to drive the other children around.

1. Why is it important that you act on what Kacper would like to do as soon as possible?

2. What areas of learning could this activity incorporate?

Using summative assessment to shape learning opportunities

Summative assessment will take place at two points in the EYFS: the progress check at age 2 and the EYFS profile. Here is a reminder of what these involve.

- **At the progress check at age 2** summative assessment will be used to gain a picture of the child's learning and development in the three prime areas. Summaries of progress at this stage should also include further details about the child's learning, including their strengths.

- **At the end of the EYFS, with the child's EYFS profile** a detailed report is produced by the reception teacher or early years practitioner in the final term of the year in which the child turns 5. The child's level of development in each of the early learning goals must be recorded along with a summary of their skills and abilities against the three characteristics of effective learning.

While both of these assessments will shape learning opportunities, the progress check at age 2 is more likely to be helpful to you, as it takes place during the EYFS. The EYFS profile report comes at the end of the EYFS stage, and looks more to the future beyond it, shaping learning opportunities as the child enters Year 1.

How a child's goals and targets support positive outcomes

Once the goals and targets have been set by early years professionals, the child and others, it should be clear how practitioners and parents will work together in order to support the child's achievement. The goals and targets will need to be SMART (Specific, Measurable, Achievable, Realistic and with a Timescale for completion) so that all those working with the child are able to focus on targets that support the child's progress and lead to positive outcomes. All those working with the child will need to have a copy of the plan so that they are able to work on this and review on a set date. (There is more information about developing a plan in learning outcome 5 of this unit.)

Explain the action to take if atypical development is identified

Atypical development is development that does not follow the expected pattern. If you or your colleagues identify atypical development when you are assessing children, it is important that you act as soon as possible. This is because you will need to access specialist help and support from others.

Depending on your role and your setting, you should have access to a variety of services.

If you are a working in a nursery or other early years setting, you should have an early years SENCO or area SENCO, who will be able to advise you about support that is available. They may need to help you to arrange further assessments with others, who could include:

- healthcare workers
- speech and language therapists
- occupational therapists
- physiotherapists
- family support services.

See Unit 1, learning outcome 4 for more information on multi-agency work. You should also consult parents and carers and ask them about any support or guidance that their child has received in the past, as this may still be available, giving them continuity of support.

Figure 5.9: Why is it important to consult parents or carers about the support available to them or their children?

If you are a childminder, support and guidance is available through the Professional Association for Childcare and Early Years (PACEY). Staff there will be able to put you in touch with specialist services in your area. You will need to carefully consider the needs of each child on an individual basis, and access the advice of other professionals who will be able to help you to set up a development plan to best support each particular child.

5 Be able to discuss children's progress and plan next stages

Discussing progress and planning learning with others

You will need to be able to discuss children's progress with colleagues and parents so that you can plan their next steps for learning. It is important to ensure that you make time to do this on a regular basis so that it becomes part of the teaching and learning cycle. Some practitioners find it easy to make time each day, while

others prefer to write down children's responses and discuss weekly. You may find that it works better for you to chat to other staff during breaks and then note down key points. Whatever you do, it is important to remember to write things down so that you can act on them and use them to plan children's future learning.

Your setting should also have a system for recording next steps for learning, whether this is a paper-based or a computer-based tracking system, and all staff should have access to this. If the child is not making expected progress or is a cause for concern, you will need to have a development plan for them and to hold regular progress reviews.

However, there should be both formal and informal opportunities to talk about and discuss children's progress and learning with a range of different people.

- **Key person** – The child's key person should speak to parents and carers on a daily basis and should be the first person to go to if you need information or have a query or comment about a child. They are likely to know about anything that has happened to the child and be aware of any transitions that have affected them, such as moving home, the birth of a new sibling, or other significant changes in their circumstances.

- **Colleagues** – Your setting should have systems in place so that everyone is aware of what to do if they need to distribute or find out specific information about a child's learning. Colleagues should also be available for you to discuss children's progress and plan next steps for learning. You can hold these discussions as issues come up, or you can call a team meeting if necessary to talk about a specific issue.

- **Parents and carers** – Parents and carers should know what to do if they need to discuss their child's learning with you. In some settings there is an open-door policy, whilst in others it may be necessary to make an appointment. You should be able to talk to parents and carers and plan the next stage in their child's learning. This may have a formal basis, for example following the progress check at age 2, or be part of your regular communication with them.

Case study 5.6

Colleen is working in a day nursery where there are a number of different staff who work shifts. There is no regular discussion time in the setting because of this, and staff do not have set routines for passing on information about children to one another. One day, Colleen needs to speak to a child's key person about something that has happened and they are not present. She passes on the information to another colleague and asks her to tell the child's key person but the colleague forgets all about it.

1. Why is it important to have a system in place in this situation?

2. How could you ensure that this did not happen in your setting?

These discussions should as far as possible take place on a day-to-day basis. However if you have a specific concern about a child or there is an aspect of their development that you feel should be addressed, you may need to discuss with colleagues and then plan a meeting with the child's parents or carers to set up a learning development plan.

In all cases, there should be a free flow of information about children where it is needed, while respecting the need for confidentiality.

Reflect

How do you discuss children's learning with colleagues in your setting? How do you ensure that this is used to plan children's future learning?

Case study 5.7

Sammi is the child of a teenage mum who lives with her parents. The family are also under the care of social workers. You and your colleagues have had some concerns about Sammi's speech and language as he is 3 years old and has poor communication skills. He has just started a block of speech therapy, but he has not attended regularly. You have decided to set up a meeting with all those who work with Sammi so that you can put in place a development plan for him.

1. Who do you think should be present at the meeting?
2. Why is it important to try to develop a plan for Sammi?

Developing a plan with the child and others to meet their needs

In some cases you may need to develop a plan so that you can work with others to meet the child's needs. This may happen in situations where the child has particular health or development needs, or if the child has spent some time with carers or foster carers. Once you have discussed the child's needs with parents and carers, colleagues and other professionals, you will need to develop a plan carefully, bearing in mind all those who need to work together to support the child.

Understanding and agreeing aspects of a development plan

You should make sure that all those involved in the plan have fully understood its objectives, so that you are all working towards the same outcomes. Ultimately the goal should be that the child is happy and settled in your setting, and is making progress towards the early learning goals.

Your targets will need to be SMART and you should not include more than three or four of them, in order for them to be achievable in the timescale you have set.

Take a look at Figure 5.10. In this case the child, Bhumika, has been in your setting for almost two months and is finding it difficult to settle and interact with others. There have been a number of recent changes in her life, including moving house, and she is reluctant to join in with learning activities or leave her key person during the morning. After discussion with her parents at an initial meeting you have decided to set up a development plan so that all concerned are aware of Bhumika's specific targets. You have also spoken to Bhumika about her targets, and her parents are working with you to support her in achieving them. You should also record how you are intending to work towards the targets on the plan. For example, under target 1 you could say that you are going to encourage the carer to leave promptly after bringing Bhumika to the setting, as she has been staying for some time to try to settle her.

LEARNING DEVELOPMENT PLAN		
Name: Bhumika Gohil	**Date of birth:** 2 Jan 2011	**Date:** 26 Oct 2014
Targets		
1) To be able to leave carer calmly in the mornings		
2) To play cooperatively with a familiar adult		
3) To start to play alongside other children and interact with them appropriately		
Date for review: Feb 2015		

Figure 5.10: What should targets in a learning development plan be like?

LEARNING DEVELOPMENT – REVIEW		
Name: Bhumika Gohil	**Date of birth:** 2 Jan 2011	**Date:** 16 Feb 2015
Review of targets		
1) Bhumika is now much more settled in the mornings and her carer is able to leave her without concerns.		
2) Bhumika will play alongside her key person and one other child but is still working on her interaction with other children.		
3) See review of Target 2. Target 3 is ongoing.		
Signature: A. Morris		

Figure 5.11: An example of a learning development plan review.

Reviewing the achievement of goals and targets

When setting up a development plan, you should always set a date for its review. In this way all those involved will be aware of when it is to be revisited. At the review, you will need to consider what progress has been made against all the goals and targets, and then record it on the review form.

There may be some targets that are ongoing. Make sure that you record this fact, so that targets can be continued on the following plan. Figure 5.11 gives an example of a learning development plan review form.

Reviewing plans and planning methods to evaluate their effectiveness

You should make sure that you review your setting's plans and planning methods on a regular basis as this should be part of the teaching and learning cycle. In this way you can evaluate the extent of their effectiveness when looking at children's achievements towards the early learning goals, while also being able to plan next steps.

Here are some factors that you will need to consider.

- **EYFS framework coverage** – It is good practice to look at the framework coverage within each of the seven areas of learning, to make sure that it is broad enough to suit the learning needs of each child.

- **Progression** – You should think about how each child can progress towards early learning goals within each area of learning and look at the opportunities they have to do this.

- **Children's needs and interests** – Your plans should be flexible enough to allow children to explore their own needs and interests within the planned activities. There should be a good mix of adult-led and child-initiated tasks. However, be careful not to overplan and make sure you allow yourself some time for observations and assessments that emerge as children are playing.

Find the balance

SueAnn, childminder: 'I have found it really tricky to know how many records to keep and what I should write when making observations of children's progress. When children first come to me, I record as much as I can so that I can build up a picture of each child. I have set up a Learning Journey folder for each child and make sure that I file everything as soon as I can. After I have got to know the children well, I only note down anything that is unexpected or that I would not have known about their learning, and this saves me a lot of paperwork.'

Make accurate and productive use of assessment in early years settings

Further reading and resources

Publications

- Barber, J. and Paul-Smith, S. (2012) *Early Years Observation and Planning in Practice,* London: Practical Pre-School Books

- Department for Education (2013) EYFS profile: exemplification materials – a series of materials for practitioners assessing children's development at the end of the EYFS – available online at www.gov.uk/government/publications/eyfs-profile-exemplication-materials

- Department for Education (2013) *Early Years Outcomes* – non-statutory guide for practitioners and inspectors, to help inform understanding of child development through the early years – available online at www.gov.uk/government/publications/early-years-outcomes

- National Children's Bureau (2012) *A Know How Guide: The EYFS progress check at age 2* – handy guide produced in association with the Department for Education to support practitioners – available online at www.foundationyears.org.uk/files/2012/03/A-Know-How-Guide.pdf

- Tassoni, P. (2012) *Penny Tassoni's Practical EYFS Handbook* (2nd ed.), Oxford: Pearson

- Walker, M., Hobart, C. and Frankel, J. (2009) *A Practical Guide to Child Observation and Assessment* (4th ed.), Cheltenham: Nelson Thornes

Websites

- Professional Association for Childcare and Early Years: www.pacey.org.uk – a standard-setting organisation that promotes best practice and supports childcare professionals to deliver high standards of care and learning

Develop effective and informed professional practice in early years settings

Unit 6

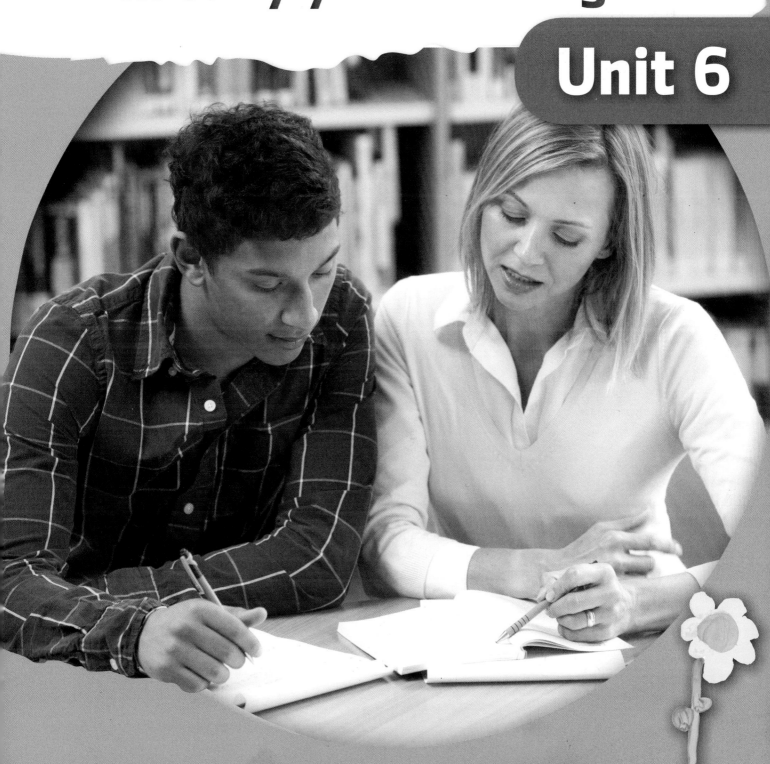

This unit focuses on you and your practice. It will challenge you to look carefully at what you do in your work as an early years practitioner and will help you to identify what you need to focus on in order to develop and become more effective in your role. The content will provide you with the skills, knowledge and support to become more professional, more confident and more reflective. This unit, in short, will help you take control of your professional development.

Unit 6

Before you start

Think about the different aspects of your role in your setting. How could you improve your effectiveness as a practitioner? What about the way you communicate with children and adults? Do people always understand what you are trying to convey? Do children or parents sometimes misunderstand you? Why do you think this is?

Are there parts of the job that you don't think are your responsibility or that you can't change? When you find something in your practice that needs changing, do you know how to make the right changes?

Learning outcomes

By the end of this unit you will:

1. **use effective written and spoken communication in the workplace**
2. **understand the importance of continued professional development**
3. **be able to plan for and monitor own professional development**
4. **be able to engage in reflective practice.**

1 Use effective written and spoken communication in the workplace

One of the key elements of any effective practice in early years is communication. As an early years practitioner, you will be dealing with a range of different people, of different ages and backgrounds, all of whom have a message they need to receive or want to communicate. Effectively communicating with parents, colleagues, other professionals and supervisors is an essential element to working in any childcare setting.

Communication tends to follow a general pattern. One model that helps us understand the communication process, for both oral and written communication, was put forward by M. Argyle in 1972. This model is a useful tool to help you identify how you can communicate effectively, and how and why some of the messages you send are misinterpreted or misunderstood. Figure 6.1 shows the pattern.

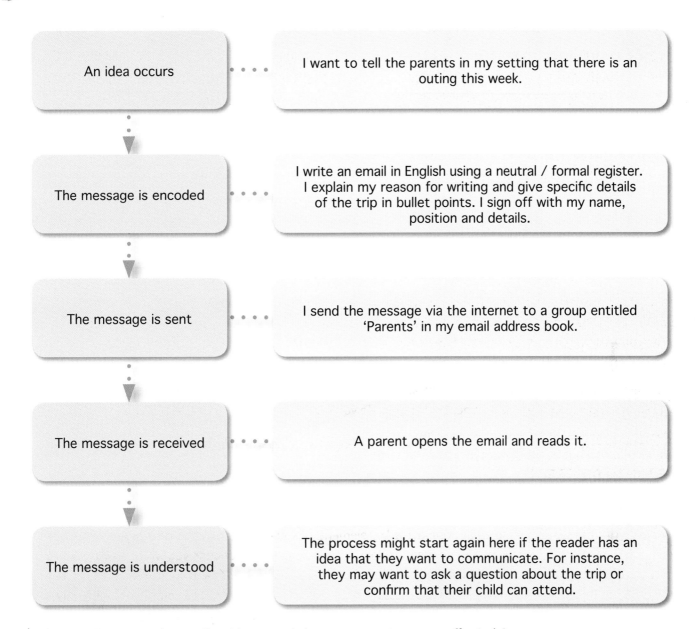

| An idea occurs | ····· | I want to tell the parents in my setting that there is an outing this week. |

| The message is encoded | ····· | I write an email in English using a neutral / formal register. I explain my reason for writing and give specific details of the trip in bullet points. I sign off with my name, position and details. |

| The message is sent | ····· | I send the message via the internet to a group entitled 'Parents' in my email address book. |

| The message is received | ····· | A parent opens the email and reads it. |

| The message is understood | ····· | The process might start again here if the reader has an idea that they want to communicate. For instance, they may want to ask a question about the trip or confirm that their child can attend. |

Figure 6.1: How can understanding this process help you communicate more effectively?

Barriers to communication

At any stage of the communication process a block could occur. Being able to identify the obstacle is a useful way to make sure that your communication is clear. Here are some possible barriers.

Style of language

Sometimes professionals use technical language, assuming that their audience will understand. Abbreviations can be a good shorthand method of communication, but they only work if both participants understand the code. You use EYFS, for example, in your everyday practice, but some parents would not know what this abbreviation means.

You will take many words and concepts for granted because you use them every day in your setting. However, you need to remember that expressions like 'cognitive development', 'reflective practice' and 'care routines' are ones that non-professionals might not understand.

Listening

If the person you are communicating with is not listening or can't listen, they will not be able to understand what you are trying to say. For example, if you are talking to a parent while they are reading a text message, they may not be taking in what you are telling them about their child.

Impairment

Physical impairments to hearing or sight might be barriers to communication. However, it is important not to presume that this will be the case. For example, if the parent with whom you are talking is deaf, this does not necessarily mean that communication will be difficult.

Conflicting messages

If a person's non-verbal communication doesn't match the actual words they use, there will be confusion about what they are communicating. For example, in a meeting someone might say they agree with a proposal but be sitting with their arms crossed and frowning.

Technology

Not everyone has easy access to email accounts or computers, but we tend to take this for granted. Settings often try to communicate using these methods but this could discriminate or exclude people. For example, if a nursery produces a newsletter and only makes it available via email, this could disadvantage those who don't have daily email access.

Clarity

Expressing yourself clearly when writing or speaking, whatever the context, is vital. When people are not direct or precise in the words or phrases they use, their message might get lost. If you are describing to a parent an accident that has happened to their child during the day, you need to make sure you include the key elements of what happened, why and what actions were taken. Extra details, like descriptions of emotions and reactions, are not important.

Inappropriate style

Some ways of communicating could prevent your message being communicated effectively. For example:

- handwriting that is hard to read
- a style of writing or speaking that is too informal
- using the wrong fonts on signs
- being too assertive
- using slang.

Using the wrong style in your communication might give the wrong impression. For example, using a font like Comic Sans for an entry in the accident log might not be appropriate, as it suggests that you are not taking the subject seriously.

Environment

The place where the communication occurs could be a barrier. If you are discussing a child's behaviour in a busy cloakroom, the parent might not hear or want to discuss the matter. Also, if you are having a conversation with someone over the phone, you can't see their facial expressions or other non-verbal cues, so you may miss important details.

Figure 6.2: Consider the environment in which your conversations with parents take place.

Language preference

Not knowing or not being confident in a particular language might present difficulties in communication.

Even aspects of one language, like dialects or accents, can have an impact on the clarity of the message.

Messages not received

It could be that a sign is not seen on the noticeboard, an email is not received or a letter is lost in the post. A voicemail may be missed or something could be misheard in a meeting. All these could have an impact on effective communication.

Communication in written documents

Many different forms of written communication are used in early years, such as:

- policies and procedures
- observations
- child profiles
- reports
- accident reports
- emails
- signs and notices
- newsletters
- website updates
- social networking media (Facebook, Twitter, etc.)
- texts
- forms.

Using standard English

Each type of writing has its own conventions, with different registers, tones, layouts, length, vocabulary and abbreviations. For example, you would use different language for a narrative observation and for a child's profile. You might use shorthand or notes for the observation, but be more formal for the profile, using more sophisticated vocabulary. It is important that you consider who your audience is for each piece of writing, as this will dictate both the style and content. Are you writing to a colleague, your supervisor, a parent, a G.P. or the general public? Will your register be formal, informal or neutral?

Using correct grammar, punctuation, vocabulary and structure has an impact on how people perceive you and your setting. Mistakes in written communication can lead to misunderstanding and confusion, or even create the impression that you are unprofessional.

Unit 6

Jargon buster

Font – a set of type with a particular style.

Grammar – the rules that govern how we put words together to form language.

Non-verbal communication – transmitting messages through actions, gestures, posture and facial expressions.

Register – the type of language expected in a particular social situation (for example, formal, informal or neutral).

However, getting it right can be powerful and can make sure that your message is conveyed as you intend. Accuracy in your written communication is something that parents and other professionals take note of. It is important when you are involved in educating children, even if you are supporting children who are just starting to learn basic literacy skills.

Producing written documents

Here are some things that could help you make your written communication effective.

- **Think about your audience.** Who are you writing to? What do you want them to know or do?

- **What is the exact message you wish to communicate?** Plan carefully, especially if your document is going to be read by a wider audience than just colleagues. Note the main points before you start writing and put things into a logical order.

- **Check your spelling and grammar.** You might use your word processing software here, but you could also ask someone to check your writing. Mistakes do happen, but you must do your best to minimise them. Develop a reputation for producing documents with a high standard of English using a good vocabulary.

- **Be direct.** Don't allow your writing to be sidetracked. Be as clear and factual as possible.

- **Be consistent with your register.** Don't change from formal to informal halfway through. If you are being formal, try to avoid contractions, abbreviations and rhetorical questions as these tend to be used in informal writing such as texts, notes and emails to colleagues.

- **Keep it looking simple.** Most software packages offer a host of options, with different fonts, colours, backgrounds and even sound clips. Use these to make your document visually effective, but make sure you don't get carried away – they could distract people from your main message.

- **Punctuate well.** Avoid lots of exclamation marks, as this implies informality. Capital letters and full stops are vital. Good use of commas, semicolons and colons can help you write with precision. Make sure you divide your work into meaningful paragraphs to help the reader understand your argument.

- **Begin and end properly.** Make sure you address the audience correctly. Are you writing to Mr/ Ms/Mrs/ Miss? What details are required: dates, addresses, phone numbers, a heading or title? The opening of your document is important, as it sets the context and tone of your communication. Remember the conventions of letter writing, such as using 'Yours sincerely' for named people (for example, Mr Smith) and 'Yours faithfully' for unnamed people (for example, Dear Sir) when ending your piece.

Jargon buster

Contractions – combining two words by the use of an apostrophe, such as changing 'do not' to 'don't'.

Rhetorical question – a question asked for effect, but not really to get an answer (for example, 'Don't you agree?').

Case study 6.1

Anna, the manager at Little Scamps Nursery, has recently noticed that some of the written signs on the noticeboard have several spelling mistakes. She even overheard some parents laughing at announcements that included the wrong words, making them sound funny. 'Early Tears Foundation Stage' was obviously a typing error, but there were other grammatical errors and even spelling mistakes of children's names.

1. What impact do you think this might have on the manager and the setting?

2. What can you do to make sure your own written communication is accurate?

3. What steps could Anna take to ensure this doesn't happen again?

Communicating effectively when speaking

There are many situations where you will have to communicate by speaking to parents, carers and colleagues. Information needs to be shared efficiently and effectively, and talking is one of the easiest ways to do this.

Talking in person

This may be the first time you have been expected to adopt the role of a professional, knowing that the person asking you for information assumes you will respond appropriately. The way you speak – your words, tone, expressions and style – represents your setting as a whole. Getting it wrong could have a negative impact on how parents and carers view the setting, and will definitely have an effect on how adults view you. It is vital that you speak in a manner that is professional, supportive, confident and knowledgeable. Look for positive role models in your setting to see how you should speak to adults.

Reflect

Speaking to parents or carers can be more intimidating than speaking to children – especially when you start working in early years. Think about the different adults practitioners have to speak to on a daily basis. Why is it easier to speak to some adults than others? Think about practitioners you have seen who communicate effectively when they speak to adults. What is it about their communication style that works? Which do you find easier: talking in person or on the phone? Why is this?

Talking on the phone

There will be times where you will have to speak to adults on the phone rather than face to face. If you are making the call, you can plan what you want to say – but you will not be able to see the person's body language to help you interpret the emotions within the message. Phone calls also tend to be short because of time constraints, so you need to approach the subject directly, rather than spending too much time with pleasantries.

Table 6.1 gives a range of factors that affect spoken communication.

Table 6.1: How do these factors affect your spoken communication?

Factor	How this affects communication
Time	• Speaking face to face can take time. If you don't have enough time to talk, be polite and offer to make time as soon as is convenient. • Parents understand that they may have to wait, but remember to return to the conversation as soon as possible. • Rushing what you have to say can lead to ineffective communication. Think carefully and take your time, especially if you feel nervous about talking to that particular person.
Language	• Use appropriate, professional language. Don't use slang, abbreviations, swearwords or taboo language, even if the person you are talking to does. • Clear, unambiguous words are vital for effective communication.
Body language	• When talking to other adults, be aware of your own body language but also the messages that they are sending with their posture, proximity, facial expressions and gestures. You can send positive messages by smiling or nodding in encouragement, but crossed arms or avoiding eye contact may communicate something negative. • Touch is a controversial issue. As a practitioner, try to avoid this even if you are a tactile person. Comforting a distressed parent by putting a caring arm around them might not be appreciated and could be deemed inappropriate.
Confidentiality	• Conversations with parents or colleagues in your setting should always remain within the boundaries of confidentiality. Never use what has been passed on to you as gossip. • Your approach should always be trustworthy and professional. It is easy to damage relationships through not keeping information confidential.
Inclusion	• Some of your conversations may be difficult because the person you are talking to does not speak or understand English. • Treat such parents, carers or colleagues with respect and show empathy when discussing issues. The information they want to pass on to you or that you need to give to them is just as important as for those who speak English. • You need patience and understanding – but also make sure that your body language and tone of voice do not communicate frustration or anxiety. • Think about how you will check that the person understands.
Message	• Take time to think about what message you want to communicate or what is being said to you. If you really don't understand, politely ask questions to check your understanding. • Spoken communication lets you question to find out more details, or to make sure the messages have been understood accurately. • Plan what you want to say, especially for a difficult conversation such as discussing a child's negative behaviour with a parent. Think about how they might react and what you might say. A little preparation can help you approach stressful conversations with more confidence.

Action planning to improve communication

Once you have identified a general area of communication you need to improve, the key is how you will do so. Writing a plan can help you really focus in on what you are going to do and how you are going to make the necessary changes to your practice.

Case study 6.2

Simon has been keeping a detailed reflective journal over the last two weeks about his communication with parents. Every day before leaving, he has been recording any communication he has had with parents either in person (perhaps when they drop the children off in the mornings) or on the phone. He was particularly focusing on any differences in the way he tended to communicate with male and female parents and whether this had an impact on how effective the communication was.

He has recently had a meeting with his supervisor to discuss his findings and they realise that he tends to speak less about a child's behaviour to fathers and more about their progress with learning. The length of conversation tends to be different, too. Mothers would usually ask more questions and so more time seemed to be spent here and there was more depth to the conversation. As a result of these findings, Simon has drawn up a short-term action plan to help him redress this imbalance. He has set himself some SMART targets and will monitor his progress, with the help of his supervisor.

1. Keep your own reflective journal that focuses on communication with parents and carers. What do you notice?

2. How can you use your findings to change your practice? Work with your supervisor to plan how you might do this.

A written plan is even something you could discuss with your supervisor or manager.

Setting SMART targets might be one way of doing this. Here, you set yourself goals that you wish to achieve but do so in a structured way. SMART stands for Specific, Measurable, Attainable, Realistic and with a Timescale. By using these measures you can check whether your action plan to improve is likely to work. For example, it is not a realistic goal to learn a foreign language in a short space of time in order to support a child whose first language is not English. A more timely, realistic and specific aim would be to learn how to pronounce and remember 10 nouns (toilet, snack, toy, etc.) that are commonly used in your setting in that language within two weeks.

2 Understand the importance of continued professional development

Working with children today is a different experience from twenty years ago. If you were to walk into a setting then, you would consider some of the practices, routines and methods you witnessed as completely alien to your own experience and training. Ask someone who has been working in the early years sector for some time what has changed since they started. You will be surprised at how different things are now. Much of this is for the better, but some changes have not been so universally welcomed.

The importance of keeping up to date

The early years sector is responsive to the ever-changing needs of children, parents, government and society. Many areas have changed fundamentally over time, including laws, qualifications and skills, training, policies and procedures, curricula, ratios, and health and safety requirements. The sector needs practitioners who can develop, progress and adapt to the flexible nature of this type of work.

It is vital that you don't become set in your ways. You need to actively ensure your skills are current and that you can undertake the role that you have been employed to do. Once you have qualified, your professional journey has only just begun. It is your responsibility, with the support of your setting, to keep your skills, practice and knowledge up to date.

Recent developments

Recent developments in the early years sector include social trends, government policy and legal requirements. Keeping abreast of them all is a challenge, but you must if you are to maintain your professional competence. How you do so will depend on the issue and its relevance to you and your professional role.

Recent developments include:

- the introduction of and subsequent revisions to the Early Years Foundation Stage in England

Case study 6.3

Shareen got her Level 3 qualification two years ago and hasn't done any formal learning since then. She is busy with her reception class and doesn't feel she has time to further her knowledge about any aspect of her practice. However, recently a boy with behavioural difficulties has started in her class. The social worker suggested his behaviour difficulties were to do with attachment and mentioned Reactive Attachment Disorder. Shareen has no knowledge of this condition.

1. Why would it be useful for Shareen to find out about this condition?

2. What methods would you suggest for her to develop her understanding of this condition and how to support a child who has it?

3. Do you think that the time spent is necessary, especially as this is not a common condition? If so, why?

- the use of information technology and social networking as a method of communication between settings and parents
- changes to state funding for childcare
- the reduction in Sure Start funding and the closure of some children's centres
- the introduction of the Children and Families Act 2014, which covers issues including caring for children with special educational needs, adoption and the rights to leave and pay for parents
- the government's move to more teaching and testing of children before they reach school age
- the introduction of the government initiative Every Child Matters in 2003, which underpins current policy and legislation in early years.

The importance of continuous professional development

Your most important professional aim is to ensure that the children you support experience the best care possible. Improving your practice is one way that you can work towards this aim.

Learning doesn't end when you have finished your qualification; it should continue throughout your professional life. Continuous professional development (CPD) is the strategy or set of activities that you establish (often with the support of your line manager or colleagues) to make improvements to your skills, knowledge and abilities.

For example, once you have participated in a training event or course, your confidence will grow – and what you have gained might be something that you could pass on to others in your setting, or even parents. Regularly adding such experiences helps you push the boundaries of your role and enhance your reputation as someone who is passionate about their job.

Relevant CPD activity can support promotion and advancement in your career. It can even help you to become an expert in a particular area. For example, if you attend a workshop on a new piece of legislation, other people around you might come to you for advice about the impact it might have for them.

Ways of continuing your professional development

There is not one optimum way of developing professionally. The method you choose will depend on what you need to learn and why. You might combine several methods before you feel competent, effective or knowledgeable about a particular aspect of your practice. Figure 6.3 shows some popular methods.

You must be active in looking for CPD opportunities. Your supervisor or manager will suggest some, but you will have to look for others yourself. Always be on the lookout for relevant courses, and contact organisations that deal with issues you feel you need to develop. Charities and voluntary organisations often run training events or offer online courses about particular subjects, so use your research skills to look for opportunities. Websites and noticeboards of libraries or county council offices can also give you useful information about upcoming events.

Some CPD events are compulsory for you. These are usually internal training events on subjects such as safeguarding, equality and diversity, along with any changes to policies or procedures in your setting. Your setting may pay for your CPD, especially if it is an essential part of your job, but you may have to fund some training yourself. Try to take advantage of the wide range of free training events on offer – but check their relevance and authenticity with your manager before starting. You don't want to start an expensive course only to find that it doesn't develop the skills you were expecting or isn't applicable to your practice.

Recording your CPD

It is important that you keep a record of all CPD activities you undertake. Your record should list what you have done and when it happened. The more detail you have, the better, as it will remind you of what was covered during the event. Some people keep their notes, handouts and certificates of attendance together in a folder, with their CPD record at the front, to refer to in the future.

If your record is long, you could divide it into different sections based on the type of activity or the actual subjects you have focused on. Remember that this is a record of your professional development

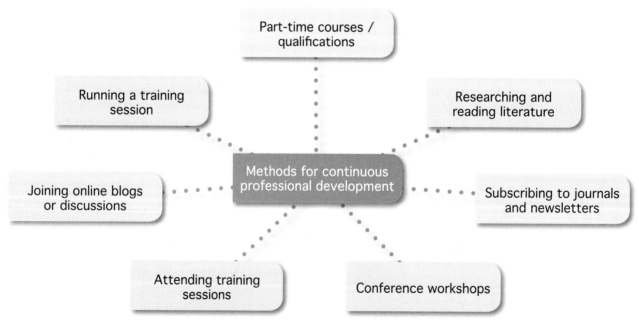

Figure 6.3: Methods for continuous professional development.

and needs to be accurate as well as professional in appearance. You might be asked to show your records when applying for a promotion, a new job or higher qualifications. A well-presented CPD record suggests someone who is organised and active in improving their professional competencies.

The importance of reflective practice

What is reflection?

When you look in a mirror you see your reflection and notice different things about yourself: your hair, your facial expression, your clothes, your mood. Some of these things you like, some you might want to change and others you simply notice. Perhaps there are things you haven't noticed before or you are checking because someone pointed them out to you. Once you have looked or noticed, you might decide to make improvements to the way you present yourself to the world, such as smoothing your hair, changing your clothes or smiling.

Reflection on your practice works in a similar way. When you look at what you do and how you do it, you can get an idea of what you like and what you want to change.

When working in early years, this sort of reflection is vital if you are to become a better practitioner.

Before exploring how to reflect, it is important to make a distinction between routine actions and reflective actions. Some of your actions are routine – simply part of what you do each day, such as setting up the snack table or tidying up before lunch. However, there are other actions that you could reflect on because you want to analyse how effective you are at something and how you can improve.

Donald Schön was influential in developing the theory and practice of reflective learning. He said that this reflection can happen in one of two ways:

- when you are actually involved in doing something
- when the event has happened and you are thinking back to what happened.

For example, you could be reflecting on your communication with a baby while you are in the process of changing the baby's nappy; or you might reflect later on how you communicated in different ways during the nappy-changing routine. Part of your reflection might even be about how other practitioners

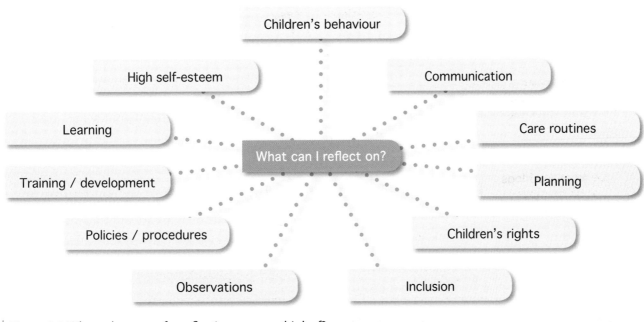

Figure 6.4: What other areas for reflection can you think of?

communicate and the reaction of the babies to different communication styles.

Themes and topics for reflection

If you're not sure where to start, here is a checklist of general themes for reflection. Everyone can do this, and the themes can be applied to almost any situation.

- What do you know?
- What can you do?
- What do you think or believe about something?
- What do you feel about something?
- What do you want to change about your practice?

You could apply the checklist to any of the issues in Figure 6.4, or to any others that are relevant to your work.

Case study 6.4

In a team meeting, a discussion was held about how children are treated differently because of their gender. People had noticed that boys were generally expected to take more risks on the climbing frame and girls were more often told to be careful or expected to tackle less dangerous activities. As a result of the meeting, Magda, a room leader for 3 to 4 year olds, decided to reflect on her own practice. She wanted to find out whether, unconsciously, she had different expectations of boys and girls.

1. In what different situations might Magda reflect on her practice throughout the day?

2. Why might it be useful to observe or notice the expectations of other practitioners?

3. How do you think that this area of reflection might help change Magda's practice?

How can I reflect?

Most practitioners use a 'reflective cycle' to support the development of their practice. This is a systematic way of looking at one particular area, giving a clear structure

that can help you make sense of your thoughts and work out how to improve your performance. There are various cycles that you might use, but they generally follow a similar pattern. Figure 6.5 shows an example of a reflective cycle.

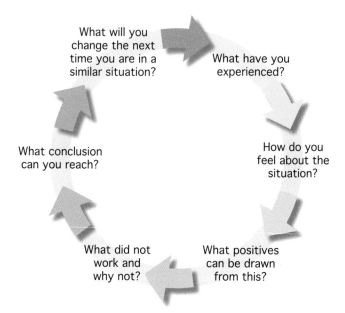

Figure 6.5: Can you think of any other stages you might include in a reflective cycle?

You might keep a reflective journal that includes your notes as you use this cycle. It is also useful to discuss this with your supervisor or a colleague who you feel will support you in your professional development. For this to be an effective learning tool, you must be honest. What you discover when reflecting might be surprising or difficult to handle, but it can be a powerful way of making changes to the way you deal with situations. Even minor changes can have a significant impact on outcomes for children.

Reflection from different perspectives

It is important that you think about your practice from different points of view, otherwise your reflection will be one-dimensional. Think about children when they are being dropped off in the morning. What are their main concerns? They are thinking about leaving their parent or carer, what toys or activities have been set up for the day, what important things they want to tell their key person. What about from the adults' perspective? They are thinking about whether they feel welcomed, and whether there is any news they should know about. Is it warm and safe? Are all the staff there, ready to look after their children? What about from your perspective? Is your plan for the day prepared? Who are you going to observe today? Are there any children absent? Is there anything you need to know about who is collecting a child at the end of the day?

When you view just one event – the start of the day – you can see there are different priorities, needs and concerns. If you reflect from different points of view, you will be able to see the bigger picture and your reflections will be more detailed and insightful.

Brookfield (2005) describes these perspectives as 'lenses'. He says that there are four lenses we need to use to focus on the area of reflection if we are to make powerful changes to our practice:

- **self lens** – your own point of view
- **child's lens** – how a child or children might see the situation
- **peer lens** – the view of your colleagues or the setting as a whole
- **literature lens** – the view of information about your area of reflection, as well as articles from newspapers or journals, books, television and so on.

Tips for effective reflection

- Be honest and fair. This is not about celebrating how great you are at doing something, but about looking at which aspects of your practice are effective and which need to be developed. Reflection is a tool to help you realise your potential.
- Keep your information confidential. This means both what you record and how you store your findings.
- Choose your areas of focus carefully. There will be some areas that you know you need to work on – don't be afraid to tackle them.

- Discuss your reflections with your supervisor and colleagues. They might add important insights into your actions and practice.
- Don't forget that the aim of reflecting is improving your practice.
- Don't be too self-critical. This process is about change and development, not just highlighting your deficiencies.
- Make time to record your reflections and keep a journal. Get into the habit of doing this regularly and it will become less of a chore.
- Observe others (colleagues, managers, other professionals, parents). They will provide invaluable insight, and you can learn from their actions and experiences.

Understanding the limits of your own competence

You work as part of a team and each person within that team has different roles and responsibilities. Together, your aim is to provide quality early years care. You will have your own limits in terms of your skills, knowledge, qualifications and understanding of your setting's expectations of you. Understanding your limits will make your appreciation of your own role clearer. For example, unless you are a qualified first aider, trying to apply a sling to a broken arm could make the situation worse, with serious consequences for you and the setting, even though your intention is positive.

However, remember that using your initiative is an essential part of your role. Even if there is not a person who is 'officially' responsible for every single incident, there are certain questions you need to ask to determine whether you are the right person to deal with a given situation.

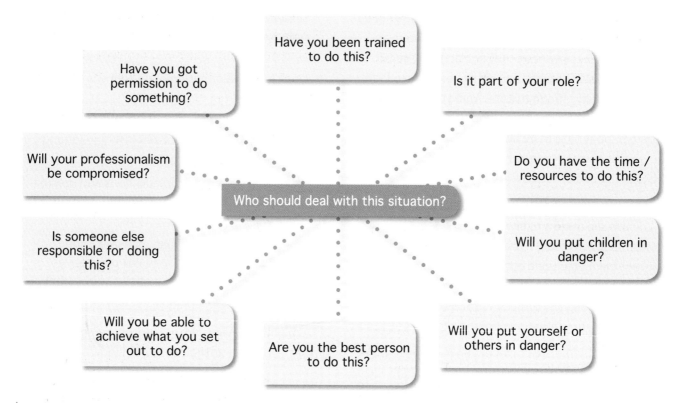

Have you been trained to do this?

Have you got permission to do something?

Is it part of your role?

Will your professionalism be compromised?

Do you have the time / resources to do this?

Who should deal with this situation?

Is someone else responsible for doing this?

Will you put children in danger?

Will you be able to achieve what you set out to do?

Are you the best person to do this?

Will you put yourself or others in danger?

Figure 6.6: Why is it important that you deal with situations in the right way?

Case study 6.5

A child in your setting is playing outside and is stung by a wasp. She starts to feel dizzy and her lips have swollen. You are concerned as you know that she has anaphylaxis and the sting could be life-threatening. The child's key person has been trained in how to use the EpiPen®, but is in a meeting with a parent. You haven't had this training.

1. What might happen if you don't give the injection?

2. What might happen if you do?

3. Are there any situations that you have been in where you didn't feel able to deal with them yourself? What are they and why did you feel you were unable to carry out the task?

Identifying your limits

Developing a professional understanding of the limits of your role may take some time, but there are certain steps that can help you. Here are some ways you can check the limits of your responsibilities.

- Read your job description carefully.
- Make sure you are aware of your organisation's structure and how different people's roles fit together.
- Check the setting's policies and procedures to see who should be doing something.

Jargon buster

Anaphylaxis – an extreme allergic reaction, which can be life-threatening.

EpiPen® – a pen-style device for giving injections.

Supervision – confidential, private support sessions with an experienced practitioner in your setting.

- If in doubt about whose responsibility something is, don't be afraid to ask.
- Use team meetings to clarify what different team members are expected to do.
- Get expert advice from an Early Years Advisor, Ofsted, other agencies and other professionals.

Don't use your lack of knowledge about people's roles as an excuse not to take responsibility for something. If you do, the issue might not be dealt with at all. Being a flexible member of the team is a positive attribute – but be aware that there are consequences if you attempt to do something when you are not competent to do so.

3 Be able to plan for and monitor own professional development

Planning to improve your practice is vital if you are serious about making changes and becoming a more effective professional. There are three important components to this:

- identifying what you want or need to develop
- finding the right support to help you make improvements
- checking and monitoring your progress throughout the process.

Remember that a plan is only the framework to help you change; real development takes place when you actively follow the goals and aims you have set yourself. Your own application and engagement is vital if you are to become an improved professional, but use the support around you – you are not expected to achieve this progress alone.

Professional supervision in early years

There are times working in a setting when you might feel confused, worried, vulnerable, disillusioned or anxious about how to deal with a situation – or even whether you are doing the right thing.

Supervision by another professional is an effective way of helping you talk about your emotions and explore solutions to your problems. Supervision is something that professional counsellors have used for many years to allow them to share difficult problems they have to cope with. They do so with another professional who is not emotionally involved with the situation, who can give impartial, objective guidance on how to support clients.

Supervision in early years allows you to:

- have time out from problems
- reflect on problems and discuss why they have occurred

Theory in action

Think back to when you had a child whose behaviour you found very difficult to manage, or who you found difficult to work with because they didn't respond to your instructions. It might have been that you didn't know what strategies to use to help them modify their behaviour. You might have worried that you should know what to do and were too scared to ask your colleagues for advice, in case you looked incompetent.

This situation could cause you stress and anxiety and, if it is not dealt with, the problem might escalate – and this is where supervision would be useful. Supervision sessions would give you the opportunity to outline your concerns and explore how you might deal with the issue. Speaking to an independent person and sharing your worries is a great starting point for finding solutions. It often turns out that others in the setting have the same experience with the child, and that there needs to be a more consistent approach across the setting to managing the child's behaviour. The result is that you feel supported and should leave the session equipped with different ways to approach the situation.

- get empathy from someone who is experienced at dealing with similar situations
- get advice and guidance on different strategies to deal with issues
- build positive relationships of trust with your supervisor
- take risks that you might not take if you were working independently, such as making changes to an established environment to enhance children's experience.

Table 6.2: Try to personalise the areas of practice in your own skills assessment.

Areas of practice	How effective are you? Rank all areas from 1 to 16, where 1 = most effective and 16 = least effective
SKILLS	
Observing	
Planning activities	
Reflecting	
Communicating with adults	
Writing reports	
PRACTICE	
Praising positive behaviour	
Including all children	
Dealing with accidents	
Liaising with external agencies	
Communicating with parents	
SUBJECT KNOWLEDGE	
Knowledge of EYFS	
English, mathematics, music, history, world religions, science, other languages	
Health and safety legislation	
Developmental milestones	
Theories of play	
Current trends in the early years sector	

The Early Years Foundation Stage framework recognises the growing importance of the use of supervision: 'Effective supervision provides support, coaching and training for the practitioner and promotes the interests of children' *(Source: Statutory Framework for the Early Years Foundation Stage, Department for Education, 2014, p.20).* However, the quality of supervision depends on the approach of the two people involved. For example, if one person doesn't engage in the process constructively, the effect on the other person's practice might be minimal.

Most settings offer some level of supervision and this might be more intensive when you start your career in early years. Appraisal, however, is a particular form of supervision that is in widespread use and not only within the caring professions. This is usually an annual review meeting of a staff member's performance by a supervisor and the employee. The aim is to evaluate their work in the previous year and set specific goals for the employee to achieve in the coming year. It is often the case that developmental needs are identified and a plan of how to achieve them is established. The major difference between appraisal and supervision is that an appraisal is normally a one-off meeting and the agenda is directed to a greater extent by the supervisor.

Identifying areas for development

Before you can make improvements to your practice, you must decide what needs changing or developing. Start by analysing your abilities, dividing the areas into skills, practice and knowledge. Table 6.2 gives examples of the areas you might include, but make sure you use areas that are relevant to your own practice.

Remember that topics such as English, mathematics, science, history and religion might be areas that you feel you need to know more about because children could ask you questions. There might be themes or topics you are covering where you need more personal knowledge, so that you feel confident enough to explain them to others.

Once you have listed your areas of practice, rank them in order of how effective you are at each of them. This will help you identify specific areas to focus on. You could ask a colleague to complete the ranking exercise for you, as this might give you a different perspective.

After ranking the areas, choose the bottom three and complete Table 6.3.

Now show your chart to your supervisor or someone who has a good working knowledge of your abilities. Ask them to add comments or examples. This will help you to pinpoint the specific changes you might need to make in order to improve your practice.

Creating an action plan

Once you have identified what skills, practice or knowledge you wish to develop or improve, you need to construct an action plan.

Remember the following points when action planning.

- Make your targets SMART (see learning outcome 1 of this unit).

- Break down an overall aim into smaller, more manageable stages.
- Have your plan checked by someone to make sure it is valid.
- Stick to the timings and don't be distracted.
- Tick off or highlight tasks you have achieved.
- Keep going. If you miss a deadline or something takes longer than expected, adjust your plan. You might even set new goals if your original one was unrealistic.
- If you feel that you have reached your goal, ask your supervisor or a colleague to confirm that you can do something or know something new.

Discuss your progress with the people who are supporting you, such as your supervisor, line manager or room leader. It might be agreed that you need more support to achieve your goals. Make regular reviews of your action plan so that you can see your progress. This can be motivating and can encourage you to continue.

Table 6.3: Make sure your targets are realistic and achievable.

Area for development	Why do you feel this area needs developing? What evidence do you have for this?	What changes to you feel need to be made and why?
Knowledge of EYFS		
How to deal with accidents		
Planning activities		

4 Be able to engage in reflective practice

In learning outcome 2 of this unit you looked at reflection and why it is vital to improve your practice. As part of this process, you will be asking yourself some searching questions to establish whether you are performing your role well, or if there are areas of your practice that you need to improve. What are your strengths in the setting? What do you get recognised for? What do you feel you do better than others? What do you feel are your weaknesses? What evidence is there that you are right about this?

How effective is your practice?

Evaluating your practice and how effective you are is a key part of the reflective process.

For example, you might feel confident with creating activities that support a child's development. Your team might praise you for activities you have introduced. However, you feel unconfident about carrying out observations with older children. You think that your narrative observations are too brief or don't focus on the specific area of development required. You find it difficult writing down a detailed account of what you see and this is something that your supervisor has mentioned to you a few times.

Jargon buster

Evaluate – assess or make a judgement about something based on its positive and negative elements.

Sources of information about your own practice

You are usually focused on the daily task of meeting children's needs, immersed in the setting's routine, so you might have blind spots in your practice – points that you simply can't see because your attention is

Theory in action

There will be times in your professional career where you are working with children from similar backgrounds, cultures and social contexts and you will find communicating with these children and their parents very easy. You will start to identify strategies to deal with their needs and there might be a chance that you become complacent in your role. However, if a child comes to the setting with different behaviours, from a different background or has vastly different needs from the rest of the cohort, your skills may become challenged. Your comfortable daily life is shaken and you now have to evaluate your practice so that you can adapt your skills to meet these new needs. To ensure the child is included and their needs are met, you must examine your own practice carefully and change the way you have done things.

Think about a child who started attending your setting who presented challenges to the way you carried out your duties.

1. When you evaluated what you were doing, what changes did you make to your practice?

2. Did the changes work? What is the evidence for this?

3. What support did you receive from others in your setting?

elsewhere. For example, you might not realise that you respond more favourably to one child than to another, unless you are made aware of this. You may feel that you know how important inclusive practice is, but you have not realised that your behaviour doesn't always reflect your understanding.

There are several ways you can find out about your own practice, which can help you reflect on things that you weren't aware of.

Sometimes the truth can be painful and difficult to acknowledge. Try to accept any feedback you get on your performance in a constructive way. It is your *practice* that needs to improve, not *you* – so don't take feedback personally. Wanting to learn and improve shows a professional, mature approach to your role.

Information about your practice could come from the following sources.

- **Staff appraisals** – Generally, these are annual one-to-one meetings with your supervisor to identify successes and areas for improvement. CPD opportunities are usually discussed here too.
- **Peer observations** – Colleagues observe you or you observe them. You might be interested in a particular aspect of your practice and could ask your colleague to carry out observations on this area. For example, you might want an objective view of whether you communicate or show compassion differently to boys and girls.
- **Professional discussions** – These might take place between you and the room leader or other members of the team, especially if there is an issue that needs to be addressed urgently.
- **Evaluation feedback** – Many settings ask parents (and sometimes children) for their feedback on different aspects of the childcare provided. You can use this as a source of information to find out about your own practice.

Factors that can affect your role

Your competence in your role is not based solely on your own abilities and approach to work. Some factors are beyond your control and influence, yet play a vital role in shaping your practice. You need to take account of these when you are reflecting. Other factors might affect you personally and are external to your setting. When personal circumstances change, this can have an impact on your daily work. Here are some examples.

Dynamics in the setting

Teams in settings are made up of different personalities, and the combination of different people produces a unique dynamic. If there is in-fighting and people are frustrated with each other, this will impact on you too. It is difficult to remain neutral and upbeat if your team members are undermining each other. Negative dynamics produce a negative atmosphere and can make you less effective at meeting children's needs.

Stress

Your role can be stressful, as you try to improve, meet your deadlines, deal with confrontational parents and adapt to new educational frameworks. When you are under stress, you tend not to perform to the best of your ability. This can affect your whole persona, making it difficult for you to cope with the demands put on you.

Emotional involvement

Becoming too attached to the children or too involved in their circumstances can affect your practice. It might be that you get too close to the child and can't deal with them objectively or, indirectly, favour them over other children.

Changes to circumstances at work

You might have to change rooms and be working with a different age group, or have new, challenging children to deal with. You might have a new supervisor or manager in your setting. These changes can affect how you perform at work positively or negatively, depending on how you feel about them.

Relationship with colleagues and parents

You will not get on well with everyone you work with, but the aim is to be professional in your relationship with all of your colleagues. Some parents will be easy to work with, but you might find others more challenging and this can affect the quality of your practice. You need to understand that personal differences must not affect the way you support the children who come to the setting. This could be an important area for you to reflect on.

Personal life

Things outside work can have an impact on your practice. Life events and circumstances such as marriage, death, divorce, money issues, housing, health, diet, friendships and relationships may, at times, occupy you and affect how effectively you perform your role at work.

Further reading and resources

Publications

- Argyle, M. (1994) *The Psychology of Interpersonal Behaviour*, London: Penguin – good background to the broad area of interpersonal behaviour

- Brookfield, S. and James, A. (2014) *Engaging Imagination: Helping Students Become Creative and Reflective Thinkers*, London: John Wiley & Sons – discusses why nurturing creativity and innovation helps children at school and beyond, with tested approaches and tools

- Canning, N. and Reed, M. (2009) *Reflective Practice in the Early Years*, Thousand Oaks: Sage Publications – encourages you to consider your own practice and examines practice in a wide range of settings

- Cooper, J. (2010) *The Early Years Communication Handbook: A Practical Guide to Creating a Communication-friendly Setting in the Early Years*, London: Practical Pre-School Books – easy-to-read guide offering expert advice on improving children's speaking and listening skills

- Cortvriend, V. *et al* (2008) *Advanced Early Years Care and Education: For Levels 4 and 5* (2nd ed.), Oxford: Heinemann – covers the content of the 12 core outcomes at a useful depth and breadth, for a complete grounding in the basics of the subject

- Department for Education (2014), *Statutory Framework for the Early Years Foundation Stage* – available online at www.gov.uk/government/publications (document reference: DFE-00337-2014)

- Lindon, J. (2012) *Reflective Practice and Early Years Professionalism: Linking Theory and Practice* (2nd ed.), London: Hodder Education – explores the nature of reflective practice and shows you how to apply this for the benefit of children and families

Websites

- Foundation Years: www.foundationyears.org.uk – for a broad range of information and resources developed by government, professionals and the voluntary and community sector, plus the latest news

- I CAN: www.ican.org.uk – information service that provides help with speech, language and communication, with *Stages of Speech and Language Development* poster available for download

Articles and magazines

- Smith, M. *Communicating with Customers*, Nursery World, 21st November 2001

- Vollans, C. *Supervision – Speaking Personally*, Nursery World, 24th February 2014

Promote the health, safety and wellbeing of children in early years settings

Unit 7

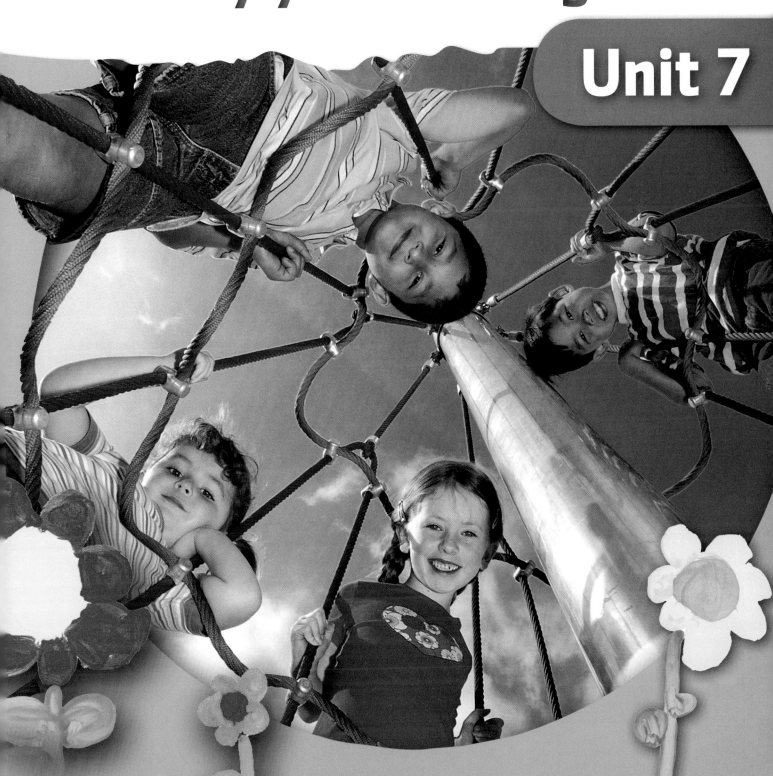

Promote the health, safety and wellbeing of children in early years settings

Ensuring the health and safety of the children you work with is crucial. In this unit, you will see how current health and safety legislation shapes and informs the policies and procedures in your setting – and underpins every aspect of your own work. Making sure you fulfil your own role and responsibilities – from assessing risk to maintaining records – is what makes health and safety happen in practice.

Before you start

Think of some of the ways you have promoted health and safety in your own setting. For instance, have you taken part in a fire drill? Have you assisted children in hand washing or responded to a child who has had an accident? If so, you are already aware of some of the ways to promote the health, safety and welfare of children in your care.

Learning outcomes

By the end of this unit you will:

1. understand health and safety legislation and regulations
2. understand how to carry out physical care routines
3. understand why health and wellbeing is important for babies and children
4. understand how to keep children safe and secure in early years settings
5. understand how to respond to accidents and emergency situations
6. understand prevention and control of infection in early years settings
7. understand how to assess health and safety risks in early years settings
8. understand how to maintain records and reports.

1 Understand health and safety legislation and regulations

Children have a right to be kept safe, so at the heart of all work with children there must be a commitment to their health, safety and security. This means that in every early years setting there are health and safety policies that everyone must follow. Policies are governed by laws and regulations. Knowing about and understanding current legislation, regulations and guidance will help you appreciate why you should follow policies and procedures in your own setting.

Implementing legislation and regulations

Legislation

The Health and Safety at Work Act (HASAWA) 1974
This was introduced to protect the health, safety and welfare of everyone in any workplace. In your setting, this means the staff, the children and their families and other people who may visit.

The employer, for example the nursery manager or head teacher, has specific legal responsibilities that include a duty to:

- put into place safe working practices
- maintain equipment
- display the approved poster or provide each practitioner with a leaflet on healthy and safety responsibilities approved by Health and Safety Information for Employees Regulations (HSIER)

- provide personal protective clothing
- provide information and training for staff.

You and all other adults working in the setting have a shared legal duty towards maintaining the health and safety of yourself and others by:

- following safe working practices
- using equipment safely and using protective clothing that is provided
- reporting concerns
- not putting others in danger from your own actions.

European Standard for Fixed Play Equipment

This governs all types of fixed playground equipment in the EU (including the UK): for example, swings, slides, cable runways, carousels and rocking equipment. The safety standards cover the equipment itself and the requirements for installing, inspecting, maintaining and operating it. They also apply to the surfaces under and around the play area and equipment.

Figure 7.1: Check the fixed playground equipment in your setting. How do you know it is safe to use?

Duty of care

A duty of care describes the standards of care that are expected of all adults employed in the early years sector. A duty of care is a legal obligation to act in a way that promotes the best interests of the children and keeps them safe from harm. As a practitioner in early years, you also have a legal duty of care towards adults you come into contact with in your work.

Agreed ways of working

You may have a contract or 'agreed ways of working', setting out your role and responsibilities and the expectations that your employer has of you. This covers the way that you meet your legal obligations in the workplace. Policies and procedures will explain what to do in different situations.

You should know the limits of your role and responsibilities, as you may not be equipped to deal with some situations. For instance, if you tried to deal with a serious accident without calling a first aider, you could put a child at risk.

The Children Act 1989 and 2004

The 1989 act was an important piece of legislation that aimed to provide better protection for children. It included a requirement for services to work more closely together and with parents to improve outcomes for children. This act required children to be put at the centre of any planning and support by introducing a new concept called the paramountcy principle – that is, the needs of the child are of paramount importance,

Jargon buster

Guidance – advice about what you should do or how you should behave.

Legislation – a law or group of laws.

Paramountcy principle – the needs of the child are of paramount importance, above those of parents and professionals, so must come first in any decisions about their needs and the support they receive.

Regulations – rules made and maintained by an authority.

Safe working practices – procedures to ensure children are protected from abuse during care routines and adults providing care are protected from allegations of inappropriate behaviour.

above those of parents and professionals, so must come first in any decisions about their needs and the support they receive.

Even with the 1989 legislation in place, there followed serious cases where the system failed to protect children from harm. The Children Act 2004 extended the 1989 act to try to improve the planning, commissioning and delivery of children's services. The act gives local authorities increased responsibilities for protecting children, requiring them to:

- put into place partnership working arrangements across all children's services
- put into place procedures for sharing information between services and professionals
- produce a Children's and Young People's Plan
- set up a Local Safeguarding Children Board.

It also tried to provide a more consistent approach to promoting the welfare of children by establishing:

- a Common Assessment Framework (CAF) to support multi-agency work
- a local database to identify children's needs
- earlier intervention for children who are 'in need'
- five outcomes for children (*Every Child Matters*) that all children's services must work towards.

Childcare Act 2006

The aim of this act was to transform the availability of childcare and improve the quality of early years services in England, by:

- charging local authorities with the responsibility for increasing the availability and flexibility of childcare services including, for example, children's centres and 'wrap-around' services in schools
- providing better information services for parents
- improving the quality of service through a better qualified workforce
- the introduction of a framework for inspection
- the introduction of an Early Years Foundation Stage (EYFS)

- improved access to childcare by reducing inequalities for preschool children, such as family tax credits and extending free entitlement.

Jargon buster

Commissioning – finding any services, professionals or resources required.

Common Assessment Framework (CAF) – a four-step process used by all children's services to identify the individual needs of children and to coordinate services to provide support.

'In need' – a legal term for children who are unlikely to maintain, or be given the opportunity to maintain, a reasonable standard of health or development or whose health or development could be impaired without the support of children's services.

Partnership working – when different services and professionals work together to meet the needs of children and families.

Wrap-around service – the provision of childcare for before school, from 8 am, and after school, up to 6 pm.

The Regulatory Reform (Fire Safety) Order 2005

This requires each workplace to appoint a person with responsibility for general fire safety precautions. There must be adequate, signed escape routes and sufficient measures and equipment, such as smoke detectors and alarms.

The Control of Substances Hazardous to Health 2002 (COSHH)

This protects people in the workplace against the dangers of hazardous substances. In early years settings this could be cleaning materials or adhesives. Settings must carry out risk assessments on the storage and use of hazardous substances.

The Data Protection Act 1998

This regulates the collection, storage and use of personal and sensitive information. It was introduced to

Figure 7.2: Do you know where the fire exits and alarms are in your own setting?

prevent personal information being passed on without an individual's consent or, in the case of children, consent from a parent or carer.

Safeguarding Vulnerable Groups Act 2006 (amended by Protection of Freedoms Act 2012)
The 2006 act introduced the requirements for more thorough checks into people's backgrounds before they can work with children or vulnerable adults, and the introduction of a register of those who are unsuitable. The amended 2012 act set up a new body called the Disclosure and Barring Service (DBS) to carry out criminal record checks and to make decisions on people who should be barred. People applying for work in early years must complete and submit an application for a criminal record check to the DBS, which then provides a

certificate which must be shown to the employer. For more information on legislation to safeguard children, see learning outcome 1, Unit 8.

Health and Social Care Act 2012: Code of Practice on the prevention and control of infections
This code gives the legal requirements for the prevention and control of infection in primary medical environments where there is higher risk of the spread of infection. It describes stringent hygiene procedures that all those working in the sector must follow.

How legislation is implemented

Health and safety legislation underpins everything that happens in your setting. Although your manager has particular responsibilities for providing a safe environment and putting safe working practices into place, all adults working in the setting share the responsibility for implementing health and safety legislation.

This means that you have a personal responsibility towards everyone in the setting: yourself, the children, your colleagues and others who may visit. Even before you started to work with children, the law required the setting to carry out checks to ensure you were a suitable person to work with children.

Think about different ways you have taken part in or observed legislation being implemented in your own setting.

- Before children play, has someone checked that the environment is safe and all materials and equipment are well maintained?
- Have you or others reported a health and safety concern, such as finding a gate unlocked or a tricycle with a loose wheel?
- Have you taken part in a risk assessment or reviewing procedures, perhaps when taking children on an outing or cooking with a group?
- Have you dealt with or observed others dealing with an accident, injury or emergency?
- Do you know safe procedures and follow them when handling and preparing food?

- Do you know safe procedures when disposing of clinical waste or bodily fluids?
- Are you trained in how to lift and move heavy objects safely – and do you do this?
- Are any health and safety training sessions available?

All of these are examples of health and safety legislation being implemented in an early years setting.

Find the balance

It is not always easy to remember everything that you do each day. Keep a log or notebook with you at all times. Briefly note down each time you are involved in activities that promote or maintain health and safety. Get your manager or supervisor to sign it. You can then use this information as evidence of some of your knowledge and skills.

Regulations

Regulations are also a legal requirement, but they give greater detail of the roles and responsibilities, as well as how you should implement them in the workplace. Regulations relevant to your work in an early years setting are listed in Table 7.1.

Just how regulations apply will be different depending on the particular environment and the activities that take place there. Policies and procedures guide staff on how to implement regulations in their own setting.

Here is one example of how these different layers work together.

Act of Parliament
The Health and Safety at Work Act 1974, Section 5 places a duty on employers to prevent and control harmful, noxious or offensive emissions into the atmosphere.

Regulation
COSHH states in detail what employers must do to carry out their duty outlined in Section 5 of the act, including to:

- identify the hazardous substances that are kept or used in the setting
- assess the risk to the individuals who work in, or visit, the setting
- put controls in place for the use and storage of hazardous materials
- put emergency procedures in place to deal with accidents or incidents.

Policy and procedure
In a particular setting, these could state that:

- a risk assessment in the use and control of hazardous substances must be carried out and reviewed annually
- hazardous cleaning materials must be stored in the locked cupboard in the nursery kitchen
- resources used in the setting must be non-toxic and ordered from an authorised source
- staff must follow procedures for dealing with bodily fluids and dispose of materials in designated covered bins
- staff must attend annual training in responding to incidents and emergencies.

How regulations are implemented

Table 7.1 identifies relevant regulations and gives examples of how these may be implemented in early years settings.

Jargon buster

Near miss – an event or accident that did not cause injury, but had the potential to do so.

Table 7.1: Implementation of regulations in early years settings.

Regulations and orders	Purpose	How they may be implemented in early years settings
The Management of Health and Safety at Work Regulations 1999	Relate to Health and Safety at Work Act giving information on what employers must practically do to ensure health and safety of employees and others in the setting including working offsite	• Risk assessments carried out • Information available on posters and through training • Suitable hand-washing facilities and protective gloves and aprons available • Procedures in place for outbreaks of diarrhoea and vomiting • Risk assessments and training held for personal safety, including procedures for lone working • Facilities provided for securing personal property while at work
The Manual Handling Operations Regulations 1992 (as amended in 2002)	• Relate to activities in workplaces that involve lifting, lowering, pulling or carrying • Employers must carry out risk assessments on these activities	• Safety information provided for lifting or carrying (e.g. use of steps to reach higher objects, bending knees rather than back to move equipment or lighter furniture) • Training for staff required to move heavy loads (including lifting children)
The Lifting Operations and Lifting Equipment Regulations 1998	• Cover wide range of lifting equipment from cranes on construction sites to patient hoists in healthcare • Training must be provided in the use of equipment	In settings with children with mobility problems, staff trained to use lifting equipment (e.g. hoists or vehicle tailgates)
Workplace (Health Safety and Welfare) Regulations 1992	Give detailed guidance to employers on HASAWA for all aspects of the welfare of staff and others using the environment	• Temperature, lighting and ventilation appropriate for children and staff • Curriculum identifies time for rest and play • Dedicated hygienic area for nappy changing and toileting
Personal Protective Equipment at Work Regulations 1992	Cover duty of employers to provide personal protective equipment (PPE) relevant for job and provide training in its use	• Gloves and aprons provided with guidance given for use (e.g. for nappy changing, dealing with bodily fluids)
Health and Safety (First Aid) Regulations 1981	Require employers to provide suitable facilities and equipment and a qualified person/s to ensure staff or children get help if ill or injured	• Member of staff trained in first aid • First aid box available • Written procedures for reporting illness and accidents
The Health and Safety Information for Employees Regulations 1989	Set out duties of employers towards employees in providing information on roles and responsibilities	• Posters on health and safety displayed • Mandatory training in health and safety
Reporting of Injuries, Diseases and Dangerous Occurrences Regulations (RIDDOR) 2013 (as amended)	• Require employers to keep records of injuries and any near misses • Set out duty of employers to report serious injuries that happen in workplace or work-related deaths • For accidents to children in early years settings, requirement is to report to Ofsted – see information on EYFS below	• Accident book for staff to complete in cases of accident or near miss • Procedures for reporting accidents to person with responsibility for health and safety in setting
Control of Substances Hazardous to Health Regulations (COSHH) 2002	Place duty on employers to identify substances that may be hazardous to health (including cleaning materials or exposure to bodily fluids) and put into place controls to reduce possibility of children or adults becoming ill or injured	• List of hazardous substances available to staff • Locked cupboard out of children's reach to store hazardous substances • Procedures/information on purchase of e.g. paints, adhesives • Procedures, clinical bins and PPE available for dealing with bodily fluids

Continued

Continued

Regulations and orders	Purpose	How they may be implemented in early years settings
Motor Vehicles (Wearing of Seat Belts) (Amendment) Regulations 2006	Prescribe wearing of seat belt or child restraint and types that should be used by children under 14	Professionals check children are using appropriate child seats or restraints for age/size when being transported by car or bus
Smoking Ban 2007	• Stems from Health Act 2006 • Total ban on smoking in enclosed work and public areas was introduced in 2007	• No smoking anywhere near children – even outdoors • 'No smoking' notices displayed in and around setting
Early Years Foundation Stage 2014 (EYFS)	• Arises from Childcare Act 2006 • Sets statutory standards for all registered early years providers • Includes learning and development and assessment requirements. Section 3 (safeguarding and welfare requirements) relevant for this unit including staff:child ratios • Gives legal responsibility for reporting serious accidents and injuries to children in setting to Ofsted or relevant childminding agency	• Professional identified to lead responsibility for safeguarding and welfare • Children adequately supervised (meeting staff:child ratios) • Steps taken to ensure risks to children's safety are minimised • Risk assessments carried out when taking children on outings • Records relating to health, safety and security maintained • Accident book maintained
Food Hygiene Legislation 2006 (European Directives) Food Hygiene (England) Regulations 2005	Set out basic hygiene principles for environments where food is stored, prepared and served	• Food stored at correct temperature • Hand-washing facilities provided • Training for staff who prepare and serve food • Cleaning procedures displayed in food preparation areas
Health Protection (Local Authority Powers) Regulations 2010	• Give powers and duties to prevent and control risks to health from infection or contamination • Local Authorities given powers to deal with outbreaks of infection or contamination	• List kept of illnesses requiring children to be kept away from setting (e.g. sickness, diarrhoea) and notifiable diseases that must be reported (e.g. measles) • Staff carry out disinfection or decontamination of setting if requested

Jargon buster

Notifiable diseases – illnesses that must be reported to the local authority because they pose a serious risk to the public.

Current guidance for planning healthy and safe environments

Many different organisations play a role in providing information about health and safety.

- **Health and Safety Executive** – Works with local authorities to inspect and enforce legislation. It advises on how to implement legislation and regulations in the workplace and provides data on health and safety.

- **British Safety Council** – Works with the government to influence policy and provide information and training on current legislation and regulations.

- **European Commission** – Initiates EU legislation and ensures that laws are upheld by each member country. It also provides information on EU legislation and regulations.

- **Department of Health** – Leads on the development of legislation and policies that promote health in the UK. You can find its reports on the promotion of health and safety on the Department of Health's website.

- **Ofsted** – Inspects and regulates children's services, including for health and safety. It is also responsible for keeping information on childminders, such as identity checks and qualifications. Ofsted obtains enhanced criminal records checks and monitors barred lists of childminders (and people who live or work in the same premises). You can find information on their role, the reporting of serious accidents and injuries and inspection reports for individual settings on the Ofsted website. Childminding agencies take on the checking and reporting responsibilities where childminders are registered with them.

- **Public Health England** – Focuses on working to improve the health of the nation and reduce inequalities. You can search for policies and reports relating to different aspects of health and safety on their website.

Theory in action

Make your own table with two columns. List all the relevant regulations you can think of in the first column. In the second column, give an example of how each regulation has been implemented in your setting.

2 Understand how to carry out physical care routines

Physical care routines

Figure 7.3 shows examples of different kinds of care routines. Which of these do you carry out on a day-to-day basis?

Nappy changing routines

The nappy changing area should be easy to clean and be away from food areas. Everything you need must be to hand: disposable apron and gloves, nappies, cotton wool, creams, bags and nappy disposal bin. This is important as, once the baby is lying on the nappy changing table, they must never be left – even for a second – as even young babies can wriggle off.

Leaving babies in wet or soiled nappies can cause a rash and may lead to infection, so they should be changed regularly. Remove the dirty nappy and clean the baby's bottom area from front to back, using a clean piece of cotton wool each time you wipe. Use barrier creams if requested by the parent.

Nappy changing areas are a breeding ground for infection so you must follow procedures carefully.

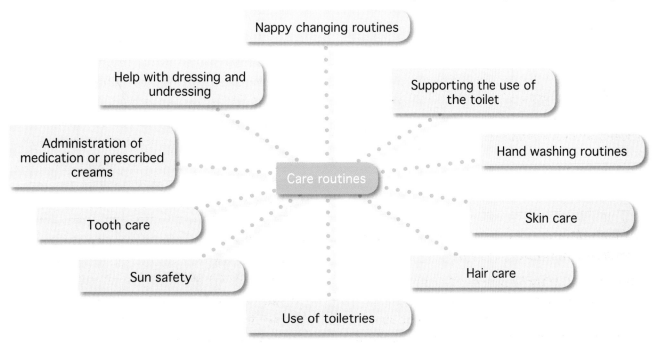

Figure 7.3: Which of these routines do you regularly carry out in your setting?

- Always wear a disposable apron and gloves and dispose of them immediately after use.

- Wrap the dirty nappy immediately in a sealed bag and place it in a designated lidded bin.

- Wash your hands thoroughly before and after.

- Do not use creams directly from the tube or jar – use a disposable spatula.

- Clean the nappy changing area with hot, soapy water after each use.

- Empty bins and clean and disinfect them regularly.

Washable nappies are increasingly being used. If your setting has facilities for washing, you must keep dirty nappies sealed, in a lidded bin with appropriate disinfectant. If they are being returned to parents or a laundry service, you must put them in sealed bags. For more information on routines for children under 3, see Unit 20.

Figure 7.4: Why is it important to follow correct procedures for nappy changing?

Supporting children with toileting

The toilet area should be cleaned regularly to reduce the risk of infection. Children may need support in cleaning themselves when they have used the toilet. As with nappy changing, you should wash your hands well and use protective gloves and an apron before supporting the routine. After using the toilet, children should be shown how to wash their own hands. Remember to dispose of protective clothing and to wash your own hands as well.

Skin care

The skin of babies and young children is delicate so you must take care. If you work in a nursery, it is unlikely that you will bathe babies, but you will need to clean their face and nappy area. Use cotton wool or a child's own flannel for washing the skin, to reduce the risk of cross-infection. It is important that you dry the skin well but gently after washing, particularly in the folds of the skin – leaving the area wet may result in fungal infection. You must know the child's individual needs and their parents' preferences. Only use creams, oils or toiletries if provided by the parents.

Tooth care

Brushing should start as soon as babies get their first milk tooth at around the age of 6 months. A smear of toothpaste can be used on a baby brush (a pea-sized blob for children over 3), twice a day, including just before bed time. Fluoride paste is recommended by the NHS, but paste should be agreed and provided by parents. As children get older they will want to brush their teeth themselves but may need some guidance to ensure that they brush correctly and for around 2 minutes. Get children to spit out the paste but avoid rinsing with water or the fluoride will not be effective in preventing tooth decay. Parents should be encouraged to take children to the dentist regularly as soon as teeth appear.

Hair care

Babies and young children normally have their hair washed when bathing. If you work in home-based care, you may need to carry out hair washing routines. Shampoo should be suitable for babies and only used with the parents' consent. Brush hair regularly, using the child's own brush. As you brush, check for head lice or nits (lice eggs that attach to the hair). If you find any, report this to the parent with advice on treatment. Children of African Caribbean heritage may require oils rubbed into their hair to prevent drying.

Sun safety

Children can quickly be affected by the sun if precautions are not taken. Keep babies out of direct sunlight, and follow NHS guidelines for young children. Remember that children are susceptible to sunburn even on cloudy days.

Ensure that children wear sunhats that shade their face and the back of the neck

Sunglasses protect eyes. To be safe, they must have met the British Standard (BSEN 1836:2005) and have the CE mark

Organise play activities in the shade

Dress children in loose-fitting clothing that covers the shoulders

Cover any exposed parts of the child's skin with sunscreen that is a high factor and effective against UVA and UVB

Figure 7.5: What could happen if you don't follow good practice when children are out in the sun?

Administration of medicine and prescribed creams

Some children in your setting may need to use medication. This can be for short-term illnesses (for example, antibiotics for an ear infection) or for a long-term condition (such as an inhaler for asthma). Whatever the reason, the same procedures are needed.

- An authorisation must signed by the child's parents or carer.

- Medication must be in the original container, clearly labelled with the child's name, date of birth and correct dose.

- Medicines containing aspirin must not be administered unless prescribed.

- Medicines must be stored securely.

- Records must be kept of the precise time medicines are given and prescribed creams are used, with the practitioner's signature.

- Staff giving medicines that require medical or technical knowledge must be trained.

Dressing and undressing

When supporting children with dressing routines it is important that you talk to them about what you are doing. As children get a little older, they can give consent. For example, don't just start to undress a child but say, 'Shall I help you to undo your trousers?' By doing this you ensure the child's dignity.

You should encourage children to dress and undress themselves as soon as they are able. Follow your setting's procedures and only help or touch a child in an appropriate way, so that you do not leave yourself open to accusations of improper conduct.

How to plan and carry out physical care routines

When planning routines there are a number of factors that you need to take into consideration.

- Does the child have a care plan in place and is this reviewed regularly? Children with a disability or an individual need may need a greater level of personal care. There could also be additional factors that you need to take into account, such as an allergy to particular products or a requirement for prescribed creams for a skin condition.

- What is the child's age and stage of development? Consider what they need help with and what they can do for themselves. For example, are they at a stage where they can care for their own teeth, hair and skin?

- Do you know the preferences of the child's parents? For example, they may prefer washable rather than disposable nappies and/or want barrier cream to be used at every nappy change.

- Are you aware of any cultural or ethnic needs the child may have, for example particular creams for skin care?

- Are you aware when personal protective equipment should be used when there is a risk of coming into contact with bodily fluids, such as during nappy changing?

Routines should be familiar and carried out in the same way each time so children get to know what is happening and don't become anxious. Consistency in your approach also encourages children to become independent as they begin to anticipate what happens next. For example, after lunch children get to know that hand and face washing is next and will be prompted to do this themselves. Makaton signs help babies and children with learning difficulties to understand routines or to indicate their needs.

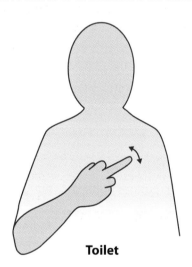

Toilet

Figure 7.6: This sign helps children to indicate that they need to use the toilet.

The key person system helps children to receive consistent care as children have the same person supporting their routines. As a key person you will get to know their preferences and what they can do for themselves. You will also be able to notice any changes in a child you are familiar with, such as

their behaviour or skin infections. It is important that you keep records of any changes that you notice so that you can report them to the child's parents and your manager. This will ensure that the child receives appropriate support.

> ### Reflect
>
> What action would you take if you were concerned about changes in a child's behaviour or health when carrying out a routine?
>
> Find out:
>
> - who you should report to
> - where and how you would record the changes.

Balancing children's rights and choices with health and safety

While it is important that you support routines safely, you must also bear in mind the rights of children to:

- dignity
- confidentiality
- safety (including safeguarding)
- privacy.

Dilemmas can arise. For example, children have a right to privacy for personal care routines, but they should not be taken into private enclosed spaces where colleagues cannot monitor safe practice.

Children can exercise their own preferences and may at times refuse to wash their hands or face, or clean their teeth. You can make it fun and encourage them through praise, but you shouldn't force children to comply. As children get older and understand, you can explain the risk of germs or tooth decay.

Finding a balance is difficult but it is important that children are given challenges so that they learn to understand and manage risk themselves. Children choose play with risk attached, but they can take part in risk assessment too. Discuss the hazards with them, such as burns, choking or falling, and point out ways they can control the risk themselves: for example, by demonstrating how to use scissors or showing where to hold on when climbing up the slide. Children should choose their own freedom where possible but this does not mean unacceptable risk. For example, you would not allow them to walk along the edge of a riverbank with a risk of drowning, but it is important that they are allowed to decide on actions where risks are acceptable, such as climbing on tree trunks or how fast to ride their tricycle.

Figure 7.7: What risks must you consider when allowing children to play outdoors?

You cannot eliminate all risk but you can assess and minimise it by carrying out risk assessments for the environment and the activities that take place there, to identify hazards and risks. This can be difficult, as decisions must be made about whether risks are acceptable or unacceptable. Many decisions are clear cut, such as not giving children under 3 years old toys with small parts. Other decisions are more difficult, however. For example, do you prevent children from using a climbing frame because one child has fallen?

Some procedures and actions must always be followed, because they are set down in legislation and regulations. For example, hazardous materials must always be stored in a locked cupboard, and hands must be washed before handling food. Non-compliance will mean that you are putting children and other people in the setting at risk. You will read more about the risk assessment process later in this unit.

3 Understand why health and wellbeing is important for babies and children

The EYFS states: 'Children learn best when they are healthy, safe and secure, when their individual needs are met, and when they have positive relationships with the adults caring for them'.

(Source: Statutory Framework for the Early Years Foundation Stage, 2014, Department for Education, p.16)

The importance of health and wellbeing

In Unit 1 you explored how areas of development are interlinked and how children's health can affect all other areas of their development.

Healthy physical development usually progresses through crawling, walking and climbing – skills that are essential for children to develop mobility, coordination and balance. Ill health can delay these skills, impacting on children's ability to explore the world around them, affecting their cognitive and language development and their levels and rate of achievement. Recognising health or developmental delay is critical. It ensures that, if necessary, specialist intervention is put into place early, reducing the impact on children's overall development.

Children who are unhealthy may be less likely to follow normal patterns of emotional development, which includes the development of self-esteem and self-actualisation (see Figure 1.8 in Unit 1). Poor health can affect the building of relationships between parent and child, and how the child feels about themselves. Children who are ill are likely to be more reliant on parents and others, resulting in a lack of confidence and independence.

Jargon buster

Self-actualisation – the process of coming to terms with who we are and our own potential.

Promoting healthy lifestyles

Promoting a healthy lifestyle for babies and children involves working in partnership with colleagues, the child and their family. Policies and procedures in your setting will provide you with the guidelines for ways of working. As a role model in your setting you will influence the choices that the children make. Think about the importance of:

- **role modelling** – such as demonstrating how to wash hands or eating with children and choosing healthy foods
- **active participation** – planning safe but challenging and creative play activities that encourage physical, emotional, social and cognitive development
- **assessing children's progress** – identifying their needs and working out how best to support those needs
- **getting to know children and their families** and advising and supporting them to choose healthy options.

Promotion of breastfeeding

Breast milk is the healthy option for babies because it:

- provides all the nutrition that a baby needs in the first 6 months
- passes antibodies from the mother that reduce the risk of illness
- helps to promote a bond between the baby and mother
- is more hygienic because it doesn't involve washing and sterilising bottles and teats.

Knowing the benefits will help you support mothers when choosing between breast and bottle.

4 Understand how to keep children safe and secure in early years settings

Learning outcome 1 of this unit explained the shared duty of care colleagues have to follow your setting's procedures and policies based on legislation and regulations governing health and safety. Here you will look at your role in making sure children are safe and secure.

Your role

Your role includes:

- obtaining and using personal and sensitive information appropriately and keeping it secure, in order to maintain confidentiality
- providing play and learning activities that challenge children, but balancing the risks to their health and safety through proper risk assessment and protection measures
- supervising, supporting, reassuring and role modelling to children to encourage them to keep themselves safe
- being aware of health and safety requirements and following safe working practices set out in policies and procedures for health and safety and safeguarding
- reporting and recording any concerns about an individual child, colleague or about the environment or activities that take place ('whistle blowing')
- understanding your own role and responsibilities, including the boundaries

Case study 7.1

Read the following scenarios. What advice would you give each member of staff and why?

1. Sameerah works in a private nursery in the toddler room. After lunch she answered the door to the school nurse who had popped in for a moment to collect some paperwork. She told the nurse that she didn't need to sign in as she would only be there for a moment and the children were all having a nap. She left the door on the latch, asking the nurse to drop the latch when she left so that she wouldn't have to get up.

2. Mike is a student at a children's centre. Procedures state that he must be supervised when carrying out personal routines with children. He is quite confident and the nursery is short-staffed so his supervisor Claire suggests that he helps children with their toileting before lunch.

- observing and monitoring your own ways of working and safety awareness, and getting training if needed

- helping to maintain security in the setting, such as signing in or keeping doors locked

- being a role model by following safe practice in everything you do.

Your responsibilities

As a member of staff, even if you volunteer, you have a duty of care to the health and safety of children and yourself. It is important that you understand and can apply each policy and procedure – and ask your supervisor or manager if you are unsure about anything. If you ignore procedures or don't understand them, you can put children and yourself at risk.

When you start to work with children you must attend induction training in health and safety so that you can meet your responsibilities from day one. Health and safety legislation requires you to cooperate with colleagues to ensure the health and safety of yourself and others. From time to time you will be offered further training to update you and develop your skills and knowledge of:

- risk assessment

- the use of protective clothing

- safeguarding

- responding to emergencies

- food handling and preparation.

Attendance will be mandatory if you are to meet your legal obligations.

Some tasks should only be carried out by staff who are trained to do them. These include manual handling and administering first aid or medication. These responsibilities may require you to use specialist equipment such as hoists or an EpiPen®. You should not attempt these unless they are within the limits of your responsibility as set out in your job description.

Other tasks have special risks attached to them, such as food handling and preparation, and healthcare

procedures. Here you must understand the requirements for reporting and recording, and the correct use of equipment, as well as the correct procedures.

Theory in action

Look through your job description and any other information you have been given about your role. Also familiarise yourself with health and safety procedures for all staff. What responsibilities do you have in relation to health and safety?

Monitoring and maintaining health and safety

Having policies, procedures and codes of practice is important but these cannot be put into place and then forgotten. Within a setting, there should be one person with overall responsibility for health and safety; this may be the manager of the setting or it may be someone else.

Monitoring

Policies and procedures must be reviewed regularly by managers and professionals in the setting with health and safety responsibility, to ensure that they continue to meet best practice and comply with legislation and regulations.

Maintaining

Health and safety can be maintained by:

- seeking feedback on procedures from colleagues, children and their parents

- reviewing and evaluating practice regularly

- having an accident book to record accidents and 'near misses'

- providing regular training in health and safety

- having procedures in place to enable staff to report concerns

- Ofsted inspections.

Risks, hazards and safe working

There are various ways that those working in a setting can be made aware of likely hazards and risks. Written policies, procedures and codes of practice give guidance on how to work safely so must be made available for all. There will also be posters that inform staff of particular risks and procedures.

Safe working practices can be encouraged by:

- knowing your own role and responsibility
- being familiar with your setting's codes of practice
- seeking feedback on your own practice and skills – and acting on it
- getting regular training and attending meetings
- being supervised by a qualified early years professional
- observing, shadowing or being mentored by colleagues, who act as role models for good practice
- taking responsibility for giving health and safety advice to children, parents and visitors.

Jargon buster

Hazard – something that may cause harm (for example, a trailing cable).

Risk – the likelihood of someone being harmed by a hazard (for example, tripping over the cable).

Find the balance

Ask permission to take digital photographs of the safety notices in your setting. Print them out and note how each notice helps you maintain health and safety.

Ask your manager or supervisor about training opportunities for health and safety in your setting.

Add this information to your portfolio.

COSHH - Do you know all you need to know ?

Under COSHH or the Control of Substances Hazardous to Health Regulations 1988, all persons at work need to know the safety precautions to take so as not to endanger themselves or others through exposure to substances hazardous to health. Below are four general classifications of risk - know the appropriate symbols, their meaning and their safety precautions.

Meaning

Toxic / Very Toxic
May cause serious health risk or even death if inhaled, ingested or if it penetrates the skin.

Safety Precautions

1. Wear suitable protective clothing, gloves and eye / face protection.
2. After contact with skin, wash immediately with plenty of water.
3. In case of contact with eyes, rinse immediately with plenty of water and seek medical advice.
4. In case of accident or if you feel unwell, seek medical advice immediately.

Corrosive
May on contact cause destruction of living tissue or burns.

1. Wear suitable gloves and eye / face protection.
2. Take off immediately all contaminated clothing.
3. In case of contact with skin, wash immediately with plenty of water.
4. In case of contact with eyes, rinse immediately (for 15 minutes) with plenty of water and seek medical advice.

Harmful
May cause limited health risk if inhaled or ingested or if it penetrates the skin.

1. Do not breathe vapour / spray / dust.
2. Avoid contact with skin.
3. Wash thoroughly before you eat, drink or smoke.
4. In case of contact with eyes, rinse immediately with plenty of water and seek medical advice.

Irritant
May cause inflammation and irritation on immediate or repeated or prolonged contact with the skin or if inhaled.

1. In case of contact with eyes, rinse immediately with plenty of water and seek medical advice.
2. In case of contact with skin, wash immediately with plenty of water.
3. Do not breathe vapour / spray / dust.
4. Avoid contact with skin.

Figure 7.8: What health and safety posters have you noticed in your setting?

5 Understand how to respond to accidents and emergency situations

Your setting's health and safety policy will include what to do in an accident or emergency situation. It is important that you know when to call a first aider or other helper. Your setting will have someone with first aid training but, if they are not available immediately, you may need to give basic first aid yourself. Even if you are first aid trained, get others to help when there has been an accident. They can assist the injured child, call an ambulance or reassure other children.

Accidents and emergencies

With any accident or emergency, you must stay calm. This will help you to deal with the incident professionally and will keep children and others calm too. Always inform the manager or senior member of staff immediately, and make sure you follow your setting's policies, procedures and ways of working.

Accidents

The most common accidents among children are trips, falls, injuries, choking and burns.

If you are the first one on the scene, you are the best person to note any changes in the injured child's condition or behaviour. For example, has their breathing become more laboured? Has their pain increased? Make a mental note of the time the accident occurred, what you observed and any action you took so that you can make a full verbal report straight away, and a written report as soon as possible afterwards.

Reflect

Do you have a first aid qualification? Find out how to achieve one at your training centre or college, or by contacting the Red Cross or St John's Ambulance.

Emergencies

In your work, you may encounter emergencies such as:

- illness
- fire
- flood
- a gas leak
- a terror alert
- an intruder in the setting
- a child going missing.

Illness

Call a first aider to assess the nature of the illness. Record the symptoms and any changes in the child's condition, then contact the parents. Children who show signs of infectious disease should be isolated but kept under constant supervision.

You must call 999 immediately if the child:

- is not breathing
- is having difficulty breathing or is choking
- is unconscious or does not seem aware of what is happening
- has had a fit for the first time.

Fire, flood, gas leak, terror alert or intruder

These incidents will require emergency evacuation of the whole building or, for a flood or intruder, to a different part of the building. Familiarise yourself with the alarms so you can alert everyone immediately if needed. Make sure you know the escape routes and where to assemble. Regular practice runs will help you to understand your responsibilities in helping children to safety.

If you are aware of an intruder it is important to get children out of the way of possible harm and call for help immediately. The usual escape route may not always be the most appropriate so becoming familiar with the layout of the setting is important.

An appointed member of staff or the manager will be responsible for contacting the emergency services but there could be situations when you need to make a 999 call yourself. To do this make sure you have to hand:

- the address and postcode of the setting (or venue if off site)
- the service you require
- the number you are calling from
- what has happened and who is involved.

Missing child

If a child goes missing, there will be clear steps to follow. Inform the manager or senior professional, who will initiate a search. A child could be hiding, or may have been collected but not signed out. If the child is not found quickly, the emergency services must be contacted and the parents informed.

How to avoid injuries

Safe ways of working can avoid many common injuries.

- Provide adequate supervision at all times.
- Carry out a risk assessment of the environment and activities taking place.
- Maintain equipment and check before use: for example, broken parts, sharp edges.
- Keep doors and gates locked and check them regularly.
- Provide toys and equipment that meet current safety standards.
- Before each play session, check outdoor areas for glass, needles, secure gates, etc.
- Provide toys and equipment suitable for the age and stage of development of the children.
- Remove anything with long ribbons or cords, such as long ribbons on dressing-up clothes.
- Keep the area clear and tidy by clearing up discarded toys.

Make sure you are aware of everyone's roles and responsibilities, and keep up to date with harm reduction training.

Figure 7.9: This symbol means that a toy might be dangerous for children under 3 years and can help you pick out suitable toys for your setting.

Recording and reporting accidents

Any accident to children or staff should be recorded in your setting's accident book. Serious accidents to children must also be passed on to Ofsted (or RIDDOR if it involves a member of staff). Make sure you know the correct forms to use, and use them.

An accident report is a legal document, so information must be detailed and clearly written. Take a good look at the accident report form in Figure 7.10, noting carefully what information needs to be filled in.

Reflect

Get a copy of the form for reporting accidents from your setting. Make notes outlining the purpose of each piece of information and with whom the information is to be shared.

Using the RIDDOR and Ofsted websites, research and list the types of accident and injury (for an early years setting) that are deemed serious. Outline the procedures for reporting them.

6 Understand prevention and control of infection in early years settings

Germs that cause illness spread rapidly in early childhood settings. You must follow effective hygiene procedures to eliminate or reduce the sources of infection.

Preventing the spread of infection

You can do a lot to help prevent or reduce the spread of infection. Three key ways are:

- personal hygiene
- effective cleaning routines
- immunisation.

One of the main ways to prevent infection is regular and thorough hand washing. You should wash hands after using the toilet, after sneezing or blowing your nose, preparing and serving food and always before and after carrying out care routines.

Name of child:	Date of birth:
Date of accident:	Time of accident:

Description of what happened:

Adult(s) in attendance:

Injuries to child:

First aid treatment given:

Other actions taken:

Parents contacted: Yes [ ] No [ ]	Method:
Signature:	Date:

Figure 7.10: Have you ever filled in an accident report form?

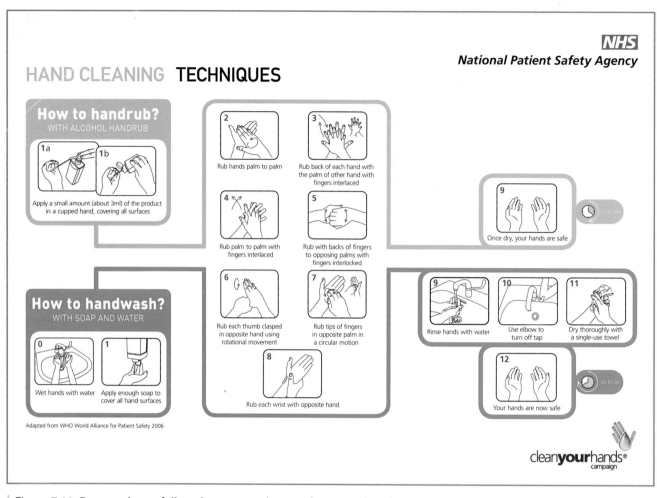

Figure 7.11: Do you always follow these steps when washing your hands?

Good practice in preventing the spread of infection

- Follow personal hygiene – cover your mouth and nose when coughing and sneezing, dispose of tissues safely and wash your hands correctly (see Figure 7.11).

- Follow cleaning routines – of play areas, toys, equipment, surfaces, nappy changing areas, toilets and food preparation areas.

- Clean items regularly – toys, equipment, furnishings, sand pits and water trays.

- Use correct personal protection (PPE) – wear disposable gloves when dealing with bodily fluids or soiled laundry, and when handling foods and food waste.

- Dispose of bodily fluids safely – use designated clinical waste bins for blood, faeces, saliva, vomit and nose discharge.

- Dispose of waste, such as foods that can cause disease, in covered bins that are emptied and cleaned regularly.

- Clean spillages immediately using PPE and dispose of this in a covered bin.

- Promote immunisation – inform parents of the immunisation schedule, encourage them to have their children immunised, and keep up to date with your own immunisations.

- Follow exclusion periods for infectious diseases for children and adults.

- Be able to identify the common childhood illnesses (for more information on childhood illnesses, see the next section).

Childhood infections

Most children will contract an infectious disease in the first few years of life. It is not your responsibility to diagnose infections and ill health, but you do need to be able to recognise the signs during your day-to-day work.

You should know when a child should or should not be kept at home, and be clear about which illnesses should be reported. For instance, a child with chickenpox should be excluded, but if they have a common cold this is not necessary. A case of measles must be reported to the Health Protection Agency.

Check the advice in your setting on exclusions and illnesses that must be reported.

How infection can be spread

Where children and adults come into close contact with each other there is an increased risk of spreading infection.

Table 7.2: Common childhood infections and their symptoms.

Infection	Symptoms
Measles	• Incubation period 7–12 days • Cold-like symptoms and dry cough, fever, eyes sometimes red and sensitive to light • Before the rash appears, may be Koplik's spots in the mouth • Reddish brown rash starts behind ears and spreads to head and neck then rest of body • Serious complications may occur, such as pneumonia or even death
Chickenpox	• Incubation period 7–21 days • Generally feeling unwell, slight temperature, sore throat and headache • Red spots start on face and trunk, spreading to arms and legs • Spots form pustules before forming scabs, which fall off
Mumps	• Incubation period 14–21 days • May start with headache and pain when swallowing or joint or tummy ache; may be fever • Children have swollen parotid glands on each side of face
Whooping cough	• Incubation period 6–21 days • Starts with cough and cold • Coughing increases after two weeks; may make whooping noise when coughing • Babies may have breath-holding attacks or turn blue
Influenza (flu)	• Fever and aching muscles, headache, stuffy nose, dry cough and sore throat • Can be complications such as bronchitis, pneumonia or middle ear infection
Pneumonia	• Cough producing thick mucus, difficulty breathing, pain in the chest, fever, shivering, loss of appetite
Ear infection	• Temperature, pain in the ears – ears may look red and children may pull at them • Hearing may be affected afterwards
Urine infection	• Fever, more frequent passing of urine, pain or burning sensation when passing urine • Children may appear more sleepy or irritable
Cold	• Runny nose and cough – children usually have a number of colds each year
Cold sores	• Small blisters on lips that give tingling, itchy or burning sensation
Fungal infection	• Red, cracked or itchy skin between toes or nappy area
Sore throat	• Difficulty in swallowing, fever, headaches

Infection may be transmitted by:

- direct contact with an infected person or animal (e.g. scabies, chickenpox)

- direct contact with a person's blood or other bodily fluids (e.g. HIV or hepatitis) or with faeces (e.g. gastro-intestinal infection)

- indirect contact through surfaces in the environment that are contaminated by unwashed hands or cleaning cloths – germs can be transferred to food or hands and then ingested

- self-infection (e.g. from gut organisms)

- consumption of food or water that is contaminated, or has been carried to the mouth on unwashed hands (poor food handling)

- breathing in minute droplets from the air caused by talking, coughing or sneezing, or skin particles carried in the air

- insects or other pests depositing germs or caused by their bite.

You must also be aware of children in your care who are more susceptible to infection, such as children with cancers or other conditions.

Jargon buster

Ingested – to take in by breathing or eating.

Legislation, regulations and guidance

You may think that the procedures outlined in this unit are common sense. As with safety in the setting there are a number of laws, regulations and guidance that apply to infection prevention and control.

Legislation

Earlier in this unit, you read about three important pieces of legislation that are intended to prevent and control the spread of infection – HASAWA, COSHH and RIDDOR. HASAWA requires your employer to ensure that the environment is clean and to provide you with protective clothing. As an employee you have a duty to cooperate by following cleaning procedures.

The Health and Social Care Act 2008 was introduced specifically to control infection in healthcare and adult social care environments. It introduced a code of practice that must be followed, including the need to:

- provide and maintain a clean and safe environment including surfaces, equipment and toys

- carry out risk assessments and review how procedures are preventing and controlling the spread of infection

- identify those who may have an infection

- provide information about infections to service users and visitors.

Regulations

Food Hygiene (England) Regulations 2005 state the minimum hygiene standards that must be maintained. The focus is on assessing the risk in a particular setting. For example, the risks in a takeaway café will be different to those in a nursery that prepares formula for babies. Regulations may be applied differently, depending on the risks.

In early years settings, you will need to:

- assess the risks in relation to food storage, preparation and serving of food

- keep all surfaces clean

- have a supply of clean drinking water

- have adequate hand-washing facilities, separate from food preparation areas

- have facilities for:

  » cleaning and sterilising equipment

  » storing different types of food

  » the removal of food waste.

The Health Protection (Local Authority Powers) Regulations 2010 give local authorities powers to intervene where there is a particular risk to health in maintained schools and nursery schools, to protect the community and society at large. In consultation with the Health Protection Agency and the NHS, local authorities can require:

- a child to be kept away from the setting if they have an infection that is a serious risk to others and if parents do not comply with the setting's request
- a manager or head teacher to disinfect or decontaminate the premises when there is a particular risk, such as an outbreak of food poisoning
- a list of children who attend the setting when there may be a risk that a contaminated person has been in contact with children in the setting.

Reflect

The Health Protection (Notification) Regulations 2010 give details of reportable diseases.

1. Which of these diseases might you come across in your setting?
2. How should you report cases and who to?

Guidance

There are a number of government and other agencies that provide guidance on infection prevention and control.

- **Public Health England** – Provides information on health issues and supports children and families by working closely with health visitors and school nurses.
- **Department of Health** – Provides information on promoting and protecting children's health, including the immunisation programme.
- **Ofsted** – Is responsible for setting standards, regulation and inspection of children's services including early years care and school.
- **National Day Nurseries Association (NDNA)** – Works closely with local authorities and childcare providers to offer information, advice and guidance. You can get publications, factsheets and resources on infection control from their website.

- **Infection Prevention Society** – Gives guidance to managers and practitioners on infection prevention strategies. It provides a range of resources including materials to use in staff training activities, and produces the *Journal of Infection Prevention*.
- **Health and Social Care Act 2012** – Includes a Code of Practice on the Prevention and Control of Infections, with detailed guidance on good practice for infection control in health settings.

Theory in action

Look at the Healthy Child Programme on the Department of Health website. In what ways does this programme support the health and welfare of children?

The immunisation programme for children

Immunisation forms an important part of the overall policy of infection control. The purpose of immunisation is to reduce the spread of serious infection by vaccination (giving vaccines), usually by injection. Vaccines contain a small amount of the virus or bacterium that causes the disease. Giving the vaccine triggers the baby's or child's immune system to make antibodies so their bodies learn how to fight the disease.

Jargon buster

Immunisation – a way of protecting against serious diseases by making our bodies better able to fight these diseases if we come into contact with them.

Vaccination – exposing the body's immune system to a weakened or harmless version of a pathogen, in order to stimulate white blood cells to produce antibodies.

Table 7.3: The usual schedule of childhood immunisations.

Age	Immunisation	Diseases protected against	Method
2 months	5-in-1 (DTaP/IPV/Hib) vaccine, first dose	diphtheria, tetanus, pertussis (whooping cough), polio, Haemophilus influenzae type b (Hib)	1 injection in thigh
	Pneumococcal (PCV) vaccine, first dose	pneumococcal infections that can lead to pneumonia, septicaemia and meningitis	1 injection in thigh
	Rotavirus vaccine, first dose	an infectious stomach bug causing diarrhoea	oral vaccine by dropper
3 months	5-in-1 (DTaP/IPV/Hib) vaccine, second dose	as above	1 injection in thigh
	Meningitis C	meningitis and septicaemia (but not caused by meningococcal group B bacteria)	1 injection in thigh
	Rotavirus vaccine, second dose	as above	oral vaccine by dropper
4 months	5-in-1 (DTaP/IPV/Hib) vaccine, third dose	as above	1 injection in thigh
	Pneumococcal (PCV) vaccine, second dose	as above	1 injection in thigh
Between 12 and 13 months	Hib/Men C booster, containing meningitis C (second dose) and Hib (fourth dose)	as above	1 injection in thigh or upper arm
	Pneumococcal (PCV) vaccine, third dose	as above	1 injection in thigh or upper arm
	MMR combined vaccine, first dose	measles, mumps and rubella	1 injection in thigh or upper arm
2 and 3 years (in some areas up to 10 years)	Flu vaccine (annual)	influenza	nasal spray
3 years and 4 months or shortly after	MMR combined vaccine, second dose	as above	1 injection in upper arm
	4-in-1 (DTaP/IPV) pre-school booster, given as a single jab	diphtheria, tetanus, whooping cough (pertussis) and polio	1 injection in upper arm

(Source: Public Health England, licensed under the Open Government Licence v1.0)

Immunisation has been successful in eliminating some serious diseases. Smallpox was once a serious threat, but has now been eradicated worldwide; polio is no longer a threat in the UK and is rare worldwide. Measles and mumps are still with us, but their incidence has been dramatically reduced since the introduction of the MMR vaccine.

When a high percentage of children have been immunised it reduces the likelihood of the disease passing to others who have not – referred to as 'herd immunity'. Surveillance and monitoring outbreaks of disease and the uptake of immunisation is important for the health of the whole community. When the percentage falls below around 95 per cent this immunity is no longer effective – so you should always encourage parents to have their children immunised.

7 Understand how to assess health and safety risks in early years settings

Risk assessments are an essential tool for keeping children healthy and safe. They are carried out to identify the hazards and risks connected to the environment – indoors and outdoors – and the activities that take place there.

Research shows that most accidents occur in the home, particularly in the kitchen, so childminders working in their own home will have to consider the particular hazards there.

The risk assessment process

You have a legal responsibility to keep children safe by ensuring that risks in your environment are minimised. One strategy is to carry out a risk assessment.

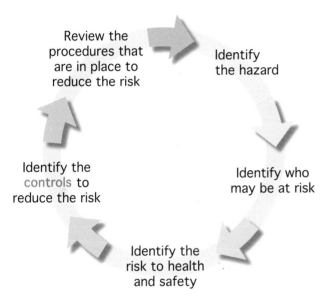

Figure 7.12: What could happen if you do not carry out a risk assessment properly?

Carrying out a risk assessment and risk management

To carry out a risk assessment you need to be aware of hazards that exist in the setting. You then need to consider the stage of development and abilities of the children in your care, and the types of accidents and injury they may sustain. Use this knowledge to go through the five stages shown in Figure 7.12.

> ### Jargon buster
>
> **Controls** – things that are put into place to eliminate or reduce the risk of harm, such as procedures, supervision or safety equipment.
>
> **Immunity** – the ability to resist a particular infection.

Carrying out a risk assessment

1. Identify the hazards. These may relate to the environment, such as wet floors, or in routines or activities, such as cooking with children.

2. For each hazard, identify who might be at risk. Some may be hazardous for all, but others may be a particular hazard for a certain age group. For example, toys with small parts may be suitable for older children but not for children under 3.

3. Evaluate the severity of risks associated with each hazard and the possible impact. Having an understanding of common accidents, injuries and illnesses will help you recognise what the risk might be. For instance, falls from a climbing frame may result in head bumps or broken bones, while nappy changing has the potential for spreading infection. This can vary depending on the stage and capability of the children.

4. Decide which controls to put into place to reduce the likelihood of injury or illness. For example:

   » supervision to ensure you have the correct ratio of staff to children and that practitioners are competent to undertake the role

   » getting safety equipment such as socket covers and pan guards

   » choosing resources that are safe and appropriate for the age of the children

   » clarifying procedures for cleaning routines or wearing protective clothing

   » having training in evacuation procedures or food preparation.

Any new controls must be recorded, and everyone who works in the setting must be told these agreed ways of working. They then have a responsibility to follow them.

Practice and procedures must be reviewed regularly and amended if the controls are not having the desired effect.

Assessing infection and safety risks

For information on assessing infection and safety risks for personal care routines, see learning outcome 2 in this unit. For information on assessing infection and safety risks for cleaning and maintaining the environment, equipment and toys, see learning outcome 6 in this unit.

Figure 7.13: What controls will you need to put in place once a baby learns to crawl?

Play and learning experiences

Even common play and learning experiences may pose a safety risk.

- Cooking activities – burns from hot surfaces, cuts from knives
- Dressing up – strangulation from long ribbons or ties
- Water play – drowning, slipping on wet floors
- Climbing frames – head bumps, bruising or broken bones from falling
- Junk modelling – cuts from scissors, puncture wounds from staplers
- Outdoor sand play – infection from animal faeces, sand in eyes
- Toileting – cross-infection from toilets, basins, taps and door handles
- Nappy changing – cross-infection from germs present on changing mats, hands and protective clothing

Find the balance

Use a risk assessment template from your own setting or produce your own using the headings in Table 7.4.

Carry out risk assessments for:

- a play and learning activity with a group of children
- a care routine.

After you have carried out the activity and routine, review your risk assessments and amend them if necessary. Use these to describe to your assessor how you carried out and reviewed the risk assessments.

Table 7.4 shows an assessment relating to a play activity and routine in a nursery setting.

Table 7.4: A sample risk assessment form for some common activities in a nursery.

Hazard	Risk	Who could be injured	Controls to minimise risk	Review
Water play	Drowning Slipping/falling	Children	• Constant supervision • Place on non-slip surface • Mop up wet floor immediately • Empty water tray after use	
Nappy changing routine	Cross-infection Falling	Babies	• Clean changing area before and after use • Adults wash hands before and immediately after routine • Adults wear disposable gloves and apron and dispose of immediately in designated bin • Do not leave baby unattended	

For some activities you need to consider the ways to reduce harm as it is not always possible to eliminate all risk. For example, removing outdoor climbing frames would prevent children falling from a height, but children need opportunities to climb to develop their physical skills. A more realistic action would be to put controls in place to reduce the risk of injury by making sure that the frame meets EU safety standards, having a safe surface beneath the frame and supervising children as they play.

Provision of food

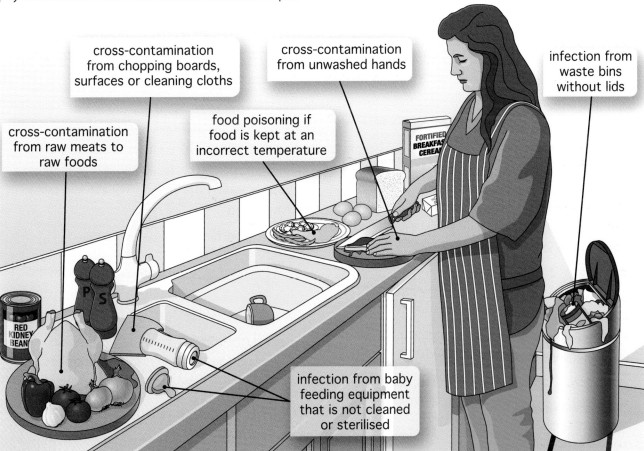

cross-contamination from chopping boards, surfaces or cleaning cloths

cross-contamination from unwashed hands

infection from waste bins without lids

cross-contamination from raw meats to raw foods

food poisoning if food is kept at an incorrect temperature

infection from baby feeding equipment that is not cleaned or sterilised

Figure 7.14: What risks are there when providing food?

Assessing the risk when taking children on outings

You must always carry out a detailed risk assessment before children are taken off site, even to the local park. The risks will depend on the venue and how the children will travel. Visit the venue beforehand so that you can fully assess the risks, taking into account:

- **travel** – age and stage of children, route and method of transport
- **toileting** – if there adequate facilities including hand-washing facilities
- **illness and accident** – what access there is to a phone, what the emergency contact number is, whether a first aider is available to accompany the group, whether there is a first aid box, what resources are required for dealing with bodily fluids
- **weather** – whether children have suitable clothing, such as waterproof coats and boots or sunhats and sun protection
- **food and drink** – if there is access to clean drinking water, a suitable place to eat, how food can be transported safely
- **abducted or lost children** – whether there are enough adults to children for close supervision
- **activities** – what children will do and what controls will be needed, such as climbing on play equipment or stroking animals
- **individual needs** – whether any children in the group have particular needs, how they will be identified and supported, how to get parental consent.

8 Understand how to maintain records and reports

Records and reports are a legal requirement. You will be expected to maintain a range of records and reports to promote and support health and safety in your setting.

Accuracy and coherence

All the information about children, their families and staff used in your setting is confidential. Parents, carers and staff have a right to know what information is being held about them and how it will be used. All those working in a setting have a duty of care to obtain information with regard to the rights of individuals and not to share information without gaining consent.

The personal information you gather about children must be accurate and up to date to be of use in protecting their health and safety and welfare. You must review this information regularly as it is always changing. For example, does your setting have the latest emergency contact numbers for parents? Are there changes to the health of any of the children? Not updating information about children can have serious consequences.

Maintaining records and reports

It is essential that the information is written clearly. Reports and records do not have to be lengthy, and are more easily understood if they are to the point. They will be read by others who need to act upon the information so they must be in sufficient detail, without any ambiguity. They must be ethical, written fairly and meeting the standards and principles of the sector. Templates are often used for records and reports such as the accident report shown in Figure 7.10. These are good practice as they include headings that ensure all the necessary information is included. When writing reports, bear in mind that they may be passed on: for example, to parents or to an outside agency that monitors health and safety such as Ofsted.

Professional records and reports must be:

- legible
- accurate
- complete and up to date
- signed and dated
- stored securely so that only those who need them have access to them.

Keeping records confidential

In learning outcome 1 of this unit, you learned about the Data Protection Act 1998. There are eight principles in the act giving guidance on protecting data. Information must be:

- used fairly and lawfully
- used for specific, limited purposes
- adequate, relevant and not excessive
- accurate
- not kept longer than necessary
- handled in accordance with rights
- kept safe and secure
- not transferred outside of the UK unless there is sufficient protection.

Although the act is clear on how data can or cannot be used, consent does not have to be given before passing on information if there are concerns that a child may have been abused. However, confidentiality must still be observed and information must only be passed to those who need to know, such as the professional with child protection responsibility in your setting and in social services.

Much of the personal and sensitive information kept about children needs to be accessible as it is in constant use. For example, care plans need to be referred to frequently. Even so, this information must be kept secure and never left around the setting for others to read. Not doing so will break down trust between parent and setting, making parents less willing to share information – and it could even put children at risk.

The principles in the 1998 act do not state how data is kept, just that it must be safe and secure. Your setting's policy and procedures must set out how it will do this. Written records must be kept in locked, hard-to-access cabinets, probably in the manager's office. Today a lot of confidential information is kept electronically, so safe, password-protected systems are vital for accessing or passing on information.

Further reading and resources

Publications

- Cole, P. (2010) *Keep it Clean and Healthy: Infection Control Guidance for Nurseries, Playgroups and other Childcare Settings*, Huntingdon: Pat Cole Ltd – accessed online at www.ifh-homehygiene.org/

- Communities and local government (2008, updated 2013) Fire safety in the home – guidance on how to keep your home safe from fire – available to download at www.gov.uk/government/publications/fire-safety-in-the-home

- DK Publishing (2014) *First Aid Manual* (10th ed.), London: Dorling Kindersley

- Parker, L. (2011) *The Early Years Health and Safety Handbook* (2nd ed.), Oxford: Routledge

- Tovey, H. (2007) *Playing Outdoors: Spaces and Places, Risks and Challenge (Debating Play)*, Maidenhead: Open University Press

Websites

- British Red Cross: www.redcross.org.uk – videos on basic first aid and training courses offered (including Baby and Child courses) at your workplace

- Cancer Research UK SunSmart: www.sunsmart.org.uk– information about sun safety

- Department for Health: www.gov.uk/government/organisations/department-of-health – news and information on how the government is shaping and funding health and care in England

Case study 7.2

Nathan is the deputy of a private nursery. He is the key person for two children with special needs. He works long hours and is under pressure at work, so sometimes he works at home. He is behind with reports for these children so he puts their information on a memory stick so that he can work at the weekend. He is particularly concerned about one of the children, so plans to discuss their needs with a friend who works as a speech therapist.

1. What could be the confidentiality issues with this practice?
2. What could be the impact for the children and for Nathan?

- Foundation Years: www.foundationyears.org.uk/eyfs – a useful section of this website for resources, information and support on the EYFS

- Health and Safety Executive: www.hse.gov.uk – guidelines and advice about health and safety including latest legislation

- National Day Nurseries Association: www.ndna.org.uk – advice and information for nurseries and early years practitioners

- Ofsted: www.ofsted.gov.uk – for information about EYFS Ofsted requirements and the schedule for inspections of early years providers

- Public Health England: www.gov.uk/government/organisations/public-health-england – for news, policies and information about public health issues

- Royal Society for the Prevention of Accidents: www.rospa.com – information on the types of accidents that happen to children and ideas on how to prevent them

Articles and magazines

- Nursery World magazine: www.nurseryworld.magazine.co.uk – news, articles and information on best practice in childcare, the EYFS and early years education and jobs

Child protection and safeguarding

Unit 8

Child protection and safeguarding

In relation to your role in keeping children safe you will come across the terms 'child protection' and 'safeguarding'. All children have the right to be protected from abuse or neglect so child protection is an important aspect of your role. In this unit you will learn how to recognise the signs that abuse may be happening and what to do if you suspect that a child has been abused.

The role of safeguarding encompasses child protection but it is far more than this. Your responsibilities extend to preventing impairment to children's overall health, development and wellbeing. To do this, you must explore ways to provide consistent care in an environment where children feel safe and secure. Safeguarding is about ensuring that all children attain the best possible outcomes in life.

Before you start

Talk to the safeguarding and health and safety representatives in your setting and ask about their additional responsibilities and that of other staff towards child protection. Before you speak to them, jot down a few questions to ask. For example, what do you do if you are a bit worried about a child's safety but not quite sure? Remember they cannot speak to you about individual cases because information must be kept confidential.

Learning outcomes

By the end of this unit you will:

1. understand the legal requirements and guidance on safeguarding in early years settings
2. be able to carry out own responsibilities in relation to safeguarding
3. understand types and indicators of child abuse
4. understand how to respond to allegations that a child has been abused or harmed
5. be able to maintain confidentiality of information
6. be able to maintain the safety and security of children in own work setting.

1 Understand the legal requirements and guidance on safeguarding in early years settings

Laws and guidance determine the way you must work with children in your setting to promote their welfare and protect them from abuse and harm.

- Legislation gives a broad directive on what must be achieved in regard to child protection and safeguarding.
- Statutory guidance is more specific and gives details on how the law should be implemented in early years settings and services.

Laws and statutory guidance are mandatory and must underpin policies and procedures that you use in your setting.

Legal requirements

Children Act 1989

This establishes the duty of early years practitioners to identify and meet the individual needs of children and to keep them safe. It introduced the principle of the child at the centre of planning: that the child's welfare is 'paramount' when decisions are being made about them. This act also identifies the responsibilities of parents in keeping children safe.

There are two sections that relate specifically to the duty of the local authority with regard to child protection.

- Section 17 states that services must be put into place to 'safeguard and promote the welfare of children within the (local authority) area who are in need'.
- Section 47 states that the local authority has a duty to investigate when 'there is a reasonable cause to suspect that a child is suffering or likely to suffer harm'.

Children Act 2004

This was introduced in response to the high-profile case of Victoria Climbié, who died in 2000 in terrible circumstances following abuse by her carers. The case highlighted the failures of services to work together effectively.

The 2004 act introduced a requirement for:

- increased responsibilities of local authorities to oversee the integration of children's services
- services to work more closely to share information and support the needs of children and their families
- earlier identification of needs and support to be given to parents to reduce the risk of abuse or harm
- the introduction of a shared process for gathering information about a child and their needs
- a shared database for information relevant to the safety and welfare of children
- a Local Safeguarding Children Board (LSCB) to be set up in every area, to support and monitor children's services and investigate and report on serious child abuse cases

- the legal framework *Every Child Matters*, introducing shared outcomes that all children's services must work towards.

Education Act 2002

This identifies the responsibilities of local education authorities, governing bodies, head teachers and those working in schools to ensure that children are safe and free from harm.

Safeguarding Vulnerable Groups Act 2006 (amended by Protection of Freedoms Act 2012)

The 2006 act was introduced on the recommendations of the Bichard enquiry, following the Soham murders in 2002. Huntley, who was convicted of murdering the two girls, had previously been investigated for sexual crimes, but this information had not appeared on the police database when he was appointed to a position in the girls' school.

The 2006 act introduced the requirement for more thorough checks into people's backgrounds before they can take part in regulated activities with children or vulnerable adults. Originally, the Criminal Records Bureau (CRB) carried out checks and the Independent Safeguarding Authority (ISA) kept a register of those barred from working with children or vulnerable adults. The amended 2012 act brought the work of the CRB and ISA together under a new body called the Disclosure and Barring Service (DBS). Anyone applying for work in early years must submit an application to the DBS, which provides a certificate that must be shown to the employer. The DBS also keeps records of people who are barred from working with children or vulnerable adults, and makes decisions about who should be placed on or removed from the list.

Jargon buster

Regulated activities – types of activity that take place with children that are specified by the DBS.

Guidance

Working Together to Safeguard Children (2013)

This important guidance sets out the duty of care for all organisations (including voluntary ones) that provide services for children up to the age of 18 years. Schools, social workers, health services, leisure services and the police must adhere to the framework. It focuses on the importance of shared responsibility and how agencies should cooperate to safeguard children and promote their welfare.

Two key principles of the framework are that:

- safeguarding is the responsibility of all those working with children
- a child-centred approach is essential for services to be effective in keeping children safe and promoting their welfare.

Working Together to Safeguard Children is the framework that the Local Safeguarding Children Boards must refer to when monitoring children's services.

Reflect

Download the relevant sections from the EYFS (2014) and Working Together to Safeguard Children (2013) from the Department for Education website. Highlight the sections that are important for you to know for your own practice.

Safeguarding Disabled Children: Practice Guidance (2009)

Anyone working with disabled children should read this alongside Working Together to Safeguard Children. It provides the additional information and support they require, as it takes into account the vulnerability of children with disabilities and the unequal access to children's services they and their families often experience.

The impact of legal requirements on own role

Everyone working with children shares the responsibility to protect them from harm and to promote their welfare – even if they are not employed by the setting.

To make sure you meet with legal requirements you must:

- be familiar with and understand the policies and procedures of your setting
- comply with all safeguarding policies and procedures
- attend training in child protection and safeguarding
- follow your setting's confidentiality procedures
- share any concerns about a child's health or welfare with the professional with safeguarding responsibility in your setting.

If you don't follow policies and procedures, it could affect a child's health and wellbeing and even put them at serious risk of harm or abuse – and you would face disciplinary proceedings.

Children's rights to be safe

The United Nations Convention on the Rights of the Child (1989)

This treaty identifies the rights and freedoms of all children in a set of 54 articles. Article 19 provides for the right of children to be kept safe from harm and to be protected from all forms of abuse by those looking after them. The countries that signed up to the treaty, including the UK in 1991, are legally bound to implement legislation that supports each of the articles.

Duty of care

'Duty of care' describes the standards of care expected of adults who work with children. Adults have a legal obligation to act in a way that promotes the best interests of the child and keeps them safe from harm, and to do nothing that might harm a child, through actions or negligence.

Safe recruitment

When you first applied to work with children, you will have been asked to complete a DBS application form (or a CRB form before 2012). This is a legal requirement for enhanced disclosure required by the Safeguarding Vulnerable Groups Act 2006, amended by the Protection of Freedoms Act 2012. (This act has been covered in more detail earlier in the unit.)

All services and settings that provide early years care or education have a legal responsibility to recruit staff suitable to work with children. They must check that applicants:

- have appropriate qualifications to carry out their role
- have experience appropriate to their role
- have an identity check
- do not have a criminal record that would bar them from working with children.

Where there is no employer (as for a childminder) Ofsted (or childminding agencies) are responsible for checking a person's suitability. Settings must also have a system for the ongoing assessment of the suitability of the staff, including procedures for investigating and reporting concerns about them.

The Early Years Foundation Stage

The framework for EYFS gives statutory guidance for those working with children aged 0 to 5 years in registered settings. Section 3 of the framework explains the safeguarding and welfare requirements for early years settings, including the duty to:

- provide a stimulating environment where children can grow and learn

Unit 8

Jargon buster

Registered setting – most childcare settings for children under 8 must register with Ofsted or a childminding agency (exceptions include when care is delivered for less than two hours per day or carers are family members).

Figure 8.1: Why do children have a right to play in a safe and stimulating environment?

- promote good health
- keep children safe and secure
- take steps when there are concerns about a child's safety and welfare.

The EYFS gives guidance on how you must work towards maintaining children's safety and welfare, including:

- having a policy and procedures for safeguarding which meet the requirements of the Local Safeguarding Children Board (childminders do not need written policies, but they do need to have clear working practices that they can follow and explain to parents and Ofsted)
- a requirement for staff to follow *Working Together to Safeguard Children*
- having a lead professional who has designated responsibility for safeguarding
- ensuring regular training for all staff in child protection, including recognising signs and symptoms of abuse and how they must respond to concerns
- having safe recruitment procedures, including DBS checks, to make sure that people working at the setting are suitable to carry out their role and responsibilities.

2 Be able to carry out own responsibilities in relation to safeguarding

Legislation and guidance give all those working in children's services wide-ranging responsibilities for promoting and maintaining children's safety and welfare – including you.

Your responsibilities

Your responsibilities include:

- maintaining confidentiality
- safeguarding children
- promoting the welfare of children
- protection of yourself and others.

Maintaining confidentiality

In your role you will have access to a great deal of information. Some of this will be confidential. Confidential information is data that is not available in the public domain and includes personal information (such as a child's date of birth) and sensitive information (such as their care plan).

Children and their families have a right to privacy, so it is critical that you maintain confidentiality at all times. The law is clear that you should not pass on information about a child or their family unless you have been given consent. The exception is when there is a concern about a child's safety – but even then information must only be shared with the professional who has safeguarding responsibility in your setting.

Remember to:

- familiarise yourself with your setting's confidentiality policy
- treat all information as if it is confidential

Figure 8.2: How could repeating what you have overheard put a child at risk?

- only access information if it is your responsibility to do so
- never repeat what you have overheard
- ask advice if you are worried that a child is at risk of harm or abuse.

Safeguarding children

Safeguarding children should be viewed in its broadest sense. It is not just about protecting children from ill treatment, but also preventing impairment to their health and development. To be able to safeguard children you need to:

- understand the risks to children in your setting, in their homes and elsewhere
- recognise each child as an individual and know their particular needs
- be able to recognise when a child is not thriving or may have been abused
- know how to work with other professionals, children and families to provide for children who need support to maintain their health, safety and wellbeing
- know what action to take if you have concerns about a child.

Promoting the welfare of children

Safeguarding means that you must take positive action to promote the welfare of children, as well as protecting them from harm. Aim to do this in everything you do, including how you organise the environment, plan routines and provide support.

One way you can promote the welfare of children is by maintaining a safe and secure environment, through carrying out routines in a safe and consistent way. Risk assessments will be routine, but you need to be constantly on the look out for hazards that may arise as children play. Then you can take any action needed to keep children safe.

Building effective and trusting relationships with children is critical. You must be approachable and value what children say. This will help you to get

to know the child, their likes and dislikes and any problems they or their family may have. Knowing the child well will help you to recognise their feelings and notice any changes in their behaviour that might indicate that they are failing to thrive.

You have personal responsibilities, but you are also an essential part of a team that includes the child, their family, your colleagues and outside agencies. Everyone in the team that surrounds the child will contribute to promoting their welfare, and effective team working is essential to get the best outcomes for children.

Protection of self and others

It is important for you to build a relationship with children in your care – but remember that this is different from the relationship between a child and their parent. You must work within professional boundaries. Comforting a child when they are upset or hurt is acceptable, but make sure that the way you do it is appropriate for their age and stage of development. You must always be open in your contact with children. Never take them into an area or room where your actions cannot be monitored by others.

Figure 8.3: Why should you be open in the way that you approach and comfort children?

You may need to carry out personal or intimate care of babies and young children. This will be part of their care plan, and only in response to their particular needs.

Always:

- follow policy, procedures and guidance
- be clear on the care plans of individual children
- work in an open and transparent way
- encourage children to become independent – for example, to use the toilet, dress or wash themselves.

Never:

- become overfamiliar with children or show favouritism
- ask a child to keep a secret.

Maintaining accurate records

You will be required to record information about the overall welfare of children in your care, including:

- concerns about their health and welfare
- records of discussions about their health and welfare, including face-to-face conversations and telephone calls
- records of what a child has disclosed
- observations
- assessment of a child's needs.

You must make sure that the information you enter in a child's file is clear and accurate. Missing out a key piece of information or handwriting that cannot be deciphered could have serious consequences for a child's safety and welfare. Inaccurate information could even affect the outcome of a court case where there has been abuse.

Case study 8.1

Read the following scenarios that describe the practice of adults working in an early years setting and answer the questions.

Scenario 1

Naomi works in the toddler room of a private nursery. The manager has carried out risk assessments including one for play in the outdoor area. Each member of staff has a copy. Each afternoon Naomi takes the toddlers outdoors so that they can play with ride-on toys. She always follows the procedures set out in the risk assessment.

1. Why is it important that Naomi follows the procedures for outdoor play?
2. What else should Naomi do before she takes the children outside?

Scenario 2

Marek is a student on work experience in a reception class with children aged 4 to 5. He enjoys working with this age group and children respond well to him. One of the children, Pria, who is usually quite shy has come out of her shell. She is now willing to be involved in activities. Throughout the week, Pria has gained confidence and has started to show signs of being unkind to another child within the group. You notice Marek and the teacher seem to have ignored this several times.

1. How might Pria feel now that she has been allowed to behave in this way?
2. What advice would you give to Marek about his practice?

Each piece of information about that child, such as their behaviour or an injury, helps build up a picture of the child's developmental welfare – a bit like a jigsaw puzzle. This picture will give the person with safeguarding responsibilities in your setting an overview of concerns, so it is vital that your information is accurate.

The importance of protecting children from harm in your setting

Parents expect their children to be safe from harm or abuse when they are being cared for in an early years setting. While most early years practitioners protect children from harm, some actually cause harm to the children they are meant to be caring for. This may be through intentional harm or abuse or through negligence because they have not followed policy and procedures.

Abuse or harm can seriously affect children's health and every area of their development: emotional, social, physical and cognitive. Children who have been abused may be underweight or take longer to crawl, walk or talk compared to children of the same age. The early years are critical, so anything that prevents a child from learning may have lasting consequences for their attainment.

Active listening

In 2008, an Ofsted evaluation of child protection highlighted that, in most serious case reviews, practitioners fail to see situations from the child's perspective. This happens when adults consider that they know what is best for the child without taking the child's own feelings into account.

Active listening is essential if you are to avoid this. When you listen actively, you:

- listen first
- consider what has been said
- then respond.

Remember that your body language can indicate whether you are genuinely interested.

In your work, active listening is part of being vigilant to what the child needs and how they feel, and will help you notice when they are worried or feeling ill.

Figure 8.4: How can this child tell that the adult is actively listening to her?

Unit 8

Remember to give children one-to-one time, as well as group time, so they can talk more freely – and you can listen more actively.

Reflect

Daniel Pelka died in 2012 as a result of abuse by his parents. The report on this case states that there was little evidence that he was spoken to about his own feelings and wishes. Children know when we are interested in them and are attending to what they say. When we are, they will be more likely to voice any concerns they have.

1. How might the outcome have been different if people had listened to Daniel?

2. Why might children be reluctant to express their fears?

Jargon buster

Serious case review – review carried out following a child's death from abuse or neglect, where there are concerns about the practice of professionals in working together to safeguard.

3 Understand types and indicators of child abuse

The different types of abuse

Four types of abuse are recognised in child protection: physical, sexual, emotional and neglect. Many children who are abused experience more than one type of abuse. For example, a child who is sexually abused is often emotionally abused too as they are threatened not to tell.

Physical abuse

Physical abuse happens when a child is physically hurt or injured. Hitting a child with hands or implements and kicking, burning, scalding, suffocating, throwing or shaking a child are all forms of physical abuse. So too is poisoning or any act that makes a child ill.

Sexual abuse

Sexual abuse happens when a child is forced or persuaded into sexual activities or situations by others. It may involve physical or non-physical contact.

- Physical contact may be penetration (rape) or touching the child's body for sexual gratification, even if this is outside their clothing.

- Non-physical sexual abuse involves forcing or enticing a child to look at sexual materials and sexual activity, or watching a child undress. This is not always by adults who are in close proximity to a child; there is a growing problem of sexual abuse via the internet.

Emotional abuse

Emotional (or psychological) abuse happens when the child suffers persistent ill treatment that affects their emotional development. It may involve making the child feel frightened, unloved, worthless or in danger. Emotional abuse may happen on its own, but it often takes place with other types of abuse.

Neglect

The legal definition of neglect is 'the persistent failure to meet a child's basic physical and/or psychological needs'. This happens when a child is not given adequate food, shelter, clothing or medical care. It also includes not providing for their developmental, educational or emotional needs.

Another type of abuse: domestic abuse

Domestic abuse happens between adults in the family rather than being directly aimed at children. You may think that this will not affect children in the same way. However, research shows that when children witness domestic abuse, it is likely to have a profound impact on their welfare. It can affect children even if they do not witness it directly but hear it happening or see the result, such as a parent who is upset or injured. Children living in a household where domestic abuse happens are also more likely to be subjected to abuse themselves. Domestic abuse may be physical, sexual, psychological or neglect, and is often a combination of these.

It is notable that the Adoption and Children Act 2002 extended the definition of 'harm' in the Children Act 1989 to include witnessing domestic abuse: 'impairment suffered from seeing or hearing the ill-treatment of another'.

Indicators of abuse

A child who is being abused often shows physical signs or changes in their behaviour. Some indicators are the obvious results of specific types of abuse; others raise concerns that a child has been disturbed by something that has happened to them.

You should be concerned if you notice a child:

- becoming unusually clingy

- reverting to an earlier stage of development – for example, starting to wet or soil themselves after having been dry

- rocking their body, or twisting or pulling out their hair

- being reluctant to play with others and make friends

- becoming aggressive or more passive.

Physical abuse

Young children often have bumps or falls and as a result often have bruises or grazes, especially on their knees or forehead. Indicators of physical abuse are unusual injuries – ones that are unlikely to occur accidentally – such as frequent broken bones, cigarette burns or bruising to both eyes. Where physical injuries are unexplained or the child gives a different reason to their parent or carer or changes their story, you should be concerned.

Table 8.1 shows some of the indicators of different types of abuse. This is not an exhaustive list; any changes in behaviour or unusual physical signs should be a cause for your concern.

Be careful with these indicators. Changes in behaviour could be explained by other events in a child's life, such as the death of a grandparent. Bear in mind that it is not your role to make the decision about whether the child has been abused. It is your job to report any concerns to the professional with child protection responsibilities in your setting.

Figure 8.5: Can you can recognise the possible signs of physical abuse?

Table 8.1: Indicators of different types of abuse.

Type of abuse	Physical indicators	Behavioural indicators
Physical abuse	• Unexplained or recurrent breaks, bruising or scratches • Injuries in unusual places (see Figure 8.5)	• Changes in behaviour
Sexual abuse	• Bruising or scratches to genital area • Child complains of pain or soreness in the genital area, or there is indication of this • Vaginal discharge or bleeding • Wets the bed (after being dry) • Stomach pains or headaches	• Uses explicit sexual language inappropriate for age • Draws explicit pictures or acts in a way that indicates they have observed sexual acts • Displays inappropriate behaviour towards adults • Changes in behaviour
Emotional abuse	• Speech disorders	• Poor concentration • Particularly sensitive to the moods of parents or carers • Self-destructive behaviour • Changes in behaviour
Neglect	• Is underweight/overweight for age • Has poor personal hygiene • Has untreated illnesses • Cold injuries such as swollen and red feet or hands	• Takes food from others or from bins • Is unusually tired • Changes in behaviour

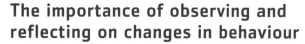
The importance of observing and reflecting on changes in behaviour

Research suggests that around half of the abuse of children goes unnoticed at the time it is actually happening. So for many children, adults are not recognising the signs. Children have told practitioners that they feel let down by adults who do not notice when things are troubling them. It may even make children assume that the behaviour toward them is normal.

Knowing the child will help you not only to observe but also to reflect on how their behaviour may have changed. Children are unique and will display how they feel in different ways. A quiet child may become aggressive, or a boisterous child more withdrawn. The differences may be subtle, as they may be trying to hide what is happening. Stay vigilant.

Theory in action

Find out about the key person role in your own setting.

1. What is the key person role?

2. What are their responsibilities?

3. How does the key person role help to promote safeguarding?

How to pass on your concerns about the practice of others

You may notice that a colleague or other professional, student or visitor to your setting is not following safeguarding procedures. When you have concerns that their practice is impacting on a child's welfare, you must report what you have observed to the professional with safeguarding responsibility or your manager.

If you have concerns that a colleague or professional is abusing a child, your actions should be the same as if the abuser were a parent, family member or stranger. You must act immediately to protect the child. Tell the lead professional who has responsibility for safeguarding in your setting, or the manager. If this is the person you have concerns about, you should contact the local authority for children's social care. It is important that you do not discuss what has happened with others who do not need to know. Ofsted offer support and advice for staff who are reporting abuse or who have allegations made about them.

This type of reporting is known as 'whistle blowing'. It is a difficult thing for anyone to do, but the child must always be your first priority. You should be pleased that you have done the right thing – but if you need support or to discuss your actions, you can speak to the professional who has safeguarding responsibilities in your setting, or a professional from an outside agency.

How abuse can take place

There are some common preconceptions about who is likely to abuse children. Many people believe that it is men who sexually abuse children, or that step-parents are more likely to abuse children than birth parents. These beliefs are unfounded. The abuse we read about in the papers is often carried out by strangers – but in fact, this is rare.

The truth is that anyone who has contact with children can abuse them. In most cases, abuse is carried out by people the child knows: a parent, family member or someone who works with the child. Adolescents may also abuse children who are younger than themselves.

Although abuse happens across all sections of society and across all cultures, there are factors in a home that increase the risk of abuse, including:

- domestic violence

- drug or alcohol abuse

- mental health problems

- lack of knowledge about child development and children's needs

- poverty or unemployment.

Babies and children who are disabled are at higher risk of abuse: these groups are more dependent on adults and may be less able to voice their worries. You need to be especially vigilant to notice the signs and not confuse them with those related to their age and stage of development or the symptoms of their physical or learning disability.

Why children need strategies to protect themselves

You cannot always prevent harm or abuse, but you can support children to protect themselves and so reduce the likelihood. Children are more likely to protect themselves if they:

- are independent
- are self-reliant
- are assertive
- are empowered
- are confident
- are able to communicate their feelings and worries
- have high self-esteem.

Finding the words

Circle time and small group activities, such as puppets, and looking at feelings cards and stories help to extend children's vocabulary. This can give them the words and confidence they need to talk about how they are feeling and to share concerns.

Figure 8.6: How can stories help children to explore their feelings?

Building self-esteem and respect for themselves and their bodies

You can help children understand that their body belongs to them and they can make decisions about how or if they are touched. One strategy used in early years is the underwear rule, which teaches children that the parts of their body covered by their underwear are private. See the NSPCC website for information on how to use the underwear rule and other strategies to help children to protect themselves.

Some children may not realise that it is not OK to touch in certain ways. They may have to learn how to be assertive, so that they can say 'no' when someone touches them in a way that makes them uncomfortable. You can use songs and puppet play to help children learn about their own bodies and understand how to say 'no' to unwanted behaviour or touches.

Exploring their feelings and speaking out

Children need opportunities to talk and to explore their feelings. The key person role is particularly important here: a child is more likely to speak to a trusted person who they feel comfortable with. Very young children or those with communication difficulties will find it hard to use words to express themselves, so you need to be tuned in to their feelings. Recognising children's worries at an early stage will help you to reassure them and put support into place.

Secrets or surprises?

Children are often reluctant to 'tell' because they have been told that what is happening is a secret. You could use activities such as puppet play or drama to help children understand that it is important that they don't keep secrets about things that worry them and the difference between 'secrets' and 'surprises' such as a birthday present.

Promoting independence and empowering children

Routines are a good way to get children to do things for themselves and empower them to make their

Figure 8.7: What strategies can you use to encourage children to dress themselves?

own decisions. To promote independence, encourage children to dress and wash themselves or clean their own bottoms. Never force children, but allow them to make decisions about their own care. Before carrying out care, always ask the child by saying, for example, 'Shall I help you to take off your wet pants?' As children develop, encourage them to make simple choices such as which dress to wear or which fruit to eat – and gradually they will learn that they have a right to make choices about their own bodies. Children who are self-reliant and feel that they can make their own decisions are less likely to be harmed or abused, because they are in control of their own personal and intimate care.

Reflect

1. Write a reflective account of two strategies that you have used when carrying out everyday routines that will help children to become more confident, independent and able to protect themselves.

2. Plan, implement and reflect on two activities that help children understand about their own bodies and where they can make decisions about themselves.

4 Understand how to respond to allegations that a child has been abused or harmed

It is always upsetting to find out that a child has been harmed or neglected but it is important that you respond appropriately. You may notice signs yourself, or you may be told something by a colleague, parent or carer – or the child. This can happen when you least expect it, so it is important that you make yourself familiar with your setting's policy and procedures in advance.

Responding to concerns

Parents or other adults may approach you to tell you that they are concerned a child may be being abused. This could happen when you are busy with children or other tasks, but their concerns need your attention straight away. If you ask them to see you later, they may be put off, lose courage or change their mind. If necessary, ask a colleague to take over.

When someone approaches you with this sort of concern:

- listen carefully to what they say, checking factual information such as what they saw or heard and when and where it happened
- avoid leading questions that would encourage them to give their own opinions, rather than the facts
- ask if they have told anyone else or spoken to the parent about their concerns
- make a note of what the person has told you as soon as possible and pass it to the professionals in the setting with child protection responsibilities (or to social services if you are a childminder).

The person may tell you that they are speaking in confidence and ask you not to pass on the information. You must let them know that you will need to share any information with your manager or the person who has designated responsibility for child protection in your setting.

The importance of believing children

Disclosures may come from children themselves. Children rarely lie about abuse. It can take a great deal of courage to tell someone. If a child chooses to tell you, it is because they trust you. Children may tell you directly or may hint that they are being harmed or abused. They may even 'tell' you through their drawings or their behaviour in their play. It is important that you accept what they are telling you or pick up on hints. Comments such as, 'Are you sure?' or, 'Oh I'm sure she wouldn't do that' might make it seem as if you are dismissing what a child is saying. Ignoring their hints may make children feel that it is their fault, or that the behaviour towards them is acceptable. They will not be likely to try to confide in you again – and they will continue to be at risk.

You should also think about how you would respond if a child tells you they are being abused. Your first response is very important, as it can affect how well a child copes. You must give the message that the child has done the right thing in telling you. For example, you could say, 'I'm glad that you have told me' or, 'You have done the right thing to let me know that you are worried.' You can also show that you understand their feelings by saying that it must have made them feel scared or unhappy.

However, it is important not to show your own emotions. Facial expressions and body language can give mixed messages. If you appear shocked, the child is likely to feel that they are in the wrong or even that they 'deserved' the abuse. The child's feelings are the most important ones, and these need to be recognised and acknowledged.

You must know what to do and what to say to the child – but it is also important to know what you should not do. Your responses should be open to avoid leading the child into giving a particular answer. You may feel angry with the abuser, but you should not make comments or pass judgements on the person who has been named. Instead, you should focus on reassuring the child that the action was wrong.

Always:

- take disclosure seriously
- remain calm and listen carefully without interrupting
- reassure the child that they are not to blame
- tell the child that you will have to tell someone who can help them
- write down what you have observed or what has been said as soon as possible
- pass information immediately to the lead professional who is responsible for child protection.

Never:

- show that you are shocked
- put children off by asking them to tell you later
- investigate or ask leading questions
- promise to keep what they tell you secret
- confront the abuser.

Case study 8.2

Amina is a key person in the baby room of a private nursery. One day as she was leaving work she was approached by one of the parents, Jennie. Jennie told Amina that she thought that one of the babies who attends the nursery was being left at night when his mother went out to work.

Jennie said that she wasn't too sure about her facts so asked Amina if she could 'keep an eye' on the baby for a while. She asked her not to say anything as she didn't want to cause trouble if she was mistaken.

1. How should Amina respond to Jennie and why?
2. What should Amina do next and why?

Roles and responsibilities of agencies that may be involved

All services that work with children and families have a shared responsibility and particular responsibilities towards children who have been abused or harmed.

Each service has **shared** and **specific** responsibilities.

Shared responsibilities

Shared responsibilities include:

- reporting concerns about child abuse
- contributing to assessments to ascertain the needs of children and the ability of their family to meet those needs
- sharing information
- contributing to a child protection plan
- supporting the plan to keep children safe and improve outcomes
- monitoring and reviewing strategies
- maintaining confidentiality.

Although services must work closely together, each service also has particular responsibilities, which are outlined next.

Specific responsibilities

Children's social care

Social workers have a key role to safeguard and promote the welfare of children who are in need. To do this they must work in partnership with children, parents and other agencies. Social workers lead on assessments at each stage of the child protection process, recording information and taking decisions (with their manager) on further action. They are also responsible for conducting interviews with children and parents.

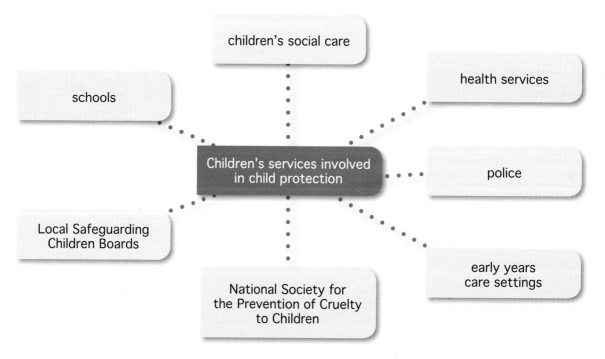

Figure 8.8: How do these services work together to protect children?

Police

All police forces have a Child Abuse Investigation Unit (CAIU), which has powers to take action such as removing the child or the perpetrator of abuse when the child is in immediate danger. The police gather evidence and interview suspected perpetrators when it is thought a crime has been committed. The police work closely with social workers.

Health professionals

Health professionals, particularly GPs and doctors in emergency departments, may examine children who have injuries they suspect to be non-accidental. They have a duty to alert children's social care when abuse is suspected. Health professionals carry out medical examinations when a crime has been committed, and may be called on to give evidence in court.

Early years professionals

All early years professionals must keep records of concerns or disclosures and if necessary present these to the case conference, to the Local Safeguarding Children Board or in a court hearing. Early years professionals carry out observations of the child's developmental needs to contribute to an assessment of needs. They put into place strategies identified in the child protection plan that relate to their own practice, and monitor the outcomes.

The National Society for the Prevention of Cruelty to Children (NSPCC)

The NSPCC is a charitable organisation that works to protect children from abuse. The NSPCC is the only charitable organisation with statutory power, alongside the police and children's social services, to take action when children are at risk of abuse. The NSPCC also:

- provides services to support families and children
- provides a helpline for people to call who are worried about a child
- provides a helpline for children in distress or danger
- raises awareness of abuse – for example, through advertising and training materials
- works to influence the law and social policy to better protect children
- shares expertise with other professionals.

Local Safeguarding Children Boards

In England and Wales, the 2004 Children Act requires there to be a Local Safeguarding Children Board (LSCB) in every local area. Each board is made up of experts from the range of children's services. The LSCB has a statutory duty to oversee the work of key agencies in the context of child protection.

An important aspect of the LSCB's work is to conduct a serious case review when a child dies as a result of abuse or neglect. The LSCB may undertake a review in particularly serious cases of sexual abuse or when a child has sustained a life-threatening injury.

How agencies work together to develop policy and procedure

Local Safeguarding Children Boards have a leading role in the development of policies and procedure for safeguarding and promoting children's welfare. Policy and procedure may concern:

- how and when to intervene when there are concerns about children
- the training requirements for people who work with children or in services that support children
- the recruitment of people who work with children
- investigations into allegations about people who work with children.

Early years settings have a statutory duty to pay regard to policies and procedures produced by the LSCB when writing policies and procedures for their own setting.

Figure 8.9: How do children's services work together to produce policies and procedures?

5 Be able to maintain confidentiality of information

The Data Protection Act 1998 protects personal and sensitive date that is obtained, stored and used by organisations including early years settings. For more information on the Data Protection Act (DPA), see learning outcomes 1 and 8 in Unit 7.

Processes to comply with data protection and handling legislation

To promote children's welfare and keep them safe, your setting needs to keep information about children and their families. This includes personal information such as their date of birth, address and GP's name, and sensitive information such as a child's additional needs. Your setting should have processes in place that are fair, transparent and in line with current legislation to keep this information safe. Remember that information flow is a two-way process – it is gathered from parents and others, and also shared with parents and others.

Processes in your setting need to relate to each stage of data handling:

- **gathering information** – how this is done, who contributes and the type of information
- **storing information** – where and how it is stored and who has access
- **sharing information** – who has a right to the information and how consent is sought
- **reviewing information** – how and when is it reviewed.

Gathering information

Before a child starts at your setting, information will need to be obtained from their parent or carer, including personal and contact details and any particular needs the child has. The parent and key person could meet to do this, with the key person making notes, or the parent could fill in a form. While the child is at your setting, further information will be gathered, such as observations of their development and health records.

The DPA states that information must be 'adequate, relevant and not excessive' – so you should only get the information needed to promote and protect the child's safety and wellbeing. For example, knowing that a child has a food allergy is essential, but details of the parent's health are not. The law also states that information must be 'accurate', so you must take care when recording the information.

Storing information

The law states that data must be kept safe and secure, so your setting must have adequate facilities to do this. Data may be stored on paper or electronically; often both methods are used. This means that there must be locked cabinets and a secure computer system that can only be accessed by people who have the right to do so.

Data is being gathered and used all the time, so there is a high risk of it being left lying around for others to see. You must return information as soon as you have obtained or used it. Sensitive information can only be accessed by professionals in your setting with safeguarding responsibilities, so it should be kept in its own file, separate from personal information.

Sharing information

Your setting must share the information it holds with parents, other professionals and children's services in order to maintain children's wellbeing. Information about children can only be shared with consent from their parent or legal guardian. Parents are usually asked to sign a form when the child enters the setting so that staff involved in their care can access personal information. Specific and limited consent would need to be obtained for sharing sensitive information with staff or outside agencies. The DPA states that information must be used 'fairly and lawfully' and for 'specific limited purposes'. For example, all staff would need to know that a child has a food allergy, but not all staff would need to know about the abuse of a child.

Reviewing information

Information must not 'be kept longer than necessary' and must be 'accurate' so your setting must have processes to ensure this. When parents tell you about any relevant change, information should be updated immediately. There should also be processes to review the information held about each child regularly.

When information can be shared

Normally, you can only pass on information told to you when consent has been given. The exception is when you believe that a child is at risk of abuse. You have a duty to pass on this information, but only to people who need to know – that is, only the people involved in child protection in your setting.

Sometimes it may be difficult for you to decide when to share information without consent. Here are some points you should consider.

- The child's welfare is the most important consideration. Ask yourself if, by not passing on information, a child might be at risk of harm.
- If a child or adult gives you information about concerns of abuse, you must pass this on. You should also tell the child or adult that you have to do this.
- Information that is passed on must be accurate, up to date and relevant.

If you are unsure when and how to pass information on, it is essential that you get advice from your manager and lead professional with responsibility for child protection or social services.

6 Be able to maintain the safety and security of children in own work setting

Risk assessment

You have a responsibility to maintain the health and safety of children and to reduce risk. Risk assessment plays an important role in the maintenance of a safe and secure environment, so you must know how to carry out a risk assessment in your setting.

Case study 8.3

Read the following scenarios and decide if the professional should obtain consent from a parent to pass on information.

- Paula works in a private nursery. She has noticed that Zayn's speech is not developing as expected for a 3 year old. She believes that his development could be helped by a speech therapist. The speech therapist will be coming into the setting in a few days' time and she intends to pass on Zayn's details.

- Marc is a reception class teacher. He has noticed that Abi, aged 4 years, who used to be very bubbly has become very withdrawn. Abi has had frequent bruises recently but her mum explained to Marc that she has a new bike that she is learning to ride. She is often collected from the class by an older brother aged 16 and Marc has noticed that she shows reluctance to go with him. Yesterday she cried, telling Marc that she wanted to wait for mum. Marc decides that he should pass on this information.

- Arisha works as a childminder. Next week one of the children she looks after, Mia, will be 4 years old. Mia's mum said that she intends to invite all the children to Mia's birthday party. Arisha decides that it would be helpful to pass on the parents' telephone numbers.

- Kalim, aged 3 years, is an outgoing boy. He loves to play in the home corner at the nursery. Recently Sara, his key person, has been concerned because he is displaying overtly sexual behaviour, touching the girls in an inappropriate way and using sexual language. She decides to pass this information on.

For more information on risk assessments, see learning outcome 7 in Unit 7. The five stages of risk assessment in Figure 8.10 will remind you of the staged process you should follow.

A good starting point is to walk around your setting observing any potential hazards – in the environment itself or relating to an activity that is taking place. Then read the policy for risk assessment from your setting. This may include a template that you could use. If not, you could produce your own, modelled on Figure 8.10.

Remember that the purpose of risk assessment is not to prevent children from taking part in challenging activities or to inhibit their curiosity, but to balance this with controls and procedures to reduce risks to their safety.

Policies and procedures for keeping children safe

A safeguarding policy is a statement that explains the setting's commitment to keeping children safe and promoting their welfare. Policies must meet the requirements of the legislation and mandatory guidance described in learning outcome 1 of this unit, and those of the LSCB policy and procedure.

Procedures give you clear, step-by-step guidance on how to achieve the aims set out in the policy. For example, the policy may state that the setting has a commitment to maintaining confidentiality and that data relating to children and their families will be kept safe. Procedures will give guidance on when and how information may be shared, how to record and store information and who may access it.

Different requirements for safeguarding may be in one policy or a number of separate ones, but overall they should cover:

- **confidentiality** – procedures for gathering, maintenance and sharing of information with colleagues, outside agencies and parents
- **reporting** – procedures for reporting concerns about a child's safety and welfare in the setting, their home or another setting

RISK ASSESSMENT				
Date:		Carried out by:		
Hazard/activity	Risk	Persons who could be injured	Controls to minimise risk	Date for review

Figure 8.10: How would you use or adapt this template to carry out your own risk assessment?

- **recruitment of staff**
- **staff training** in safeguarding and child protection
- **risk assessment** – including monitoring and review of controls
- **procedures for reporting poor and unsafe practice** (whistle blowing)
- **e-safety** – restrictions and monitoring procedures for computers, mobile phones and cameras
- **complaints** – procedures for dealing with complaints from parents, staff and others.

Find the balance

Make a list of the policies and procedures relevant to your own role. For each, make a note of how you have implemented it in your setting. For example, have you taken part in safeguarding training? How has this supported you in your role?

Supporting children's resilience and wellbeing

'Resilience' describes how well children deal with things that happen in their lives. Change may be caused by expected life events (such as starting school) or unexpected life events (such as illness or the death of a person close to them).

You cannot prevent change in children's lives, nor would you want to. As much as you try to protect children, they will still have to cope with events that may trouble them. However, you can support children's resilience and wellbeing to help them overcome difficulties and come to terms with events. Table 8.2 lists some ways to help support children's resilience and wellbeing.

Reporting procedures for poor practice or safety concerns

There are procedures for checking the suitability of staff before they start to work with children – but you still need to be vigilant. The EYFS identifies practice and behaviours that should raise cause for concern, such as not following safe practice, undertaking tasks that are not within one's own responsibilities or

Table 8.2: Ways of supporting children's resilience and wellbeing.

Method of support	What this means in practice
Help children see that change is part of life	• Help children prepare for expected life events by encouraging them to try out new things. • Talk to children about events that have happened or are expected to happen – this will help them share their anxieties and come to terms with their feelings. • Stories about children who have dealt with unexpected events, such as bereavement, are a way of helping children to explore change and develop ways of coping.
Provide a safe and secure environment with familiar routines	• Children need to feel safe and secure. A familiar environment gives children this sense of security. • Feeling secure is particularly important when there are other things happening in children's lives that they do not understand. • Routines help children understand what is happening now and anticipate what will happen next.
Build strong, trusting relationships	• Having a strong bond with an adult outside of their family is important for building children's resilience. • It is important for children to have a trusted person to keep them informed about what is happening and what is likely to happen to them.
Help children to be in control, become independent and make decisions	• Children need opportunities to make their own decisions and solve their problems to help them to feel in control of each situation. • Consult children about what they want to happen and how they will be supported. • Get children involved in tasks and helping others to promote their independence.
Promote children's confidence and self-esteem	• Children who feel confident in their own ability will be able to overcome challenges and difficulties. • Use frequent praise – this helps children feel good about themselves. • Point out things that children can do and how they are progressing – this helps children develop a 'can do' attitude.

capabilities, or showing inappropriate behaviour such as making sexual comments or giving a child excessive attention. It is also a cause for concern if a member of staff is under the influence of alcohol or drugs.

Your setting must have policy and procedures in place for reporting concerns (whistle blowing) about staff or other adults from outside agencies who work in or visit your setting.

Reflect

In 2009, Vanessa George was found guilty of sexually abusing young children in her care at a nursery where she had worked for three years. Even though she had begun to take children to a separate area to change them in private, none of the staff had raised concerns about her behaviour. During a review it was found that there was no whistle-blowing policy in place in the setting.

Read about what happened and the subsequent recommendations that were made in the serious case review on the Plymouth City Council website.

Never ignore poor practice or assume that someone else will notice. Read the procedures in your setting and reflect on how these would help you to:

- **report concerns** – for example, setting out in writing what it is about the person's practice or behaviour that may be putting children at risk of harm or abuse
- **know who to report concerns to** – for example, the manager or the professional with responsibility for safeguarding
- **gain support or advice after reporting concerns** – in line with the protection given under the UK Public Interest Disclosure Act 1998.

Your setting's policy should also include:

- information on what happens following an allegation, including the investigation and if appropriate the disciplinary procedures

- procedures for reporting to the Disclosure and Barring Service that a member of staff has been dismissed because they have put a child at risk or have harmed them.

Although childminders do not have to have written procedures, they must by law report any allegations about any person in the home setting to Ofsted or their childminding agency.

Further reading and resources

Websites

- Foundation Years: www.foundationyears.org.uk/eyfs – a useful section of this website for resources, information and support on the EYFS
- Ofsted: www.ofsted.gov.uk – for information about EYFS Ofsted requirements and the schedule for inspections of early years providers
- Professional Association for Childcare and Early Years: www.pacey.org.uk – a standard-setting organisation that promotes best practice and supports childcare practitioners to deliver high standards of care and learning
- Department for Education publications: www.education.gov.uk
  - » *Working Together to Safeguard Children* (2013)
  - » *Safeguarding Disabled Children* (2009)
  - » *What to do if you're worried a child is being abused* (2006)
- National Society for the Prevention of Cruelty to Children: www.nspcc.gov.uk – charity dedicated to ending cruelty to children in the UK
- Barnardo's: www.barnardos.org.uk – charity working to transform the lives of the most vulnerable children across the UK through services, campaigning and research
- Kidscape: www.kidscape.org.uk – UK charity established specifically to prevent bullying and child sexual abuse
- National Association for People Abused in Childhood: www.napac.org.uk – provides advice and support for people abused in childhood through bullying advice, a helpline, information, anti-bullying resources and training

Partnership working in early years

All early years settings need to work in partnership with parents or carers and other professionals in order to be able to meet the needs of all children. Parents are the most important primary educators of their child. They have a wealth of knowledge, which needs to be shared to support children making the transition into the setting and throughout their learning and development.

Before you start

Some children need extra support to reach their full potential and early years practitioners need to work together to achieve this.

How many colleagues does your setting work with to support the children you care for? Think of some recent examples where you and a colleague have worked together to support an individual child. What did you do? Was the experience positive? Would you do anything differently next time?

Learning outcomes

By the end of this unit you will:

1. understand how to work in partnership in early years settings
2. be able to work in partnership in early years settings
3. be able to work with parents and/or carers in early years settings.

1 Understand how to work in partnership in early years settings

As well as being be able to work effectively with colleagues in early years settings, you need to understand how and why this is important for children. You should understand the roles and responsibilities of colleagues you work with, so that you know how their involvement might lead to better outcomes for children. (For more information about this, see 'The roles and responsibilities of colleagues' later in this learning outcome.)

Parents' experiences, views and rights also have an impact on partnership working. (You will find out more about people who might work in partnership with early years settings in the roles and responsibilities section of this unit.) You need to consider these fully to help give children the best possible start in life.

Policies, procedures and guidance

All early years settings have a duty to work with parents and other professionals to support children's care, learning and development. In England, this is a legal responsibility under the statutory framework for the Early Years Foundation Stage (EYFS).

Relevant policies and procedures

Special educational needs and/or disabilities

All settings have a responsibility to ensure that children with special educational needs or disabilities (SEND) have their needs met. This might mean making reasonable changes, such as employing an extra member of staff or adapting the environment. Sometimes the extent of a child's needs is not clear until they start at your setting. The EYFS framework makes it clear that you must think about whether children need specialist support and must support families to seek appropriate help.

Your settings may have an inclusion or equality of opportunity policy, with procedures for providing access and support for children with specific needs. This may involve having a named member of staff to take responsibility for working with them, usually known as a special educational needs coordinator, or SENCO. Their role usually includes referring children to specialists outside the setting after consulting the parents. Your policy might also outline the setting's responsibility to help parents find extra support themselves – for example, by giving them details of the local health visitors or speech and language therapists.

Working with parents and carers

Your setting may have a policy and procedure for working with parents and carers, outlining intentions and ways of working. This might outline how the setting values them and wants to include them in children's learning and development. Under the EYFS framework, you need to take into account observations that parents or carers share with you. Most settings will want to make sure that they include them as much as possible in children's learning. Ways to do this include holding parent consultations or asking parents to share special achievements they have observed at home.

There are other important times when you need to work closely with parents, such as sharing information about care needs, discussing medication and accidents, or deciding when a child might need further support. When you are completing the progress check for children aged between 2 and 3, you need to make sure that parents have the chance to contribute their own knowledge of their child's abilities.

Key person

The EYFS framework also explains the requirement for all early years settings to assign a specific key person to each child. In its policies and procedures, your setting may explain how their key person approach works in practice, with examples of how the key person works with families and other professionals, and how key groups are decided. The role of the key person varies from setting to setting and even, in larger nurseries, from room to room.

The procedure might also outline what steps would be taken if the key person needed to change, perhaps because staff leave or the child has formed a closer attachment to another member of staff.

Guidance in the setting

Each setting will have its own guidance about partnership working. It might be the sole responsibility of senior staff to liaise with outside professionals. However, you also have a role to play in sharing information about children's learning and development with other staff and parents. It is important that you follow your setting's guidance, so that parents and professionals have consistent information. Incomplete or inconsistent information could confuse or get in the way of effective partnership working.

How integrated working delivers better outcomes

Integrated working happens when all those involved in supporting children and families work together, putting children's needs and rights first. When everyone

> **Jargon buster**
>
> **Integrated working** – all those involved in working together, in a coordinated way.

works together, children get consistent care. This makes them more likely to be able to make good progress, particularly in areas where they need extra support.

Case study 9.1

Claire is an early years practitioner covering for staff absence in the toddler room. When Lauren's mum dropped her off at nursery two weeks ago, she mentioned to Claire that she was worried about Lauren's speech. Over the weekend, Lauren had played with her cousin who was 6 months younger. Her mum had noticed that he used many more words than Lauren. Claire promised she would speak with Lauren's key person later that day.

Claire discussed Lauren's speech with her key person, who said she had noticed that Lauren wasn't saying many words and that she uses pointing to express herself. After speaking with Claire, the key person made a note of this to discuss with Lauren's parents at her upcoming progress review. She also decided to ask the nursery SENCO to attend the review.

Two months later, Claire was covering in the toddler room again when Lauren was dropped off by her dad. He handed Claire an information sheet from the speech and language therapist with games to play at nursery to help promote her speech. He said he had noticed that her speech had started to improve already. Claire observed that Lauren copied her, saying, 'Bye-bye, Daddy,' as she waved him off.

1. What did Claire do to help Lauren to get the support she needed?

2. What action do you think was taken as a result of Lauren's progress review with her parents?

3. What was the impact of the action taken and how did it benefit Lauren?

Better outcomes for children

The benefit of ensuring that all those involved in children's care work together is that they can all play their part in helping children to achieve the same outcome.

One example is when children are toilet training. When children are starting to master this complicated stage of development, all those who care for them should use the same approach. Parents, early years practitioners and particularly key people need to share information and recognise the signs that the child needs to use the toilet. Sharing information will help parents decide whether current approaches are working.

Children are more likely to receive the care they need meaning they will not feel excluded.

With integrated working, each individual can share their particular area of knowledge or expertise. For example, you may find caring for a child with a severe food allergy for the first time daunting, but a dietician may have seen many cases before. They can support you and other staff to make sure there are plans in place for the child's snack and meals.

Better outcomes for families

Parents and families feel reassured that children are receiving the care they need.

It can be upsetting for parents to hand over their child to someone else to care for, especially if the child has specific needs. When you work with professionals who are already involved with the family, the family can be reassured that the care is consistent.

Families are often relieved if they have had a concern about children's learning or development that an early years practitioner recognises.

Parents might have concerns about an aspect of their child's learning and development and could feel supported when staff identify this too. They might have been unsure how to seek support, so when your setting refers children to other professionals or signposts them to parents, it may be a huge relief.

The responsibilities of partnership working

You have a responsibility to work with integrity and to a high standard in partnership with others.

Respect the views and opinions of others

When working in partnership with others, there is bound to be a range of differing views. This can be difficult to manage. However, regardless of whether or not you agree with the views of others, it is important that you respect their views and opinions. (For more information on the difficulties, see later in this learning outcome.)

Be non-judgemental

It is important that all those who work together adopt a non-judgemental approach. Working with other professionals you will encounter people with different qualifications, experience and skills. You should not make assumptions about what other professionals do or do not know. For example, a highly qualified member of staff will have in-depth general knowledge, but may

not know as much about a specific child as their key person. Similarly, an unqualified member of staff might not have had formal training, but might have a wealth of personal experience in supporting children.

> ### Jargon buster
>
> **Integrity** – the quality of being honest and having strong moral principles.
>
> **Non-judgemental** – not critical of others, not judging what they do.

Maintain confidentiality

Working with children and families you will become party to information that needs to be kept confidential. Working in partnership with others you may not be told all information. Generally, information is shared on a 'need-to-know basis' – if you don't need to know it, you may not be told it. You should respect this. The information discussed among professionals is sufficient to make sure children and families get the support they need, but outside of professional circles information must be kept completely confidential. There may be special ways to exchange information to help maintain confidentiality, and it is essential that you follow the guidance you are given.

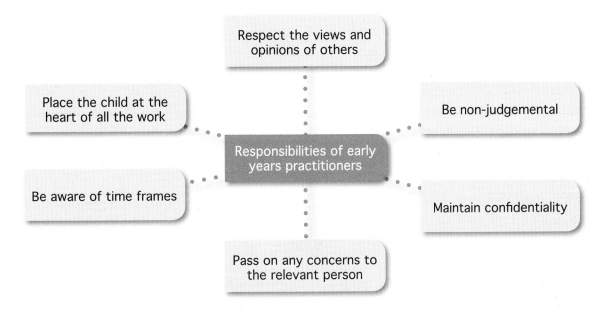

Figure 9.1: Do you know your main responsibilities as an early years practitioner?

Pass on concerns

It is important that you pass on information to the right professional. Some aspects of work may fall outside your remit, or you may not feel able to deal with them. You must be confident in passing on any concerns, particularly about safeguarding.

Be aware of timeframes

This is a basic but very important aspect of partnership working. All professionals are busy people, governed by timeframes – whether it's to complete a child's progress file or to meet a deadline for a funding application. If you have been given a task, it is important to complete it in the given timeframe. Delays could have a serious impact and stop children and families getting the support they need. The same applies to attending meetings. Be on time. People have busy schedules and may have to start without you, meaning you miss vital information or, worse, cannot share something important.

Place children at the heart of your work

This is obvious, but can never be overstated. Sometimes, the right thing to do is not the easiest. For example, you may find it hard to share difficult information with parents with whom you have developed a close professional relationship, such as discussing a child's negative behaviour. However, it is essential that you communicate freely and clearly to support children to make good progress.

The roles and responsibilities of colleagues

In integrated working you are likely to come into contact with a wide range of professionals (see Table 9.1). You may not be familiar with their titles, but it is

Jargon buster

Cohort – group of children with a common feature, such as age or class.

Table 9.1: Roles and responsibilities of early years practitioners.

Colleague	Role	Responsibilities
Special educational needs coordinator (SENCO)	Organise the care of children with special educational needs	• Support parents and carers of children who have special educational needs • May train or advise other staff • May contact other professionals and make referrals to outside agencies • Usually involved in developing individual plans for children's care and learning • May support transition between settings when children move on
Key person	Take individual responsibility for working with a child or group of children	• Usually meets and greets parents when they are settling in • First point of contact for parents and carers • Usually responsible for observing and assessing the child and organising their learning journals • Develop close bonds of attachment with children as they spend most time with them
Early years teacher	Promote the education of babies and young children	• Vary significantly from setting to setting • Usually plan, deliver and monitor the quality of teaching and learning in a setting • May offer advice and guidance to other staff or be responsible for delivery themselves • May be responsible for tracking cohorts of children
Early years professional	Lead and shape the quality of early years practice	• Vary greatly from setting to setting • May be responsible for the setting in a managerial or leadership role • May work with more than one setting and advise other early years educators about teaching and learning • Usually monitors the work of others in some way

Continued

Continued

Colleague	Role	Responsibilities
Teacher	Educate children in schools	• Responsible for delivering the National Curriculum and sometimes the Early Years Foundation Stage • Provides children with the knowledge they need to pass through school life successfully • Teaches numeracy and literacy among other subjects and measures the progress children make
Social worker	Support children and families during times of difficulty	• Helps families to stay together by guiding them and offering extra support at difficult times • Sometimes has to take the difficult decision to remove children to ensure they receive the care and support they need or to protect them from harm
Police liaison	Provide a link between police work within the community and children and families	• There might be differing roles a police liaison undertakes • May go to a setting on a matter of child protection (for more information on child protection, see Unit 8) • May go to a setting to help children understand police are available to help them and learn about safety issues, such as road safety and 'stranger danger' • May go to a setting to advise parents about road safety and parking or to alleviate concerns about local crime
Family support worker	Give families emotional and sometimes practical support (perhaps attached to children's centres, schools or nurseries)	• Usually supports families who have extra needs – for example, the arrival of a new baby, parents separating or dealing with children's illness or difficult behaviour • Not usually involved in making decisions, but may contribute to assessments
Health visitor	Support children and families with advice on issues such as immunisation, feeding and weaning	• Often takes over support and guidance to families after the midwife – so usually develops relationships with families with young children • May support mothers suffering from postnatal depression • May weigh children and check to make sure they are developing well • Later, responsible for continuing to monitor the growth and development of very young children
Speech and language therapist	Assess children's ability to talk and communicate and provide strategies for overcoming communication delay and difficulty	• Helps children who have speech delay or a stammer – but also do much more • Supports children who had an operation on their mouth, have problems feeding or have hearing difficulties • Provides exercises and games to help a child develop their speech and communication skills
Dietician	Advise and support individuals to make healthy food choices	• Usually works within hospitals or the community • Helps children and families understand the right food for them to eat • May develop an eating plan or list of foods that can and cannot be eaten, perhaps because a child has an allergy or intolerance, has a medical condition such as diabetes, or needs to lose weight
Educational psychologist	Study children to determine whether they have a special educational need and advise early years practitioners about support	• Gets to know children, building up a picture of their behaviour and needs • Assesses whether they have a special educational need • Suggests ways early years staff can help the child make progress in their learning and development
Counsellor	Help children and families to understand their feelings and emotions by talking	• Helps children and families to talk about things that are difficult or painful in order for them to understand them better • Helps individuals to understand why they feel the way they feel, without offering solutions

Unit 9

213

important that you have a basic understanding of their roles and responsibilities so that you know how they can support your work with children.

The difficulties of working in a multidisciplinary team

As you have seen, when all professionals work together in a **multidisciplinary** team, they achieve better outcomes for children. However, working with other professionals is not always easy.

Figure 9.2: What challenges might you face while working as part of a multidisciplinary team?

Personalities

Some personalities clash, for all sorts of reasons. For example, it could be that you feel someone dominates discussions or doesn't listen to others, which makes it difficult for you to get along with them. You can't get along with everyone you work with, but it is essential that you always show professional courtesy and respect. Remember that your shared aim is to work together for the benefit of children. Establishing ground

rules and agreeing good practice can help alleviate the problems created when personalities clash.

Differing opinions

When professionals come together, they bring along a wealth of knowledge and experience. This is what makes multidisciplinary teams so effective – but it makes them challenging too. For example, professionals may have differing ideas about how to diagnose a child's needs and what way forward to suggest, but they need to agree in order to give consistent messages to the parents and the setting. Agreeing a care plan can take time, and you may feel that important time is being wasted. However, it is vital that all those who contribute towards children's care feel that they have been able to share their views and ideas.

Availability and time

Coordinating meetings can be difficult when people are busy. People may not be available because of their working hours or other commitments. It is important that everyone who can be flexible is flexible. In order to get professionals together, you might need to attend evening meetings or arrange for cover during the day. Some professionals may only be able to attend for a limited time, but a structured agenda can enable them to say what they need before leaving. Meetings should have clear aims. Everyone who attends will have to be accommodating and respectful of timeframes, and must stick to the agenda. Some professionals might waffle or talk about issues unrelated to the objective of the meeting. Focusing on the aim will help you avoid this.

It can be frustrating when you are waiting for a response or report from another professional if this is delaying access to support for children. Having deadlines for actions makes everyone aware of their responsibility and means it is easier for you to ask people to move things along.

The impact of parents' rights

Families come in all shapes and sizes and it is vital to respect and uphold the rights of all parents when working with children. This will often involve finding out more about families and how best you can help parents feel included.

Parental rights

Parents must always be your first point of contact and discussion when raising concerns about children's learning, development and wellbeing. It is important that you establish productive working relationships with parents who are partners in children's care and education. You should not take any action without discussing and agreeing it first with parents (except where there are child protection concerns). Some parents might be reluctant, and it is the role of your setting to find ways to share information and communicate that parents are comfortable with. The setting must always uphold parents' wishes and views, unless a child may be at risk of harm by doing so.

Reflect

1. How does your setting support parents who are living apart? Is there equal information sharing between both parents?

2. What extra measures does your setting put into place to help all parents to feel included and welcomed?

You might like to use these questions to develop a plan for improving parent partnerships.

Working parents

Some parents work long hours and rely on childminders and nannies to care for their children on a day-to-day basis. Often these parents can't attend appointments and activities during the day. Communicating through their caregivers is acceptable for passing on information, but working families need to have an opportunity to contribute to their children's learning and feel part of the process. Some settings have introduced weekend workshops and parent consultations to make sure that all parents have a chance to come to the setting.

Looked-after children

Some children are not able to live with their parents, for a short or longer period. Remember that, where parents retain parental responsibility, you need to value and respect their wishes. Your setting needs to make sure that information is shared with these parents and that they are consulted about any change in care, along with the child's caregiver. You should make every effort to welcome parents who are not caring for their children – for example, by having meetings and discussions at times when children are not present.

Jargon buster

Estranged parents – parents not living with their child.

Multidisciplinary – covering a range of different professions or services.

Parental responsibility – all the rights, duties, powers and responsibility that a parent of a child has in relation to the child and his or her property.

Estranged parents

As part of settling-in procedures, your setting should establish who the child lives with. If parents live apart, your setting should find out what access the child has to their estranged parent. If you are the key person, this could be your role.

When parents live apart, it is good practice to invite both parents to attend settling-in sessions. If parents can't attend together, you might be able to arrange a separate session for the parent who does not normally live with the child. This benefits the child as both parents will find out about the new environment and can give their support. It also establishes from the start that both parents are welcome and can feel included in the child's learning and development.

This approach should continue. This might mean arranging two parent consultations, or sending out two copies of progress reports and two newsletters,

Figure 9.3: How can you make sure that all parents feel welcomed and included in their children's care and education?

for example. Don't take it for granted that one parent will pass information to the other; it is the duty of the setting, not the parents, to organise this.

Same-sex parents

Some children might have same-sex parents. Here it is important to establish the family arrangements early on, and definitely before the child starts at the setting. This should include what children call their parents and whether they have contact with any other parent.

The impact of parents' views and experiences

Parents can't share their views if there are no structures in place to help them do so. You may need to find different ways of communicating with different parents.

Parents can contribute their views by:

- joining a parent partnership group or committee
- completing questionnaires about the quality of care and education
- giving their ideas in suggestion or comments boxes

- contributing to a wishlist for resources
- being involved in fundraising
- attending steering meetings about important changes
- sharing their observations of their child's learning at home, so that these can be included in the child's development profile
- being able to discuss and challenge staff evaluations of children's progress.

Case study 9.2

Some parents at Little Chickens Nursery have noticed that some children are playing boisterously, sometimes leading to younger children getting pushed over and hurt. The children do not say sorry when this happens. While waiting to collect children at the end of the day, the parents have discussed how they manage children's behaviour at home.

The parents have told staff that they use a 'naughty step' at home, where children sit on their own for a short time so they know they have been naughty. The parents have asked the nursery to use a naughty step for the children if they play too roughly.

Two weeks later, the nursery has not introduced the naughty step. A well-meaning parent has brought two child-sized steps for the nursery to use. However, when she gives them to a member of staff, she is told that a naughty step does not conform to the nursery's positive behaviour management policy.

1. Why do you think the setting did not respond to parent's views and experiences on this occasion?

2. How might this situation have been handled better by staff at the nursery?

3. What action plans could be drawn up along with parents, to support children's behaviour?

Table 9.2: Possible impacts of parental experience on partnership working.

Parental experiences	How this impacts on partnership working	Good practice
Being a first-time parent	The parent will have no experience to draw on; everything may be new for them. They may not understand what is expected of them.	• Help all parents understand clearly how they can contribute – for example, by showing them documents, or reminding them of groups or events they can be involved with.
Having had a poor experience of another setting in the past	The parent might be mistrustful of the staff, distant and not find it easy to establish a working relationship.	• Encourage the parent to build a relationship with their child's key person. • Give the parent extra time and reassurance.
Having strongly held views on parenting or religion that affect their expectations	The parent may have expectations or a desire for the setting to operate in a way that differs from the setting's policy.	• Make sure that policies and procedures are freely available and easy to read. • Make sure parents know, understand and agree to follow the policies and procedures that underpin the work of staff.
Having had negative experiences with education or professionals	The parent might be wary of staff and fail to disclose important information through fear of being judged.	• Be clear and honest about why you need to know certain information. • Help the parent by sharing in ways they find comfortable, such as text message or email.
Wanting to be highly involved because of previous work or experiences	The parent might be able to share their enthusiasm and experiences for the benefit of the setting.	• Find useful ways to use parent's knowledge and skills, such as fundraising projects. • Welcome ideas and show they are of value by seeking opinions or trialling ideas.

Table 9.2 gives a range of experiences that parents or carers may have had and shows the potential impact of these on partnership working.

2 Be able to work in partnership in early years settings

It is important that you not only understand, but also can apply the practices and procedures of partnership working. You need to develop a wide range of skills and be able to stick to strict codes of practice in relation to confidentiality.

Working in partnership

You need to be able to plan and reflect on your work with other colleagues and professionals in order to be able to develop and improve. A good way to approach this is to think about who you work with and why. You might like to develop a plan for partnership working with other professionals like the one shown in Figure 9.4.

You may be able to adapt the same approach for reflecting on your work with other professionals. If you don't usually work with other professionals, you could think about what other professionals you are aware of and how you could engage with them to support children. Reading through Erica's summary might give you some ideas.

Find the balance

Erica, Early Years Practitioner: 'I had seen many different people come in and out of the setting and knew that they were supporting different children but I wasn't ever involved. Then last week I did a water play activity and noticed that one of our children who has special educational needs took part for the first time. I made a note of this and showed my line manager. She suggested that I talk about it with the SENCO. I did, and he asked me to repeat the activity and observe the child again. The SENCO included my observations in the child's individual learning plan and discussed them with the parents and the speech and language therapist at the child's review meeting.'

Plan for partnership working

Week beginning:

Which colleagues will I work with this week?

Name and job title	Why I need to work with them	What they need from me
Room leader	To take guidance about duties and any issues which arise (e.g. making sure parents have returned permission slips for farm trip)	List of names of any children who have not returned their permission forms. Feedback about any individual children if needed, feedback from any parents if needed

Reflection

How did I do?

Were there any issues which meant that I needed to seek further advice or support from colleagues?

One thing which I did well this week was:

My target for working with colleagues next week is:

Figure 9.4: How can a plan like this help you to work effectively with other people?

Following laws and codes to maintain confidentiality

Information about children and families is sensitive. You need to make sure that you help to protect children and families from the risk of their information being shared with the wrong people or misused. This could have serious implications for children and their parents. Here are some examples.

- Children and families might experience prejudice or discrimination.

- Families could lose trust and confidence, damaging their relationship with the setting.

- The information could lead to children not getting the care they need.

- In the wrong hands, information could lead to criminal activity such as identity theft, or to safeguarding concerns, putting children and families at risk.

Your setting will probably have a policy and procedure on confidentiality. Many settings insist that staff read and sign this to be sure they abide by it. Some teams of professionals will reinforce their policies or codes of conduct at the beginning of meetings and discussions by reminding those present of their responsibility to maintain confidentiality. Some documents, such as medical reports and assessments, might need to be stored more securely. When you are photocopying material, take care not to leave it on the copier, and destroy any partial or damaged copies in a suitable way.

Legislation

The Information Commissioner's Office (ICO) is an independent authority that works to uphold information rights in the public interest. It offers guidance to individuals and organisations, and keeps a register of who gathers information about people, to make sure they process information according to the Data Protection Act 1998 (DPA).

The DPA covers the handling of other people's information. It sets out some basic principles, such as:

- excessive information should not be gathered
- information must be kept securely
- information should not be exchanged with anyone who does not need to know it.

This is the legal framework all professionals must adhere to, including you.

Personal responsibility

All professionals working with children and families have responsibilities in their work that extend into their private life. You must think carefully about the information you put in the public domain, especially via social media, such as Facebook or Twitter.

Your setting may have policies and procedures outlining the expectations of staff not to discuss their work. Even if children's and families' names are not mentioned, information about supporting children and families can unintentionally lead to individuals being identified. This can cause distress and upset.

Case study 9.3

Tiana and Safia had been friends before they started working at Prickles Day Nursery together. After an argument while out at the weekend, both started to post negative comments about each other on a social networking site. Each made accusations about the other, escalating into a slanging match littered with swear words. By Monday morning, they had forgotten the argument and become friends again.

However, the comments were seen by a parent who is a friend of one of Tiana's friends and by the manager of the nursery who is a friend of another work colleague who Safia has as a friend. The parent has made a formal complaint as she feels that neither should be working with children because of the accusations made. The manager is concerned about the impact on the good reputation of the nursery.

Both Tiana and Safia are now waiting to see what action will be taken and cannot believe that such a silly argument has caused so much trouble for them both.

1. Why do you think the parent is so concerned about the comments she read on the social networking site?

2. What action do you think the manager should take?

3. Why do you think such incidents might damage the reputation of the nursery?

3 Be able to work with parents and/or carers in early years settings

All settings must work with parents and carers to help children experience good transitions in and out of the setting, make consistent progress in their learning and development, and be happy and settled with the staff who care for them.

Guiding parents and carers to take an active role

Engaging parents actively and successfully is vital to children's ability to do well and make good progress. You should encourage parents to feel comfortable and confident in engaging in a two-way flow of information with you.

Play and learning

Parents need to be able to understand the benefits for children of learning through meaningful play. It is helpful for them to understand children's play: for example, the different stages and types of play children might exhibit. You need to be creative and find ways for parents to engage in play themselves, so they can understand how important it is for children.

You could help parents to learn about play by:

- inviting them to stay-and-play sessions
- inviting them to share a talent, or cultural aspect of their religion
- having 'at home activities' – setting challenges for children to complete at home with their parents
- inviting parents to 'Messy Mondays' or 'Sensory Saturdays', when they can come with their children to take part in activities such as playing with different messy media
- having 'Today's play' display boards for parents to read, outlining some of the benefits of the activities they have enjoyed that day
- having a 'What's in the bag?' activity, when children pick a simple object, such as a toilet roll tube, for parents and children to use in role play at home.

As parents begin to understand more about play, they will see what children learn from it. You can offer parents guidance about the EYFS framework, in bite-sized, easy-to-read chunks, with details about where to find further information. This will help them understand the range of learning that takes place in your setting, and at home too.

Figure 9.5: Why do people say that play is children's work?

Development

You need to reassure parents that assessment of a child's development is not a race to achieve goals. Children develop at their own rate and each child will be very different from the next, with different areas of strength. Parents can be anxious about how well their child is progressing, and often compare their own child with the child of friends or relatives, which can be unhelpful. You need to help them focus on their individual child's development, while using milestones (such as those outlined in the Department of Education's *Early Years Outcomes*) to help monitor whether a child needs specific support. You can identify a child's next steps in learning and share these with parents, then focus together on the aspects of learning that best help the child to move forward.

Recognising and valuing parents' contributions

It is important that settings do not just ask for parents' contributions, but value and respect them too.

Parenting has a big impact on children's wellbeing and ability to be successful in their learning. The more effective the partnerships with parents, the better the outcomes for children.

Health

Children's health can be a cause for concern for parents. They might have read or heard conflicting information about what is best for children. An example of this was the effect of media reporting on immunisations in 1998. Parents concluded that the measles, mumps and rubella immunisation was unsafe due to widespread reporting of a now-discredited research paper. Many decided not to immunise their children, some of whom went on to contract the illnesses.

Parents want what is best for their children, but sometimes misinterpret guidance or make bad decisions due to lack of understanding. Obesity among young children is a concern for medical professionals. Your healthy eating advice needs to be consistent and helpful. For example, rather than simply telling parents what can't be in children's lunchboxes, explain why and suggest alternatives.

Parents also need to know the benefits of outdoor play to understand why children are encouraged to be outside in winter months or when it is raining.

You need to tackle parents' attitudes to their children's health sensitively and with full knowledge of any cultural or personal beliefs, as well as of any medical conditions. If parents want their child to follow a vegan diet, you need to understand their reasoning and respect their wishes. Any advice and guidance you give should not assume that parents deliberately or willingly make bad choices for children's health. Instead, you should encourage discussion and understanding.

Wellbeing

Parents know their child best. Coming to your setting may be the first time that parent and child have been apart for regular periods. Parents will be in the best position to predict how children may react, so you should base your planning for the transition around what they expect. Give parents the opportunity to share the child's home routines and help your setting to accommodate these. What happens at home will affect children's wellbeing. The more open the relationship between the setting and the parent is, the better you can plan for changes or events that may unsettle the child.

Children's sense of identity and self-esteem will be developed through their associations with other people and their relationships within their families. You can promote children's sense of wellbeing by finding out about, and valuing, their individual identities and backgrounds. (For more information on diversity, equality and inclusion, see Unit 3.)

Learning and development

You need to make sure that you promote and welcome the information parents and carers share about children's learning and development. One way to reflect on the effectiveness of this process is to review what information you gather and how you use it.

Information when a child first starts at the setting
Think about what information you gather, why and how it is used.

Does the information include:

- a breakdown of the child's home routines?
- the child's likes and dislikes?
- their favourite toys, comfort items or comforting habits?
- their family's beliefs, celebrations and values?
- their current interests?
- who is involved in their daily lives – friends, family, siblings and pets?
- the parents' assessments of their child's stage of development and any areas where they need extra support?

After gathering all this information, you will be able to evaluate how it is used. For example, do you use parents' assessments of learning as starting points to build on? Do you use daily routines to plan an individual timetable for the child? Do you plan for children's interests using the information parents have shared?

Ongoing sharing of information

After parents have shared all this useful information, how is this good practice continued? What further information do you ask for? You should not 'take over' assessing children's learning and development. Instead, regularly encourage parents to share information in as many and varied ways as possible. This is particularly important when feeding into reviews of children's progress, such as when completing the progress check for children at age 2 or the EYFS profile.

Effective communication with parents and carers

Parents and carers can only communicate effectively with you when you communicate effectively with them. You need to be as imaginative and creative as possible in finding ways for parents to share their knowledge and observations of children, and make sure that you share information in differing ways to meet parents and carers differing needs. For example, some parents and carers might:

- not be able to read letters
- not have time to come to your setting for parent consultations
- not have internet access.

Using a variety of communication methods is crucial. Here are some suggestions.

- Give parents and carers regular access to development records and encourage them to write feedback or comments.
- Have a daily diary that goes between home and your setting, giving a brief outline of activities and basic care practices.
- Hold parent consultations where key staff can discuss with parents and carers face to face.
- Make time available at the start and end of each session for any immediate concerns or achievements.
- Produce a regular newsletter giving an overview of any important dates, celebrations and activities.
- Create a webpage to share policies and procedures, planning and information about the setting and staff.

- Use text message alerts for important events or reminders.
- Display photographic picture frames when parents arrive and drop children off to show them what activities children engage in.
- Put out newsflashes of achievements, successes and general snapshot information.
- Have a 'Today's play' noticeboard outlining some of the learning objectives behind activities children have enjoyed during the day.
- Have a staff noticeboard with photographs, to help parents and carers identify who staff are and be able to address them by name.

Figure 9.6: How can you communicate effectively with children's parents or carers?

Reviewing your own performance and developing action plans

In this unit you have looked at the different ways you communicate with parents and why you communicate. To review your own practice, first you need to think about all the ways you communicate with parents, what you communicate and why it is important. You could do this by thinking about how you share information about play, learning, health and development. Bear in mind factors that may impact on the quality and effectiveness of your communication, such as:

- the amount of time parents have to stop and talk about children
- whether information is clear and easy to read

- any physical or practical barriers to communication (for example, parents who do not speak English)
- whether the advice you are sharing is relevant.

Developing an action plan

Now you can start to think about developing an action plan for improvement. This could be about how you share information, what information you share, or when you share it.

For example, it could be that you have identified that sometimes you are not giving parents advice or information in ways they can easily understand. Your action plan might be to find differing ways to communicate, such as exploring the use of pictures, diagrams and flow charts in newsletters and displays.

You might like to structure your action plan like the one shown in Figure 9.7.

What would I like to improve?	Why do I need to improve this and who will be involved?
How will I improve?	**How will I measure the effectiveness of my improvements?**

Figure 9.7: Have you completed an action plan like this before?

Further reading and resources

Publications

- Gasper, M. (2009) *Multi-agency Working in the Early Years: Challenges and Opportunities,* London: Sage Publications – suggests ways to draw together the different professional ideas, methods and targets to get multi-agency working right

- Sylva, K. *et al* (2004) *The Effective Provision of Pre-School Education (EPPE) Project: Final Report* – first major European longitudinal study of a national sample of young children's development between the ages of 3 and 7 years, to investigate the effects of pre-school education – available for download at www.ioe.ac.uk/RB_pre-school_to_end_of_KS1(1).pdf

- Whalley, M. (2007) *Involving Parents in their Children's Learning* (2ⁿᵈ ed.), London: Sage Publications – story of the pioneering work of the Pen Green Centre for children and families, showing how early years practitioners can collaborate effectively with parents

Websites

- Department for Education (2013) *Early Years Outcomes* – non-statutory guide for practitioners and inspectors, to help inform understanding of child development through the early years – available online at www.gov.uk/government/publications/early-years-outcomes

- Foundation Years: www.foundationyears.org.uk/eyfs – a useful section of this website for resources, information and support on the EYFS

- Information Commissioner's Office: www.ico.org.uk – independent body that upholds information rights, promoting openness by public bodies and data privacy for individuals

Articles and magazines

- Crowley, M. and Wheeler, H. 'Working with Parents in the Early Years' in Pugh, G. and Duffy, B. (2013) *Contemporary Issues in the Early Years* (6ᵗʰ ed.), London: Sage Publications

- Pre-school Learning Alliance: www.pre-school.org.uk/providers/research/352/roles-responsibilities-of-sencos-in-early-years-settings – report on roles and responsibilities of SENCOs in early years settings from the Pre-school Learning Alliance, a membership organisation and provider of childcare and education

Understanding how to promote play and learning in the early years

Play is always an enjoyable experience for children but it is also a great way for them to learn and develop. This unit will introduce you to some of the theories of play that influence practice and the play opportunities and resources that support the early years framework. Knowing how children develop and learn will help you to plan effective and challenging play activities that meet the needs of all children in your setting.

Before you start

'Play is often talked about as if it were a relief from serious learning. But for children play is serious learning. Play is really the work of childhood.' Fred Rogers (educator and children's TV presenter).

Before you begin this unit, take some time to think about what Rogers means in this quotation. What does it tell you about the importance of play-based learning? Do you agree with him – and if so, why?

Learning outcomes

By the end of this unit you will:

1. **understand how children from birth to 5 years learn through play**
2. **understand the play and learning needs of children**
3. **understand how barriers to play-based learning can be overcome**
4. **understand how to support play and learning activities**
5. **understand the principles of managing risk in early years settings.**

1 Understand how children from birth to 5 years learn through play

Understanding different theories and approaches will help you to appreciate the importance of play for children from birth to 5 years. A range of theoretical perspectives has influenced the way your setting plans for and supports children in their play. You will recognise these influences as you explore theories and approaches in this unit.

Theoretical perspectives

Piaget

Jean Piaget (1896–1980) was one of the first psychologists to study the cognitive and language development of children. When working on intelligence tests he discovered that children think in very different ways to adults. This led him to carry out observational studies to find how children develop their reasoning and thinking skills. He discovered that children pass through four distinct phases up to 15 years. Table 10.1 describes the first two stages for early years.

Table 10.1: The first two of Piaget's stages of cognitive development.

Stage and approximate age	Description of stage	How this influences play
0–2 years Sensorimotor	Babies and young children understand the world through their senses and movement. By around 1 year, they understand that objects exist even when they cannot be seen.	Children hold and manipulate toys and objects. They use all their senses to explore the environment. By the age of 1 they will hunt for something that is out of sight, such as a hidden toy.
2–7 years Preoperational	Children think symbolically. They are developing memory and will imitate things from past experiences. Children are still seeing things from their own perspective (egocentric).	Children take part in 'make believe' play. They take on different roles such as a doctor or shopkeeper. Through their actions they show that they have remembered things they have seen or experienced previously. They use objects to stand for other objects – for example, a broom as a horse. By the end of this stage, children are beginning to see things from others' perspectives.

Piaget believed that children construct their understanding of the world through hands-on experience during play. This theory, known as constructivism, is influential in learner-centred learning. Figure 10.1 shows the process.

Assimilation
Children construct an understanding about something (a schema)
For example: 'Sand is dry and pours from containers.'

Equilibrium
The child's experience with sand fits into their understanding
For example: as they tip the sand from the bucket, it pours and levels out again

Accommodation
The child's understanding changes to accommodate the new information
For example: 'Wet sand does not pour but keeps its shape when tipped out of a bucket.'

Disequilibrium
Something happens that upsets the child's understanding of the properties of sand
For example: Water is added to sand

Figure 10.1: How does Piaget's theory relate to your experiences of children's play and learning?

Figure 10.2: How do children construct their understanding of the properties of sand?

This process is shown as a cycle: children accommodate the new information, and develop a schema, then gain new learning – and the process continues. In Figure 10.1, the schema is about the properties of wet and dry sand. Later on, children may come across different materials that they can shape or pour.

Theory in action

Produce an example of your own of how children construct their understanding of the world through their play.

Psychoanalytical theories

Psychoanalytical theories are based on the belief that early childhood experiences influence what we become as adults. Sigmund Freud (1856–1939) developed a theory based on his belief that there are three aspects of personality. He recognised a conflict between a child's wants and their needs and how they can be satisfied. He believed that conflicts in childhood are stored in the unconscious mind and determine personality in later life. For more information on Freud's theory, see learning outcome 2 in Unit 1.

Erik Erikson (1902–1994) was greatly influenced by Freud's theory of personality development. However, he believed that the social environment had more influence over the development of personality than psychosexual influences. Erikson proposed five stages of personality development to the age of 18 years, describing each as a time of 'conflict'. Table 10.2 describes the stages relevant to early years.

Maslow's hierarchy of needs

Maslow set out to find what motivates people. He came to the conclusion that people had inborn or 'innate' motivation that was not influenced by rewards or by unconscious desires. In 1943, Maslow developed his hierarchy, similar to that shown in Figure 1.8 in Unit 1, to explain these stages of motivation.

Table 10.2: Erikson's first three stages of personality development.

Psychosocial conflict	Stage/age	The influences of personality on play
1. Trust versus mistrust	Birth to 18 months	Erikson refers to this stage as 'psychosocial crisis'. The child is uncertain and relies on their parent or carer to give them security. If they form strong attachments they will develop a sense of security (trust); if not they may develop a sense of insecurity (mistrust). He believed that the result of experiences would affect how children view the world in later life. Negative experiences may cause anxiety and affect an individual's ability to form relationships.
2. Autonomy versus shame	18 months to 3 years	Children are becoming independent (autonomy). They should be encouraged to make choices, such as what they play or what they wear. Erikson believed that the way the parent or carer responds to the child's desire for independence affects their development. For example, being critical or making a child feel as if they have failed will affect their self-esteem (shame).
3. Initiative versus guilt	3 years to 5 years	Children are beginning to assert themselves (initiative) and develop interpersonal skills. They enjoy playing and socialising with other children. They constantly ask questions. If they are made to feel that they are being a nuisance or doing something wrong (guilt) it will inhibit their curiosity.

Maslow believed that the needs at one level of his hierarchy must be met before an individual can move on to the next. This has implications for your setting. Children need to have their basic needs met and feel safe and secure before they can progress. They need to develop trusting relationships so that they can move on to develop positive self-concept, achievement and confidence through their play. The highest level Maslow referred to is self-actualisation or self-fulfilment but recognised that not everyone can reach this stage of meeting their full potential.

Other theoretical perspectives

Many other theoretical perspectives have been developed that have a bearing on your practice and your setting. Table 10.3 describes the main perspectives and their implications for how a child learns through play.

Approaches to play

In the mid-20th century a number of early educators were developing educational programmes and approaches based on cognitive theories that recognised the value of play for children's learning, health and wellbeing. Each approach identifies the important role of a challenging environment, both indoors and outdoors.

Hymes play

James Hymes (1913–1998) developed his approach to learning in the 1960s. He believed that children reached their full potential through play. To Hymes, play was not something that children do for leisure but was the main vehicle for learning and solving problems. He believed that children would be successful because, through play, they are in control of their own learning. Through observing children at play, adults can understand how they think and what their interests are, then provide them with age-appropriate opportunities for play, indoors and outdoors.

Reggio Emilia approach

Reggio Emilia is the Italian city where this approach was introduced in the 1940s. Started by parents, the Reggio Emilia nurseries have at their heart a partnership between parents and educators. The environment is viewed as the third most important element (after the early years educator and the child's parent). The early years educator is there to listen and to guide children, but not to dominate or control their play. This approach soon spread across the world – you may know of a local Reggio Emilia nursery. You will certainly recognise elements of this approach in your own programme of teaching and learning.

Freely chosen play

Freely chosen play takes any direction the child chooses. The environment must be interesting and challenging, providing children with a wide range of natural and man-made areas and resources. Assuming that children are intrinsically motivated, freely chosen play happens when:

- there are no set goals or rewards
- it is supported by but not led or controlled by adults
- children follow their own interests
- children choose how they play and why
- children can explore their emotions.

In the 1970s, Fraser Brown, a play worker, became concerned at the lack of opportunity for children to play as freely as they had in the past. He believed that this was borne out of a sense of 'risk aversion' – the fear of children hurting themselves, 'stranger danger' or risks from traffic.

His observations led him to conclude that a child's development is closely linked to the environment. His 'compound flexibility' theory supposes that an environment that supports 'flexible and adaptable' play results in children becoming more flexible and adaptable, which means they become more resilient throughout their life.

Jargon buster

Resilient – more able to cope with difficult events in their life.

Table 10.3: Other theoretical perspectives.

Theory	Description	Implications for learning through play
Humanistic	Based on work by Carl Rogers, this looks at the whole person and from their point of view. Rogers believed that individuals have free will and can choose their own actions. Individuals who have respect and value themselves will be able to strive towards self-fulfilment.	Children need to choose their own play and follow their own ideas. They should be encouraged and praised to help them to develop self-esteem and confidence through their play.
Social learning theory	This is based on the belief that behaviour is learned by watching others. Albert Bandura carried out experiments where children watched an adult hitting an inflatable doll (Bobo doll) to show that they learn behaviour from others.	Children learn from others and adults during their play. Adults should model positive behaviours when supporting children in their play.
Behaviourist approach	John Watson (1878–1958) founded this. Influenced by Pavlov's experiments on animals, he believed that children's behaviours could be trained or 'conditioned' by the environment and what happened to them (classical conditioning).	Children may respond to certain stimuli. For instance, by playing music at 'tidy up' time children will soon make the association and not have to be asked to tidy up.
Operant conditioning	Influenced by Watson, B.F. Skinner (1904–1990) carried out well-known experiments on rats. He concluded that animals and humans learn their behaviours through the consequences of what they do. If they receive positive reinforcement, they are more likely to repeat the behaviour; if they receive negative reinforcement, they are less likely to (operant conditioning).	Positive reinforcement (such as praising or giving stickers) will encourage children to repeat wanted behaviours. Negative reinforcement (for example, sharing toys with other children to avoid being left out of the game) will also encourage them to repeat wanted behaviours.
Social pedagogy	This is based on the belief that the child is at the centre of their learning and development and should control this. It emphasises a shared responsibility in the care and education of children that includes the child, their parents and society as a whole.	Early years practitioners understand the needs and interests of the child when planning for play and activities, and involve children and their families.
Multiple intelligences	Howard Gardner proposed that there were different types of intelligences or abilities: linguistic, logical-mathematical, spatial-visual, musical, bodily-kinaesthetic, interpersonal and intrapersonal. Gardner believed that these described preferred ways of learning. This theory questioned how intelligence is measured, proposing that a variety of methods should be used to reflect different aspects of intelligence.	Children have different strengths and abilities, expressed in different ways, and they learn in different ways. Knowing individual children and how they learn best helps professionals to plan effective play and learning activities.
Information processing theory	This explains the way that we think and learn through three types of memory: • sensory memory – incoming information • working memory – gives meaning to the incoming information using thought processes • long-term memory – stores information for the long term.	This helps you to understand how children think. Children begin to recall information from the age of 2 years and use it to relate to new information. You may see this in their play as they act out what they have observed. As children grow they develop long-term memories that help them recall what has happened to make decisions and solve problems.
Social-cultural cognitive theory	Lev Vygotsy's theory focuses on how social interactions with an adult who is more skilful contribute to a child's cognitive and language development. He believed that children internalise language throughout their interactions, which enables them to express their thoughts at a later stage.	Like Piaget, Vygotsky believed in hands-on play and learning experiences, but he stressed the importance of the adult in extending children's thinking and language by modelling certain behaviours or by teaching and supporting (scaffolding) the child.
Language acquisition theories	Skinner believed that children acquire language through imitation and reinforcement. Noam Chomsky suggested that Skinner's theory does not explain language development. He believed that all children have an innate sense of language. He called this our Language Acquisition Device (LAD). The LAD enables children to use language when they have acquired vocabulary.	Adults can reinforce children's language development through interaction and responding to children's first sounds and words. Children need opportunities for developing vocabulary through their play. Adults are role models so must use speech and language that is clear and grammatically correct.

Brown's research led to the development of principles for Play Work. Look at the nine principles in Table 10.3. Consider what activities there are in your own setting to support these.

How children are competent learners

Children are naturally curious. How they satisfy that curiosity and develop understanding depends to an extent on their biological development. A baby who cannot yet crawl is restricted to what they have around them – but as soon as they can explore their environment, their 'world' expands. Children also need language to be able to internalise new concepts and make links to previous knowledge.

Birth to 12 months

Babies use all their senses – touch, sight, sound, taste and smell – as well as movement to explore their environment, but still depend on their parent or carer. From birth, babies turn to the light and respond when they hear their mother's voice. Gradually babies show more interest in what is happening around them, responding to and recognising different sounds and pictures. You may have noticed how babies frequently mimic facial expressions, and imitate sounds and actions. By 8 months they develop the concept of 'object permanence' (Piaget): if you hide objects or adults leave, they understand that they are still there. At this stage babies' brains are developing quickly. When they respond to experiences, new connections called neural pathways are being formed in the brain. These help to develop thought processes and language.

As babies develop their fine motor skills they can hold objects to explore them in a sensory way, by mouthing and touching. Developing motor ability enables them to physically explore more of their environment. By 12 months, as speech and language develops, they can understand and respond to simple requests.

12 months to 2 years

Piaget described this stage as 'exploratory play'. Now that they can say words and use short sentences, children can think and organise their ideas, as well as controlling and exploring their world using language. They can remember things they have seen or done before and build on this. They understand more words than they are able to speak so will respond to simple commands such as, 'Give me teddy'.

Children begin to walk, run and climb. This increased motor ability gives them more freedom to gain first-hand experiences, indoors and outdoors. They see themselves as independent beings, which gives them confidence and eagerness to try out new things.

2 to 5 years

Around the age of 2 years, children progress toward what Piaget describes as 'mastery play'. They use symbols in their play to represent and develop their thoughts and ideas. As their vocabulary develops, they start to ask questions and share their thoughts with others. Language is critical for:

- making connections between ideas
- drawing on past experiences to predict what might happen
- comparing
- categorising, classifying and searching out patterns.

Around the age of 3 years, children begin to take part in social play, talking about and planning their play, cooperating and taking turns. Learning by trial and error is important at this stage: for example, what happens when you blow into a tube in water play or walk through autumn leaves? Taking part in a range of activities such as drama, dance or drawing enables children to express their feelings and come to terms with who they are and what they can do. At this stage children enjoy sharing a book with an adult and can retell favourites. They are developing their imagination and you will observe their creativity through their drawing, paintings, music activities or drama.

By the age of 4 years children are speaking quite fluently. They are recognising patterns in language and using adult speech sounds. Although they are mastering grammar they may still make errors such as 'I goed' rather than 'I went'. They can now use language to express their thoughts and solve problems.

2 Understand the play and learning needs of children

Play provides a wonderful opportunity to promote all areas of a child's learning and development. Take time to watch children as they play and you will see how absorbed they become if allowed to choose and develop their play.

Play is important for holistic development, but some types are more helpful in developing a particular area of learning: for example, sharing a story for promoting language development, or wheeled toys for physical development. Children need experiences and resources to develop their learning in each of the three prime areas and the four specific areas of learning in the EYFS framework.

Types of play that support learning and development

Jargon buster

Dramatic play – acting out scenes from real life that are familiar.

Imaginative play – play such as home corner or dressing up.

Small-world play – creating 'worlds' using resources such as farm animals, small figures and toy cars.

Figure 10.3: How can these types of play support learning and development?

Communication and language

The EYFS guidance states that the learning environment must include 'opportunities to experience a rich language environment'. Play is the key way to give children these opportunities. Skinner describes how from birth, babies respond with coos to an adult speaking and singing to them. This, he suggests, reinforces language development, as children are rewarded by their mother's response. Later they join in with peek-a-boo, actions songs and rhymes and eventually trying out new vocabulary.

Figure 10.4: How can play help children learn how to negotiate and share?

As children's language develops they enjoy experimenting with new vocabulary in their play. Reading and sharing stories and rhymes is a good way to introduce new words and support language skills. They will go on to explore language in their writings. You may have heard children adding a commentary, even when playing alone; for instance, in the water or sand play and often when drawing. They give voices to small-world toys or puppets. Piaget observed that children in the preoperational stage, between 2 and 7 years, often think aloud as they play, showing a close link between cognitive and language development. Playing with natural materials, construction play and outdoor play makes children curious, which encourages them to ask questions. According to Vygotsky, when children are supported by an adult who can discuss new concepts and introduce new vocabulary as they play, they will internalise language and learn to carry out tasks independently.

Once children begin to socialise they understand the importance of communication and language to resolve conflicts and plan their play. Imaginative, dramatic and role play are fun ways for children to practice their communication skills.

Physical development

Physical development includes how children grow and develop their mobility, coordination and balance.

Table 10.4: Aspects of physical development supported by play.

Aspect of physical development	Types of play	How this promotes physical development
Growth	Free play and outdoor games and activities that require children to run, jump and climb	• Improves lung capacity and promotes health and stamina • Aids healthy appetite and helps children sleep
Fine motor skills	Small-world play, construction toys or sand, water or dough/ clay play	• Develops small muscles in hands and fingers as children manipulate objects
Gross motor skills	Climbing frames, wheeled toys or taking part in dramatic or imaginative play	• Develops large muscles in children's arms and legs promoting mobility, coordination and balance
Hand–eye coordination	Scribbling and drawing, table-top toys such as puzzles and shape-posting boxes	• Develops control of fine movement as children use eyes to guide hands as they manipulate and place small objects

Personal, social and emotional development

This involves supporting children to develop a positive self-image, build effective relationships with others and manage their feelings. From birth, play between parent and child promotes the bonding process: it is enjoyable and makes children feel safe and secure. Play experiences such as scribbling, creative play, painting, play dough or using musical instruments are all ways of expressing emotions. Children come to terms with their own feelings and understand the feelings and needs of other children. Play is sometimes used as therapy with children who have emotional difficulties.

Through dramatic and imaginative play, music and singing, and reading and shared stories children develop the skills to interact and socialise with others. Table-top toys and games encourage sharing and cooperation. Role play helps them learn how to negotiate and share in situations where they feel comfortable.

Play activities do not have a set outcome. For example, you may have observed how each time children play with small-world toys or with sand or water, their play develops differently with different outcomes. Children will always achieve in these types of play because they decide on what happens next and how to conclude their play. Having this control gives children confidence in their ability and leads to high self-esteem.

Literacy

Literacy involves linking the written form of letters to the sounds they make and then developing skills in reading and writing. Young children can be helped to develop these skills through play activities.

Reading skills

You may have used a large storybook with children. Pointing out the letters and words as you tell the story helps children to link letters and sounds in a playful way. Gradually children will recognise letters, sounds and whole words and point these out in the environment. Providing comfortable seating areas with a selection of picture books and storybooks will encourage children to choose to read books alone or share books with others. Children love to listen to stories. It's fine to retell the same favourite story as children can readily join in. Stories can also be used to inspire dramatic or imaginative play.

Writing skills

Any play such as threading beads or puzzles that requires fine motor control helps children to develop the physical skills needed for writing. Children also need to understand the written form of writing. Through play they can explore different mark-making materials, crayons, felt-tip pens, pastels and finger paints. You will start to see the beginnings of shapes or letters appearing in their scribble, which is preparing them for formal writing of letters and words.

Opportunities for writing should be available through different types of play, such as:

- a notepad by the telephone in the shop or the home corner
- coloured folded card in the creative corner for children to make greetings cards
- magnetic letters and boards on table tops
- chalks for writing outdoors on pavements or walls.

Mathematics

Mathematics involves numbers and counting and simple calculations, as well as shapes, space and measures. There are many opportunities for developing mathematical knowledge through play. Here are a few.

Numbers and counting

Key activities for developing knowledge of numbers and counting include:

- table-top games that involve matching, sorting, classifying, counting, ordering and using dice
- number action rhymes and songs, books and stories
- role play and dramatic play, such as shopping games that include using money and labelling
- outdoor play such as writing numbers on pavements using chalks, or in sand using a stick.

Space, shape and measures

Key activities for developing knowledge of shape, space and measures include:

- sand and water play using differently sized containers to explore volume and capacity

- construction play, using different 3D shapes both indoors and outdoors to explore concepts of shape and size

- creative play such as pattern-making activities, cutting and pasting, colouring and painting to understand 2D shapes and position

- small-world play to help understanding of position, such as under, behind, next to, over.

Understanding the world

Understanding the world involves children learning about the physical world around them, their community and uses of technology that impact on their lives.

The physical world

Children are naturally inquisitive so they will be eager to take part in play activities that involve exploring the world around them. Babies and young children use all their senses as they play so will become engrossed in exploring a basket of natural objects, referred to as heuristic play.

If you have ever watched a child jumping in a puddle, kicking up autumn leaves or catching snowflakes on their tongue you will appreciate the importance of opportunities for free play and games outdoors in order for children to truly understand the natural world. The outdoor area needs to be carefully planned for encouraging play, such as having areas for digging and growing and for observing insects. Indoors, children can explore a range of natural materials such as sand, water, clay or dough.

Figure 10.5: Why is outdoor play critical for children to develop an understanding of the world?

The community

Play will help children extend their experience and knowledge of people beyond their immediate family and community. Stories and books are a good way to introduce ideas about their own family and people from different cultures and in different roles. Dramatic and imaginative play can offer opportunities to develop an understanding of different people and their roles. You may also see children role-playing situations they have observed or using small-world toys and construction materials perhaps following a visit to a farm or a fire station. This type of play is important for them to come to terms with their experience.

Jargon buster

Heuristic play – play about discovery and finding things.

Technology

Young children are often very quick to learn how everyday technology works. They are becoming increasingly confident in using computer programmes or digital cameras. Babies love toys with levers and knobs and soon understand what happens when they are turned or moved. Table-top activities such as a tray with torches, programmable toys, audio recorders, or construction materials with knobs or pulleys encourage children to persevere as they can develop their knowledge through trial and error.

Expressive arts and design

Expressive arts and design is concerned with children learning about different media and materials and in developing their creativity.

Children need access to a wide range of resources for design and technology and creative and art play to enable them to use all their senses to learn about texture, colour and shape. Junk modelling, dough and clay, construction materials and materials for writing, painting and drawing should be freely available. Try to think about new ways to present experiences, such as painting with rollers or sponges as well as brushes, setting up painting walls or areas for floor painting or chalking.

Children's imagination can be fostered through play that involves exploring music using instruments or objects that make sounds. Their ideas for play can be stimulated by listening to music or looking at works of art. Space and time for small-world, table-top, dance, dramatic and imaginative play give children the freedom to explore previous experiences and develop their ideas.

The effect of lack of play on learning

The first few years of life are the most critical for brain development. Research has shown that stimulating play and learning experiences help to build connections in the brain called neural pathways,

Case study 10.1

Naomi works with children aged 4 years in a reception class. It is Mother's Day soon, so she decides to plan a creative activity with the children. She makes a card herself with a flower made of tissue paper and a painted plant pot.

She shows the children her card and tells them that they can make one to take home for their mothers. She places all the resources that the children will need on the table.

1. Why might having a set idea of the outcomes of the activity restrict children's creativity?

2. How would you present the activity to encourage children to develop their own ideas?

3. How could you engage with the children, while following their lead, to extend their knowledge of materials and creativity?

essential for cognitive development. Not having these opportunities for play restricts the development of these pathways, slowing or delaying learning in the short term and affecting a child's chances later in life. For more information on neural pathways, see learning outcome 1 in Unit 1.

Figure 10.6: What are the physical, emotional and social effects of play?

Play is one of the main ways that children interact with others, form friendships and most importantly have fun. Without social interaction children will not be able to learn how to cooperate, develop confidence and problem-solving and thinking skills. Children's development can be slowed or delayed if they do not play, which can have serious consequences for their life chances.

The lack of play may be observed in changes in children's physical health because they have fewer opportunities for developing movement skills and coordination. Mental health can also suffer if they are unable to be physically active and let off steam. Lack of play can lead to obesity, poor health and wellbeing. This can have a serious impact on children's happiness and self-esteem.

Personalising children's play and learning

A personalised approach to play and learning relies on the adult's understanding of the individual needs and interests of the child. The key person approach enables early years practitioners to carry out a focused assessment of each child's needs because they get to know the whole child, their family and their interests at home and elsewhere.

Children's development is individual and they have different strengths and weaknesses. Observation of children during their play and learning is therefore essential for providing an appropriate learning environment and resources to support effective play. For instance, does the child tend to develop their play or quickly move on? If they appear to lose interest easily, is the play sufficiently challenging for the child or are the resources unsuitable because they are difficult for them to use? The knowledge about the child enables you to decide on the best pedagogic approach and to identify learning objectives to be worked toward. Progress towards the learning objectives need to be continuously monitored and then reviewed to ensure that planning continues to meet each child's needs.

Key features of an effective play-based learning environment

The learning environment describes the whole experience offered to the child, not just the physical room, furniture and equipment. You need to create an enabling environment – so called because it enables children to make their own choices and take control of their play and learning.

An effective play-based learning environment will be one where:

- the routine allows for children to take part in uninterrupted play
- the layout includes different spaces created to allow for different types of play and for rest
- play opportunities are planned and take account of each child's interests and needs
- there are opportunities for safe and secure indoor and outdoor play
- children are able to choose personalised activities that challenge them and are appropriate for their age and stage of development
- children can choose and access a range of stimulating resources independently
- resources are safe and fit for purpose
- curiosity is fostered by providing interesting resources that change regularly
- resources are age appropriate, safe and take account of children's individual and cultural needs
- there are enough experienced adults to monitor, support and review learning and development.

Jargon buster

Key person – the person designated with the responsibility for a child's welfare.

Table 10.5: Benefits of different types of play.

Benefits of adult-initiated play	Benefits of child-initiated play
• Adults can give guidance and support children toward play and learning activities that will challenge children to develop specific skills. • Adults offer play and learning activities that start from what the child knows and can do, to challenge and extend their thinking in a particular direction. • Adults can introduce children to new ideas and new ways of playing and learning to develop their skills. • Adults provide a more structured programme of teaching and learning ensuring that all areas of their development are targeted and that children experience all areas of learning in the EYFS framework. • Play activities can be initiated to introduce new vocabulary.	• Children feel free to explore and can follow their own interests, imagination and creativity. • They can learn at their own rate and in different ways. • Play is non-threatening so children feel more able to try things out and risk making mistakes, which develops their self-esteem. • Children are more likely to develop independence and persevere when they are in control of their own learning. • Children can use their own creative ideas in their play and decide on their own goals.

Adult-initiated and child-initiated play and learning

An effective early years educational programme will maintain a balance between adult- and child-initiated play and learning activities. Both approaches have their place because each has clear benefits for children – see Table 10.5. At birth, the adult or carer will usually initiate playful activities until the baby is more aware and mobile and begins to initiate play themselves.

Adult-initiated play

Adult-initiated play occurs when the adult plans and introduces play and learning activities that will direct children toward particular goals. The adult may initiate and not be involved or control and lead the play towards a particular goal.

Child-initiated play

Child-initiated play is play that is spontaneous and experiential. The child will decide on where to play and who with and choose the resources to use in their play. Adults may engage in play that the child has initiated but will not control the play. The child will decide upon the goals.

3 Understand how barriers to play-based learning can be overcome

Barriers to play-based learning

There are many possible barriers to play-based learning, including:

- **attitudes** – people may not value play-based learning because of their experience or culture
- **the environment** – access to indoor and/or outdoor play may be limited
- **resources and equipment** – they may be insufficient or inappropriate to support play
- **health and safety** – there may be concerns about children's safety
- **additional needs** – for example, disability or communication difficulties may restrict access
- **health and wellbeing** – children may not be able (or may believe they are not able) to take part because of physical or mental health problems, bullying or abuse
- **poverty and social disadvantage** – experiences at home may affect children's motivation and confidence to engage in play.

How to overcome the barriers

Before you can begin to break down the barriers to play-based learning, you need to understand why they exist. You could carry out an access audit that might find, for example, children not getting the opportunity to play outdoors because the outdoor area is overgrown and unsuitable, too few staff to monitor them or parents and/or staff being over cautious and worried about children having accidents. Monitoring what is happening in the setting is an effective way of finding out why children are not taking part in play. Inspection is a formal process of monitoring and reviewing the quality of provision, but informal monitoring and reviews should also be taking place.

Audits of available resources and equipment may highlight where these are insufficient or unsuitable to support effective play. One answer may be to seek funding from local councils or charitable organisations such as *Children in Need*. Lack of resources may be overcome by being more imaginative. In fact, children's play can be more successful when the resources are open-ended rather than having a specific purpose. Children do not need expensive equipment. A basket of

Figure 10.7: Expensive play equipment is not always needed to give children a challenging play environment.

natural or everyday objects will satisfy the curiosity of toddlers; dens can be built with large cardboard boxes and fabric or tarpaulin.

Lack of space should not be a barrier as it can be adapted to meet the needs of all children. Space should be flexible: for example, trays used for sand or water can later be covered to provide a table for small-world toys. If outdoor space is limited, consider how play that usually takes place outdoors can be organised indoors, bringing in pots for planting or moving furniture aside for ride-on toys. If there is a lack of room for role play indoors there is no reason why it cannot take place outdoors.

Attitudes may be more difficult to overcome but should be challenged. Parents may not understand the importance of play for learning because of their own experiences or their culture. They may need written information or opportunities to visit the setting and talk to professionals to understand the reasons for play-based learning and the benefits for their child.

In line with the requirements of the EYFS, staffing levels should be sufficient for monitoring and supporting a range of indoor and outdoor play opportunities. Play activities that have higher risk will need additional supervision, so need to be well planned at a time when qualified practitioners and support staff are available rather than not providing challenging play. The introduction of the Early Years Educator qualification, alongside regular training and development and good recruitment, will ensure that staff have knowledge and expertise in planning for play-based learning.

How children with additional needs can participate fully

Play is important for empowering children in a way that means they can feel in control. This is particularly important for children with additional needs as this often affects how they feel about themselves. Their inclusion is important. Children can be helped to participate by a well planned and, if necessary, adapted environment that reflects their needs.

Planning

Take children's additional needs into account at the planning stage by:

- finding out what the child knows and what they can do (assessments, involvement of parents, carers and specialists)

- finding out whether the child is able to take part in any of the play opportunities (observations of children during play, reviewing plans to identify possible barriers)

- identifying health and safety requirements over and above that faced by other children (risk assessment considering the child's individual needs)

- making sure that activities are open-ended, enabling all children to achieve at their own level of development.

An environment that enables play

The layout in your setting – perhaps the lack of space between equipment or furniture – could make access to some areas difficult. Lighting needs to be sufficient for children with visual impairment. Some children need quieter areas with fewer distractions to take part in play.

Adapting resources and activities

Having smaller groups or grouping particular children together may help children with language or communication difficulties to take part. Resources may need to be changed or adapted: for example, including larger paint brushes or construction equipment that is easier to grasp. There are some amazing specialist toys, resources and equipment available nowadays. Professionals, such a physiotherapists or sensory specialists, can advise on ones that are suitable for children in your setting.

Support

Although it is important to help children to be as independent as possible, they may still require support from an adult. For some this means emotional support through reassurance or encouragement; others need physical help: for example, support to climb up rungs of the ladder of the slide. You could even become a play 'buddy' for children who find it difficult to join in play with others, although it's important that you follow the child's lead.

Case study 10.2

Kyle, aged 3½ years, attends nursery. He has cerebral palsy. Kyle can walk unaided but has difficulty using his left arm and has a problem with mobility and balance. The nursery has a large outdoor area. Staff are planning an outdoor role-play area that includes space for climbing and for wheeled toys such as prams and carts.

1. What do the staff need to take account of when planning the play environment?

2. What are the health and safety considerations?

3. How can the staff support and encourage Kyle to play independently?

4 Understand how to support play and learning activities

Effective play-based learning depends on detailed planning, and the provision of a stimulating environment and imaginative resources. When planning and supporting play, you must take account of the different ways that children play, including:

- **playing and exploring** – play that encourages curiosity and exploration of resources and environment

- **active learning** – play that gives first-hand experiences

- **creating and thinking critically** – play that encourages children to think and develop their own ideas.

(Source: Statutory Framework for the Early Years Foundation Stage, Department for Education, 2014, p.9)

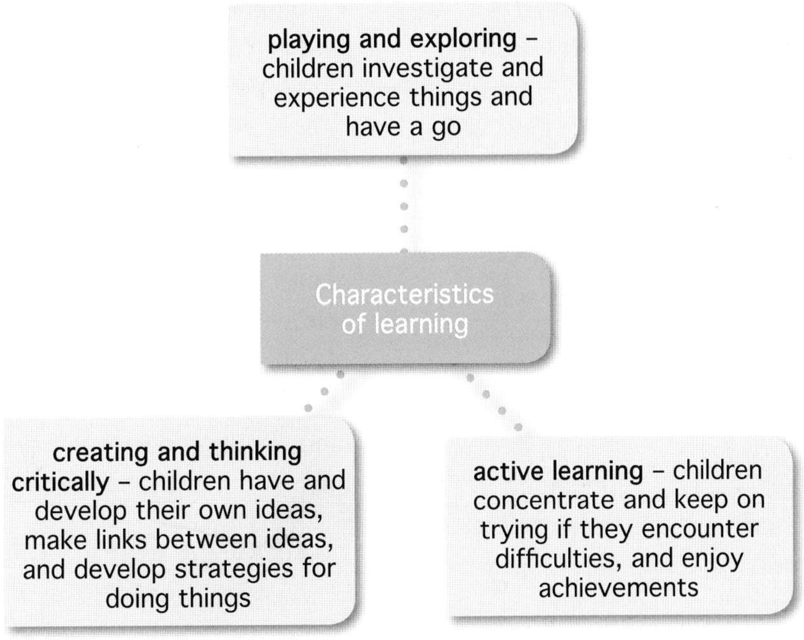

Figure 10.8: How can considering the characteristics of learning help you to plan play activities?

Planning for a play-based approach

Planning starts with the child. Children of the same age may be at different stages of development and learn in different ways. Information about the child is gained through observing them and by talking to parents, carers or colleagues. Knowing each child's needs ensures that the educational programme is structured so that each child has the opportunity to fully participate in a range of play activities.

When planning for play you need to ask the following questions.

- Is the environment safe with adequate heating, ventilation and lighting?
- Are there sufficient activities and resources to support children in all areas of learning?
- Are there visual and tactile activities, resources and displays to enable children to use all their senses and encourage exploration?
- Are activities and resources appropriate and accessible to meet the needs and abilities of all the children?
- Are there opportunities for monitoring, assessment and review? This is important for future planning.

Supporting a play-based approach

You are a facilitator for children's play, there to help them achieve their full potential. Children may not always want adults to be involved in their play but they do need them to be there for them, for reassurance and a feeling of security.

Getting to know individual children's needs and abilities helps you to decide on the type and level of support they need. Children who are more reticent may need consistency in approach and encouragement to take part in play. This can be done by modelling the play: for example, pretending to have a cup of tea in the home corner, making a model with dough or building a tower with blocks. You will soon find the child joining in alongside you. Alternatively, talking with the child about what play is available and what they would like to do gives them ideas for play and confidence to try things out.

When play is underway, spend some time observing before becoming involved. Children may just need encouragement or praise that indicates they are doing well. At other times, engaging with children as they play is beneficial as it can help to extend and challenge their play by:

- joining in with play – playing the role of the customer in the 'shop' and asking how much items cost
- providing additional or different resources so that the play can develop
- making suggestions for extending their play ideas
- helping a child to join in with others or socialise.

Whatever type of support is given it is important that the adult is sensitive to the children's needs and wishes to avoid taking over or putting their own ideas into place.

Sustained shared thinking

Supporting play can be a good way to involve children in sustained shared thinking. This means getting the child to think more deeply about their play and what they are learning. Rather than praising a child ('You've made a lovely model car'), you could ask 'How did you join the wheels on so well?' You could get children to predict what might happen next in a story or think about their resource choices. At the end of a period of play, you should show you are interested in what children have achieved, encouraging them to think more deeply about what they have done and getting them to suggest what they might do next.

Evaluating materials and equipment

There is a wide choice of toys and equipment on the market for children. Often these have been produced

Table 10.6: Materials and resources that can be used to support play-based learning.

Materials and resources	Examples	How it supports play-based learning
Natural materials	Sand, water, wood, shells, digging materials, soil, bark, gravel, stones, heuristic materials	• Children use all their senses • Triggers curiosity and engages children in exploratory play • Promotes physical control • Develops mathematical concepts of volume and space, sorting and classifying
Role-play resources e.g. home, shop, clinic	Furniture (tables, chairs, bed/cot); props (pots and pans, cutlery, telephone, dolls, empty food boxes, bags, dressing-up clothes, small-world toys)	• Children plan and develop ideas or 'story plots' • Children explore and develop language • Role play promotes cooperation, sharing and friendship
Constructional apparatus and equipment	Blocks of different sizes, small construction materials that link together, planks of wood, logs, crates, mats, slides, cardboard boxes	• Children develop spatial awareness, gross and fine motor skills and hand–eye coordination • Develops mathematical concepts of shape, space and measures
Creative resources and materials	Musical instruments, objects that make noise, paints, chalks, mark-making materials, boxes for junk modelling, different types of paper and card, glue and paste	• Supports children to express feelings, use imagination and develop ideas and creativity • Promotes decision-making • Aids colour recognition • Promotes hand–eye coordination
Malleable materials	Play dough, clay, gloop	• Enables expression of feelings • Develops imagination and creativity
Imaginative play	Fabrics, dressing-up clothes, puppets, small-world toys	• Encourages planning, language development, creativity and problem solving
Books	Story books, rhymes, non-fiction, pop-up books, tactile books	• Children use their senses • Children develop their communication skills and vocabulary • Children use ideas from books to develop ideas for play

for a particular type of play and will lead to a specific outcome for children and may not be the most effective for developing children's imagination. Open-ended resources such as cardboard boxes, pieces of fabric and natural materials can be used in different ways. Including them in play enables children to take their play in any direction they wish. Some of the materials and resources that support play based learning are given in Table 10.6.

Think how these materials may be used in different ways. Small-world toys can be used with sand or water and play dough used as 'food' to develop play in the home corner.

The role of the adult

Adults have many roles, including:

- supervising and monitoring children as they play, to make sure they are safe and get the most from their play
- observing play to assess children's learning and skills for future planning
- giving encouragement by commenting on children's play and showing interest
- engaging with children and asking questions to reinforce and extend learning
- praising children to promote a sense of achievement and self-esteem
- keeping records of and reporting on achievement and development
- carrying out risk assessments and safety sweeps and following controls and procedures to keep children safe.

5 Understand the principles of managing risk in early years settings

Too often we hear that children have been stopped from challenging play because of a belief that all risk must be eliminated – or a fear of litigation. There will always be some risk involved in play. What is important

is to identify risks that are acceptable or unacceptable. The Health and Safety Executive recognises that children must be given opportunities for challenging play but that this needs to be managed. Their advice is that controls must be 'sensible and proportionate'. Controls that prevent children from visiting woodlands because they may trip or hurt themselves would not be proportionate, but controls that include children wearing long trousers and having adequate supervision would be sensible.

Why children need to take risks in play

Children derive many benefits when taking risks in play. They will gain a sense of freedom when exploring and trying out new activities. Children can develop their own rules and boundaries as they play and push themselves to the limit of their ability. Using planks to build bridges and ramps involves risk, but has the physical benefits of improved balance and coordination and the emotional benefits of high self-esteem. Risk taking in play gives children opportunities to develop and express themselves, be creative and learn how to become self-sufficient. They gain confidence and independence because they have to make decisions and overcome difficulties and challenges.

Theory in action

The philosophy of Forest Schools is to inspire children through challenging outdoor play. Find out about Forest Schools and their approach to risk taking in play at www.forestschools.com.

The role of play in managing risk

Your environment must be safe – but that does not mean that it has to be boring. Children need to take risks. If they are not allowed to do so in a safe, managed environment, they may take risks elsewhere to gain excitement. If children do not learn how to manage risk at an early age, how will they cope in later life?

Including children in your risk assessment process helps them learn about and deal with risk. When children identify controls themselves they are more likely to remember them: for example, discussing how many children can play safely on the climbing frame or where to walk to avoid being hit by a swing. Simple posters recording the agreed controls can be used near the play activities as a reminder.

During play you will notice children applying their own controls after testing out things for themselves. A child who falls from the tricycle when going round the corner slows down the next time, or perhaps changes to a smaller tricycle.

Praising children when they control risks encourages vigilance for their own and others' safety. However, it is important not to worry children unduly or they will be put off from taking part. Monitoring, observing, recording and assessing how children play will help you understand how they manage their own risks and ways to involve them at the planning stage.

Risks and hazards in your setting

Where hazards are identified, it is important that the risks for children are balanced against the benefits.

Figure 10.9: Why is it important for children to have access to outdoor play?

Risks refer to the likelihood that a person may be harmed. It is what may happen to compromise their health and safety. This could be injuries such as head bumps or trapped fingers, or risks relating to their health and welfare.

Table 10.7: Are you aware of the hazards and risks of outdoor play in your setting?

Area for risk assessment	Hazards	Risks
Indoor and outdoor environment	• Broken fences or gates • Discarded materials e.g. glass • Stinging or poisonous plants • Activities involving water • Poor lighting	• Becoming lost, road accidents, abduction • Cuts, infection • Rashes, pain, poisoning • Drowning • Trips and falls
Space and flow	• Lack of space around apparatus causing children to bump into each other or to fall onto objects or equipment	• Bumps and bruises • Cuts and breaks
Equipment and resources	• Poorly maintained toys and equipment • Dangerous substances • Climbing equipment	• Entrapment e.g. fingers, limbs, head; cuts, abrasions • Poisoning, burns • Falls causing head injury, breaks or bruising
Staffing/supervision	• Insufficient numbers of staff • Untrained staff (not understanding/following safety procedures)	• Children taking part in unsafe play leading to injury

Hazards refer to those things that may cause injury or ill health, such as using equipment or hard surfaces. Some of the hazards and risks of outdoor play are given in Table 10.7.

Principles of a risk and benefit assessment proforma

The risk and benefit proforma and assessment procedures (see Figure 10.11) are similar to the risk assessment process in Unit 7, but include an additional stage requiring you to consider the benefits for children.

- Identify the hazards.
- Decide who may be harmed and how.
- Identify the benefits to children of taking part.
- Evaluate the precautions that can be taken to minimise the risks.
- Record the assessment and inform staff so that procedures can be followed.
- Review the benefits and precautions taken considering if precautions are adequate or require updating.

Figure 10.10: What are the advantages of weighing up the risks and benefits of play activities?

Where the risks to children are reasonable or can be minimised to a reasonable level, the benefits will outweigh safety concerns. However, remember that where the level of risk is too great, the benefits will not outweigh the risks – so the activity should not take place.

RISK AND BENEFIT ASSESSMENT					
Activity: Building a den in a natural outdoor area (4–5 year olds)					
Hazard	**Who may be at risk**	**Risks**	**Benefits**	**Control measures to reduce risks**	**Review**
Children will be carrying, moving and positioning a range of natural materials including small planks of wood in an outdoor area	Children aged 4–5 years old	Splinters from wood Bumps / bruises from falling wood Fingers being trapped between pieces of wood	Skills of negotiation and planning Promotes thinking skills and language Supports physical control and mobility Builds self-esteem and gives a sense of achievement	Check area for glass or sharp objects before the activity begins Talk to children about their plans and how best to carry materials Close monitoring by a member of staff Check wood for splinters Restrict numbers to 4 children at a time	

Figure 10.11: You can use a proforma like this one to carry out a risk and benefit assessment for a challenging play activity.

Reflect

Using the proforma, carry out a risk assessment of your own for a challenging play activity. You can use this to talk through the principles of managing risk with your assessor.

Legal framework and current national guidelines for safety

The requirement for ensuring that play is delivered safely within a safe and secure setting is set down in a range of legislation and regulations. Your setting will have policies and procedures in place that help you to follow regulations. The Health and Safety Act 1974 is a key piece of legislation. Statutory guidance on how this legislation is implemented in practice is given in the Management of Health and Safety at Work Regulations 1999 and guidance specific to early years settings in section 3 of the Early Years Foundation Stage.

For more information on relevant legislation and regulations for health and safety, see learning outcome 1 in Unit 7.

Further reading and resources

Publications

- Duffy, B. (2006) *Supporting Creativity and Imagination in the Early Years* (2nd ed.), Maidenhead: Open University Press – good practice and practical guidance for encouraging exploration, invention and discovery

- Early Education (2012) *Development Matters in the Early Years Foundation Stage (EYFS)* – non-statutory guidance material for practitioners implementing the statutory requirements of the EYFS – available online at www.foundationyears.co.uk

- Featherstone, S. (2013) *The Little Book of Role Play*, London: Featherstone Education, Bloomsbury Publishing plc – hundreds of ideas for role play,

grouped so you and the children can incorporate linked themes into your setting

- Harries, J. (2013) *Role Play (Play in the EYFS)*, London: Practical Pre-School Books – covers every aspect of role playing, from planning for the EYFS, to managing play and helping children create their own props

- Moyles, J. (2010) *The Excellence of Play* (3rd ed.), Maidenhead: Open University Press – clearly illustrates key play theories in practice

- Playwork Principles Scrutiny Group (2005) *The Playwork Principles* – a professional and ethical framework for playwork – available for download at www.playwales.org.uk

- Tassoni, P. (2012) *Penny Tassoni's Practical EYFS Handbook* (2nd ed.) Oxford: Pearson – practical handbook for applying the EYFS by an early years expert

- Tassoni, P. and Hucker, K. (2005) *Planning Play and the Early Years* (2nd ed.), Oxford: Heinemann

- Cummings, A. and Featherstone, S. (2009) *Role Play in the Early Years*, London: Featherstone Education – to help you deepen your understanding and plan successful activities

Websites

- Health and Safety Executive: www.hse.gov.uk – an independent body that regulates health and safety in the workplace

- Play England: www.playengland.org.uk – an organisation that promotes play, supports children's rights to play and provides information and training to improve play practice

- Professional Association for Childcare and Early Years: www.pacey.org.uk – a standard-setting organisation that promotes best practice and supports childcare practitioners to deliver high standards of care and learning

Articles and magazines

- *Nursery World*: www.nurseryworld.magazine.co.uk – includes articles about approaches to play and ideas for play activities that are usually linked to the EYFS framework

Understand how to work with children in home-based care

Unit 12

Understand how to work with children in home-based care

Home-based care may be provided by childminders (self-employed and working from their own home) or by nannies (employed by parents to work in the family's home). This unit aims to develop your understanding of the value of this sort of care, and how to establish a safe and healthy home-based environment for children. It looks at how you can develop play for differing ages and meet different children's needs in a home-based environment. Finally, the unit explores the importance of working in partnership with parents, carers and other agencies.

Before you start

As a home-based childcarer, what do you think makes the service you offer children and families different from the service offered in centre-based care? What are the challenges you face, working alone in a domestic setting? What advantages does your small-scale, homely setting offer children? How are you able to relate to organisations and other professionals in the interests of the children?

Learning outcomes

By the end of this unit you will:

1. **understand the value of home-based care for children and families**
2. **understand how to establish a safe and healthy home-based environment for children**
3. **understand how to provide play for differing ages of children in a home-based environment**
4. **understand how to meet the personal, social and emotional needs of children in a home-based childcare environment**
5. **understand the role of parents and/or carers and other agencies as partners in home-based childcare.**

1 Understand the value of home-based care for children and families

Home-based provision has special characteristics that mean it has much to offer families.

The importance of consistent care

Feeling safe and secure is essential to young children's emotional wellbeing. Being in a comfortable and familiar environment, with the support of well-known adults within a structure of predictable routines provides that sense of security. Emotional stability underpins other aspects of their development, such as making social relationships and becoming confident and independent enough to make choices, and enables them to achieve through their learning.

Consistent care by a small number of well-known adults is especially important for babies and children under 3.

In centre-based care, staff turnover, leave and shifts may mean that children are not always looked after by the same person. Home-based care may offer a child more consistent care.

Case study 12.1

Ros explains why she chose a childminder rather than a nursery for her baby: 'Toby and I chose Shaeeda carefully and we trust her. We can be sure that Connie is in her care every day. We hope Connie will stay with Shaeeda even when she starts to go to nursery school part-time and eventually to school.'

1. How do you think Connie's development is likely to be helped by consistent care?

2. Why is trust so important in home-based care?

Case study 12.2

Miranda talks about her childminder: 'Andy and I have busy work lives and it helps so much that we only have to take both the two girls to and collect them from one place at one time. And it's cheaper too as Sandra charges less for the older one.'

1. Why is it likely that a child feels more secure in the same setting as their sibling?

2. What benefits might there be for the childminder?

The benefits of flexibility

Parents who have irregular or unsocial working hours need childcare to be flexible, but centre-based provision can rarely meet their needs beyond the 'normal' working day. Childminders can often be flexible in their hours, offering 'wrap-around' care either side of the school day, in holidays and as emergency cover. Nannies particularly can provide care as and when parents need it.

Home-based childcare is available in the family's own community, and parents can feel reassured that their child has the continuity of consistent care, while they focus on their work role.

The benefits of siblings being together

When a sibling (a child's brother or sister) is part of a child's childcare environment, they have more continuity and consistency of experience with the family's home. They feel more secure and reassured.

The benefits of smaller groups

In a home-based setting, a child will be a member of a smaller group and so is likely to get more individual and personalised attention than is possible in centre-based provision, even with the key person system. A childminder or nanny can more easily see each child as an individual, identifying and meeting their particular needs. A child in a smaller group is likely to be more closely monitored and observed, and young children can more easily become confident enough to interact when they are with a small number of others with whom they are familiar.

The importance of home-based care during transition

Young children can find it difficult to deal with transitions, as you saw in learning outcome 5 of Unit 1. They are better able to cope with changes if they have a part of their lives that is consistent. Home-based care can offer children stability, security and comfort at these points.

It is especially important to show acceptance during times of transition, to ensure that children feel comfortable talking to you or expressing their emotions freely in response to these changes. Your support will be particularly important if the transition involves changes at home – for example, parents' separation.

Case study 12.3

Sadia describes how her 4-year-old son was anxious about starting school, but says: 'What made it easier for him to cope with was knowing that Cath was going to meet him on the days that I work, and he was going back to her familiar and cosy home, where he's been going since he was a baby'.

1. Why do familiar and stable surroundings help a child cope with change in part of their lives?

2 Understand how to establish a safe and healthy home-based environment for children

Managing risks in home-based care

You learned about assessing risks in Unit 7. You should apply this to carrying out a risk assessment in your home-based setting, as part of your duty of care towards children and your responsibility to keep them safe and healthy. You have to achieve a balance between limiting risk and enabling children to experience challenge in their activities. Remember that you could be held liable if you had not taken appropriate precautions to avoid risks and that this would damage the reputation of your business.

Case study 12.4

Manjit carried out a risk assessment, walking through her house and round the garden, noting potential hazards. She noted:

- slippery rugs on her polished hall floor
- the main staircase rising out of her sitting room
- the open fireplace in the sitting room where she sometimes lights a fire in cold weather
- several exposed power points
- a rickety garden fence
- a broken catch on the garden gate so it would not shut
- the pond in the back garden.

1. What actions should Manjit take?

2. How might risks vary according to the time of year?

Figure 12.1: What hazards can you see in these rooms?

Safeguarding in home-based care

Safeguarding children is a wide-ranging aspect of your work. It includes not only child protection, but also having policies and procedures to assess risk and implement precautions, as well as taking action if things go wrong. Besides considerations of health (to control the risk of infection) and safety, you need to think about e-safety (protecting children who go online) and the possibility of a child getting lost or going missing.

There are specific factors to take into account in a home-based setting in relation to:

- health and safety accidents and incidents
- child protection.

Health and safety

Food preparation

Meals and snacks for children must be prepared in hygienic conditions. When storing, preparing and cooking food:

- cover or wrap food in the fridge and keep raw meat at the bottom (to prevent blood dripping onto other foods)
- never use food after the use-by dates
- take care to defrost frozen food fully before cooking
- never re-freeze food that has been thawed
- keep implements and utensils used for preparing food, tea towels and working surfaces clean, and never allow pets on working surfaces
- run the fridge at 4°C or 5°C, and the freezer at minus 18°C (to stop bacteria multiplying)
- cover pet food stored in the fridge, and wash up and store pets' feeding bowls separately from utensils used by humans
- never change babies or put toddlers on the potty in the kitchen.

Waste disposal

Disposing of waste in a home environment must be done hygienically.

- Empty rubbish bins frequently and clean them thoroughly.

- Wrap disposable nappies individually and put them in the dustbin outside the house as soon as possible, not in the kitchen bin.
- Tip the potty down the toilet (not the hand basin).

Pets

If there are pets in your setting, take care to:

- clean the floor after a pet has been fed (to prevent bacteria multiplying or pests being attracted)
- keep pets' feeding dishes and litter trays out of reach of the children
- keep animals clear of fleas, wormed and inoculated
- exercise dogs away from the garden
- keep the sand pit covered when it's not in use to prevent animals getting into it
- never leave a child alone with a dog or other animal such as a reptile which might harm them.

Hazardous materials

Store these objects and materials in the home out of the sight and reach of children:

- gardening, car maintenance and DIY equipment and materials
- medicines and tablets
- matches and sharp objects, such as knives and razor blades
- household cleaners
- polythene bags
- alcohol and cigarettes.

You may also need to put house plants which could be poisonous on high shelves.

Supervision of children

To keep them safe, children may need:

- constant supervision – watch them every moment
- close supervision – watch them most of the time, ready to step in and take action if their safety is at risk
- general supervision – check on them regularly and keep a watchful eye from a distance.

Understand how to work with children in home-based care

Equipment

When you buy equipment, always check for standard safety markings.

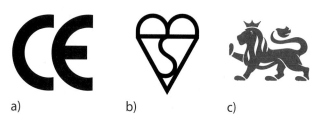

a)   b)   c)

Figure 12.2: Do you know what these standard safety markings mean?

Safety equipment like car seats should not be bought from second-hand shops, car boot or nearly new sales where you can't be sure of the quality and safety of the equipment for sale.

All equipment can be used in a safe or unsafe way. Make sure you familiarise yourself with the correct way of using and storing your equipment.

- Use equipment as the manufacturer says it should be used. Unfold a buggy so that all the safety clips are in place – otherwise the buggy might collapse and trap a child inside, possibly injuring them.

- Use equipment that is suitable and safe for the size and stage of development of a particular child. It

would be unsafe to put an 18-month-old child into a car seat designed for a 4 year old. Be alert to warning symbols on toys that say 'not suitable for children under 36 months'.

- Make regular checks of toys for sharp edges, pieces working loose, etc. and repair or throw them away; check that swings don't work loose; check that brakes are working on prams and buggies.

Accidents and incidents

In spite of your efforts to keep children safe, accidents may happen from time to time. You must plan procedures for dealing with accidents, illness and emergencies, including:

- your access to a phone

- circumstances in which you would contact outside assistance such as emergency medical services

- arrangements with someone who can care for the children if you have to leave them (if you have to take one to hospital, or if you are the emergency)

- how you would evacuate the house if there was an emergency, and the safe place you would gather the children

- how you would react if a child went missing from your setting

- keeping emergency contact details for parents (home and work) readily available

- keeping your first aid box easily accessible and ensuring it is kept properly stocked

- how to record accidents and incidents.

Registered childminders are required to hold a current first aid certificate and be prepared to deal with an emergency, and other home-based practitioners should also complete such a course.

Childminders need to be aware that a high-risk time for children to have an accident is when they arrive and when parents come to collect them and it may be unclear which adults are responsible for the children.

Children's illness and medication

Childminders' policies on children's illness should make it clear that ill children cannot be admitted to their setting because of the risks of passing on infections.

You should never give a child any form of medication without the written instructions of a parent; you may not know about a child's allergies or possible over-reaction to medication. When you administer medicines:

- give the doses in the amounts and at the times set out in the instructions given by the parents
- make a note each time you give a dose of the amount and time, and get parents to sign your record to show they have seen it.

Child protection

You learned about protecting children from abuse in Unit 8. To safeguard children, you need knowledge of signs that might indicate that a child is experiencing abuse or bullying, and you must know what action to take to protect them. Don't think that you could never encounter a child experiencing abuse because you work with 'nice families'; child abuse happens in all social and cultural groups in our society.

You should have a policy setting out what you will do if you have reason to suspect that a child is being harmed or abused, making it clear that:

- you will take action to protect the child, putting their interests and welfare first
- if a child starts to tell you about harm they are experiencing, you will listen carefully to what they say, but will allow them to communicate in their own way and at their own pace, explaining to them that you have to share the information with other people to try to help them
- in certain circumstances, you might take action without informing parents (if a child has told you that it is a parent who is harming them).

Share this policy with parents when their child joins your home-based setting, so they are fully aware of what you would do if you suspected abuse.

You should also have procedures to follow in the event of suspicions of harm or abuse, including:

- who should be informed about suspected abuse (social services department/police)
- how you would record your concerns, writing down factual information about what you've seen and observed, with dates and times

- how you would maintain confidentiality
- how you would inform your regulating body
- how you would keep your focus on the care of the child, giving warm, calm comfort and reassurance
- the actions you must take if allegations are made about harm or abuse occurring in your setting.

In group settings, practitioners discuss their concerns with a manager or other senior colleague, but most home-based practitioners are lone workers and have no one at hand to explore how seriously a possible situation should be taken, and the appropriate actions.

Case study 12.5

Elaine is a childminder who developed concerns about the welfare of one of the children she worked with but she was unsure whether to report the situation to children's services. She says: 'I had some suspicions but I couldn't believe that an adult, someone I knew, who was related to the child, could deliberately harm a child. I wrote down the changes in the child's behaviour that first made me aware that all was not well, and also what the child had said to me. I had no one I could talk to about my suspicions, and I felt very lonely and worried. When I contacted the NSPCC, I didn't have to give them any details, but they listened to what I was saying and took me seriously. I was very relieved to get advice and help with thinking through my concerns. The conversation confirmed for me that I was right to be concerned and that I should take action to protect the child. I am so glad I did so – things moved quite quickly and I think the child is now safer.'

1. If you were in Elaine's position, what might you have done?
2. How do you think you might feel?

Safe recruitment in home-based care

If you are considering employing an assistant, start by deciding what role you want your assistant to play and so the knowledge and skills you need them to have. Do you want them to take on one particular aspect of your work such as caring for a baby, or supporting the learning of older children? This will help you decide what experience and training to look for.

You might advertise or approach someone who has been recommended to you. If you advertise, be aware of the care you must take in checking out where someone has worked before by taking up references. Some people with bad intentions towards children seek out opportunities for working with them so you will have to arrange for an enhanced Disclosure and Barring Service check before an assistant starts to work for you.

Check out all your responsibilities as an employer concerning employer's insurance, paying the minimum wage, and deducting national insurance and income tax on the PACEY website.

Confidentiality in home-based care

Any professional practitioner must be very vigilant about confidentiality, as you learned in Unit 7.

Jargon buster

Confidentiality – not sharing with other people or passing on personal information about the families you are working with, except when it is in a child's best interests to do so (for example, you may have to share information with another professional in order to protect a child).

As you get to know families well, you acquire a lot of information about them, especially if you are a nanny, living with the family. You should always treat information about parents' financial and business matters, relationship difficulties and health issues as confidential.

Because home-based carers are so embedded in their local community, you may find you experience pressures from other people that make it difficult to keep information confidential. Parents of other minded children, your friends, neighbours, even other childminders or nannies may be curious about the children you care for and their families.

Case study 12.6

When Mel found herself under pressure from other childminders to tell them things that should remain confidential, in a gossipy way, she adopted the strategies of:

- being firm in stating clearly that she could not give the information they sought
- explaining that it would be unprofessional to break a confidence
- bringing the conversation to a swift conclusion
- if necessary, moving away from the person.

1. You may find yourself in Mel's position at the school gate or at a childminders' drop-in. Are there other situations when this might happen?
2. What strategies can you use to maintain confidentiality?

If you record information about children and families, you must comply with the Data Protection Act 1998 by:

- keeping written information about children and families securely in a lockable personal record box so no one in or visiting your home can have access
- using password-protected computer files to keep records.

The lone worker and child protection

Members of a childminder's family can be vulnerable to allegations of harming a child.

Case study 12.7

The father of one of the children Julie cares for accused her teenage son, Aaron, who has learning difficulties, of causing the bruises on his daughter's back. Aaron was away staying with respite carers for two days before the allegation was made, and Julie had noticed the bruises earlier in the day and made a note about them in her accident and incident book.

Julie knew she must comply with the EYFS requirements and informed both local children's services and Ofsted about the allegation, but she also contacted PACEY for help and support in dealing with the situation.

1. What effect do you think these accusations had on Julie and her family? Think about their feelings of anxiety and shock, how their privacy and dignity was affected by the investigation of the accusation, the impact on Julie's confidence and the way she thought about herself personally and professionally.

2. If you were required to suspend your childminding during an investigation, how would this affect the reputation and finances of your business?

3. What actions could you take to help protect yourself and members of your family from the effects of such allegations?

Healthy lifestyles

You learned about promoting healthy lifestyles in Unit 7. Home-based practitioners are well placed to do this by setting a good example (modelling behaviours), establishing healthy routines for meals, activity and rest, and weaving conversations into everyday life. Talk about how:

- the good food we eat helps to give us energy and grow strong bones but sugar can damage teeth

- rest and sleep help us to be able to be energetic, and being active and being outdoors keep us well

- germs make us poorly so we must wash hands before meals, and after going to the toilet or handling animals.

3 Understand how to provide play for differing ages of children in a home-based environment

Different children's play needs

You learned about the role of play in children's learning in Units 4 and 5, and you can find out more in Unit 10.

To be able to provide suitable play activities and experiences for each child, you need to observe (or monitor) each child, interact with them and talk with their parents to:

- assess what stage of development they have reached (what they are already capable of doing) and what they are ready to progress to

- find out what they are particularly interested in.

Case study 12.8

When Bronnie first became nanny to Charlie aged 4 and Maisie aged 16 months, she watched and listened to them carefully for the first few days, and talked to their parents about the milestones they had reached. She discovered that Charlie was intrigued by the diggers on a nearby building site. She observed that Maisie was fascinated by putting objects into containers and taking them out, over and over again.

1. How could Bronnie use this information to plan play activities that each child would enjoy and that would help them on to the next stage of their development?

2. How should she continue to gather information and work in partnership with the parents?

The importance of play

Healthy children play from their earliest days, and children of all ages should have daily opportunities to play. Play is how young children learn – how they discover the nature of the world they live in and practise skills, both practical and social. Play should allow children to:

- have first-hand experiences of the real world
- explore and make discoveries
- experiment, trying something out (an idea, a feeling) to see what happens
- practice skills
- think creatively, solving problems
- express ideas, including fears and anxieties
- take risks and become independent
- interact and cooperate with others.

These are powerful ways of learning essential life skills and support all aspects of children's development.

Measuring and recording progress

In Unit 5, you learned about assessing children's progress. The key to this is active observation. However well you know a child, it is worth setting aside specific times to spend quietly watching and listening, taking time to focus specifically on the individual child, to collect evidence that will help you identify what they can do and how they are behaving. This can indicate to you:

- what each child is capable of doing and when they develop new skills
- how they behave and any changes in their behaviour
- what particularly interests them
- their reactions to new situations and opportunities.

When you reflect on this information alongside your knowledge of the expected path of children's development, you can assess or measure whether each child is progressing at a rate and in ways that are usual for children of their age. Commercially produced checklists are of less value than your close attention to individual children.

Home-based practitioners sometimes feel daunted at the idea of carrying out observations but, in fact, childminders and nannies observe children closely all the time, often without being consciously aware that they are doing so, and know each child well as an individual. However, they have less need to make extensive observation records since they do not have colleagues to pass on information to.

Case study 12.9

Karen kept blocks of sticky notes and a pen in various corners of her setting, so she could grab them and quickly jot down any key observations, without unduly interfering with her interactions with the children. She made very brief notes and during quiet moments – nap time, or while the children were engaged in an absorbing activity – she stuck the stickies in the appropriate child's file and read what she had written.

1. Try this method and reflect on what your observations tell you about children's progress over time. Be sure to date your notes.

2. How can you share your observations with parents?

You might choose to write some more detailed observations to share with parents from time to time, or to create some examples to demonstrate to an inspector how you make use of your observations. Although your notes may only be legible enough for you to read, these more detailed records must be clear and readable by others. Don't get too hung up on keeping masses of observation records, taking your time away from the children. That is not the purpose of observation!

Planning play activities

You don't have to provide a mini-preschool or nursery in your home-based setting – it is important to maintain the home atmosphere. However, providing play activities and experiences appropriate to each child can play a significant part in enabling them to progress to the next stage of development.

The key here is planning. If you simply offer the same range of play activities all the time, you may not be providing what is suitable to help a particular child's development at any given time or covering all aspects of development. If you use your observations to build up a picture of the stages of development each child has reached, you will be in a position to identify suitable play to help this to happen.

Making plans involves you thinking about the resources you need. That may mean buying new equipment, or borrowing from a toy library, or improvising things from household objects: cardboard boxes, wooden spoons and old saucepans have great play potential, as does a tablecloth draped over a clotheshorse.

Think about how you will arrange equipment and materials to make an activity attractive to the child concerned. It may also mean adjusting routines so that you ensure there is sufficient time for a child to

Figure 12.3: What everyday objects do you use for play?

complete an activity without interruptions, or going out of your setting to make use of local facilities like a playground or drop-in group. Remember that the most important resource for a child's play is you, and the support you can provide.

If you don't make plans like these, you may continue to provide play in a rather haphazard way, and lose opportunities to support children's progress. However, don't be too rigid in your plans – be prepared to adjust them if necessary.

Early intervention and children's development

If your observations show you that a child is not making the sort of progress in an area of development at the rate that would usually be expected, it is important that you take action. This action should take the form of:

- making more observations to confirm your assessment, in case the apparent delay in development is just related to an occurrence, such as poor health, or an upheaval in the child's life such as the birth of a sibling
- making careful notes of what you observe and how that links to your knowledge of expected development
- talking with the child's parents and checking if they have made the same observations.

If you and the parents share concerns, they might consider discussing the matter with their health visitor or GP, who may be able to arrange some suitable professional help – for example, speech and language therapy for a child whose communication skills seem slow in emerging. Together, you could plan some strategies to help the child make progress. For example, if a child is not developing habits of concentration, you might make sure they have opportunities for quiet activities that particularly interest them, free of distractions.

What is important is that you don't delay taking action. Areas of development such as communication and concentration underpin other aspects of development, and the longer such aspects of a child's development are not moving forward, the longer lasting the negative effects are likely to be as they begin to interfere with other areas of development. A child who cannot communicate finds it difficult to form social relationships and may become isolated, which will impact on their emotional development. A child who cannot concentrate will have problems with all aspects of cognitive learning.

Intervening at an early stage can help you and the parents to tackle problems before they get too serious and make sure that the child's progress is not impeded in the long term.

Everyday activities to support play

'Play' isn't just about the sort of activities provided in centre-based provision. Children enjoy being involved in 'grown up' tasks, and there are many opportunities for children's development and learning in everyday activities in the home setting.

- Laying the table involves counting and sorting, and so does hanging out and bringing in washing.
- Helping to prepare food can develop hand–eye coordination and weighing ingredients for cooking is early mathematics.
- Watering plants and watching them grow is early science.
- Helping with the washing up (non-breakable and non-sharp things) is a form of water play.

Play for children of different ages

Most home-based settings cater for children of a range of ages: nannies care for the children of a whole family, and many childminders offer out-of-school care as well as for babies and pre-schoolers. Forethought and planning is needed to make sure that you provide a variety of play activities so all the children have the chance to enjoy play that is appropriate to their stage of development, and that does not interfere with the other children's play.

Balancing child-initiated and adult-led play

While it is important for practitioners to plan play to be sure that each child is offered chances to make developmental progress, you should also value the play that comes spontaneously from children's own interests and motivations. Play does not always have a tangible end-product – it is the doing and being that matters and that enables the learning to happen and creativity to blossom.

Children whose every move is planned and directed by adults do not learn independence or self-reliance; they find it difficult to take responsibility for themselves. If children disagree with one another during their play, it is often better to let them sort out their own disputes, rather than imposing an adult solution.

Figure 12.4: How can everyday activities be used as learning opportunities?

Case study 12.10

Lucy is a nanny who looks after baby Arthur, 3-year-old Molly and 7-year-old Oliver. Molly and Oliver get cross if Arthur upsets or interferes with their activities. When the older children get very active, Lucy has to keep Arthur safe. Molly sometimes gets frustrated that she can't keep up with her big brother. Oliver gets annoyed with the little ones holding him back from 'big boys' play. Lucy has to juggle time, equipment and materials to give all three children the opportunity to play in ways that suit their stage of development.

1. What play activities can Lucy set up for Molly and Arthur when he is awake and crawling about?

2. What activities can she provide during school holidays that will enable Molly and Oliver to play alongside one another, each benefitting from the play according to their stage of development?

3. How can she give Oliver time for his play that frees him from the constraints of his younger siblings?

This all means that adults should know when to step back and let children play independently. The adult's role is to provide interesting equipment and materials – and then to stand back and let children use them in the ways their own imagination and inventiveness takes them. Practitioners need to keep a watchful eye on the level of detail of their planning and make sure that they do not try to lead all of children's play.

Showing that play is valued

When children are absorbed in play and find satisfaction in what they have done, there is often little need for adult reaction. However, it is important to let children know that you do not regard their play as a trivial activity of no importance. It should be respected and valued, and never be dismissed as 'just playing'.

Your interest, praise and encouragement (feedback) is essential to children. You can offer to join in their play, but be sure to do so on their terms – don't take over or try to steer. You can make suggestions and offer additional equipment and materials, but be prepared to withdraw if they are rejected.

4 Understand how to meet the personal, social and emotional needs of children in a home-based childcare environment

Recognising individual needs

In Unit 3, you learned that it is essential that you see each child as a unique individual so you can avoid making assumptions about them. To be able to meet the social and emotional needs of each child, you have to assess those needs in each individual child. Each child is a unique combination of characteristics, each has had different experiences in life so far, and each develops at a different rate, so each has different needs and likes and dislikes.

Forming secure relationships

In order to be able to meet children's social and emotional needs, you must establish a secure relationship with them and begin to form a bond which will help to meet their attachment needs (as you learned in Unit 1). Home-based carers often look after very young children so you need to be aware that as babies approach the age of one, they may experience 'stranger anxiety', and many toddlers feel 'separation anxiety'.

Jargon buster

Separation anxiety – children under 3 years often find it difficult to cope with being separated from the familiar adults in their lives.

Stranger anxiety – from about 8 months, it is usual for children to become wary of people they don't know.

When you first start caring for a child, they will need help in adjusting to the new relationship and in developing trust in you. The strategies you use to ensure you communicate effectively with them and get your relationship off to a good start will depend on their stage of development and previous experiences, and whether you are caring for them in the familiar surroundings of their own home or in the unfamiliar environment of your home.

Case study 12.11

Childminder Kim describes how she helps a child to feel emotionally secure in her care: 'I arrange for the child to spend time with me with a parent and, when they're ready, progress to short stays without the parent. I make sure everything is calm and welcoming, and give the new child lots of individual attention – I stay close by and offer them reassurance. I try to give them food they are used to and I make sure they have their comfort object or "cuddly" if they need it, so they have continuity and consistency from their parents' care.'

1. How do you establish a good relationship with a child new to your care?

2. How does this vary between forming relationships with a baby and a 3 year old?

Figure 12.5: Why is it important to give a child individual attention when you first start caring for them?

You may find that you relate more easily to some children than others, but in your professional role, you must ensure that you give all children equally good care and focus on building a secure relationship with each.

The impact of a new child

As you focus on a child new to your care, this has can have a disruptive effect on the other children you look after. This applies in all settings, but is particularly intense for children in a home-based setting since they usually get so much individual attention.

A child who is confident and secure in their relationship with you may enjoy helping to welcome the new child, especially if you have prepared them for the new arrival and involve them in providing a welcome. However, a less secure child may feel unsettled by a change in routine or getting less of your time and attention and children with poor self-esteem may even feel that you do not care for them as much as you did before. You may find that they 'play up' or regress in their development which may indicate that they are anxious, and you will have to reassure them that you still value them.

For childminders, it can be particularly difficult for your own children. They may have to adapt to different routines, and have to get used to sharing their parent and perhaps some of their toys with other children, so they need careful explanations and reassurance. They may want to store some of their treasured possessions away in a part of the house the childminded children don't have access to.

Including children in decision making

Childminders and nannies can involve children in making decisions about what happens in the home-based setting, offering them choices according to their stage of development. You might offer options about what to have for meals. Thinking about what they like to eat and what is healthy to eat contribute to their ability to plan ahead and think creatively. Other decisions about what games to play today can involve logical thinking about whether the weather is suitable for playing outdoors and what resources need to be gathered together.

Decisions involve thinking through the advantages and disadvantages of the range of options and realising that having one thing may mean doing without something else. The process of making decisions is a way of taking responsibility and builds up confidence and independence.

Reflect

Think of the decisions you enable children to make during your everyday routines with them while protecting them from the consequences of poor decisions.

What support do they need from you to be able to think through the consequences of their decisions?

Children's emotional needs

You learned about children's emotional needs, including attachment, in Unit 1. The small group and individual attention that characterises home-based childcare is especially suited to meeting the emotional needs of young children. The sort of quiet, intimate conversations you can have in your setting, using stories and puppets, can help children to think and talk about their feelings in a relaxed and comfortable environment where they feel safe and secure. The consistency, security and closeness of the relationship you offer support all children's confidence and the emotional resilience needed to become independent.

Close communication with parents is essential; you need to share the information you gather by observing the child's emotional wellbeing and tackle together any problems such as a child becoming unsettled by a life event, like the birth of a new sibling or moving house.

Managing children's behaviour

You learned about children's behaviour in Unit 4. You need to make it clear to children the sort of behaviour which is and is not acceptable in your home-based setting (your 'house rules'). Setting boundaries or limits for the way they behave can be very reassuring to children. Discussing this framework (set out in your behaviour policy) with parents before you start caring for their child will help you agree a shared approach.

'Rules' are often expressed in a negative way, so children feel that adults are always telling them what they shouldn't or mustn't do, but they may not be clear about what adults *do* want them to do. 'Expectations' describe how you do want them to behave in a positive way, and this provides children with something to aim for.

Achieving continuity and consistency in handling children's behaviour involves working closely with parents. The best situation for the child is one in which you have shared rules and shared strategies.

You may find that some parents expect rules that are different from the ones you usually work with, or have attitudes to punishment that are different from yours. It can be difficult for nannies if the child has two sets of rules within their own home. If children face totally different expectations from their parents and from you, it can be confusing for them, so you may need to negotiate a compromise with parents. You will find it helpful to record what you observe of children's behaviour and share the information with parents.

Unit 12

Case study 12.12

Debbie's expectations indicate to children how they can avoid doing things that:

- are dangerous, hurtful or offensive to others
- are a danger to the children themselves
- will make the child unwelcome or unacceptable to other people
- damage other people's belongings.

She and the children have drawn up a list.

- We try to be kind to one another, so we don't fight or hit, bite or scratch one another, or call each other names.
- We share.
- Everyone helps at clearing up time.
- We hold hands when we're out, and don't run into the road.
- We don't touch dangerous things like electric sockets.
- We sit at the table to eat a meal.
- We don't swear or use rude words.
- We don't run about indoors or climb on furniture.
- We take care of toys and books.

1. What 'rules' do you use in your setting? Have the children helped to set expectations that everybody can agree to? If you are a childminder, do you have the same expectations and rules for your own children?

2. How do you model behaviour to show children appropriate ways to behave?

For childminders, one potential flashpoint for children to let their behaviour slip is at the beginning and end of the day when children move from the care of their parents to you and back again. This is when the need

for you and parents to have a united front about what is and is not expected is most essential – otherwise the children will play you and their parents off against one another.

The importance of inclusion

In Unit 3 you learned about how a setting can be inclusive, making rights to play and learn available to all children in order to give them equal chances for development and achievement, and to protect them from prejudice and discrimination based on gender, ethnicity, social or family background, or disability.

Reflect

1. How do you ensure that the play environment you provide is accessible and welcoming to all children?

2. How do the play experiences and activities you offer avoid stereotyping and give each individual child an equal chance to participate and learn?

3. How do you challenge any prejudice or discriminatory behaviour that arises promptly and firmly?

5 Understand the role of parents and/or carers and other agencies as partners in home-based childcare

Working with parents as partners

You learned about working with parents in Unit 9. Parents are the most important people in a child's life because:

- they have a long-term and permanent role in their children's lives
- there is strong attachment between parents and their children, and parents usually have the child's interests most at heart

- parents care deeply about their own children and know their own child better than anyone else does.

Working closely with parents is in the best interests of children. It is essential to exchange information regularly about how children's development is progressing, as well as what they eat, their sleep and rest, trips to the toilet and other practical matters to ensure their health and welfare. When you and parents work as a team, you are more likely to identify and be able to tackle any concerns that arise about a child's development or behaviour, and ensure the continuity that is necessary for their emotional security.

Home-based carers have close relationships with parents; nannies live in the parents' home, and parents come into childminders' homes. If you approach the relationship positively, there is great potential for a beneficial partnership.

Supporting parents

There may be times when your observations of a child lead you to have some concerns about their development or behaviour. In learning outcome 3 of this unit, you saw the advantages of taking early action if you have concerns, in order to seek appropriate support.

Often, if you raise a concern, parents feel a sense of relief since they already have anxieties and are comforted that a professional has also spotted that there is something that needs attention. You can help the family by explaining why you think that there is a matter that needs to be pursued further, and making some suggestions about where they might go for further advice. If you write down what you have observed, the parents can show this to a health visitor, doctor or therapist. Say that you are willing to cooperate in carrying out suggestions from other professionals.

However, given their strong feelings for their child, some parents may be reluctant to contemplate the idea that their child has a developmental problem. They may feel that your expectations are unrealistic or your 'rules' too severe. In this situation, be tactful and understanding. Gently explain why you think the child needs some additional help, and what you would

usually expect the pathway of a child's development to be. Reassure the parents that many children need an extra bit of help and that taking action in the early years can prevent longer-term difficulties.

Making links with home learning

It has been established for many years that children's learning is enhanced by their parents' involvement. Keep parents well informed about the learning activities and experiences children are having in their time with you so they can carry on that learning at home. This is all part of ensuring continuity and consistency in children's lives.

It is equally important that you listen to what parents tell you about what children have been learning at home; remember they spend more time there than in your setting. Follow up the ideas and themes that emerge from this information and plan how to build on the child's learning. Young children need to revisit new information and experiences many times in order to be able to strengthen the connections in their brains and consolidate their learning.

Case study 12.13

Jess, a nanny, heard from Ethan's parents about the castle they had been to look at over the Bank Holiday weekend when she was away, where they had seen a battle re-enactment. Jess borrowed a book about a knight, *Sir Charlie Stinky Socks,* from the library and read the stories to Ethan.

Becky, who is a childminder, heard from Lauren's parents about the excitement of seeing newborn pigs on her uncle's farm. She encouraged Lauren to draw some pictures of the piglets.

1. How do children benefit from the ways you extend their learning at home?

2. In what other ways could Jess and Becky use these events to extend the children's learning?

Working with other agencies

You learned about working with other professionals and how that can benefit families in Unit 9. You need to be open to sharing information with professionals in other agencies and to be ready to work in partnership with them, taking advantage of the expertise and specialist resources they can offer.

Case study 12.14

Chloe is 3 years old. She spends two days a week at home with her mother, and three days with a childminder. She goes to pre-school two half days a week – her mother takes her one day and her childminder takes her the other. Chloe has cerebral palsy; she sees a physiotherapist and a speech and language therapist regularly.

Tyrone is 6 years old. He attends a local primary school and goes to a childminder until his parents get back from work. His asthma makes him susceptible to infections so he sees his GP and the practice nurse quite often.

1. Both Chloe's and Tyrone's childminders are experienced and knowledgeable. What is being added to their care and welfare by the other agencies involved?
2. How might their childminders be able to work with the professionals in the other agencies towards the aims they all share for the children?

Childminders and nannies are usually comfortable communicating with other childcarers and people like family support workers and foster carers, but sometimes feel unsure about communicating with practitioners in other disciplines, especially those who work in large organisations (such as social workers), or feel daunted by the nature of their expertise (such as psychologists). If you feel like this, keep at the forefront of your mind how much a child and their parents could be helped by getting access to the right expertise at the right time. And also remember, that no matter how well qualified and highly skilled the professionals in other agencies are, you know the individual child far better than they ever can because you see them every day and have a close relationship with their parents. Draw confidence from this and recognise the value of the unique contribution you can make.

Linking with other settings

The children you care for are likely, as they get past the baby stage, to spend part of their time in other settings such as pre-school/nursery school and then school. Just as it is essential to work with parents to sustain continuity from home to your setting, so it is important to develop working relationships with the other settings. You may also find other settings a source of support and guidance in your work.

Be sure to introduce yourself to the practitioners in the other settings and make clear that you are open to working in partnership with them, so you can communicate relevant information and enable children's learning to be transmitted from one setting to another. Present yourself confidently as a fellow professional and, if necessary, explain that you, like they, have knowledge of the EYFS and work towards the same outcomes as they do. Take advantage of opportunities to network and have ongoing communication with practitioners in other settings in your area, attending any meetings you are able to get to.

Respecting boundaries

The close contact between home-based carers and parents can make it difficult to keep relationships with parents on a professional partnership footing – business-like, within a friendly atmosphere. There is a difference between being friendly and becoming friends.

Case study 12.15

Childminder Sunita has always had pleasant conversations with Kate about her son, and enjoyed chats over a cup of tea about how their weekend went. Recently this has progressed to Kate confiding personal health information to Sunita, and now she has asked Sunita to come to see a film with her.

Nanny Emily gets on well with Nicola, mother of the little boy she cares for. She has become aware that there is tension between the parents and Nicola has started to drop hints about their disagreements.

1. Where should Sunita and Emily draw the line in their relationships with Kate and Nicola?

2. How can they make their position clear while keeping the relationship cordial?

Sharing your policies with parents will emphasise your professional role.

Understanding ethnicity

You learned in Unit 3 about the importance of taking a child's ethnicity into account in your interactions with them and their family in order to ensure that your practice is inclusive and that you support children's self-image and self-esteem. The sort of personal and physical care given by home-based childminders makes it especially important to consider the individual needs that arise from ethnicity, such as skin and hair care and dietary requirements.

Case study 12.16

Amarjit describes the care she takes of Ngozi:

'Ngozi has tight, curly hair which she wears in braids close to her head. If she gets sand in her hair, it's a nightmare for her and her mum. I want her to enjoy playing in the sandpit just as much as the other children do, and gain from the learning opportunities it offers.'

1. How can Amarjit make sure Ngozi avoids getting sand in her braids?

Various cultures and religions have rules and customs about food, and devout followers of many religions may fast (abstain from eating certain foods or at certain times). However, don't assume that because a child is a member of a particular ethnic group, they and their families stick to the dietary rules and traditions of a specific culture or religion. Always discuss what a family wants and clarify with parents which religious practices they want their child to follow. It is essential to comply with what is agreed with parents about their children's diet. It would be lacking in respect for the family's religious beliefs and values to be disregarded and the child given a food which is excluded by the traditions the family follows.

Further reading and resources

Publications

- Lee, A. (2007) *The Childminder's Companion: A practical guide to looking after other people's children*, Oxford: How to Books
- Lee, A. (2008) *Childminder's Guide to Child Development*, London: Continuum International Publishing Group
- Lee, A. (2007) *Childminder's Guide to Play and Activities*, London: Continuum International Publishing Group

Websites

- EYFS documentation: www.education.gov.uk/eyfs – information and guidance on using the EYFS
- Food Standards Agency: www.food.gov.uk – government website showing current research in food safety, nutrition and food-related disease
- Professional Association for Childcare and Early Years (PACEY): www.pacey.org.uk – a standard-setting organisation that promotes best practice and supports childcare practitioners

Articles and magazines

- *The Childcare Professional*: www.pacey.org.uk/about/benefits_of_membership/the_childcare_professional.aspx – magazine for members of PACEY
- *Practical Pre-school*: www.magonlinelibrary.com/toc/prps/current – a magazine covering childcare

Lead and manage a community based early years setting

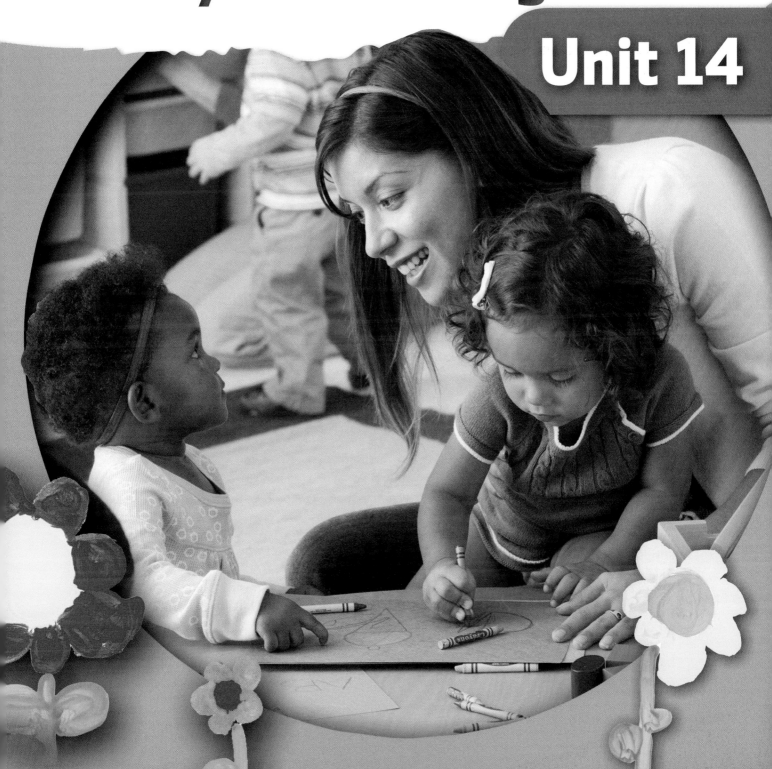

This unit is about providing effective leadership and management in a community based early years setting that promotes the engagement, involvement and participation of parents. Being a parent is a difficult job and the support of a well-managed community based early years setting can make all the difference.

Before you start

Think about the support families have today and how this may differ from when your parents or grandparents were little. Who helps families to cope with childcare, parenting and advice? What are the challenges faced by parents today? What are the benefits of helping parents develop the skills to bring up their children in a safe and healthy environment?

Learning outcomes

By the end of this unit you will:

1. understand the purposes, benefits and key features of community based early years provision

2. be able to lead teams in a community based early years setting

3. be able to engage parents and/or carers as partners in the community based early years setting

4. understand how to involve parents and/or carers in the management decision-making processes of an early years setting

5. understand the provision of learning opportunities to support parents' and/or carers' participation in a community based early years setting

6. be able to manage the resource, regulatory and financial requirements for a community based early years setting.

1 Understand the purposes, benefits and key features of community based early years provision

Community based early years settings were introduced in the late 1990s as a support for families in deprived areas. They soon became a source of support and guidance for all families with young children. However, recently there has been a move away from universal, locally-based provision to a more targeted approach, focusing on priority families once more.

The purpose and key features

Local authorities are responsible for improving outcomes for young children and reducing inequalities between young children in their area. They aim to improve the wellbeing of young children by:

- promoting physical and mental health and emotional wellbeing
- protecting them from harm and neglect
- providing education, training and recreation
- enabling and supporting contribution to society
- supporting social and economic wellbeing.

Integrated services

The Childcare Act 2006 outlines the duty on local authorities to make sure that their early childhood services are integrated so that as many children, families and carers can access and benefit from them as possible. Some services are provided by the centre itself, such as baby clinics and toddler music sessions or the provision of healthy eating advice. Others are outreach services for families that find it difficult to attend the centre for a variety of reasons. Centre staff also help families and carers access other local services, such as literacy classes and Jobcentre Plus.

Figure 14.1 shows how integration can provide good-quality services for all the family.

Jargon buster

Integrated – professionals working together, at a single location, to deliver frontline services for children and their families.

Outreach – visiting and providing services to people who might otherwise not be able to access them.

Targeted services – services for children and families with additional and multiple needs but who fall below the threshold for specialist support.

Universal services – services offered to meet the needs of all children, where specialist or targeted support is not required.

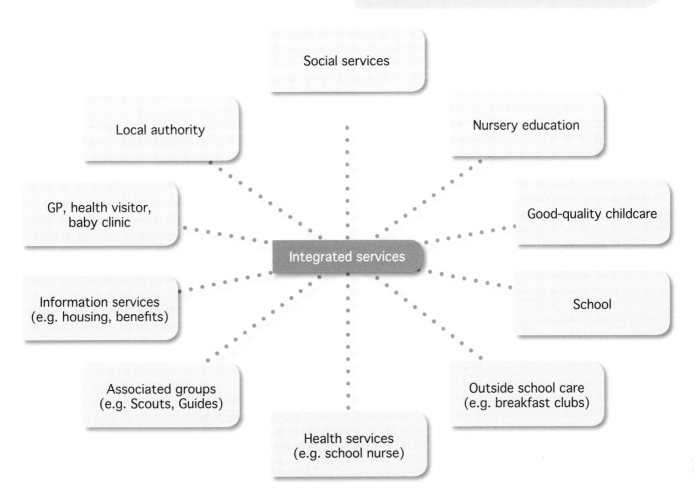

Figure 14.1: How do these services provide for families?

Multi-agency approach

Community based early years provision uses a multi-agency approach to improve outcomes and reduce inequalities for young children and their families in:

- child and family health and life chances
- parenting skills
- child development and school readiness.

Early support and advice in a community context makes sense to families. They can access many of the services they need through their local children's centres, including early education, childcare and health services. Parents and carers can also find support to help them develop life and work skills, such as literacy, numeracy and job-seeking skills.

Other services include:

- drop-in sessions
- antenatal care
- breastfeeding support
- healthy lifestyle planning
- baby massage
- pregnancy club
- parenting classes
- special needs programmes.

The services promote inclusion. The users of a setting determine which services it provides, and these change often to meet their specific needs and interests.

Jargon buster

Inclusion – the process of ensuring equality of opportunities and access to services for all.

The benefits

Community based early years settings have a positive impact on children, parents and carers, as well as the local community. It is hard to measure the benefits

Reflect

1. How effective is the provision in your setting in meeting the needs of the children and their parents and/or carers?
2. What evidence do you have to support your view?
3. How do you measure effectiveness?
4. What strategies are in place to ensure an inclusive approach to implementing services?

exactly but one thing is for certain: the wellbeing and quality of life for the children and their families would be significantly reduced if they did not have access to the high-quality care, support and guidance provided by centres.

For children

Children who attend community based settings benefit from the range of activities and experiences on offer. Their confidence and skills grow as they socialise with other children and adults. Their play and learning is also encouraged as their parents develop the skills necessary to support their child. The health and life chances of children attending community based early years settings are greatly increased. This is mainly due to children benefiting from the early identification of any existing or emerging additional needs and the support put in place to help them. Children who attend centres are more prepared for entry in to school as the centres work towards school readiness.

Figure 14.2 shows the potential impact community based early years settings have on children.

For parents

In the past, parents and carers developed their own range of services by drawing on the expertise and support of grandparents, relations and neighbours through a strong community network. However, society today is quite different. Families may be

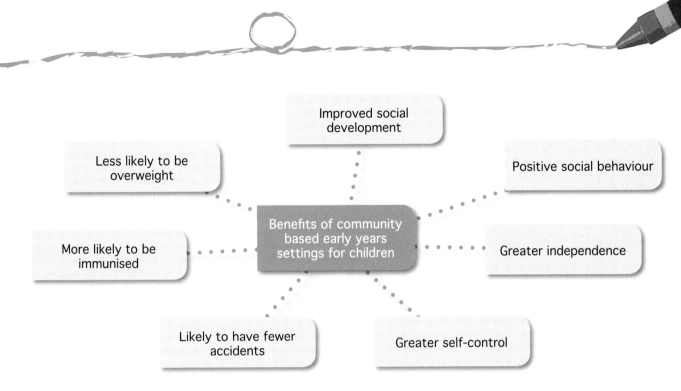

Figure 14.2: Can you think of other benefits for children of community based early years settings?

The mind map shows "Benefits of community based early years settings for children" with the following benefits:
- Improved social development
- Positive social behaviour
- Greater independence
- Greater self-control
- Likely to have fewer accidents
- More likely to be immunised
- Less likely to be overweight

spread across the world and no longer part of a close-knit community.

Most families do not need help much of the time, but there are families who find themselves in crisis for different reasons and in desperate need of additional support. Community based early years settings offer a wide range of benefits for these families. Firstly, they provide support and advice that is specific to the individuals' needs. Well-organised parenting programmes give parents the opportunity to talk to trusted, knowledgeable, non-judgemental professionals. These conversations are vital in enabling families to avoid a crisis and supporting them through one.

Parents, especially those bringing up a young family in challenging circumstances, do not always have consistent, positive role models. Community based early years settings offer parents the chance to be surrounded by highly trained professionals who can model ways to be a parent and show them a range of strategies they can use. These settings employ a variety of professionals including health visitors, midwives and early years practitioners, with a wide range of skills and expertise for support and advice.

As community based settings serve their immediate area, families can meet each other, developing friendships and support networks that might have been impossible if the centre did not exist.

Figure 14.3 shows the potential impact community based early years settings have on parents.

Reflect

In whose interest do you think it is for community based early years settings to support parents through professionally organised parenting programmes, employment skills and life skills workshops?

An agent of community development

Local authorities analyse the data gathered by community based early years settings to measure their impact. When this is put together with other social data, you can see that these settings have had a significant impact on community development in most neighbourhoods.

Figure 14.3: Can you think of other benefits for parents of community based early years settings?

Reported developments locally include less litter and people taking greater pride in maintaining their property. It is reported that having more young families moving into some areas creates more of a community feel. Research data also indicates that there is less dependence on benefits, fewer burglaries, less anti-social behaviour and greater social cohesion.

Jargon buster

Cohesion – working together productively towards a mutual goal.

Social cohesion – communities sharing common values and having greater trust between members.

Other reported improvements where there is community based early years provision include:

- fewer accidents
- significantly better child health
- an increase in the identification of children with a special need or disability, probably due to improved screening

- higher school attendance and achievement – a likely result of successful parenting and behaviour management programmes.

Through quality partnerships, better education, and sharing expertise and experience, the life chances of children and families have improved greatly.

Reflect

1. Do we focus too much support on families who have reached a crisis point, rather than supporting them beforehand to avoid a crisis?

2. How can settings identify families that need additional advice and support but are not yet at a crisis point?

2 Be able to lead teams in a community based early years setting

The children, their families and the staff team are at the heart of any setting, and the way they are cared for and managed will have a significant impact on how the setting is viewed by the service users as well as those in the community. Strong and responsive leadership is key to ensuring high quality practice that offers outstanding services for children and their families.

Ofsted views the quality of leadership and management as a key area, expecting that settings will:

- understand their responsibilities for learning and development, and for the safeguarding requirements of the EYFS
- oversee the education programme and ensure that it is delivered in its entirety and that children's progress is assessed and used to inform planning
- promote equality and diversity and have a clear overview of the potential and progress of all the children who attend
- evaluate the service and have high expectations for the quality of what their team provides, and set challenging targets for service improvement
- have effective systems in place for safe recruitment, continuous professional development (CPD) and staff performance
- work in partnership with parents, professionals and associated organisations
- ensure that children, parents and staff are safeguarded and that they maintain secure and comfortable environments in which children can thrive and where safeguarding is embedded into aspects of practice
- have tackled highlighted weaknesses from the previous inspection.

A common goal

Leaders of community based settings often find themselves managing teams made up of professionals from different agencies, and have to take into account varying working conditions, skills and professional principles. This can be challenging, but when groups of professionals come together to work with young children and their families they share one common goal. They are all working towards the best possible outcome for the child and their family and it is this shared goal that underpins how you lead and manage a team to work effectively together.

The government's 'common core of skills and knowledge' sets out six areas of expertise that all professionals working with children and their families are expected to have:

- effective communication and engagement
- knowledge of child and young person development
- knowledge of safeguarding and promoting the welfare of each child
- effective skills for supporting transitions
- multi-agency working skills
- good practice for sharing information.

Reflect

1. Reflecting on the Ofsted inspection criteria for leadership and management, what skills and attributes do you think are essential for a leader of a community based early years setting?

2. Do you have all these skills? What evidence can you draw on to support this?

3. If you do not have all the essential leadership skills, how could you develop them?

Leadership skills in practice

To be a good leader, you need to understand what makes a good team.

What makes an effective team?

There are four key characteristics of effective teams:

- a sense of purpose and clear objectives
- a good balance of roles
- committed and effective leadership
- good communication.

Creating a sense of purpose and clear objectives
Working towards a common vision or aim can ensure the team's cohesion. If the team shares common values and beliefs, this makes working together much

easier. Although you can't assume that everyone holds the same values and beliefs generally, you can assume that most people working in early years settings will be working to the same set of key principles that guide their practice as highlighted in the EYFS.

Your team's aims and objectives may be written down in a formal mission statement, but what really counts is everyone seeing them evolving in the team's everyday practice.

Getting a good balance of roles

Teams that provide services for children and families need a balance of individuals to provide different skills, attitudes and personal qualities. You need to build an understanding of the personality traits of the different team members, making sure that harmonious working relationships are created and maintained. You also need to establish where there are skill gaps in the team, supporting continuous professional development for those who need to develop their skills.

Making your leadership committed and effective

As a leader of a community based early years setting you are not only accountable to the children and their families but also to the team, the community and to yourself. In order to deliver the best possible services, you must reflect on your leadership skills on a regular basis. Through reflection you will be able to evaluate the effectiveness of your leadership style and consider how you could modify it to suit the needs of your setting.

There are key leadership skills that have been identified as essential in leading high-quality practice in community based early years settings, which could be used to measure your own practice. These include:

* effective communication
* negotiation and empathy
* consistency and fairness
* leading change and modelling good practice
* effective conflict management
* coaching and facilitation skills.

Good communication

Good communication skills are essential in order to lead and manage a community based early years setting effectively. You will need to be able to communicate effectively with a range of children, people and professionals on a daily basis. Communication is key to getting things done. The

Case study 14.1

Alice is a new member of the team. She is an early years practitioner with five years' experience in a community based early years centre. Her previous setting was in a less deprived area. During the weekly team meeting the leader of the setting announces that she has secured some additional funding to help them engage dads in activities with their children in the setting. Alice suggests a song and story session where the dads can take it in turns to select a story with their child and lead the session. Most of the team don't feel that a song and story session like this would be appropriate for their families. One member of the team suggests asking the dads what sort of activity they would like. Alice is keen to point out that it worked well in her last setting, and doesn't feel there is a need to ask the dads.

1. As the leader of the setting how would you deal with this situation?

2. Why do most of the group feel that Alice's idea is not appropriate for their setting?

team need to know what is expected of them as well as be informed and listened to.

Good communication aids decision making, enhances a setting's reputation and helps the effective running of systems, policies and procedures. Poor communication can result in misinformation and misunderstanding as well as poor workplace relationships.

Reflect

1. What do you consider to be your key roles and responsibilities?
2. Which leadership skills do you use to carry out your role?
3. Which skills do you think you need to further develop? Why?
4. How are you going to achieve this?

Planning activities for good practice

It is essential that you take part in regular activities that promote the understanding of good practice. One of your responsibilities as a leader is to hold regular supervision meetings and appraisals with your team. These enable you to identify any gaps in the team's skills, areas that need improvement or updating and any training that is needed.

You can share and promote good practice through a number of activities, including:

- continuous professional development (CPD)
- specialist courses – for example, language and communication, outdoor play, infant and toddler activities
- attending industry conferences
- industry-related shows and exhibitions
- group reflection
- shadowing the work of a more experienced practitioner
- mentoring and coaching
- end-of-the-day shared evaluation

- visits to other early years settings rated 'outstanding' by Ofsted
- shared training with local settings.

Effective teams work collaboratively on a journey of continuous improvement, so it is important that any practitioner who attends training shares it with the team afterwards. To support this, you could give the practitioner a means of documenting:

- what was covered
- what the key points for practice were
- where to find additional information and resources.

This would help them when they feed back to the team.

Creating and maintaining a team culture

In community based early years settings the main resource for service delivery is the team itself. A well-trained, motivated and committed team who enjoy their jobs and work well together will deliver high-quality practice. As leader, it is your responsibility to create and maintain a strong team culture, so that people with different personalities and strengths can work well as a cohesive team.

Remember that building a team culture is not a one-off event, but a continuing process. Different groups of people will make up your team: not only the professionals working directly with the children and families, but also the parents, outside professionals, maintenance staff and site managers. They will all need to feel they are part of the team and valued and respected as such. As leader it will be your responsibility to identify the specific training needs of each member of the team and to ensure the team works well together.

Here are some ideas for embedding a strong team culture.

Team-building exercises

Team-building exercises can give members of a team the opportunity to stand back and reflect on their own skills and consider ways of improving them. They can also help leaders distinguish different viewpoints and identify people who work well together. However, the real work begins afterwards, when the knowledge must be used to strengthen the team.

Team development

There are a number of ways to look at how a team has come to a certain point in its development. A group of people working together can take time to form into a team, and some groups may never become a cohesive team.

To build a strong team, you will need to:

- ensure everyone has the opportunity to share their views and opinions
- ensure everyone understands their own roles and responsibilities and how these relate to each other's
- support teams through change and new developments
- foster an environment that respects and values each role
- be aware of team morale and act promptly
- have clear, shared goals and objectives.

Figure 14.4 shows some of the common features of strong teams.

Implementing principles

High-quality early years services delivered through community based settings are essential in improving outcomes for children and their parents and/or carers, particularly those in greatest need. Ofsted complete inspections of community based services at five-yearly intervals, which helps to raise standards. Part of the inspection process looks at the quality of the leadership and management of the setting with a focus on how:

- management of the financial resources made available to the setting are carried out effectively
- young children, parents and prospective parents in the area served by the setting, who would otherwise be unlikely to take advantage of the services on offer through the centre, are identified and encouraged to take advantages of those services
- the needs of young children, parents and prospective parents who attend, or are likely to attend, are identified and evidence-based services are delivered to meet those needs
- appropriate policies, procedures and practices for safeguarding and promoting the welfare of young children who attend are adopted and implemented.

Figure 14.4: Can you think of any other features of strong teams?

Principles of practice

The most successful community based early years settings fulfil five key principles of practice:

- leadership
- coproduction
- partnership
- citizenship
- effective data sharing and analysis.

Leadership

High-quality leadership means delivering high-quality services that reduce inequalities and turn around the lives of families experiencing difficulties. You have just read about essential leadership skills for this role, but leaders working with vulnerable families also need excellent communication skills and a commitment to excellence.

Coproduction

Genuine co-production seeks to engage families in a way that makes good use of their expertise and values their input into the creation of policies and procedures that impact practice.

Partnership

Working in partnerships with parents, sharing expertise and building on existing strengths is far more productive than telling parents what to do. You can explore appropriate and achievable solutions, so that the outcome is more likely to be successful. By delivering services in a way that gives families control, you can promote greater engagement. Working in partnership, families can become advocates for your setting and will be more likely to influence other families in the community to use the centre.

Not all families will be willing or able to actively engage in the services your setting provides. One of the hardest tasks for leaders of community based early years settings is to ensure connectivity across the community, making sure that all local families have the opportunity to access the setting. Many settings keep in contact with local families through newsletters or offer invitations to special events. Newsletters have

been reported to be particularly successful, especially for those families who were not aware of outreach work and home visiting. Once your setting has established contact with a family, it is easier for you to identify their particular needs and make sure these are provided for.

> ### Jargon buster
>
> **Connectivity** – how far the different aspects of something are connected or interconnected.
>
> **Coproduction** – a way of working where people who use services, families and service providers work together to create a service that works for them all.

Citizenship

Community based early years settings provide opportunities for isolated families to become better connected with their community by actively promoting citizenship through volunteering programmes and peer-to-peer support schemes. Networks are developed between local families by providing a range of programmes that enable families to connect with their community. Local families who act as advocates for their local community based early years settings are an important part of a thriving community and are hugely influential in engaging isolated families.

Data sharing and analysis

By sharing data, teams supporting young children, parents and carers can identify local families, especially those who are less visible. Data sharing can play a crucial part in your centre reaching its potential by:

- ensuring your services meet the needs of families
- ensuring your services are targeted effectively
- enabling your team to identify priority families
- enabling your team to assess and evaluate their services
- enabling your team to measure the outcomes for children and their families.

It is also your responsibility to analyse the effectiveness of implementing the principles of practice, as a continual process. Regular discussions with staff, informal interviews, surveys and observations can help you to analyse your practice and make any improvements.

The importance of reflection

Reflective practice is vital in working with young children and their families. In early years practice, embedded reflection is becoming a key expectation to help you develop and improve your practice. Through regular reflection you will be able to analyse the effectiveness of implementing the principles of community based early years provision, and consider what improvements you can make.

Being prepared for change

In this line of work, you need to be prepared for frequent change. Many of the families that centres support are bringing up children in very challenging circumstances. However, the majority of these families find that, with the correct support and advice, their personal situations change for the better – and so their need for support changes. Change shows that your services are being targeted correctly and are successful.

Case study 14.2

Jay leads a community based early years setting providing services for over 100 families. During the weekly team meeting, he informs the team that they will be making a few changes to the services they deliver. Based on a review of positive outcomes for children and their families, only those services that have proved to be highly successful will continue to be delivered; those with limited impact or poor attendance will not continue. Jay explains that they will also be implementing a strategy to develop relationships with a wider group of professionals, and that they will be participating in data sharing too. Jay is enthusiastic about these changes but quickly realises that the team doesn't seem so keen. He asks the team what their initial thoughts are. The team's main concerns are that their workload is going to increase and that they'll be expected to have more training in order to be able to deliver the new services.

1. How do you think Jay should deal with this situation?
2. Why do you think the team feel this way?
3. How can Jay encourage his team to embrace the necessary changes?
4. Can you explain why these changes need to be made?

3 Be able to engage parents and/or carers as partners in the community based early years setting

Centres offer differentiated support to young children and their families, according to their needs by:

- offering access to integrated information and support to all prospective parents, new parents and existing parents of young children
- encouraging and providing access to early intervention strategies and targeted support, for those young children and their families who experience factors that place them at risk of poor outcomes
- helping families who are experiencing difficulties and have young children to access appropriate wider and specialist support to meet their needs.

However, there is no point in any of these services being available if people do not use them. As a leader, it is part of your role to engage parents and work with them in partnership, so that children and families get the greatest benefit from the services you offer.

Working in partnership with parents and carers

Professionals working with young children agree that a positive relationship with families has a significant long-term impact on the child's learning and development. You can promote partnerships with parents and carers who use your setting in a number of ways, including:

- ensuring opening times and availability meet the needs of local families
- engaging with hard-to-reach families
- encouraging families to be centre advocates
- analysing data from parent questionnaires, surveys or interviews to understand local needs
- recognising and valuing different parenting styles
- conducting home visits
- encouraging parents to:
  - » work or volunteer in the setting
  - » be on the management committee or governing body
  - » help run workshops or courses
  - » share their skills and expertise.

Reflect

1. What do you think may be the issues around ensuring that the opening times and availability of the services meet the needs of the families?
2. How can these issues be addressed?
3. How would you go about deciding on opening times and which services to run when?

The foundation of a successful partnership is mutual respect and sharing of information, responsibility, planning and decision making. The more involved parents and carers are, the more guidance and support early years practitioners can provide. This level of interaction means that you are more available to answer questions on matters such as child development and parenting. It also gives you the opportunity to act as a role model on an informal basis.

Developing confidence and trust

The idea that good parenting is just common sense is a misconception. There are times when parents and carers may be in crisis or dealing with emerging issues and need some additional support. This support can develop their confidence and competence, which in turn produces confident and competent children.

However, no matter how well targeted, planned and resourced the support is, it is meaningless unless parents engage with it. A strong, positive relationship between you, the children and their parents or carers will allow trust and mutual respect to develop.

Once families feel respected and valued, they are more likely to engage positively with the range of support you have to offer, and to receive the best support for the family's situation.

Barriers to accessing support

Parents may not engage with their child in the way that they would like. Extensive research shows it is not that parents lack an interest in their child's development and learning, but that barriers make it more difficult for them to support it. These may include:

- work pressures, such as working long or unpredictable hours
- lack of skills, knowledge or confidence to access support services
- stress
- poverty
- mental health issues
- single parenthood
- disability or illness.

By recognising some of the barriers parents face, you can understand the needs of families, develop positive relationships with them and enable them to engage with your setting.

On top of this, some people may find it hard to ask for help. Figure 14.5 shows some of these reasons.

Providing feedback on a child's progress

Parents want practitioners who are confident and well informed, but also show an interest in them and their lives. Your feedback helps overcome barriers and ensures that your support is appropriate and effective.

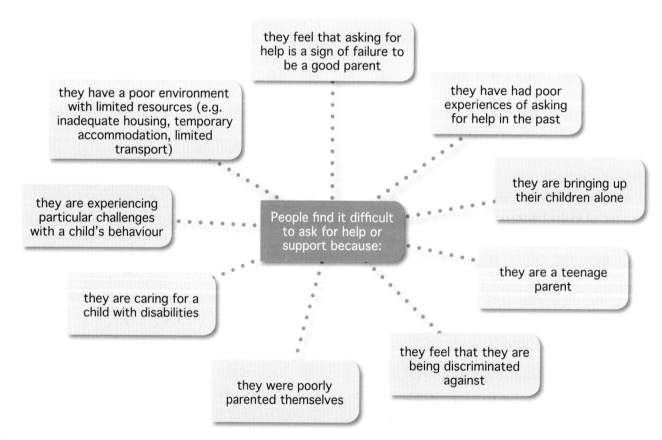

Figure 14.5: How can you help people to overcome the barriers shown here?

Your setting has a responsibility to monitor the progress of each child. Detailed records of children's progress should be maintained and shared with parents or carers. This helps you all to celebrate a child's progress and highlight any areas of concern. Photos, learning journals and observations can be used as evidence as you feed back to parents about their child's progress.

You have a responsibility to:

- feed back to parents information gained from observations
- explain the purpose and objectives of activities and how they support and encourage development and learning
- involve parents in the formulation of plans to progress the child's learning and development.

Informal feedback to parents about their child's progress is always welcome, no matter how small. Pointing out a newly developed skill or sharing their excitement about an activity or story helps to develop strong relationships with parents.

Displaying children's creative work, collating learning journals and sending completed work home are all ways you can provide informal feedback to parents.

Progressing a child's learning and development

As parents or carers are the most influential people during a child's formative years, it makes sense to involve them in their child's learning as much as possible. It is widely agreed that practitioners need to recognise the role parents have already played in the early education of their child, and that their continued involvement has a positive impact on future learning.

You can learn a lot about an individual child from the child's parents or carers. It is not only good practice, but essential to reflect on the information gathered from parents when you plan for their child's learning and development.

How to work with parents to plan for learning and development

Regular informal planning meetings with parents enable them to have their say in what is planned for their child's learning and in any decision making.

If you engage parents in deciding which activities to plan for their child, they are more likely to engage in their child's learning both in the setting and at home.

Case study 14.3

Bradley is 3 years old and attends nursery five mornings a week. He loves storybooks and will often sit in the book corner and 'read' to other children or by himself. On library day he chooses the book that was read at story time. He excitedly shows his mum the book when she arrives to collect him. She asks Bradley to choose a different book as they already have the chosen book at home. Bradley gets upset and insists that he wants to borrow the book. Mum can't persuade him to choose a different book and eventually gives up and takes it home. The following day Mum reports that Bradley spent much of the afternoon with both books meticulously checking every detail on every page. He was deeply engaged in comparing and contrasting the pictures and words in both books and enjoyed doing so. Mum's feedback prompted much discussion between the team and Mum about what Bradley was gaining from the experience and how it was extending his learning.

1. How do you think this informal approach helped Mum support Bradley's learning at home?

2. How do you take advantage of opportunities to explain how children learn as they arise?

How to help parents support their child's learning at home

Early home learning encompasses a wide range of experiences that help children flourish and achieve their full potential. You should share with parents the importance of:

- developing positive adult-child relationships, recognising success, building confidence and self-esteem
- giving children the opportunity and encouragement to explore with support, including real experience, everyday routines and playing together
- storytelling, sharing stories, making up stories, engaging in reasoning, speculation, description and making connections between concepts
- talking about words, letters and sounds seen at home and out and about.

The benefits of supporting home learning

Strong working partnerships provide the opportunity to support home learning. There are benefits to both the parents and the child if this is done effectively.

- Learning activities in the setting can be revisited and reinforced at home.
- Parents are more confident taking an active role in their child's home learning once they have experienced the activity in the setting.

Many settings provide follow-up activities for home that link to learning in the setting. These include:

- additional home activities
- songs, poems or rhymes
- simple recipes
- 'look what I did' sheets.

Remember that some families find resourcing activities difficult, so you need to be creative in what you provide. It is well worth providing simple craft packs and materials to complete the activities sent home. Settings that do this report a higher level of engagement.

Reflect

1. What systems and procedures are in place to make time for sharing information with parents and carers about their child's learning and development?
2. How are parents encouraged to share information?
3. How is the information that parents share with the setting used?
4. How do parents know the information they have shared has been taken into account?

Activities that involve parents and carers

When establishing a two-way partnership with families that enables parenting capacity, it can be helpful to consider the following key principles.

- All parents are made welcome and can see evidence of an inclusive approach.
- Parents, carers and practitioners are considered equal partners, and treated with respect and consideration.
- Parents usually know their child best.
- Parents have the right to be consulted on changes and issues that may affect their children.
- Practitioners must recognise the need for confidentiality when dealing with parents and carers.
- Parents can contribute to the assessment of their children and to the planning of their child's learning.

Involving parents and carers

There are a number of ways you can involve parents and carers in your setting. Using parent's skills and expertise can benefit everyone. Encouraging parents to be responsible for activities in the setting builds relationships and uses and develops skills.

Figure 14.6: How can you involve parents and carers in your setting?

Consider asking parents to take responsibility for:

- supporting a new family
- being a parenting mentor
- breastfeeding support
- arranging social events
- maintaining the parents noticeboard
- assisting during play sessions, music time or reading stories.

4 Understand how to involve parents and/or carers in the management decision-making processes of an early years setting

The involvement of parents and carers is not only essential to the success of any early years setting, but is also a feature of quality provision and professionalism.

Successful settings involve parents in the day-to-day activities as well as working in collaboration with them. Genuine and close working relationships enable teams to meet both the statutory requirements of the EYFS

Theory in action

Romy started attending the centre on a regular basis after experiencing mild post-natal depression following the birth of her second child. Her health visitor put her in contact with the centre where she received specialised support. Romy had a special interest in the centre's library as she used to work in a school library before having children. When the opportunity to help with the refurbishment of the library came up, Romy was keen to get involved. She was invited to advise on the purchasing of new furniture and books. Romy suggested that the centre developed a home/centre reading scheme to help parents support early reading. The centre manager welcomed the idea and the project was a huge success.

1. What do you think were the benefits of being involved with this project for:

- Romy?
- her children?
- the centre?

as well as safeguarding protocols. This close working partnership means that parents feel respected, valued and genuinely involved with the setting and the services provided.

Leaders need to set the expectation that parents will be involved in the setting and find ways to ensure an inclusive approach.

Reflect

Making sure that all parents' views and opinions are welcomed and valued is important for developing practice and delivering services. How can leaders of community based early years settings foster an inclusive approach to ensure all voices are heard?

The parent management committee

A key feature of a successful community based early years setting is the quality of the relationship between the setting and the families that use the services. Establishing a parent management committee is an effective way to involve parents in all aspects of running the setting. Initially you may need to invite specific parents to make sure that all groups are represented. However, the committee should be open to all parents. The committee can be used to shape many aspects of the services your centre provides and to inform your planning of future services and events.

The exact function of the parent management committee depends on the setting, but the committee should aim to:

- have a genuine impact on how the setting is run and which services are provided
- enable parents and carers to have a voice in how the setting is run
- enable parents to take part in the recruitment process by sitting on the interview panel
- represent the views of all service users.

Case study 14.4

When Vandu first attended Butterflies community based early years setting she was invited to join the parent management committee. She was reluctant to do so as she felt she did not have the necessary skills to make any worthwhile contribution. Jo, the centre manager, offered to attend the meetings with her so that she could meet the other members and see how the meetings were run. Jo provided support during the meetings, explaining things in an informal way. Over time, Vandu grew in confidence and volunteered to take responsibility for taking the minutes and distributing them. Some months later, Vandu told Jo that she was planning to look for a part-time job and that the confidence to do this had come from her experience of taking part in the committee.

1. What other skills do you think Vandu had gained from taking part in the committee?

2. How else could you encourage different people to join a committee?

Involving parents and carers in the committee

Parents' and carers' views on how the setting is run and which services are provided are vital to its success. You must explain the role and responsibilities of the committee in terms parents can understand, avoiding jargon. The idea is to attract them to take part, not put them off. You can offer appropriate support or training, or the chance to shadow someone, to help them take part effectively.

You will need to use a range of strategies to engage parents in running the setting. Many settings report that social media have been a successful way for parents to share their views without having to have more formal, face-to-face contact. However, you need to manage this well. Remember that it is not a substitute for face-to-face contact, but an additional way for families and the setting to communicate.

Reflect

1. What do you think the barriers to taking part in a management committee may be for some parents?

2. How could these barriers be minimised?

3. What are the benefits of taking part in the management committee to:
   - the setting?
   - the parents and carers?

5 Understand the provision of learning opportunities to support parents' and/or carers' participation in a community based early years setting

Providing learning opportunities that support parents' and carers' participation in your setting has multiple benefits. Parents and carers can develop skills and knowledge to cope with daily living, and at the same time develop skills and confidence to support their child's learning at home. Reports show that activities aimed at improving parenting, budgeting, numeracy or literacy skills give parents the confidence to continue their own learning. They may progress to a short course, enrol on further education programmes or take GCSEs or A Levels.

To decide which early interventions work best for your local families, you need to combine evidence with professional expertise.

Learning opportunities for children from parents' participation

When children see their parents valued and respected, they feel valued and respected too. You can promote informal learning opportunities by:

- giving formative feedback to parents during activities
- modelling behaviour management and strategies
- modelling positive adult-child interactions
- explaining how play opportunities can be continued at home
- building on family interests
- giving encouragement.

The benefits of parents' participation include:

- improved educational outcomes for children
- parents feel engaged in their child's learning and the life of the setting
- improved relationships between parents and children
- parents' first step back into learning.

Reflect

1. What sort of evidence could you use to decide which early interventions work best for local families?

2. What could happen to activities that are not based on evidence?

3. How would you manage a difference in professional opinion when it came to determining which activities to provide?

Jargon buster

Formative feedback – feedback that is ongoing or continuing.

Safeguarding protocols – the procedures in place for protecting children from harm, abuse and neglect.

Developing an understanding of the curriculum

It is helpful for parents and carers to have an understanding of the curriculum or framework that you are following, so that they can support their child's learning. One of the most effective ways to do this is to give parents the chance to experience the EYFS framework at first hand. You could invite parents into sessions, highlighting the prime and specific areas of learning in action and how they relate to each other. Don't assume that just giving parents copies of the EYFS framework is enough.

Figure 14.7: Displays relating to the programme of studies at your setting can help parents to feel involved in their children's work.

Many settings display the EYFS statutory framework on a noticeboard and make clear links between the activities on offer and the areas of learning in order to support parents' understanding of the framework.

Reflect

How might your team engage parents and carers in learning activities that develop their understanding of the EYFS learning and development requirements?

Encouraging parents and carers to participate in learning

There are many examples of good practice that encourage parents to feel part of your setting, including:

- producing parent information in a magazine format with pictures, top tips, news updates and diary dates
- identifying areas of specific learning needs and modelling activities and games to do at home, as well as providing the resources for these
- inviting parents in to help
- welcoming siblings too
- having a parent noticeboard with news, dates and information about upcoming events – parents can contribute too
- actively seeking their ideas and opinions
- setting up an online social network account.

Family learning in community based early years settings enables parents and carers to develop the skills and confidence needed to support their children's learning at home, through play and everyday activities. Family learning could include short courses, activities or workshops where families learn together and where there are planned outcomes for both children and parents.

Reflect

Carry out a 'dad audit' and identify how many men have contact with the setting versus women.

1. Why is engaging dads with your setting important?
2. What barriers prevent dads from getting involved?
3. How can your setting be more 'dad friendly'?

Ensuring dads feel part of the setting too

Fathers play an important role in young children's lives. Children do better emotionally, socially and educationally when dads are actively involved in their children's learning and development. A positive male influence is not just limited to fathers but includes stepfathers, grandfathers, uncles or older male siblings.

Helping parents and carers participate

As you saw in learning outcome 4 of this unit, involving parents in the management committee brings a positive contribution to the design of your services, and gives parents ownership of your centre. However, they will need information and resources to enable them to do so effectively. These include:

- dates and agendas in advance
- crèche facilities
- tea and coffee facilities
- a role to play in the meeting
- an appropriate room to hold the meeting
- the support of a team member.

If a community or group can't represent their own views at the committee, you should ensure that these families have their views heard in some other way, perhaps through their outreach worker.

If people have a positive experience of taking part in the management committee, they are more likely to participate again and encourage other families to do so too.

6 Be able to manage the resource, regulatory and financial requirements for the community based early years setting

You are responsible for all aspects of your service: the day-to-day running of the setting, safeguarding, meeting inspection criteria and ensuring that outcomes

are assessed and measured. You need to constantly evaluate the service you provide, reflecting on how to develop and support ongoing improvements. You are responsible for ensuring health and safety policies and procedures are in place and are followed, to promote good outcomes for children's learning.

The regulatory requirements

You will need to work within the regulatory frameworks of:

- safeguarding
- the statutory framework for the Early Years Foundation Stage
- Ofsted inspection.

Safeguarding

Your setting must be a safe place for children and families to spend time in, and the services you provide must be safe and appropriate. Those working with children and vulnerable groups must be suitable and are required to have an enhanced Disclosure and Barring check (DBS).

Effective safeguarding arrangements in every local area should be underpinned by two key principles:

- safeguarding is everyone's responsibility
- a child-centred approach.

You must follow the statutory guidance for adults working with children and families, *Working Together to Safeguard Children*. The guidance emphasises that safeguarding systems are effective when:

- the child's needs are paramount
- all professionals who come into contact with children and families are alert to their needs and any risks to harm
- all professionals share appropriate information in a timely way
- high-quality professionals can use their expert judgment
- all professionals contribute whatever actions are needed to safeguard and promote a child's welfare, and take part in regularly reviewing the

outcomes for the child against specific plans and outcomes

- local areas innovate, making changes that are informed by evidence and data analysis.

The EYFS

The EYFS statutory framework sets the standards that all early years providers must meet to ensure that children learn and develop well and are kept healthy and safe.

Ofsted inspection

If you offer registered childcare, Ofsted must register and inspect your service. The Children Act 2006 places a duty on Ofsted to inspect community based early years settings to assess the quality of practice and identify where performance can be improved. Local authorities are responsible for responding to their findings and working with the setting to maintain or improve standards of practice.

Lines of responsibility and reporting

You are accountable to a number of people for the quality of the services you offer and your setting's success, including:

- the lead agency
- the service users – the children and their families
- the local authority
- stakeholders
- local professionals.

You need to keep detailed records of outcomes and to monitor progress to measure success. This data is important as it informs future planning and which services need to be dropped or developed.

Managing human resources

The quality of the delivery of a service depends on the quality of the team. To develop high-quality practice, your staff must be supported and encouraged to take part in continuous professional development. Effective performance management systems will enable you to

monitor and assess your team's practice and to identify areas needing further development.

You will need to:

- set realistic targets for performance improvements through a documented system of supervision and appraisal
- encourage and facilitate participation in nationally recognised training and qualifications
- encourage and facilitate attendance at early years conferences and events
- encourage a culture of peer support, work shadowing, mentoring and coaching of new team members, students and established team members with skills to be developed further
- establish a system of sharing outstanding practice between team members and other settings.

Resource management systems

You will be responsible for putting in place and running resource management systems, to maintain the high levels of practice. You will need to think ahead and plan to make sure that your budgets are not overstretched. You will also need to anticipate unexpected expenditure – for example, paying bank staff to cover staff sickness, damage to buildings, the replacement of equipment or having to employ specialist outside services.

Resources that you will need to manage include:

- specialist services from outside professionals
- staffing
- building maintenance and gardening
- equipment and materials (perishable and non-perishable)
- children's meals, drinks and snacks
- refreshments for service users.

Maintaining accurate financial systems

You will be responsible for maintaining accurate financial systems. You will be accountable to the local authority and participate in audits to make sure that funds are being well managed.

Your responsibilities will include:

- managing 'payment by results' mechanisms
- planning and monitoring how you and your team use the delegated budget
- monitoring your actual and committed expenditure
- actively controlling your expenditure against the budget
- complying with approved ordering procedures
- taking action to deliver any savings set for your budget
- taking corrective action as and when necessary to bring your spending in line with the budget.

Figure 14.8 shows some possible sources of funding or information on funding.

Reflect

Additional funding streams are always welcome, especially where much of the budget is spent on items or equipment that need replacing regularly.

1. How would you find out about additional funding?
2. What do you think you need to consider when applying for additional funding?

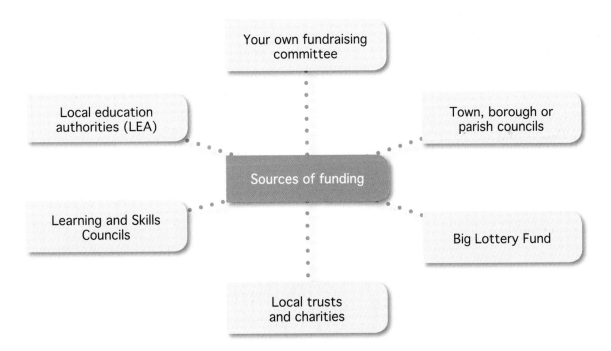

Figure 14.8: Why might an early years setting need additional funding?

Further reading and resources

Publications

- Daly, M., Byers, E. and Taylor, W. (2009) *Early Years Management in Practice* (2nd ed.), Oxford: Heinemann – skilled and experienced author team provide management guidance with real-life case studies to help you put the theory into action

- Fitzgerald, D. and Kay, J. (2007) *Working Together in Children's Services*, London: Routledge – provides a critical framework for looking at issues like the benefits and barriers of multi-agency working, current policy and essential skills for inter-professional teamwork

- Hallet, E. (2012) *The Reflective Early Years Practitioner*, London: Sage Publications – focuses on the practitioner's role, highlighting assessing and planning for children's learning, developing inclusive teaching strategies and integrated practice

- Langston, A. and Doherty, J. (2012) *The Revised EYFS in Practice: Thinking, Reflecting and Doing,* London: Featherstone Education – takes you through the new policies with vital information and practical advice on how to implement them effectively

- Miller, S. (2010) *Supporting Parents*, Maidenhead: Open University Press – practical advice on how to set up and deliver parenting services that support parents and improve outcomes for children

- Owen, J. (2011) *How to Lead* (3rd ed.), Harlow: Pearson Education Ltd – guide to the theory and practice of leadership, whatever your level in an organisation

- Penn, H. (2011) *Quality in Early Childhood Services: An International Perspective*, Berkshire: Open University Press – considers the variety of rationales that inform services for early childhood education and care

Websites

- 4Children: www.4children.org.uk – national charity for children and families, with a focus on children's services and shaping policy

- Dad Info: www.dad.info – articles, videos, podcasts and blogs plus advisors and coaching for dads in the UK

- Fatherhood Institute: www.fatherhoodinstitute.org – charitable organisation focusing on policy, research and practice, to help men be 'great dads'

- The National Association for the Prevention of Cruelty to Children: www.nspcc.gov.uk – charity dedicated to ending cruelty to children in the UK

- Ofsted: www.ofsted.gov.uk – for information about EYFS Ofsted requirements and the schedule for inspections of early years providers

Care for the physical and nutritional needs of babies and young children

Care for the physical and nutritional needs of babies and young children

Good practice in the provision of care for babies and young children is about more than providing a good diet, opportunity to exercise and protecting them from infections and accidents. Responsive, personalised care provides opportunities to develop social and emotional skills, communication and learning. Babies and young children depend on adults to meet their physical and nutritional needs – and carers rely on knowledgeable, skilled and confident practitioners to provide sensitive and appropriate care.

Before you start

Care matters to young children. Respectful care is essential to their self-respect and self-esteem. Think about the role of the key person in the provision of physical care. How can a positive approach to providing care support your effective partnership work with carers?

Learning outcomes

By the end of this unit you will:

1. be able to provide respectful physical care for babies and young children
2. be able to provide routines for babies and young children that support their health and development
3. be able to provide opportunities for exercise and physical activity
4. be able to provide safe and protective environments for babies and young children
5. be able to provide for the nutritional needs of babies under 18 months
6. be able to provide for the nutritional needs of young children from 18–36 months.

1 Be able to provide respectful physical care for babies and young children

You will need to develop partnerships with carers and communicate effectively to make sure there is continuity of care so that you can meet the individual care needs of babies and young children. This is the key person's responsibility. As far as possible, the key person will be the one who provides the physical care, ensuring babies and young children feel safe and secure by strengthening attachment. This will reassure their carers and help you to build strong relationships with families.

Theory in action

The Early Years Foundation Stage (EYFS) statutory framework states: 'Each child must be assigned a key person. Their role is to ensure every child's learning and care is tailored to meet their individual needs …'

Discuss with colleagues how this is managed in your setting.

Showing cultural and ethnic awareness

You will be able to learn about the home life and cultural background of the family and their preferences for the care of their child. This will enable you to provide respectful physical care.

Skin care

One of the primary purposes of skin is to protect the body from infection. Washing helps the skin stay healthy and unbroken, making sure that this essential function can be fulfilled. This is particularly important for babies and young children who are vulnerable to infection due to immature immune systems. The skin of babies and young children also needs protection from the harmful ultra-violet rays of the sun.

Skin varies in colour, texture and type. When caring for skin, you will need to find out from carers how they care for their child's skin.

Black skin is dry and sensitive, and needs moisturising frequently to keep it supple. There are specially designed oil-based, alcohol-free products to keep black skin moisturised. The face, arms and legs of black babies and young children need to be moisturised daily and bath oils need to be used to keep the skin in a healthy condition.

Bathing and washing

Whatever the age of the baby or child, for safety you must:

- always check the water temperature (the desired temperature is 37°C)
- never leave a baby or child alone near or in water.

Babies

Babies are often bathed once a day, either in the morning or as part of a bedtime routine – so this is not usually carried out by daycare settings. However, bathing may be the responsibility of a nanny or childminder.

It is good practice to observe another practitioner bathing a baby before you bathe a baby on your own.

Here is the correct process for bathing a baby.

- Make sure the room is warm (ideally 20°C).
- Prepare by collecting everything you will need, including clean clothes, nappy changing equipment and a towel.
- Remove your watch and any sharp jewellery and wash your hands.

- Smile and talk to the baby gently to provide reassurance.
- Undress the baby on the changing mat, apart from the nappy.
- Wrap the baby in the towel, keeping their arms tucked in.
- Wash the baby's face using dampened cotton wool.
- Add bathing preparation to the water (if used).
- Tuck the baby under one arm, supporting their head and shoulders. Hold the baby over the bath and use the other hand to wash their head and hair.
- Lay the baby back on the changing mat to dry their hair.
- Remove the nappy. Clean the nappy area with cotton wool or wipes.
- Lift the baby into the bath, supporting their head and neck in the crook of your arm and hold their upper arm; use your other arm to support their bottom.
- Keep supporting the baby's head and neck and use your other hand to gently massage the skin to clean the baby's body, using soap if preferred.
- Give the baby time to splash and kick in the water. This supports their physical development and provides a valuable sensory experience.

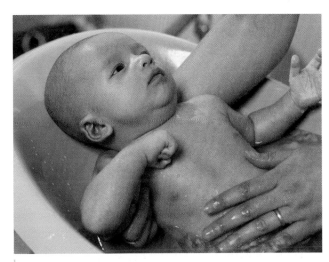

Figure 20.1: How can you make sure babies feel safe and comfortable during bathing?

- Lift the baby out, supporting their bottom, and place them on the mat. Pat the baby dry using a warm towel.
- Put on the clean nappy and clothes.

Babies who do not have a daily bath will need to be 'topped and tailed'. This involves:

- undressing the baby, in the same way as preparing for bathing
- washing and drying their face, top half of the body, hands and nappy area
- dressing them in clean nappy and clothes.

Older babies and children

A daily bath or shower is often part of the bedtime routine as it is relaxing.

- You need to check that bath toys are developmentally appropriate.
- It is good practice to run cold water into the bath first.

Young children who do not have a daily bath or shower and are no longer wearing nappies will need their bottom and genital areas washed daily, and their faces washed at night and in the morning.

Sun care

The skin of babies and young children can be seriously damaged by the sun. Too much exposure increases the risk of skin cancer later in life. Overexposure causes painful sunburn and may lead to dehydration and sunstroke.

Take the following precautions to protect all colours, textures and types of skin from the harmful effects of the sun.

- Keep babies under the age of 6 months out of direct sunlight.
- Encourage play in the shade between 11am and 3pm, when the sun's rays are strongest.
- Remember that the sun can cause damage in cloudy and overcast conditions.
- Make sure exposed skin is covered with a high factor sunscreen (factor 15 or above) or sunblock.

Your setting must have a policy for applying suncreams, including getting the carer's permission.

- Reapply sunscreen often.
- Encourage carers to supply loose clothes with sleeves, and a wide-brimmed hat to shade the face and neck.

Care of hair

Hair care is an important part of a daily routine and helps children develop good grooming habits.

Hair needs combing twice a day. This removes knots and prevents head lice by damaging any eggs on the hair shaft, preventing them from hatching. Children with curly hair will need a wide-toothed comb.

Hair needs washing no more than twice a week. You can use non-stinging products to help children who are distressed by hair washing.

The hair of children of African-Caribbean descent may need cream applied after washing and before drying, to moisturise and prevent the hair breaking. Do not over-dry their hair. Some children may have cornrows or braids. These cannot be brushed but can be gently washed and moisturised twice a week.

Care of teeth

Dental health is important for the health and development of babies and young children. Careful attention to tooth care is needed to prevent decay. Decay can be painful and may involve early loss of teeth, which affects the development of permanent teeth. The first set of teeth is essential for language development and contributes to the development of the jaw bones and facial muscles. Teeth are important for children to be able to chew and enjoy food.

Care of the teeth of babies and young children involves:

- brushing twice a day when the first teeth appear with a soft brush and fluoride toothpaste – in the morning and before bed. This is not usually carried out in day care settings but may be your responsibility if you are working as a nanny or childminder
- avoiding sugar in food and drinks between meals

- encouraging carers to take their child to the dentist for regular checks – NHS dental treatment is free for children under 18 years.

Care of the nappy area

Babies and young children wearing nappies need careful attention to their nappy areas to prevent nappy rash, which is uncomfortable and can be painful if left untreated.

You must follow the hygiene health and safety procedures of the setting for hand washing and disposal of waste.

The nappies are supplied by the carers and are usually disposable; some carers prefer towelling nappies. If carers supply creams or lotions, they will need to be labelled – they must not be shared.

Good practice in nappy changing

- Where possible, the key person changes the nappy. This helps the baby or young child feel secure by providing continuity, and makes sure the carer's wishes about skin care and toiletries are followed.
- Nappy changing needs to take place in a draught-free area separate from eating areas.
- If the changing mat is on a raised surface, a harness should be used.
- Record any causes for concern such as frequent stools, nappy rash, blood in the nappy or bruises.

Taking carers' preferences into account

Carers are usually asked for details about their wishes and preferences for their child's physical care as part of the registration process when a new baby or child joins the setting. As a key person, this will often be your role. It provides a good opportunity for carers to build a close and trusting relationship with you as the person taking responsibility for their child's physical care. You will need to record this information and pass it on to the rest of the team.

Handover times at the beginning and end of the sessions provide opportunities for carers to share with you any changes needed to the physical care of their baby or young child. In some settings, daily diaries are used for carers to record this information for practitioners.

Sometimes a carer's preferences may not reflect what you know to be best practice: for example, protecting skin from the effects of the sun. You will need to talk over any issues with carers and agree what is in the best interests of the child through friendly, respectful discussion.

In most settings, carers supply the products needed for physical care. These need to clearly be labelled – they must not be shared.

Working respectfully

Babies and young children need to be treated with genuine warmth and sensitivity when you are meeting their physical needs. This supports their emotional development, making them feel valued as individuals.

There are many ways you can achieve this.

- Tell babies and young children what is about to happen and what you are doing. Just lifting a baby up without warning is disrespectful and confusing for them. Provide a running commentary – this reassures them and supports their communication skills and understanding.
- Make sure you meet their preferences in personal care. This will make them feel valued and supports the development of their self-esteem.
- Make sure your care-giving is relaxed and unhurried as this encourages wellbeing and a sense of self-worth.
- Create opportunities for decision-making by providing choices. For example, ask, 'Which toy would you like to hold while I change your nappy?'
- Give young children opportunities to take part in their own care and praise their efforts, to encourage independence and further their self-esteem. This will take more time, but provides valuable opportunities to support learning and development.
- Provide babies and children with privacy when meeting their physical care needs. This shows respect.

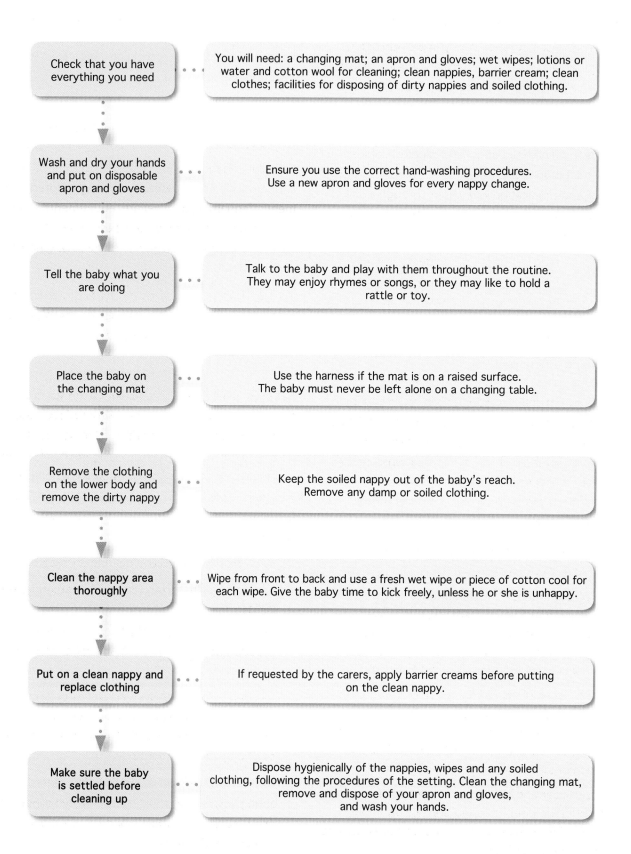

| Check that you have everything you need | You will need: a changing mat; an apron and gloves; wet wipes; lotions or water and cotton wool for cleaning; clean nappies, barrier cream; clean clothes; facilities for disposing of dirty nappies and soiled clothing. |

| Wash and dry your hands and put on disposable apron and gloves | Ensure you use the correct hand-washing procedures. Use a new apron and gloves for every nappy change. |

| Tell the baby what you are doing | Talk to the baby and play with them throughout the routine. They may enjoy rhymes or songs, or they may like to hold a rattle or toy. |

| Place the baby on the changing mat | Use the harness if the mat is on a raised surface. The baby must never be left alone on a changing table. |

| Remove the clothing on the lower body and remove the dirty nappy | Keep the soiled nappy out of the baby's reach. Remove any damp or soiled clothing. |

| Clean the nappy area thoroughly | Wipe from front to back and use a fresh wet wipe or piece of cotton cool for each wipe. Give the baby time to kick freely, unless he or she is unhappy. |

| Put on a clean nappy and replace clothing | If requested by the carers, apply barrier creams before putting on the clean nappy. |

| Make sure the baby is settled before cleaning up | Dispose hygienically of the nappies, wipes and any soiled clothing, following the procedures of the setting. Clean the changing mat, remove and dispose of your apron and gloves, and wash your hands. |

Figure 20.2: Why is it important to follow the correct procedures during nappy changing?

Providing personalised physical care

The individualised personal care you provide needs to be the same as the care at home. This is important for babies and young children to feel secure, and for parents to know their wishes and preferences are being met.

Make sure that the individual care needs of babies are recorded and kept up to date. This will require ongoing two-way communication with carers through a daily diary exchange, telephone conversations, emails or text messages.

Make sure that all personal care products – such as nappies, creams and lotions – are clearly labelled with the child's name, and stored in a way that prevents them being used for other children. This will prevent infections or allergic reactions.

Following procedures

You will need to follow organisational and regulatory procedures to ensure the health, safety and wellbeing of babies and young children, and to make sure that you are protected from false allegations. These are specified in the Safeguarding and Welfare Requirements of the EYFS, which are essential for registration by Ofsted.

Make sure you know and stick to the following policies and procedures of your setting:

- correct staff ratios – the minimum is that, for children under 2 years, there must be at least one member of staff for every three children and, for children aged 2 years, there must be at least one member of staff for every four children
- the health and safety policy and procedures, including your role and responsibilities in infection control, accident prevention and risk assessment (for more information on health and safety, see learning outcome 4 in this unit, and Unit 7)
- the safeguarding policy and procedures, including procedures for safe working practice (for more information on safeguarding, see learning outcome 4 in this unit, and Unit 8).

2 Be able to provide routines for babies and young children that support their health and development

Very young children depend on adults to meet their physical care needs and this is achieved through well-planned routines. Routines to support the health and development of babies and young children must meet safeguarding and welfare requirements – but you also need to understand the essential role they have in ensuring wellbeing and encouraging holistic development.

Caring routines should not be seen as something to do before getting on with learning opportunities, but valued as significant aspects of the day.

Planning routines

Routines give babies and young children structure to their day, which encourages a sense of security. Routines must be safe and will need to be adapted to meet the individual and changing needs of babies and young children as they grow and develop. You will need to have a flexible approach: for example, changing routines when a baby has slept poorly, is teething or is feeling unwell.

When planning routines you need to consider:

- your setting's health and safety and safeguarding polices
- the individual needs of the babies and children, including their developmental and health needs
- the carer's preferences
- how babies and children will be valued and respected: for example, by providing privacy, not hurrying, and providing choices and opportunities to develop independence
- how you will support learning and development
- recording and reporting, including details of feeds and meals, sleep, progress and achievement, and any causes of concern
- how you will review the effectiveness of routines.

Routines for babies and young children include:

- daily routines for:
  - » feeding
  - » meal and snack times
  - » nappy changing
  - » sleep and nap times
- weekly routines for regular events such as outings.

Feeding, meal and snack time routines

With plans for providing food and drink for children, you need to make sure these comply with your setting's health and safety procedures for food preparation and storage, hygiene and risk assessment. This is particularly important in relation to children's food allergies and intolerances (for more information on food allergies and intolerances, see learning outcome 6 in this unit). Bottle feeds will need to be clearly labelled with the baby's name.

Feeding babies

Babies in early years settings who are bottle-fed, with breast milk or formula, need regular feeds. As babies grow and their hunger levels change, you will need to consult their carers to find out how to meet individual requirements.

Where possible, the key person should feed the baby. Feeding times should be calm and relaxed. Make sure that the baby gets the correct feed at the correct temperature. You can warm bottles in a jug of hot water, but never in a microwave. You must throw away any feed not taken within one hour. (For information on how to make formula feeds and how to introduce a baby to solid food, see learning outcome 5 in this unit).

Meal and snack times

Well thought-out meal and snack times should be positive and enjoyable experiences. These times offer valuable health and learning opportunities as well

Figure 20.3: Why is it important that babies are fed by their key person whenever possible?

as providing for nutritional and energy needs and ensuring children keep well hydrated. (For information on appropriate food and drink, see learning outcome 6 in this unit.)

Meal and snack times can support holistic development by giving children opportunities to:

- try a range of different foods and those from other cultures
- develop fine motor skills – in food preparation and by using cutlery

- learn about healthy food choices
- share and take turns, to support their personal, social and emotional development
- develop their communication and language through interactions with adults
- develop their problem-solving and mathematics skills – when helping to set up and pouring drinks
- learn about hygiene by washing hands before eating
- develop independence by making choices and self-serving food and drinks.

For children to benefit from these opportunities, you need to make sure meal and snack times are unhurried and relaxed. Sharing food with the children at these times encourages children to try new food, as you lead by example. You can model appropriate behaviour and the use of cutlery. You will encourage children's development as you support their interactions, early understanding of concepts and independence. Spills happen when children help, but these too can be used as a learning opportunity – for example, by involving children in wiping up.

Nappy changing routine

Nappies should be changed as often as needed, and at least every three or four hours. Some settings have regular times for nappy changes, with extra changes if a baby is uncomfortable.

Figure 20.4: How can meal times be used as a learning opportunity?

Sleep and nap times

Sleep is a basic human need and has an essential role in the health and development of babies and young children.

Sleep is needed:

- for growth – growth hormones are released during sleep
- to support a healthy immune system and fight infections
- to allow the brain to process information and aid concentration
- to support emotional development by providing a sense of wellbeing.

Sleep patterns for babies and young children vary, some needing more than others. You need to get to know the individual sleep patterns of the children in your care, in discussion with their carers.

As a key person you will need to:

- find out from carers the times of sleeps and naps in relation to feed/mealtimes, comfort objects needed and any individual preferences which help sleep, such as stroking the cheek
- observe for signs of tiredness which may include not joining in, being more irritable or getting upset easily
- help the baby or young child prepare for sleep by helping them to relax, perhaps having a quiet time or looking at a book together
- settle the baby in a quiet, calm sleeping area in their own cot
- follow the health and safety procedures of the setting (for more information on health and safety, see learning outcome 4 in this unit)
- check sleeping children frequently
- give babies and young children comfort and time to recover when they wake up if they are distressed
- record sleep information for carers.

If you are working as a nanny, you may be involved in bedtime routines. Bath time is often part of this, and helps children relax before bedtime.

Find the balance

Imagine that a colleague in your setting plans lots of activities and experiences for the babies and young children. She hurries mealtimes and tries to encourage the babies to sleep at the same time so that 'they do not miss out on opportunities'.

1. How would you help your colleague to realise the value of care routines for children's holistic development?

Toilet training

For bowel and bladder control, young children need to have developed physically and be emotionally ready. Timing varies between children, but most children have bladder and bowel control in the daytime by the age of 3 years. It is important that you can recognise when children are ready, as this will ensure they are not pressurised but are successful quickly.

You will also need to ensure continuity between what is happening at home and routines in your setting. This will make sure the child feels secure and is not confused.

Sign of readiness include:

- a dry nappy for long periods
- they show you they are aware that they are having a bowel movement or passing urine
- they have the physical skills to pull down their trousers and pants and sit on a potty
- they have enough language to let you know they need to use the potty or toilet
- they have shown they are interested in not wearing nappies.

When you and the carer agree it is time to start, you will need to take the nappy off and ask the child to use the potty – this needs to be easy for the child to reach. In a group setting, children will be helped by seeing other children using the potty. Praise success and mop up any accidents without comment. For sleep times and outings you may need to put a nappy on until you are confident the child has control.

If the child shows no interest in using the potty or toilet, or is getting upset, this may indicate that the child is not quite ready. Discuss with carers the best course of action for the child, which may be to go back to nappies for a while.

Encourage children to wash their hands after using the potty or toilet. This is important for hygiene, helping children develop good habits and encouraging independence in self-care.

3 Be able to provide opportunities for exercise and physical activity

Activity and exercise are essential for health and for the development of physical skills. The benefits of exercise and physical activity go beyond physical advantages and have an important role in holistic development.

Current guidelines for physical activity recommend that once preschool children are walking they should be physically active for three hours a day. This includes light activity such as walking, moderate activity such as pushing wheeled toys or climbing, and more intensive activity such as running. It is thought that most children are not achieving this level of activity as they are involved in activities that involve sitting for long periods.

Babies who are not yet walking need opportunities for free movement on their backs or tummies, without being restricted by clothing or straps in high chairs, car seats, buggies or bouncers.

Supporting exercise and physical activity

You have an essential role in supporting children's physical skills and increasing their activity levels.

The benefits for babies and children include:

- strengthening bones, muscles and heart
- supporting development of physical skills and coordination
- encouraging appetite and improving digestion
- helping sleep
- promoting a sense of wellbeing and confidence
- helping to prevent obesity
- encouraging social interaction
- providing opportunities for exploring the environment
- aiding concentration
- encouraging good habits for being active.

Planning to support exercise and physical activity

You will need to plan carefully to make sure that babies and young children are safe and gain the optimum benefits from activities and experiences. There are many aspects you need to take into account when planning physical activities, including making sure that:

- observations, assessments and information from carers have been gathered – so you can select developmentally appropriate activities and resources, and identify individual needs and interests
- risk assessment has been carried out, including checks on equipment, resources and surfaces
- supervision levels are maintained to ensure safety and ongoing observations
- sufficient space and time have been allowed
- appropriate clothing and footwear is worn

Figure 20.5: Why do you need to provide sufficient space for children to play freely?

- indoor and outdoor experiences are planned
- free play and structured opportunities are planned
- opportunities are provided for all aspects of physical development including gross and fine motor skills and hand–eye coordination
- light, moderate and intensive physical opportunities are planned for children once they are walking
- confidence will be encouraged through challenge and support
- babies and children are not tired or hungry
- all areas of learning of the EYFS will be supported.

Table 20.1: Learning opportunities and ways in which they can aid the physical development and skills of babies who are not walking.

Opportunities for babies who are not walking	Physical development and skills
Tummy time	Strengthens muscles in arms, legs and back Head control
Baby gym	Reaching and grasping
Activity mat	Turning and reaching for objects Rolling over
Push-along toy	Pulling to stand Balance and coordination
Tunnel	Crawling
Self-feeding with cup, spoon	Development of grasp Hand–eye coordination
Treasure basket	Development of grasp Voluntary release
Action songs	Clapping, pointing Bouncing strengthens muscles in legs
Bath time	Strengthens muscles in arm and legs
Swing	Spatial awareness

Table 20.2: Learning opportunities and ways in which they can aid the physical development and skills of children under 3 years old.

Opportunities for children under 3 years	Physical development and skills
Wheeled toys e.g. prams, tricycles	Stability Coordination
Climbing frames	Balance and coordination Strength using large muscle groups Climbing and jumping Spatial awareness
Ball games involving throwing, kicking	Balance Hand–eye and eye–foot coordination
Gardening	Coordination Handle and control tools
Action songs and rhymes	Control Balance
Tidying e.g. sweeping up sand	Coordination Control Use of equipment
Sand and water play	Manipulative skills Use of tools
Obstacle course with stepping stones, low balance beam	Balance Coordination

Recording and reporting

After physical activities you will need to record developmental progress and your effectiveness to inform future planning, considering:

- the effectiveness of your observations and assessments in planning appropriate activities
- progress made by babies and children in physical development and other areas of learning
- what experiences and opportunities you could provide to further physical development
- changes you would make to improve experiences, resources or levels of support
- how you will keep carers informed about achievements and progress.

Theory in action

Physical development is one of the prime areas of learning in the EYFS.

Discuss with colleagues how exercise and physical activity support babies and young children towards achievement of the early learning goals in physical development and the other prime areas of learning.

4 Be able to provide safe and protective environments for babies and young children

Policies and procedures for health, safety and protection

Health and safety and safeguarding policies are requirements for all early years settings for registration by Ofsted. (For more information on the legislation and regulations governing health and safety and safeguarding, see Unit 7.)

Your setting will devise its own policies and procedures to make sure staff carry out their legal responsibilities. You have a professional responsibility to understand these and work within them. They will give details for all staff of what needs to be done to keep babies and young children safe. Clear policies and procedures reassure carers that everything is being done to keep their child safe and secure.

Policies and procedures need to be reviewed regularly – usually annually – to make sure they are fit for purpose.

Safety features

For information on the safety features that apply to all early years settings, see Unit 7. However, you will need to take extra steps to make sure that your environment is safe when caring for the youngest children. This is because babies and young children:

- are vulnerable to infection due to immature immune systems
- are prone to accidents as they are physically immature, are curious and lack any understanding of danger.

Protection from infection

Babies and young children are at risk from infections as they spend a lot of time on the floor, put toys in their mouths and may have accidents when toilet training. You need to know how to provide a clean and hygienic environment.

You will need to:

- follow policies and procedures for hand washing, food preparation, nappy changing and disposal of waste
- vacuum carpets daily and clean every 6 months
- mop floors with washable surfaces daily with hot, soapy water
- mop up toileting accidents with disinfectant
- clean highchairs and tables after meals
- wash soft and plastic toys weekly or if contaminated by a child who is unwell
- wash cot bedding provided for individual children if soiled, or weekly as a minimum
- maintain good ventilation to reduce cross-infection.

Organising a safe environment

Babies and young children need freedom to practise their physical skills and explore their environment safely. To minimise the risk of accidents you need to make sure that regular safety checks of the premises and equipment are carried out according to your setting's policies and procedures.

You will also need to make sure that:

- there is space indoors for children to roll, crawl, pull and push along toys
- chairs and tables are stable, as babies and young children use these to pull themselves to stand when learning to walk
- outdoor surfaces are non-slip for moving freely and using wheeled toys.

Selecting and using safe toys, resources and equipment

You need to select safe toys and use safety equipment correctly and appropriately. If you are working as a childminder, you will be responsible for buying these resources for your business.

Toys

All your toys must conform to safety standards. You will need to check for safety marks (the CE mark, Lion mark and Kitemark). Look for age warning labels that indicate whether toys are suitable for children under 3 years.

Figure 20.6: The CE mark (left) and the BSI Kitemark (right). Do you know what these safety marks mean?

Equipment

This will include:

- mattresses that fit the cots and meet safety standards
- harnesses in chairs, prams and pushchairs as soon as babies can sit up
- safety gates at the top and bottom of stairs and to prevent access to the kitchen
- covers for sharp corners
- safety glass in glass doors
- catches on windows, cupboards and doors
- finger guards for doors
- netting over ponds
- car seats correct for the weight of the baby or child.

Supervising

Staff ratios must be maintained (for more information on staff ratios, see 'Following procedures' in learning outcome 1 in this unit, and learning outcome 2 in Unit 2). Babies and young children must never be left unsupervised, in order to keep them safe and to give them the emotional support they need. Continuous supervision gives you an opportunity to observe their abilities and progress, and keep them safe as they develop skills.

Managing risk

In Unit 7, you learned how early years settings are required to have procedures for assessing risks to children's safety.

It is important to have a balanced approach to risk assessment, recognising that concern for children's safety should not prevent settings offering opportunities for babies and young children to develop and learn. For holistic development, babies and young children must have the opportunity to practise physical skills and explore their environment. If you limit these experiences, children will be prevented from reaching their potential.

It is not possible to remove all risks. All you can do is avoid accidents that are preventable. Minor bumps and tumbles will happen occasionally.

Reducing the risk of sudden infant death syndrome

You must follow the guidelines for reducing the risk to babies of sudden infant death syndrome (SIDS) in sleep routines. You will need to make sure that babies do not overheat, as research has shown that this increases the risk.

Figure 20.7 shows safe sleep practice to reduce the risk of SIDS.

To reduce the risk when babies sleep you must:

- place babies on their backs
- make sure the room temperature is between 16–20°C
- ensure babies' heads are uncovered – the blanket needs to be tucked in no higher than their shoulders
- settle babies in the 'feet to foot' position (with their feet touching the end of the cot)
- not use duvets.

You will need to make sure you keep up to date with any changes to advice. The Lullaby Trust (formerly the Foundation for the Study of Sudden Infant Death) issues up-to-date guidance.

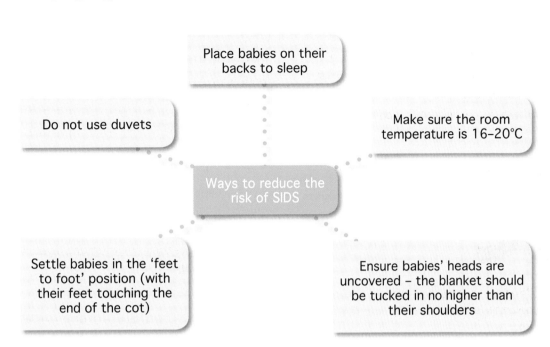

Figure 20.7: *How do you reduce the risk of SIDS in your setting?*

The figure shows "Ways to reduce the risk of SIDS" with the following points:
- Place babies on their backs to sleep
- Make sure the room temperature is 16–20°C
- Do not use duvets
- Ensure babies' heads are uncovered – the blanket should be tucked in no higher than their shoulders
- Settle babies in the 'feet to foot' position (with their feet touching the end of the cot)

5 Be able to provide for the nutritional needs of babies under 18 months

Babies grow rapidly. They double their birth weight by 4 to 5 months and triple it by a year. By the age of 2 years a healthy toddler is approximately half of his or her adult height.

Good nutrition is essential for optimum growth and development, especially for the brain.

Government guidance

The Department of Health guidelines for infant nutrition, based on World Health Organisation (WHO) recommendations, are:

- feed only breast milk for the first 6 months – weaning or complementary feeding should not be introduced until the baby is around 6 months old while continuing to breastfeed
- continue to breastfeed for as long as the mother and baby wish
- from 6 months (until 5 years) a supplement containing Vitamins A, C and D is recommended.

Jargon buster

Sudden infant death syndrome (SIDS) – the sudden, unexpected and unexplained death of an apparently well baby, also known as cot death.

Weaning or **complementary feeding** – the process of introducing solid food to the diet of a baby. Complementary feeding is a term preferred by WHO, as weaning may imply that breastfeeding should stop.

These guidelines are based on research that shows the health benefits of breastfeeding for both babies and mothers.

Remember that how a mother wishes to feed her baby is a personal choice. Breastfeeding is best, but formula milks have been designed to provide all the nutrients babies need. You have a professional responsibility to respect individual choices, and be knowledgeable about current government guidance so that you can give carers accurate information and support.

Table 20.3: Benefits of breastfeeding for babies and mothers.

Benefits for babies	Benefits for mothers
• breast milk includes all the nutrients required for the first 6 months in the correct proportions and at the right temperature • reduces risk of infection as it contains maternal antibodies • reduces likelihood of obesity later in life • less chance of developing eczema	• reduces risk of developing breast and ovarian cancer • is free – saves spending on formula milk and feeding equipment • uses up to 500 calories a day so may help in weight loss

You will be able to support breastfeeding in your setting by storing expressed breast milk to feed to babies with a bottle.

Weaning

Weaning or complementary feeding is introduced at around 6 months:

- because milk alone does not provide for increased energy needs or contain enough iron
- to introduce new tastes and flavours
- because this is when the digestive system is sufficiently mature.

You will need to discuss with carers when they plan to start weaning, which is indicated when milk alone does not satisfy the baby's hunger and the baby is able to sit up with support. To prepare weaning programmes to meet individual needs, you need to know from carers any food preferences and the babies' routines. A baby will not cope with new experiences if they are tired. A relaxed approach is essential as meal times should be pleasurable and stress free.

The weaning process needs to be gradual, allowing the baby to accept a new food on several occasions before trying another new taste. It is usual to start by giving some of the milk feed before offering a small amount of food on a spoon at one meal time. You could offer the baby rice mixed with breast or formula milk first as it is bland and gives the baby time to adjust to a spoon before trying more flavours.

At first you will need to purée the food, gradually increasing the amount. As the baby learns to manage lumps, you can give mashed or sieved food.

Gradually you will be able to reduce the amount of milk given at meal times, replacing it with water from a cup. Breast or formula milk is still an important part of the diet.

When weaning, you should avoid:

- added salt or sugar
- honey
- nuts and seeds
- eggs that are not hard-boiled
- foods that contain wheat (before 6 months).

When weaning, you must:

- never leave babies alone with food
- follow the procedures of the setting for hand washing and food preparation
- sterilise all feeding equipment.

From 6 months

- Start with one or two spoonfuls at one meal time. Suitable foods are; cooked puréed fruit and vegetables such as carrot, sweet potato, yam, peas, apple, pear; mashed soft fruit such as banana, peach, melon, apricot.
- Gradually increase the amount and range of foods, such as mashed fish, lentils or hard-boiled eggs.
- Full-fat dairy products such as fromage frais or yogurt with no added sugar may be included.
- The baby will need a breast or formula feed on waking and late evening.

From 8 to 9 months

- Continue to give the baby mashed and chopped foods and finger foods.
- Move towards three meals a day with a wide variety of foods including meat, fish, eggs, beans, fruit and vegetables, bread, rice, pasta and dairy products.
- The baby will continue to need a breast or formula feed on waking and late in the evening.

From 12 to 18 months

- Provide three meals a day which include three to four servings of starchy food, four servings of fruit and vegetables, and two servings of protein foods. Some food will need to be chopped or minced.

- Give healthy snacks such as vegetable sticks, rice cakes or toast.

- Breast milk or whole cow's milk – 300 ml a day is needed.

Preparing formula feeds

If you work in a home setting you may have responsibility for making formula feeds. The Department of Health (DH) recommends that each feed should be freshly made to reduce the risk of infection.

The DH suggests that, if feeds need to be taken to a day care setting, they can be prepared at home, cooled, transported in a cool bag and stored in the setting's fridge. Feeds must be clearly labelled with the baby's name and date, as feeds must be used within 24 hours.

Before you make the feed, bottles, teats, bottle caps, bottle and teat brushes will all need to be thoroughly washed, rinsed and sterilised.

Methods to sterilise feeding equipment include:

- cold-water solution
- steam methods using an electric steriliser or microwave – follow the manufacturer's instructions carefully
- boiling for 10 minutes.

When making a formula feed, you must:

- boil at least 1 litre of fresh (not bottled) water in the kettle
- leave the boiled water to cool for no longer than 30 minutes as the water needs to be at least 70°C when making the feed
- wash your hands and clean the feed preparation area before you start

- remove the bottle from the steriliser and rinse with cooled boiled water if using cold-water solution
- place the bottle flat on the surface and pour the correct amount of boiled water into the bottle
- check that you are using the correct formula
- loosely fill the scoop provided by the manufacturer with formula and level off with the flat side of a clean, dry knife
- add the correct amount of formula to the water in the bottle, screw the cap onto the bottle and shake well to mix.

Before feeding, you will need to cool the milk by holding the bottle under cold, running water or placing the bottle in a jug of cold water. You will need to replace the bottle cap with a sterilised teat.

Essential health and safety precautions

- Always follow manufacturer's instructions and use the scoop provided.
- Make sure the water is hot when adding powdered formula.
- Check the temperature of the formula by placing a drop on the inside of your wrist before you give it to the baby – it needs to be body temperature: warm, not hot.

Different types of formula

Most formula milk is based on cow's milk with added vegetable fats and vitamins and altered mineral content. There are several types and carers may ask you about their differences. Table 20.4 shows the differences between formulas.

Refer carers to health professionals (midwife, health visitor or family doctor) for advice about any feeding difficulties their babies are having.

Table 20.4: The differences between infant formulas.

Formula	Features
First milk	• Suitable from birth; babies can stay on this throughout the first year • Easily digested as the casein and whey balance of the cows' milk has been adjusted to match that in breast milk
Second milk (sometimes labelled as milk for hungrier babies and suitable from birth)	• Not recommended for young babies • Contains more casein which tends to produce firmer curds in the stomach, taking longer to digest • No evidence that babies are more settled or sleep longer
Follow-on formula, labelled as suitable from 6 months	• Not suitable before 6 months • Contains additional iron, but iron is more easily absorbed from food in mixed weaning diet
Goodnight milk	• Not suitable before 6 months • Follow-on milk with added cereal
Toddler milk (sometimes labelled as growing-up milk)	• Not necessary as cows' milk provides sufficient nutrients for children over 1 year as part of a balanced diet • Not recommended by government • Contains more sugar than cow's milk
Soya formula	• Only to be given on the advice of a health professional
Goat's milk formula	• Currently not approved for use in infant formula milk in the UK

6 Be able to provide for the nutritional needs of young children from 18–36 months

Planning nutritional meals

You will need to make sure children are given meals, snacks and drinks that are healthy, balanced and nutritious. This is one of the welfare requirements of the EYFS. Carers have the main responsibility for their child's nutrition, but the food you provide for children in your care makes a considerable contribution to their diet.

By planning a varied nutritious diet for children, you will:

- contribute to their growth and development needs
- meet their energy needs
- encourage healthy eating habits
- improve their health by reducing the risk of obesity and tooth decay.

Current government guidance says that, every day, a child between 18 and 36 months needs:

- four portions of starchy food – one as part of breakfast, lunch and tea and one as a snack; foods include bread, potatoes, sweet potatoes, pasta, rice, noodles, breakfast cereals
- five portions of fruit and vegetables – one portion at each meal and with some snacks (these can be fresh, frozen, tinned or dried and include juiced fruit and vegetables)
- two portions of any meat, fish, eggs, beans and non-dairy sources of protein
- three portions of milk and dairy foods, including milk, cheese, yoghurt, puddings made from milk
- 100–150 ml of fluids a day – milk and water are the only drinks to offer between meals; fruit juice should only be given at mealtimes and be diluted half and half with water.

The guidance also says you should:

- limit saturated fat by grilling or baking food, choosing lean meat, using only small amounts of sunflower, olive or rapeseed oil in cooking
- not add salt when cooking
- limit the use of processed food by cooking from scratch

Figure 20.8: How can you present food to appeal to young children?

- avoid sugary foods such as cakes, biscuits and sweets between meals
- only give dried fruit at mealtimes, to avoid tooth decay.

Case study 20.1

Alekna and her colleagues have identified a need to review the food policy in their setting to:

- improve the nutritional content of meals, snacks and drinks
- introduce children to a wider range of food
- encourage children to make healthy food choices
- increase vegetarian options as many carers are requesting their children do not eat meat or fish.

1. Suggest modifications to the food policy in your setting to meet the nutritional needs of the children.
2. How would you involve carers in the review of the food policy?
3. Why is it important to involve carers in changes to the food policy?

Information from carers

You will need to know from carers any specific dietary requirements children have. This must be recorded on your setting's registration documents, and will include:

- any allergies or food intolerances
- the carer's wishes for the child's diet.

The carer's wishes may be based on the dietary codes of cultural, religious and ethnic groups or on personal preferences. You will need to find out directly from carers just how they want these codes or restrictions to be followed.

Food allergies and intolerances

Some children have food allergies and food intolerances. It is essential that you are fully informed by carers as you will need to plan to ensure foods are avoided as the child may become ill or, in the case of severe allergies, their life may be threatened. You will also need to know how to deal with medical emergencies.

Food allergies

Children may have allergies to eggs, milk, peanuts, tree nuts, fish and/or shellfish. Symptoms come on quickly and may include:

- an itchy sensation inside the mouth, throat or ears
- raised itchy red skin
- anaphylaxis (a severe and potentially life-threatening allergic reaction) – swelling of the face, around the eyes, lips, tongue and the roof of the mouth, and breathing difficulties.

Jargon buster

Food allergy – when the body's immune system reacts abnormally to specific foods.

Food intolerance – when an individual has difficulty in digesting certain food.

Food intolerances

Children may be intolerant to:

- gluten – the protein in wheat, barley, rye and oats
- lactose – in dairy products.

Symptoms for food intolerances come on more slowly and include discomfort, stomach cramps or bloating.

Ensuring carers' instructions are met

Your plans to meet children's dietary needs must include consultation with their main carers. You can do this by:

- (as key person) discussing and recording dietary requirements at registration and keeping this information up to date if the child's needs change
- ensuring all members of the team are informed of carers' instructions
- reviewing menus to make sure individual dietary needs are accounted for
- sharing menus with carers
- informing carers about food their child has eaten, using daily diaries or informally at handover times – including if the child has not eaten well and food they have enjoyed.

Reflect

Consider your responsibilities as a key person in meeting personal care needs.

1. How have these supported children's holistic development?

2. How effectively have you worked in partnership with carers to meet the physical care and nutritional needs of babies and young children?

Further reading and resources

Publications

- Barasi, M. (2007) *Nutrition at a Glance*, Oxford: Wiley-Blackwell – succinct information in a user–friendly, well illustrated format, with coverage of topics from obesity to food policies

- Crawley, H. (2006) *Eating Well for Under-5s in Child Care: Nutritional and Practical Guidelines* (2nd ed.), St Austell: The Caroline Walker Trust – definitive advice on what eating well means for this age group, with nutritional and practical advice for those involved in the early years sector

- Department for Education (2010) *Information for Parents: Sleep*, Nottingham: DCSF Publications – examines why sleep problems may occur and gives ideas to help children have a better night's sleep – available for download at www.ncb.org.uk/media/875230/earlysupportsleepfinal2.pdf

- Duffy, A., *et al* (2006) *Working with Babies and Children Under Three*, Oxford: Heinemann – how to understand the development of babies and young children and support them, with theory and practical examples

- Lean, M. (2006) *Fox and Cameron's Food Science, Nutrition and Health* (7th ed.), London: Hodder Arnold – easy-to-read classic dealing with topics from food microbiology and technology to healthy eating and clinical nutrition

- Lindon, J. (2006) *Helping Babies and Toddlers Learn: A Guide to Good Practice with Under-threes*, UK: National Children's Bureau – aims to help practitioners value what children under 3 are learning and not rush them, with the support of examples and activities

- South East London Health Protection Unit (2010) *School Health Matters: A guide to communicable diseases and infection control* (4th ed.), London: Public Health England Publications (previously Health Protection Agency) – information on a variety of conditions and their management in group settings – available for download at www.hpa.org.uk/Publications/LaRS/LondonPublications/InfectionControl

- Virgilio, S. J. (2005) *Active Start for Healthy Kids: Activities, Exercises, and Nutritional Tips*, Illinois: Human Kinetics Publishers – covers the foundations of physical activity and healthy eating in a simple format

Websites

- Baby Centre: www.babycentre.co.uk – resource for newborn and expectant parents, with week-by-week baby development updates, thousands of articles and advice from other parents

- Baby Weaning: www.babyweaning.com – support and advice for starting babies on solid food

- Children's Food Trust: www.childrensfoodtrust.org.uk – UK organisation to improve the nutrition of school meals, providing news, information, guidance, resources and research

- Food Standards Agency: www.food.gov.uk – shows current research in food safety, nutrition and food-related disease

- Healthy Food Healthy Planet: www.healthyfoodhealthyplanet.org – advice and information on making food and lifestyle choices to protect your health and the health of our planet

- Lullaby Trust: www.lullabytrust.org.uk – promotes expert advice on safer baby sleep and provides special support for anyone bereaved through SIDS

- NHS SIDS: www.nhs.uk/conditions/Sudden-infant-death-syndrome/Pages/Introduction.aspx – NHS guidance on SIDS

- British Nutrition Foundation: www.nutrition.org.uk – provides useful advice about vitamins and nutrients in different foods

Glossary

Adult-led activity – activity set up and directed by the adult, with a specific learning aim in mind.

Anaphylaxis – an extreme allergic reaction, which can be life-threatening.

Annotated planning – planning that has handwritten comments on it to show that it has been adapted daily according to needs and interests of children observed.

Anti-discriminatory practice – actively promoting equality of opportunity.

Atypical – not typical; unusual; not following the expected pattern.

By rote – by memorising and repeating, often without really understanding.

Centre advocate – a parent who actively supports and promotes the centre to other families in the community.

Characteristics of effective learning – the different ways in which children learn: playing and exploring, active learning, and creating and thinking critically.

Child-initiated activity – activity chosen by the child and led by them.

Child protection plan – a plan identifying the intervention needed to keep a child safe from harm and improve their outcomes. It identifies the services that will support the plan and how they will work together to achieve the outcomes.

Classical – in this context, to do with an unlearned reflex such as salivating.

Cognitive – to do with acquiring knowledge.

Cohesion – working together productively towards a mutual goal.

Cohort – group of children with a common feature, such as age or class.

Commissioning – finding any services, professionals or resources required.

Common Assessment Framework (CAF) – a four-step process used by all children's services to identify the individual needs of children and to coordinate services to provide support.

Confidentiality – not sharing with other people or passing on personal information about the families you are working with, except when it is in a child's best interests to do so (for example, you may have to share information with another professional in order to protect a child).

Connectivity – how far the different aspects of something are connected or interconnected.

Continuous provision planner – planner that reflects how the environment is planned for resources, children's interests and learning, both indoors and outdoors.

Contractions – combining two words by the use of an apostrophe, such as changing 'do not' to 'don't'.

Controls – things that are put into place to eliminate or reduce the risk of harm, such as procedures, supervision or safety equipment.

Coproduction – a way of working where people who use services, families and service providers work together to create a service that works for them all.

Culture – the attitudes and values behind the traditions and customs that determine everyday aspects of life.

Decipher – decode, work out the meaning of.

Differentiated support – support specifically designed for an individual child, taking into account their needs and abilities.

Differentiation – recognising the differences in individual children's needs.

Disability – the long-term and substantial adverse effect of an impairment on a person's ability to carry out normal day-to-day activities.

Disclosure and Barring Service (DBS) – the service that checks an individual's criminal record and issues certificates to adults wanting to work with children and young people.

Discrimination – treating someone less or more favourably because they or their family are seen as belonging to a particular group in society.

Dramatic play – acting out scenes from real life that are familiar.

Early intervention strategies – ways to address the specific needs of children and/or their families as soon as possible.

Early learning goal – one of 17 EYFS goals covering each of the seven areas of development, giving the level of progress children should be expected to attain by the end of the EYFS.

Echolalia – echoing what others say over and over.

EpiPen® – a pen-style device for giving injections.

Estranged parents – parents not living with their child.

Evaluate – assess or make a judgement about something based on its positive and negative elements.

Fine motor skills – skills that involve small muscle movements, such as using a pencil.

Font – a set of type with a particular style.

Food allergy – when the body's immune system reacts abnormally to specific foods.

Food intolerance – when an individual has difficulty in digesting certain food.

Formative assessment – part of daily practice that informs how you can meet each child's requirements on an ongoing basis.

Formative feedback – feedback that is ongoing or continuing.

Grammar – the rules that govern how we put words together to form language.

Gross motor skills – skills that involve large movements of the arms, legs, feet or entire body, such as running.

Guidance – advice about what you should do or how you should behave.

Hazard – something that may cause harm (for example, a trailing cable).

Heuristic play – play about discovery and finding things.

Holistic – making links across different areas of learning and development.

Holistic development – all areas of development, including moral, cultural and wellbeing.

Imaginative play – play such as home corner or dressing up.

Immunisation – a way of protecting against serious diseases by making our bodies better able to fight these diseases if we come into contact with them.

Immunity – the ability to resist a particular infection.

Impairment – a condition caused by an injury or illness, or present from birth, which might lead to disability.

Inclusion – the process of ensuring equality of opportunities and access to services for all.

Individual learning plan – a plan to support the specific learning needs of a child, developed by practitioners, parents and any relevant professionals who may support the child.

Ingested – to take in by breathing or eating.

Innate – inborn, natural; an innate ability is something you are born able to do.

'In need' – a legal term for children who are unlikely to maintain, or be given the opportunity to maintain, a reasonable standard of health or development or whose health or development could be impaired without the support of children's services.

Integrated – professionals working together, at a single location, to deliver frontline services for children and their families.

Integrated working – all those involved in working together, in a coordinated way.

Integrity – the quality of being honest and having strong moral principles.

Key person – the person designated with the responsibility for a child's welfare.

Legislation – a law or group of laws.

Maintained school – school maintained by a local authority, funded by public money.

Makaton – a language programme that uses signs and symbols alongside spoken language.

Mandatory – required by law; not optional.

Medical model of disability – a traditional view of disability that treats the person as a sick patient and tends to focus on how to make the person more 'normal'.

Modelling – a technique by which adults show children what is expected by doing it themselves.

Monotropic – in one direction; towards one person.

Multi-agency – involving different services, agencies and teams of professionals working together.

Multidisciplinary – covering a range of different professions or services.

Near miss – an event or accident that did not cause injury, but had the potential to do so.

Neurological – to do with nerves and the nervous system.

Non-judgemental – not critical of others, not judging what they do.

Non-maintained or independent school – school that is privately run and privately funded.

Non-verbal communication – transmitting messages through actions, gestures, posture and facial expressions.

Notifiable diseases – illnesses that must be reported to the local authority because they pose a serious risk to the public.

Open questions – encourage children to think deeply and to give their opinions or express their feelings. By using words such as 'how', 'why' or 'I wonder' at the beginning of a question, you will give the child the opportunity to lead the conversation.

Outreach – visiting and providing services to people who might otherwise not be able to access them.

Paramountcy principle – the needs of the child are of paramount importance, above those of parents and professionals, so must come first in any decisions about their needs and the support they receive.

Parental responsibility – all the rights, duties, powers and responsibilities that a parent of a child has in relation to the child and his or her property.

Partnership working – when different services and professionals work together to meet the needs of children and families.

Pedagogical strategies – ways of supporting children's learning and development, such as responding to children's interests or extending their thinking through the use of open-ended questioning.

Peer – someone who is equal in terms of age, status or ability to another specified person.

Phoneme – a distinct unit of sound, such as the 'p' in 'pad'.

PLOD – possible line of development, used in developing a child's individual plan.

Portage worker – someone who helps to develop a programme to support an individual child.

Positive behaviour – the way that children actively show respect and behave well towards themselves, other children and adults.

Positive images – visual and other representations showing people who are sometimes marginalised or discriminated against in roles and activities that go against stereotypes.

Prejudice – a judgement or opinion, often negative, of a person or group, made without careful consideration of accurate, relevant information.

Progressive – in this context, a reform or change in the way in which education is delivered.

Psychosocial – to do with how social factors and individual behaviour interact.

Purposeful play – play that has meaning and enables children to make sense of the world.

Reflection – reviewing what you have already done in order to improve the way you do things in the future.

Register – the type of language expected in a particular social situation (for example, formal, informal or neutral).

Registered setting – most childcare settings for children under 8 must register with Ofsted or a childminding agency (exceptions include when care is delivered for less than two hours per day or carers are family members).

Regress – go backwards.

Regulated activities – types of activity that take place with children that are specified by the DBS.

Regulations – rules made and maintained by an authority.

Resilient – more able to cope with difficult events in their life.

Rhetorical question – a question asked for effect, but not really to get an answer (for example, 'Don't you agree?').

Risk – the likelihood of someone being harmed by a hazard (for example, tripping over the cable).

Safeguarding – all areas of keeping children safe, including considering the adults who work with them, health and safety, suitable environments, behaviour, outings, medication and child protection.

Safeguarding protocols – the procedures in place for protecting children from harm, abuse and neglect.

Safe working practices – procedures to ensure children are protected from abuse during care routines and adults providing care are protected from allegations of inappropriate behaviour.

Scaffolding – a process by which an adult or a more competent child builds on a child's existing knowledge and skills.

Schemas – patterns of thoughts or repeated behaviour that can be noticed when observing children's play. More information can be found on this in Unit 4, learning outcome 4.

Schematic learning – the use of previously learned experiences to understand or simply new experiences.

Self-actualisation – the process of coming to terms with who we are and our own potential.

Self-concept – the way in which you see and think about yourself.

Self-confidence – feeling able to do things and capable of achieving.

Self-esteem – valuing ourselves, and seeing ourselves as being of value in other people's eyes.

SEND – Special Educational Needs and Disabilities.

Sensory development – growth of awareness through the senses (sight and sound, touch and texture, smell and taste, and also body position sense).

Separation anxiety – children under 3 years often find it difficult to cope with being separated from the familiar adults in their lives.

Serious case review – review carried out following a child's death from abuse or neglect, where there are concerns about the practice of professionals in working together to safeguard.

Significant event – any event that causes disruption to the normal routine or situation.

Small-world play – creating 'worlds' using resources such as farm animals, small figures and toy cars.

Social cohesion – communities sharing common values and having greater trust between members.

Social model of disability – a more modern view of disability which recognises that discrimination against people with disabilities is created by society, not by these people's impairments.

Socio-economic – relating to a mix of social and economic factors.

Statutory – having a legal status.

Stereotypes – generalisations about a person; assumptions (usually inaccurate) about an individual because they are part of a particular group.

Stranger anxiety – from about 8 months, it is usual for children to become wary of people they don't know.

Sudden infant death syndrome (SIDS) – the sudden, unexpected and unexplained death of an apparently well baby, also known as cot death.

Summative assessment – assessment carried out at a specific period, such as the progress check for 2–3 year olds, that informs you of where the child is in their learning development and sums up the evidence gathered throughout the formative assessment process.

Supervision – confidential, private support sessions with an experienced practitioner in your setting.

Sustained shared thinking – when adults and children or groups of children engage in learning together, to talk about or explain their ideas and develop their thinking.

Targeted services – services for children and families with additional and multiple needs but who fall below the threshold for specialist support.

Transition – a period of change.

Universal services – services offered to meet the needs of all children, where specialist or targeted support is not required.

Vaccination – exposing the body's immune system to a weakened or harmless version of a pathogen, in order to stimulate white blood cells to produce antibodies.

Weaning or **complementary feeding** – the process of introducing solid food to the diet of a baby. Complementary feeding is a term preferred by WHO, as weaning may imply that breastfeeding should stop.

Whistle blowing – raising concerns about the actions of an individual, group or organisation.

Wrap-around service – the provision of childcare for before school, from 8 am, and after school, up to 6 pm.

Index

Index